THE LIVING LIGHT DIALOGUE

Volume 5

THE LIVING LIGHT DIALOGUE

Volume 5

Through the mediumship of
Richard P. Goodwin

Living Light Books

The Living Light Dialogue Volume 5
Copyright © 2012 Serenity Association

Through the mediumship of Richard P. Goodwin.

All rights reserved. Printed in the United States of America. No portion of this book may be reproduced—electronically, mechanically, or via internet transmission—without advance, express written permission of the publisher except in the case of brief quotations embodied in critical articles and reviews. No derivative work—games supplemental material, video—may be created without advance, express written permission of the publisher. For information address Living Light Books, P.O. Box 4187, San Rafael, CA 94913-4187.

Cover design copyright © 2012 by Serenity Association
Cover photograph by Serenity Association, 2012; copyright © 2012 by Serenity Association.

www.livinglight.org

Library of Congress Control Number 2007929762

FIRST EDITION

This volume of teachings is dedicated to the spirit friends who brought to Earth the Living Light philosophy. With eternal gratitude, we pray that we may demonstrate these principles and continue to bring to publication these teachings.

CONTENTS

Acknowledgement ix
Introduction xi
Consciousness Class 93 3
Consciousness Class 94 11
Consciousness Class 95 22
Consciousness Class 96 29
Consciousness Class 97 38
Consciousness Class 98 47
Consciousness Class 99 57
Consciousness Class 100 65
Consciousness Class 101 75
Consciousness Class 102 84
Consciousness Class 103 93
Consciousness Class 104 102
Consciousness Class 105 111
Consciousness Class 106 119
Consciousness Class 107 131
Consciousness Class 108 138
Consciousness Class 109 150
Consciousness Class 110 159
Consciousness Class 111 168
Consciousness Class 112 176
Consciousness Class 113 183
Consciousness Class 114 191
Consciousness Class 115 201
Consciousness Class 116 211
Consciousness Class 117 221
Consciousness Class 118 230
Consciousness Class 119 237

Consciousness Class 120 243
Consciousness Class 121 252
Consciousness Class 122 259
Consciousness Class 123 270
Consciousness Class 124 279
Consciousness Class 125 284
Consciousness Class 126 292
Consciousness Class 127 300
Consciousness Class 128 308
Consciousness Class 129 318
Consciousness Class 130 325
Consciousness Class 131 334
Consciousness Class 132 351
Consciousness Class 133 362
Consciousness Class 134 370
Consciousness Class 135 377
Consciousness Class 136 385
Consciousness Class 137 392
Consciousness Class 138 409
Consciousness Class 139 417
Appendix 429

ACKNOWLEDGMENT

Grateful acknowledgement is made to the many friends and associates for invaluable aid in compiling this book, for their helpful suggestions, for their loyal interest and encouragement.

Special acknowledgement is due to those who painstakingly and selflessly transcribed and proofread the text.

INTRODUCTION

[This introduction was written by Mr. Goodwin and originally appeared in *The Living Light*, which were the first teachings of the Living Light Philosophy published in book form. The entire text of *The Living Light* was republished in *The Living Light Dialogue,* Volume 1.]

> "Think, children. Think more often
> and think more deeply."

The teachings in this book were given as a progressive series of lessons to a group of four students who were sitting for spiritual unfoldment with me beginning in January of 1964. The communications were regular until October of that year, when nearly a seven-year silence ensued, and resumed in 1971 to the present. They were received in three ways by me as a channel. The main text was taped from a direct control of my voice in deep trance at special sittings of our group, during which I had no experience of the voice or what was being transmitted. A few scattered verses were given independently when I was privileged to see and hear our teacher clairvoyantly. I have also been a channel for this communicant when speaking from the podium at church and in answering difficult questions at our public seminars.

Nearly all we know about our teacher is contained in the lectures. He reports that he had tried for sixteen years to break through an interference barrier that the channel had to deep trance. When our conditions were in resonance with his patient wisdom, he came through ready to teach his understanding. I have seen him as an old man dressed in white with long flowing white hair. He has blue eyes, slightly smiling and deeply compassionate. I have always called him the Old Man. The students liked to call him the Wise One. He is surely one of those often called a Teacher of Light. I do not know his country, although he indicated at one time that he was from 6000 B.C., and a form of a judge in his time.

The text is often difficult, but it is complete, having been transcribed word for word from the original tapes recording the trance voice. It is presented with a minimum of punctuation to be freer for the individual interpretation of each reader. The lessons given before the long silence are phrased with many allegories often paradoxical. There are repetitions and renewals of theme, but it is explained that if an understanding is not perceived, compassion dictates that it be said again. Some of the topics have but a simple mention with little development but all are revealed, we are told, according to merit.

The Old Man is a fine teacher. He has in a hundred ways intertwined his allegory, progressive explanations, unfolding exercises, and timely references to reach a multitude of levels of individual understanding. A notable change is his more direct style of presentation beginning in 1971.

There is an endearing intimacy of person that can be felt through his lectures, a meaningful and loving encounter with a wise friend. Like an old man, he makes a mistake and conscientiously corrects himself a few paragraphs later. He listens often and carefully to our earnest discussions of his words. He consults with a group of experts on evolution and cites their learning in his lesson. His use of the direct address "children" or "my children" is not patronizing but infinitely loving and supportive.

A word must be said about the teachings. The Old Man makes clear that his lessons are not dogma, a creed or a narrow way, but simply his own understanding offered to us as a form of instruction to aid us in our own individual progression. When he speaks of Laws, he does not refer to man-made rules or moral traditions but to the cosmic and atomic way-things-are, the natural world of what-is, the universal laws of life, part of the original creative design and through which creation is fulfilled. These laws are beyond the possibility of being changed, suspended, transcended, or destroyed but they are ever a tool of mankind, not his master. First, through our awareness of the universal laws and then slowly through our developed understanding, the powers of creation are accessible to us. Not power over men's minds or circumstances, but power over whatever is selfish and imperfect in ourselves is the way up the eternal ladder of progression. When the Old Man cautions us concerning the Law of Responsibility or gives us a thinking exercise to explore the Law of Identity in a dynamic manner, he prepares us to take another step. And all move in accordance with the Law of What Can Be Borne.

Our teacher shows us how the two worlds are drawn together. In his realm, he describes, there is a great diversity of thought, many schools of understanding; but the Light is always known by the Light. Because of the interdependence of the two realms, listening to our discussions helped to clarify his teaching to others on his side of the curtain. His love and gratitude he humbly equates with ours.

The lessons to be perceived are not new, they are very old, but they are new to certain levels of our being. I would personally advise the reader, after reading this volume of discourses in full, to make a daily habit (or when there is a feeling or need) to sit quietly with the book. Open it at random and be guided to the Light by the passage that is there for the day. This technique is still used by the original students who were given the lessons and by many students after them who have studied in unfolding classes with me through these teachings.

Go beyond the words into feeling, into the immediate meanings for you. Touch into the inspiration that flows into the form of this book. It is from the Divine.

RICHARD P. GOODWIN
San Geronimo, California
June 1972

CONSCIOUSNESS CLASSES

CONSCIOUSNESS CLASS 93

Greetings, children of Earth. May the light of eternal truth shine fully in your heart.

And in keeping with the principle of bringing to you a sharing of understanding from our realms, we should like, at this time, to discuss the dream of life, the true essence of which is indeed the Law of Life.

You all know, I am sure, that what the senses feel or touch, what the eyes see, is indeed viewed by the eternal soul. And so, my children, when the senses view creation, the soul creates its viewing in what is known as the dreams of life. This dreaming process takes place not only in the conscious mind, but is recorded indelibly in what you call the subconscious or magnetic field of your universe. Whenever you view or sense anything, if there is not an established pattern or dream in your magnetic field, then, my friends, there is an experience called trauma that takes place within the magnetic field. And so we see from this process that man is ever controlled by his own subconscious, by his own dreams, which he calls experiences of the past.

Now, the Law of Life is the Law of Evolution. And the Law of Evolution is the Law of Change. And so, my friends, regardless how you try to hold to the dreams of yesterday, sooner or later they will pass, for that is the demand of evolution. Therefore a wise man does not hold to the past and he does not concern himself with the morrow, but lives in the eternal moment of now, for only in that eternal moment of now is man free or happy.

Now, when we entertain what you commonly call self-concern, an interest in self, what we are doing, in truth, is entertaining in mind consciousness the dreams of the past. When these dreams are expressed through the mind, that is known as self-will, based upon the limited acceptances or dreams and experiences of yesterday.

My good students, you have been given what is known in our world as the "Eternal Call of the Soul." We spoke to you in your year of '64 that the soul can, and does, all things create in your universe. And do you not now see that you, and you alone, are the captain of your ship, that you, and you alone, are the master of your own destiny? And so for the students who have not yet heard the "Eternal Call of the Soul," we shall give it once again. When you use it, and not abuse it, the soul rises in consciousness within your universe and, being the creator of your own dreams or experiences, it has the power to view them and put them to sleep that you may indeed—your eternal soul—be free and, being free, view the paradise called heaven, which is not a place you're going to. It is a state of consciousness that you are growing to each moment of eternity. And so, my students, remember:

Rhythm, Harmony, Balance, Peace
Hold release, Hold release.

When you use that call, you will find that the mind is still. No thought is able to enter, for your dreams are going to sleep. My good students, this, that you are in, is not the beginning of life, nor is it the ending of life. You, your soul, has always been. You, your soul, will always be.

The Law of Life is the eternal principle that all form is destined to change. And so we, once again, repeat to you: hold not to form, for form shall pass. And when your minds insist upon holding to dreams and not letting them pass your view, then you become the victim and the slave of the dreams that you dream. That is not the purpose of life. It is the abuse of life, for the mind, which ever seeks to be the king of the form, does not, and cannot, forever control your eternal soul. You have the great power within you in this moment to be the peace, the freedom, and the joy of Life herself.

So often the students ask, "If I could only understand, if I could only understand." And when understanding is presented to them, they find difficulty in accepting, because there is no reference in the mind for understanding. The mind is designed to garner up what is called knowledge. It is not, nor was it ever, designed for understanding. It is the heart, the soul, that understands. And so in all your getting, get understanding. And do not forget, my children, in all your giving, give wisdom.

We have gone through many dreams in many, many centuries. I am grateful for some awareness of that eternal journey. Dreamer children, do not entertain in consciousness that this is the only dream that you have, this dream called Earth. For you dreamed a dream before you came to Earth and, in keeping with the Law of Life, the dream you dream is your experience. And so your soul, destined by the dreams you dream, has entered your earth realm.

There is no escape from the divine Law of Evolution. But man was granted that 10 percent, that so-called free will to dream his dreams. And so your day this day is the direct effect of the dreams you insist upon dreaming. If you have experiences—which many of you do—that you do not find pleasing to your mind, be grateful, my children, for that which is not pleasing to the mind is ofttimes the joy to your own eternal soul. And when you ask of God and receive not, express the gratitude of your soul. For ofttimes when we receive not, when we are not aware of the receiving, then, my children, we are indeed truly receiving.

The universal laws of life are the divine principles of God. They are beyond change. And we, our minds, in time shall follow those principles, whether we like those principles or not. And all of eternity, my good children, is the effect of what you yourself set into motion and declare the law unto yourself.

It is stated by many that God helps those who help themselves. What a truth, my good friends, it is. God does help those who help themselves who make the effort to still the activity of their mind or so-called self-will. That's when God moves in your universe, when you are willing to surrender to a greater authority than what is known as king brain. The Intelligence that holds the stars in space is certainly well qualified and capable of clearing the path for your little soul. But it cannot, and it will not, clear the path for your soul to freedom unless you permit it to do so.

Of what benefit is it, my children, to pray to God for health, for wealth, and for happiness, when the mind, addicted to its own dream experiences, refuses to still itself to permit God to bring you, in keeping with natural law, health, wealth, and happiness? God does not bring us joy. God does not bring us sadness. God *is*. Truth *is*. We, and we alone, through our own daily efforts, become receptive to the Law of Joy or receptive to the Law of Sadness, receptive to the Law of Health, receptive to the Law of Sickness, receptive to the Law of Wealth, receptive to the Law of Poverty. Think, my students, the spoken word is life-giving energy. And what do you spend that energy in? Are you creating the negative when you, your divine right is the positive, which is the divine will called God?

Is the suffering called nightmares of reality—which is nothing more, nor less, than a dream—is that suffering intense enough for you to make greater effort to self-control? And what is self-control, but the conscious effort moment by moment to control the patterns of your mind that have already caused you great pain and suffering. My children, no soul is beyond God's watchful eye. But God, the greatest, humblest servant of all, does not interfere with your divine right to deny his service. And so does it behoove us to continue to deny the eternal truth of freedom in this eternal moment?

I believe, my children, that some of you have submitted a question or two. I will be most grateful to share with you our understanding. And before sharing that understanding on your questions, I should like you to know that your little school on Earth of the Living Light is only one of the schools of the Living Light. It is slowly, but surely, coming closer to the many schools of Living Light in our dimension and in our realms.

And remember, self-control means discipline, the discipline of personality and dreams to the surrender and acceptance of principle. And so the mind says, "What is principle?" The mind, my children, does not know principle. The mind is a dual vehicle. How does man know principle? By knowing God. And how does he know God? By becoming God, by permitting his eternal soul, which is a part of God, to speak through his own heart. There, man knows principle. There, he knows understanding, for there, and there alone, does man have total consideration. For God is total consideration. And that, my children, is where you, all of you, will find principle.

Remember and ne'er forget: whatever in all of life happens to us has, by the eternal law, been caused by us. But you may do something with whatever dream you're dreaming: You may put it to sleep or you may entertain it and suffer from it. Not all dreams are nightmares. There are some that are beautiful. Those dreams are worthy of entertaining for a time. A person may say, "Well, dreaming is an illusion." My children, what do you think reality is? Reality is your view, your dreaming process. And what is real to one is not real to another. You may say that the chair in which you sit is a real chair. And you support your dreaming theory by all the other friends you can garner up who say, "Oh, yes. That is a chair." And so man's illusion and delusion is supported by what is known as agreement.

Remember that irritation wakes the soul, not the satisfaction of someone constantly agreeing with you. If you find agreement with a friend in all things, remember, that's not a friend: it's only a mirror of you.

You may ask your questions.

The first question: Would you please trace the steps leading to the expression of revenge? How does one recognize it and how does one retrace the steps to free oneself of revengeful feelings?

Thank you for your question. In reference to the Law of Revenge, which is man's law, whenever we experience in life what we decide is a rejection, we immediately go into what is called retaliation. Now, the expression of this retaliation is known to you as revenge. Now, why do people experience what they call rejection? My good students, the soul does not reject. Rejection is not recorded in the soul, for the soul is divine will. It is the mind that is self-will, limited in its duality.

And so it is man dreams his dreams. Someone disagrees with his dreams and says, "No." When that happens to the mind, the mind does not experience the release of energy directed into the dream that he is dreaming. Not experiencing the release of this divine energy through the dreaming process of the dream, man experiences what he calls rejection. The energy goes down into his so-called computer and triggers what you call the mechanism of self-preservation: it's known as the animal instinct in man. But, my children, the animals are so much wiser.

However, this self-preservation mechanism, redirecting the energy, expresses it in what is called getting even: "An eye for an eye, and a tooth for a tooth." "You have hurt my feelings. My mind demands that I hurt yours." And so we have rejection, retaliation, revenge. But we have forgotten God's law when we do that. We have forgotten the beauty of truth: that every dog has his day in court and our day shall always come. Now, what does that mean, my children? Every dog has his day in court. Every friend of God shall face the divine justice of God and accept the eternal truth that vengeance is mine saith the Lord, the Lord, the Law of Life.

You may ask.

Second question: Please discuss more fully the process of deception, its purpose, and how it becomes more subtle in its manifestation as one unfolds.

Thank you, my student. In reference to the created law called deception, it is the mechanism of the mind in order to preserve its authority and rule over the eternal soul. For example, it is the nature of the soul to express. That is its nature. It is the nature of the soul, which is love, to love. The soul is not limited in its expression by its nature. The soul is limited by the accepted patterns or dreams of man's own mind, which is called knowledge. The truth of life is: Love all life and know the Light.

Now, God, the divine Infinite Intelligence, loves all life, and God *is* the Light. Now, until man follows the example of the demonstrable truth, which God constantly reveals, he will not know the Light, for he refuses to love all life that he may know it. He refuses because he is limited in his own expression by the patterns of acceptance of his own mind.

Now, whenever the soul starts to rise in consciousness, the mind fears that it will lose its throne, its authority to make all decisions and to limit the power of God. The mind is very, very clever. The mind justifies any and everything it wants to do. Now, all souls, being a part of God, are power. It is their divine right, for that is the soul. The created mind views the soul and senses and feels its power. The mind desires that power that it may have greater authority, that *it* may be the soul. But the mind will never be the soul, for the mind is only the temporal reflector of dreams that it has dreamed.

And so the mind deceives us as the soul strives to rise. The mind justifies all things that it chooses to do. The mind ever seeks the power of God. But the power of God is not within the possibility of attainment by the human mind. And so the sooner that man surrenders the so-called created king, the sooner he realizes that what is called deception is the mechanism of the mind to maintain and to sustain its superiority and authority over your own eternal soul. It is necessary for the mind to deceive us in order that it may remain superior.

And so it is deception, you see, my children, is the great need of the mind to be king. However, we have not been left void, without the way. The soul perceives when you put the dreams called mind stuff to sleep. You have been given the way to put them to sleep and when you do that, your soul will speak through your heart and you will be free.

The third and the last question: What actually takes place when the faculty of surrender is being unfolded?

When the soul faculty of surrender is in the process of unfoldment, man experiences the storms of life, the battle of his own mind, of his own subconscious. The mind strives to preserve its own limited dreams. It's known as self-preservation. And so it is the greater the sinner, the greater the potential of the saint. For the mind is extremely clever and devious. And when you are in the process of surrendering it, its great authority, when Caesar, sitting on his paper throne called the human mind, views that the soul is rising and he must surrender, there is great trauma; there is deep water. However, all of the ways necessary to bring you through the trauma of life to free your eternal soul have been given. If only, my children, you would accept in consciousness that God is the humblest servant of all servants. Without God, your king brain, your Caesar, would not be sustained. For it is the great kindness of God to sustain all things. And it is your divine right to choose what you are, in truth, asking God to sustain.

Look at the principle of life, my children. If it is your failing that you cannot let go, that you must hold to all things, then, my children, you guarantee to hold to something that will demand you to let go. We cannot let go, because we are not making the effort to let go. We cannot surrender, because we are not making the effort to surrender. Try to surrender the little things. Then view how great God truly is.

Good night.

SEPTEMBER 4, 1975

CONSCIOUSNESS CLASS 94

Good evening, students.

I am aware that some of my students are not familiar with what is known as total trance mediumship. The reason that these classes, that began last Thursday, are restricted and limited is simply because total trance mediumship is not something that is publicly done for very just reason. When the spirit, whoever the spirit may be, in any medium, comes in and takes control of the physical body of a medium, there is a very delicate process that takes place having to do with the blood pressure of the medium. And so it is of the utmost importance that you try to remain as silent and as quiet and as still as possible. Because each movement—the movement of chairs or coats or writing and things of this nature—is like a shock. And if you can visualize how you feel when you are halfway awake and halfway asleep—you're in that in-between state—you know what an impact any noise, movement, or sound has upon you. Now, if you will magnify that impact by about one thousand times, then perhaps you will have some understanding of what it's like to be a medium in total trance to give these classes to you. So your full cooperation is greatly appreciated.

I know that for some of you it is difficult to remain still for forty-five minutes to an hour. But stop and think, my friends. The movement of the body is only a reflection of the movement of your mind. And you are here in these classes for discipline, inner discipline, of your own mind, that you may control your mind, because through self-control, the effect thereof, is known as freedom. And so, in truth, in these classes you are given the golden opportunity to self-control, to personal, inner discipline that you may free your own eternal soul.

And I want to mention one thing else before we go into the reading of our discourse this evening and that is: all experience, all experience, my children, is in keeping with a subtle law that we, and we alone, are setting into motion. So if experiences in life are not pleasing to you, do not, for your own sake, look outward for the cause. Look inward for the cause. If you experience things that are pleasant, look inside, for you have established a law. If you experience things that are unpleasant, then look inside, for you have established a law.

Now until, as students, you make the constant, moment-by-moment effort to guide your mind inward for all experiences that you encounter, you cannot control your mind, nor free your own soul. The tendency of the human mind is to blame the cause of things outward. That is not where the cause exists. Only the effect exists outward. The cause exists inward in laws that we, and we alone, have established.

[At this point, Mr. Goodwin goes into a trance.]

Greetings, friends. Once again, we are pleased to speak with you in this way.

And this evening we should like to discuss a word that is so meaningful to the true soul of all life. The word is commonly known as *truth*. We have stated many times that an attempt to define *truth* would limit truth and you would no longer have truth. So our efforts are not in defining the word for you, for you already know, deep in your hearts, what it is. Our efforts are to show you the obstructions that stand in the way of its expression.

We have spoken many times on the minds of men and how the mind is, in truth, the great deceiver. For the mind has limited what it understands, for, in truth, it has knowledge, not understanding. And its knowledge is dependent upon what you have permitted your own mind to accept and to reject.

Now, the soul, that great eternal being that lies within all form everywhere, strives to express itself in a gentle and simple way. Whenever you have decisions to make—and decisions beset all mankind each and every moment of every day and night—when you have these decisions in your conscious awareness, look at them and listen quietly in the silence within you, and you will find the decision is based upon accepted patterns and experiences of yesterday. However, if you will be very patience, you will hear a soft, still voice that whispers eternal truth to your own mind.

We stated, in one of our classes with you, before you speak to think not once, nor twice, but thrice. To think with the conscious mind the thought, to think with the emotional, subconscious mind the same thought, and then permit your own soul to whisper the eternal truth to your mind. My good students, we have yet to find one who is making that effort for their own good, their own peace, and their own freedom.

Many times the students speak of principle, but the question must be asked, my good students, "What *is* principle?" Is principle what the mind has decided? Is principle what your earthly dictionaries dictate to you? Oh no, my friends, if that were principle, then all people expressing principle would be in total agreement. But that, my good children, is not the case. And so we must ask ourselves in honesty, "Then what *is* principle?" We have one thing to say in reference to principle: principle is the essence of truth. You know how to find truth in your own consciousness. And so when you find the essence of truth, you will then demonstrate what is, in truth, principle.

I know that many of you have tried, and continue to try, to demonstrate to some degree what has already, over these years, been shared with you. As you take that eternal inward journey, you will slowly, but surely, begin to become aware of the separation, so to speak, between the mind and the soul. Be grateful. Be not concerned that this awareness dawns within your consciousness, for the mind, called king brain, will begin to separate in your mind and you will hear the voice of the patterns to which you are addicted and in the same moment you will hear the voice of your eternal soul, which is truth. And so, my students, as greater and greater effort is made by you, this separation slowly, but surely, will increase. And that is indeed, my children, a grateful day in eternity.

Many of you are aware of the soul faculties and the sense functions. They have all been given to you, many of them, for your study and your application. You know that duty, gratitude, and tolerance is the first soul faculty, that faith, poise, and humility is the second soul faculty. Now, our teaching has always been do not annihilate the functions, which are listed in the book you have [*The Living Light* and also *The Living Light Dialogue Volume 1*], called money, ego, and sex, which is the function. And the faculty being faith, poise, and humility.

We gave to you of recent date a great eternal truth: Put God in it or forget it. How does man put God into his acts and activities? You cannot put God in if you do not know God within. And so it is when you put your soul, mind, and body into any effort, you have the power of God and divine eternal justice is the inevitable manifestation of all of your efforts.

My students, the path is not an easy one for any soul. Sometimes the students ask the question, "Why does it have to be so difficult? Why does my brain, my mind have to deceive me so frequently?" The great deceiver was not created by God. It was, and is, created and sustained by the so-called free will of man. He decided that he was greater than God. And until that decision of greatness of the mind of man bows in the fullness of humility and surrender to the true God of peace, of poise, of humility, of faith, man cannot, and will not, be free.

In reference to the nine bodies of which you are in truth, let us ne'er forget the physical body of which we are aware returns to the elements from whence it came: it is called earth. The mental body returns to the elements from whence it came and it is called mental consciousness. The astral body returns to the elements of which it was composed. The only thing that is eternal is your free spirit, your eternal soul. And it is constantly identifying and placing itself in bondage because man will not make the effort to control his own mind, his own emotions.

Heaven, we've often said, is a state of consciousness we are growing to. Let us grow, my good students, this moment. Let us learn to give it to God, that our minds may be at peace, that our soul may rise, that we may enjoy here and now the fullness, the goodness of Life herself. There is no suffering, nor pain, created by God. This is only created by the minds of men. And how does man refrain from creating his suffering? Only, my good students, from the control of the human mind.

Now, I know that you are waiting with many, many questions. And so I am going to share with you the best of our understanding in reference to the questions that you have asked. And as greater effort is made, my good students, then we can share with you the true meaning of universal consciousness, the true meaning of the seventy-two oars that move the soul of man. It is only in keeping with the divine universal laws that we have refrained from granting to you, as students, yea, even a broader horizon of your true heritage.

You may ask your questions.

What takes place between the electrical and magnetic bodies when the mind has no past tape to deal with a new situation?

The question is well put. What takes place with the electrical, which is the conscious mind, and the magnetic body, which is the subconscious mind, when there are no dreams to, as you stated, deal with a conscious experience? Is that correct?

That is correct.

When man, his eternal soul, views an experience and he is not controlled by the magnetic body, which is the dreams of yesterday, in reference to the experience, and he is not controlled by the censorship of the conscious mind, those two minds neutralize themselves and you have what is known as soul perception through what is commonly referred to as the superconscious. When that takes place, total consideration is manifest in the experience. Because man has not yet made the conscious effort to neutralize these two bodies, that neutrality may view the experience, then man is bound by the experience. When the soul views, through the perfect balance of the conscious and the subconscious minds, any given situation, the soul is freed from the magnetic-creating processes and, being freed from it, views Life, the dream that she, in truth, is. And man, his soul, is freed.

What is the spiritual responsibility when one takes the life of one of God's creatures that, in man's eyes, are insignificant, such as insects, snakes, etc.?

Thank you for your most important question. And, in truth, no man has the power to take any life. For example, man, the glory of his ego, thinks by stepping on a humble creature, he has killed that creature, say, the ant or the grasshopper. Man has not killed him. Man has simply freed him—the insect, the grasshopper, or a human being—from the bondage of what you call the earth body. You hear?

Yes.

However, this does not mean that man does not face his educated conscience. Now, the educated conscience says that man shall not kill another. And because man has that education, then man pays the price of his own beliefs. Now, that is the educated conscience. Now, the spiritual conscience dictates: do unto others as ye would that others do unto you. And so the spiritual law is an immutable law. And if you hurt another, you guarantee to be hurt, for that is the divine law that is inescapable. I do hope that's helped with your question.

Thank you. How does one perceive the principle involved in one's experiences?

By freeing themselves from the bondage and enslavement of the subconscious and conscious mind. We discussed that in soul perception a few moments earlier.

Thank you. Shakespeare wrote that all the world is a stage, etc. Would you give your understanding of how this takes place?

In reference to that wonderful philosopher, Shakespeare, that all of life is a stage and how does it take place, because man dreams, he, by the law of his own dreaming, must play the part, the effect of the dream that he set into motion. For that is the Law of Life. And so man has dreamed many dreams. Each moment of each day is revealing to him the effect of his own dreams. And only a fool would blame an experience, an effect in life, on another soul, because it would take a fool not to view the eternal truth that each and every experience in all of life is an effect of their own dreaming.

And so here we are, my children, the actors and actresses playing on the stage of life, the great illusion and delusion of our own created mind. That that is creation is a dual law. Truth is not duality. Freedom is not duality. And soul *is*.

And so it is, my students, when of your mind you seek the truth, the wheel of delusion, the playing of your dreams of yesterday, view the experience of the moment and the delusion increases more and more and more. But it takes a man of character, a man of strength and honesty, to say, "O God, here I am. A little microscopic dot in your universes looking out at your greatness and blaming you and everything else for my weaknesses." That is not the path to growth, my students. It is not the path to change or freedom. It is not the path to the expansion of consciousness, the broadening of your horizons.

Learn to let go. Learn to surrender the importance of the mind. Surrender it, and you will indeed be free.

Thank you. The uneducated ego rejects an idea which it did not originate. What, therefore, is the process of unfolding acceptance?

The uneducated ego, or ego, rejects thoughts, not ideas, for the ego does not receive ideas. Ideas come from the Godhood and they are expressed through the heart and the soul of man. Thoughts come from the brain and the uneducated ego. How does man get the ego, the uneducated ego, to accept a thought that it, itself, has not originated? It's called, my students, spiritual awareness.

Whenever you have a thought—and you have been told many times—ask yourself the honest question, "From whence cometh this thought? From whence cometh this thought that I have?" Be honest with yourself and you will start the inward journey and you will find the true cause of the thought that you are entertaining. You will not only find the true cause of the thought, but into your mind's eye, so to speak, will be revealed the dream that sent forth the thought from your subconscious to your conscious mind.

Now, that is one way that you receive thought. There are many, many ways that you receive thought. You could be, and often are, in rapport with a person, though not seeing them, you could be receptive to their level of consciousness and receive all kinds of thoughts: it's known as auric pollution.

Now, the soul expresses ideas. They are felt in the heart. They are impressed upon the mind. If the mind is not educated, in the sense that it is freed from the control of the dreams of yesterday, the impression of the soul upon the mind and the feeling through the heart, which is the vehicle of the soul, it cannot be registered. For example, ofttimes, moment by moment the soul within impresses upon the mind of man to express. Now, the mind of man looks around the world and it says, "No.

Not here. Not now." And it justifies the reason why it does not express itself in keeping with the preservation of its dreams of yesterday.

Now, my friends, evolution is the eternal Law of Life. But it is, indeed, a very slow process to evolve when the very nature of the mind is to hold and to preserve. Man's true security is not in dreams of yesterday. His true security is in maturity: that he grow up and become a man, that he no longer act like a six-year-old boy, that when he doesn't have his own way, he doesn't react emotionally—just because, when we were five or six, we were permitted to gain our own way, to do what we wanted, when we wanted, because our parents or guardians did not want to be bothered with our temper tantrums. Surely there is no benefit to our soul to be in this constant trauma and temper tantrums at the age of forty or thirty or fifty. Now think, my students. Whenever you react to what someone says, does, or doesn't do or doesn't say, you are reacting from a very immature level of consciousness, about that of a six-year-old emotional body.

Thank you. How can one truly forgive a level within oneself in order to be freed from an illness or other experience?

By first viewing in honesty the level of consciousness that exists within us. Now, ofttimes man prays and prays and prays to God to be freed from illness, from suffering, from lack and limitation, from all types of things man prays to God to be free. But he doesn't give God a chance to work. You see, God, the Divine Intelligence, the great freedom, can only be experienced within us when the obstructions are removed. *We* have to do the work. *We* have to become receptive to God. The reason we have to become receptive to God is because we have built up these mountains of obstructions. And so man prays to God to be freed from pain and he prays and he prays and the pain doesn't go away. Well, of course, it doesn't go away: he hasn't removed his own mind from it, his mind, his dream that is registering pain. Pain is registered within the human consciousness, but there is a power greater than the mind: it is called God, your eternal soul. You have the power within you to put those dreams to sleep. You have been given every way possible, but it has to mean enough to you to make the constant effort.

So often man says, "Well, I have tried this for a week and it doesn't work." What comparison is that to the mind's building of obstructions for sixty years? No, my friends, the energy must be balanced and equaled, then man may view in perspective, then man may be freed. But you see, man relies upon the mind and man relies upon what the mind has accepted. And so man has pain and he accepts a pill. But remember that God's pill is man's will and it's called sickness. But that is the right that God has granted to man. When man stops relying upon pills and things of a mental nature for freedom, then man will be freed.

Thank you. Would you please explain the process of transference?

The process of transference is dependent upon the degree of rapport that one soul has with another soul. For example, there is transference in what man calls love, for love, in truth, is the reflection in another of the goodness in oneself. And so there is a transference taking place in that respect. Depending upon the rapport that any soul has with another soul and depending upon the soul compassion for the other soul, is transference in its fullness possible. For example, ofttimes in marriage there is such a rapport established that the wife may suffer the pains and grief and sorrow of the husband and vice versa. Now, these pains and griefs and sorrows are very real, for there is an established rapport and transference.

Now, it is possible, on higher levels of spiritual consciousness, to take on, out of compassion, the obstructions existing in another mind unto oneself. But this is only possible on higher levels of consciousness and is rarely done by man.

Thank you. If a baby goes to the spirit world, what contact, if any, is maintained with its parents on earth?

A baby leaving the earth realm for the realms of spirit is cared for and guided by those mothers who have merited and earned a baby to care for. Ofttimes in earth life women are unable to have babies of their own, because of their own deep-seated and rooted subconscious rejections. Now, many times a person will say, "Well, I have a physical problem." But let us not forget, my students, that physical problems are the effect of mental problems. And so it is that a baby, entering the realms of spirit, is cared for by a mother. And this child, as it is raised by their spirit mother, so to speak, is brought to earth by the mother that she or he may learn of their true earth parents.

Thank you. Please tell us of pain, its reasons and its manifestations.

In reference to the word *pain,* we know, in truth, that it is recorded in consciousness—the direct effect of discord and disharmony within the human mind. We have stated many times that all illness, all pain, is the effect of this discord in consciousness.

Now, the soul is not a discordant note, but the soul can only express through the heart and impinge its message gently upon the human consciousness or mind. Through surrender, true surrender, man can and is freed from pain—the surrender of the dream of pain, for the mind is a dreaming process. The mind has created the dream. And that which creates a thing is capable of freeing itself from it. The soul views, the dream is created, and the mind plays the dream and the body reacts. But you cannot free man from pain or free him from sickness unless you work body, soul, and mind. And so, my friends, work with the true Power, called God, on a soul level. You can accomplish mental things with the mind. You accomplish spiritual, seeming miracles, with the soul.

Thank you, friends. Good night.

SEPTEMBER 11, 1975

CONSCIOUSNESS CLASS 95

Greetings, students. This evening we are discussing the Law of Justification, excuses, a mental process conceived by the mind for balance of the emotional body and preservation of the uneducated ego, frequently revealed in the emotionally immature adult. I know that you all are most familiar with justification and excuses. And so it is that we are discussing with you this evening the law that governs the mind as it strives to justify and to defend the position that it takes in any given situation.

My good students, you all know that truth needs no defense. You all know of the great effort that the mind constantly makes to preserve its dreams of yesterday. And so it is, my children, that balance of the bodies within does not come to any soul who does not make the constant effort to bring balance in their universes.

You know that the subconscious mind is commonly referred to as the emotional body. You know that it is the magnetic body that attracts and holds all things in your universe. And you know that the conscious mind constitutes the electrical body, which sends forth all things from your universes.

Now, my children, when you find yourselves trapped, so to speak, in the magnetic field, commonly referred to as the emotional body, you may be rest assured that you are suppressing, not expressing, the various feelings and emotions that are within you. You also know that suppression is bondage, that expression is freedom. But expression without total consideration is license and is also bondage.

When man makes greater effort to be honest with himself, to be honest with his own feelings, to bring them to the fore of the conscious mind, to look at them in the spirit of objectivity, then, and then only, will he start upon the path of reason, known as balance.

Now, you all have been taught that your soul, this moment, is encased in the nine bodies in one, which is, in truth, its own totality. The direction of the divine energy to one, two, three, or four of those bodies, limiting this energy, denying its expression through the other bodies or vehicles through which your soul is striving to express, creates an imbalance within you and you cannot have freedom and happiness, fulfillment or success. And so it is, my children, that this grounding process in one of the bodies, usually the emotional body, causes what is known as the trauma of life.

Each of the nine bodies through which your soul is expressing is directly related to the planets in the universe. And when you awaken within yourselves in consciousness to those bodies, you will then understand that you are an inseparable part of all universes.

My students, the only difficulty in expressing freedom, happiness, and success and joy is the difficulty that we alone insist upon having. For example, when we state that we are not growing, we direct energy to the obstruction created by mind in order that we may continue to receive attention and energy to one of the bodies which is almost totally depleted from the lack of directing energy to it through our own efforts.

And so it is, my children, if we would pause to think, if we would pause to listen, we would then hear, we would then see what, in truth, we are sending forth into the universe. For each spoken word, each act, each deed that we do each moment is revealing to us, and to all souls who are awakened, what our greatest need of the moment truly is. If you find yourselves discouraged, if you find yourselves hurt, if you find yourselves in despair and grief, then be rest assured you, yourself, have not, and are not, directing your attention to the higher spiritual bodies of consciousness within your own being. And you have a great need to be freed from the more gross bodies of consciousness. And so, my friends, when you feel all is lost, be of good cheer, for that is indeed a good sign: it means that finally you are reaching the bottom of the vehicle which you have over polluted from your self-concern, from your own self-interest and, having reached the very bottom, you are destined to rise in consciousness.

It is not your soul that wants to remain on the bottom of anything. It is the body itself: the emotional body, the mental body that wants to hold your soul, for it has held it already for a lifetime.

Why is it, my good students, that people who are emotional, who go into what we refer to in our philosophy as the forces of frustration, why is it when they speak the words and release the energy they feel a little better? It is because there is no room left in the emotional body for any increase of feeling and it must be released. Because of our dreams of yesterday, because of our patterns of mind, we have limited and restricted the expression of God, the Divine Energy itself. Because we have done that, we live a life of frustration, emotional forces.

As we stated earlier, justification and excuses are frequently revealed in the emotionally immature adult. The energy, my good students, must flow through the body. If you continue to restrict and limit the divine energy, you will, in time, burn out, so to speak, by your own grounding, one or more of the bodies through which God is striving to express. My dear students, no one, nothing in form or out of form is greater than the Divine Intelligence, which is the simple truth of expression.

And so, my students, can you now not see that selfless service is, in truth, the only path to spiritual illumination? For it is the only path through which man may free the divine energy in such a way that his mind is not related with it or to it. All of man's problems, all of his unhappiness, all of man's disturbances are the direct effect of the mind or will of man limiting the harmonic flow of God. And so, as you find yourselves in the forces of frustration, which seem, to us in our realm, to be a daily entertainment of earth children, remember it is only your lack of permitting God to flow freely.

You have been shown the way, my students. Only you can make the decision, if not this moment, then some moment in the great eternity. But also remember, the longer you wait, the more difficult it becomes. If you think it is difficult today, then wait for your tomorrows. For each tomorrow adds another burden as you stand in your own light and become the eternal obstruction to God.

As our little class proceeds, we will speak further on the evolution of the vehicles of the soul, of what they are constituted, and how the soul is freed from them.

At this time, we shall listen to the questions you have submitted.

Thank you. Will you please speak to us of giving?

Thank you for your question on the Law of Giving, which is so fitting to the discussion we just had. Man is not the giver. He never was, he never will be unless you understand that through man's efforts to get out of the way that the Divine Intelligence, called God, may express itself. Man, when he steps aside in consciousness and permits God to flow, when he grants God, God's divine right of expression, then man, in his ignorance of the divine law, believes that he has given something. And so it is, as man steps aside and lets God, the great beauty, rhythm, and harmony flow, God returns that to man in keeping with the divine law known as balance and reason. And so, O man, keep faith with reason, called balance, for that is when you, your mind, views the beauty, the wonder, and the glory of the true God of Gods.

Thank you. Please trace the steps leading to jealousy. How does one recognize it in himself and others? And how can it be overcome?

Thank you so much for your question. In the first place, man cannot recognize in another what he does not first recognize within himself. And so it simply means, when we view jealousy in another individual, we have first viewed it in ourselves. Now, what is it that constitutes jealousy? From what does jealousy truly stem? You have been taught in this philosophy that desire was the divine expression of God. What man does with desire is sometimes beneficial, ofttimes most detrimental.

And so it is the nature of the mind to desire that which is pleasing to the mind. But that which is pleasing to the mind is dependent upon the acceptances of the mind from all past experiences, called dreams. And so it is that the minds of men look out into the world and they see things that, to them, are desirable, but because they have created in their own minds obstructions to the attainment of the things they desire, they experience what is known as envy, what is known as jealousy. For it is their desire to possess that which they are not willing to make the effort to attain because of the obstructions existing in their own consciousness.

How is man freed from these obstructions? How is man freed from what he calls envy, jealousy, and greed? He is freed from all those things by declaring in his heart the eternal truth: "All things that I seek or desire, thou, O God of Gods, have already granted unto me. Knowing this great truth, O God, direct me with strength of character to face the obstructions in my own consciousness. Once having faced them, grant me the power to remove them, that this great truth, that all things are within me, may be made manifest in my universe."

Thank you. How is logic related to reason when used in everyday living situations?

Thank you for your question in reference to logic. Logic is an instrument of the mind, a function. Reason is a faculty of the soul. Reason has total consideration. Logic is based upon the accepted thoughts and experiences of man. Logic leads to bondage. Reason leads to freedom. When man uses total consideration of himself, then man is qualified to express total consideration for another. Logic does not grant that to man.

Thank you. Is a white lie ever justified?

That depends, my good students, on what you mean by a "white lie." If you decide to lie, you may deceive yourself and call it white or you may be honest and call it black, but the principle does not change. The principle is the essence of truth. In the world in which you live, if the motive is pure, then the method is legal. But methods, my students, are not devices. Devices are what are conceived by mind stuff. Methods are based upon soul faculties. Methods are based upon the foundation of understanding, total consideration. Methods are legal based upon the faculties of the eternal soul.

Now, many times people who do not want to see someone for some various reason or thought will use what is known as lies. They're using deception. And the mind doesn't know principle. Truth is not known by the mind. No, my students, for the mind is limited. And how can limitation know truth, which is freedom? No. And so, my students, if you choose to use lies and call them white or if you choose to use lies and call them black, lie is lie, no matter what garment you cover it with. And it shall return unto you, for it is deception and it shall deceive you, for you have mothered it, you have fathered it. It is your child. And all children know their own homes.

Thank you. When one feels rejected, why is retaliation often taken out on oneself?

My dear students, rejection is an absolute and automatic guarantee of retaliation. We must first ask ourselves the question, for example, "I feel rejected. What part of me, which body feels rejected? My mental body, my emotional body, my spiritual body, my universal body, my astral body, my celestial body, which body feels rejected?" It is the emotional body that feels rejected. And it is the emotional body that retaliates. Ofttimes with some people, because of their consideration for others, also because of their pride, they will retaliate against their own emotional body. However, usually it's the other way around.

When we feel rejected, we retaliate against that which we have any feeling for. We retaliate against the people and the places that we have some rapport with, some liking towards, or feeling for. We do not walk down the street and retaliate against a perfect stranger, usually. The reason we don't do that is because of fear: we really don't know what they might say or do. Sometimes, however, we will retaliate against the store clerk, who had absolutely nothing to do with our feeling of rejection. That is dependent upon the programming of each individual.

People who feel rejected—and we find no soul today on earth who does not experience in their emotional body in the course of one day at least one feeling of rejection, whether they recognize it as such or not. Does that not, in truth, reveal that man has over directed the divine energy to his own emotional body, that man, in truth, on earth is absolutely filled with frustrations, because he hasn't yet made the necessary effort to express his true being? Woe to the souls who retaliate against themselves when they feel rejected, for the retaliation unto oneself drives oneself deeper and deeper and deeper into self-pity and self-concern, the greatest disaster to befall the human soul.

We stated many years ago, "O man, think humble yet well of thyself, for in thy thinking is created the vehicle of the soul [*The Living Light* and also *The Living Light Dialogue Volume 1*]." Yet man insists upon thinking high and thinking low of himself. One moment in the clouds, the next moment like a gopher. Never satisfied with the hole that he insists upon digging. My good students, pray for balance. Pray for God's eternal peace, for only God can free you from the mountain of frustration in which you have trapped your eternal, beautiful soul.

Thank you. In Discourse 51, you described nine states of mind or consciousness as follows: superconsciousness, conscious, subconscious, solar conscious, celestial, terrestrial, infinite, cosmic, and universal. In Discourse 62, you described six states of consciousness as follows: self, slave, servant, student, preacher, teacher. Please elaborate on the correspondence and correlation of both discourses.

The question is a very important question. And it is for the ears of the questioner only. And may I speak at this moment in reference to a universal, infinite law which states, The secrets of the universe are never given to a blabbermouth. And so the student who has asked the question, if he has learned that universal law, may speak to me in private at a future time and receive the answer. Because their soul consciousness, at the moment of asking the question, was inspired from a higher level than can be discussed at this time, the question shall be handled in a private manner. Thank you.

Thank you. What are some practical, day-to-day methods to help one rise above likes and dislikes?

A very simple and practical, moment-by-moment, day-by-day effort and practice is to flood the consciousness with, "Rhythm, harmony, balance, peace. Hold release, hold release." My good students, I cannot overemphasize: the "Call of the Soul" frees the soul, but the mind does not understand its value. When your soul is ready, you will use, not abuse, the eternal "Call of the Soul" and you will indeed be free.

Good night.

SEPTEMBER 18, 1975

CONSCIOUSNESS CLASS 96

Greetings, students on the path. We are discussing at this time responsibility, sanity, and surrender.

Saneness is merely a perfect balance of energy between the electric and magnetic fields of the human mind. This perfect balancing of energy is possible for all mankind when he recognizes and accepts that there is a greater authority that governs all life and sustains it. And so it is when man, in the course of his experiences, which are the direct effects of his own direction of God's energy, surrenders his thought, his emotion, his disturbance to the Power intelligently expressed in all of the universes, known as God, balance is possible. However, man has made for himself a barrier between his balance of the mind and surrender of this divine energy.

We all know that all things are, in truth, energy, that man's eternal soul is expressing through what is called an energy field. When man insists upon entertaining a thought and refusing to surrender the thought to the Divine, or God, man becomes the obstruction. He blocks the free flow and balance of the divine energy. We have spoken many times that there is no lack of energy in the universes, that the seeming lack is because man has chosen to be the obstruction to the flow this divine energy. We have also spoken on the word *responsibility*—the ability to respond.

And so it is, my children, as you are seeking to broaden your horizons, to free yourselves, to enjoy life, and be happy, you must first make the initial effort to surrender the thoughts, the feelings, and the emotions that rob you of your peace of mind. For you are standing in your own eternal light, declaring that you, and you alone—your minds—have the answer to all of life. Your horizons cannot broaden until you make the tiny effort to surrender that which seems to be disturbing and plaguing you.

My good students, no life is ever lived in vain, for each life is a rung on the eternal ladder of progression. All consciousness is one. That one consciousness, all things are an inseparable part thereof. As man dreams his many dreams, he magnetically attaches in consciousness to the dream that he dreams. Once having attached, which is through the magnetic field of energy, man becomes his own dream.

It appears to some that man, in truth, enjoys his suffering, enjoys his grief, and enjoys his sadness. In a sense, this is a true statement: in the sense that all things, all creation, all form is an energy field.

When man chooses, as he often does daily, to become the obstruction of the free flow of this divine energy by directing it to a particular thought or interest to the exclusion and starvation of other areas of consciousness, those areas of consciousness, lacking their sustenance and support of divine energy, begin to cry for food and survival. And so man gains energy for those areas of consciousness through what is known as negative receptivity. Now, negative receptivity is what man has done in his mind to gain energy for areas of consciousness that, for some reason or another, he has chosen not to balance. It is commonly referred to, in your psychiatric clinics, as failure and frustration. We find the earth realm filled with negative receptivity of energy or more commonly called frustration.

And so it is the mind, the most tenacious and clever instrument ever designed, gains the energy that it needs by what is called negativity. And through these negative thought patterns, man has found that he gains attention, which, in truth, is energy. That, my good students, is not responsibility unto oneself. It is not sanity and it is the furthest thing from surrender.

I know that all of you present are seeking a path to light and freedom and happiness. But your seeking, my friends, shall ever go in vain if you are not willing and ready to make a little more effort to understand the vehicles through which your soul is, at this moment, expressing itself.

It has been said many times that honesty is the best policy. My students, honesty is the only way. Be honest with yourselves and you will free yourselves from the greatest deceiver ever designed, known as the human mind—the deceiver because man has made it so. Be honest with yourself and you will not only learn, but you will become the living demonstration of the freedom of your eternal soul. You will no longer doubt, you will no longer question, what is principle, what is truth, what is life, for you will become those very things in expression. You will become them in expression. You already are, your soul, the truth, the life, the principle.

You will not have to use and abuse, under the facade and guise of spiritual seeking or endeavors, the deception of old patterns. You will see clearly with your own eternity what the created form, through your own efforts, has done to you so far. You will no longer have to justify and to excuse yourself to yourself. You will not have to deceive yourself with those devices. You will be honest and declare the eternal truth of how much effort you are making for your own freedom and for your own peace of mind. You will no longer have to live in the clouds of illusion and delusion. You will see, in truth, where you stand in eternity. You will not have to think about failure or victory, for you will be the true be that you are in truth.

It is of no value, my students, to dream of hopes. It is of no value to look for bright tomorrows when you insist on keeping dark todays. It is of no value to look outside and blame the world when you know, in truth, that you have the power, the intelligence, the reason, and the way to help yourself to be strong of character, to be a witness for God, the only power that brings you peace, love, life, and light. When it means enough you indeed, my students, will care. You will care for that which, in truth, is yours: your eternal spirit.

Of what benefit is it to you to gain the wisdom of the ages when it does not yet have sufficient value to turn your efforts one degree to goodness and to God? It is time indeed, my good students, to look in the mirror of life, which is called experience, and be honest with yourself. You must face yourselves someday.

The longer you wait, the more difficult it becomes. Do you not yet see the benefit of facing yourselves in honest perspective today? There is no escape in any eternity, in any realm, in any dimension. There is no escape from facing your true self.

Man cries for freedom and holds with a tenacity greater than any creature on Earth to bondage. Man cries for joy and wallows in sadness. Is that not, my good students, a contradiction, a duality so diverse that it cannot help but be viewed as imbalance or more commonly known as insanity? To speak forth the word with God's energy—for it is God's energy that sustains the word—to speak forth one thing and manifest its opposite is an absolute and direct guarantee of failure. My students, is failure so pleasing to your mind that you desire, in truth, to guarantee its continuity? What does failure bring to man, but negative energy, known as pity. It does not uplift the eternal soul. It sends it deeper into the caverns of darkness.

Some of you, I know, are thinking I speak a bit strongly. But consider, my good students, it took strength to drive your soul down. It's taking strength to pull it up. For the way out of a thing is the way that you got into the thing in the first place. And it is from the direction of your self-will that your soul descends. And it is the direction of that same will, turned to God in total surrender, that will lift it up to heaven's heights.

Now, total surrender, my students, does not mean you sit back in an easy chair and say, "Well, I have surrendered, God. I have surrendered. I wait now for you to move me." God does not move through an obstruction. God moves when man makes the effort to remove the obstruction that he, man, has created. Surrendering to God does not mean no effort. Surrendering to God means to remove the obstruction that you created and placed in front of God in the first place.

And so it is, my students, that responsibility—the ability to respond—sanity, and surrender is a triune soul faculty, inseparable from and the handmaiden of faith, poise, and humility.

You all know the first soul faculty of duty, gratitude, and tolerance. And you know the second soul faculty of faith, poise, and humility. And now you know the handmaiden of both of them: responsibility, sanity, and surrender. For without that faculty you do not, in truth, have duty, gratitude, and tolerance. You do not, in truth, have faith, poise, and humility.

And now, my friends, I will be grateful to share with you our understanding on the questions that you have.

Thank you. I understand that man has mental, physical, and spiritual bodies. Do plants and the so-called lower animals also have a mental body? Please explain.

In reference to your question that man has—man is spirit and has a mental and physical body and several other bodies. Plants are spirit and have mental, emotional, and physical bodies. Rocks—or the mineral kingdom—are spirit, which, in truth, is Energy, intelligently expressing itself, called God. And so rocks are spirit and have mind and body.

Now, the question may well arise—it already has in some minds of my students—"I can possibly accept that a plant or tree has an intelligence, a mind, and a physical body. But I cannot accept that a rock has such." My friends, it's only your limited view. The Infinite Intelligence, called Spirit or God, is exactly what it says: infinite, intelligent energy expressing itself. The rock has feelings. It has mind. It has emotion, as your world is finally becoming aware, a little of it, about the plants.

Many times plants or trees have a total disagreement about who is going to share the space around them. The disagreement is so intense that one of the plants finally wilts and what you call dies. Your world is just beginning to blink its eyes and to see, to feel, and to know that this intelligence is everywhere present, never absent or away; that man, earth man, bears a great burden of responsibility, a burden because of his self-interest, his self-concern, his self-will, his self-pity. He has not, on the whole, cared for, let alone considered, the rest of creation. And yet it is man's thoughts and man's feelings, permeating the atmosphere, that have polluted the flowers, the trees, the plants, and the blades of grass, the animals and, yea, even man himself.

We have spoken many times that the word *disease* is nothing more, nor less, than discord, emanating from an imbalanced mind, called man. We have also stated that the planet Earth is the fifth planet in your solar system. The planet on which your souls have come to learn the lesson of lessons, called faith. My good students, without surrender, there is no faith. Do not deceive yourselves that you may have faith if you do not have surrender. Many a prophet has taught, if you have the faith of a half a grain of mustard seed, speak to the mountain and tell it to move and the mountain shall move. But earth men have little or no faith, for they have little or no surrender. Is it any wonder that earth men cry, like voices in the wilderness, for God and in their very crying, lack the faith, because they are not willing to surrender?

Thank you. Could you please give us the procedure for meditation?

In reference to the question on the procedure of meditation, we have given it many times to the questioner. And it is evident, because the questioner has again asked the question, that the answer we have given to the questioner has not been satisfactory or in keeping with their preconceived thoughts of what they, as an individual, choose to do in reference to meditation. And so at this time we will give unto you the one word, the only word that can free you and bring to you the meditation experience that you, in truth, are seeking and that word—three words, in truth—is surrender to God your self-will. Then you will experience the heavenly heights that you are seeking.

Thank you. Would you please speak to us of choosing the hour most proper for meditation? Does the correct hour vary with each individual?

In reference to the question, hours proceeding the noon day under the vibratory wave of the light of your planet, called Sun, is advisable. Some time ago we brought through a little saying that states clearly, "Put God in it or forget it." My good students, you can't put God in anything that you're in. You first must take your self-will out of it, so God can get in it.

Thank you. Women's liberation has been commented on often disparagingly. Isn't its goal similar to the one expressed in the teaching, "When motherhood becomes brotherhood, the children will grow up?" In this connection, please give your understanding of universal motherhood and comment upon when it may appropriately be directed for positive effects?

In speaking on the first part of your question, which is evident and obvious, a personal interest called women's liberation and in reference to your understanding that we have spoken disparagingly concerning that movement, I do sincerely pray that you may awaken and not misunderstand statements made concerning sincere spiritual efforts and not the facade of their appearances.

In reference to universal motherhood, motherhood is not limited to a certain species or sex. That is the limited view that earth men have of eternal truth. You see the forms or personalities and are blinded to the principles, which are truth. All people, so-called men or women, have a level of consciousness known as universal motherhood. And it simply means this: when the soul faculty of compassion, in its efforts to express itself, becomes obstructed by the magnetic field, then you have what is known as universal motherhood: the need, the drive, the desire, the intensity for running everybody's business but your own. When this universal motherhood becomes brotherhood, the soul faculty of compassion is freed from the magnetic field and becomes expressed through a balanced electromagnetic field and then, my students, you have the brotherhood of man, the heaven on earth.

Thank you. Is universal motherhood at the root of the ambivalent relationship between man and woman? For example, the smothering role first played by the parents and then carried on by the children in their subsequent relationships in life.

In reference to your question, dealing purely with psychology and not, in truth, spirituality, I would like to say this: our adversities become our attachments; it is an immutable, subtle law. And so it is in creation, in personality, in form, that man—and I've often said by that word I mean "humanity"—that man has chosen, by his own mind, what is. He has guaranteed, by establishing in his own thought, what is right and what is wrong. He, by his own thought, directs God's infinite, divine, intelligent energy into attachments and adversities. The law ever seeks to balance itself. As water reaches its own level by its own weight, so it is that your adversities, then, become your attachments. And so it is that your attachments become your adversities.

And all you have to do is to be honest with yourselves and look at your own world and you will see how the law, guaranteeing her own balance, is driving you eternally into your adversities and freeing you from your attachments. For reason, in which a wise man keeps faith, transfigures us. And reason is perfect balance. So remember, my students, as you speak the word and use the infinite, intelligent, divine energy, remember, the adversities you are building, you shall live to adore.

Thank you. To what degree have cultural customs been influenced by the widespread practice of universal motherhood and also so-called professional therapy and medical practice?

In reference to professional therapy and medical practice, little, very little, if any, energy has caused change in cultures. Now, this may seem to be the furthest thing from truth. But if you look at all civilization throughout the centuries, you will see that it is, in truth, the magnetic field that has caused upheavals and changes. It is the magnetic field that holds, binds, and destroys itself in time, for that is the law. And so it is that so-called universal motherhood, serving a seeming bad purpose in one way, serves, in another way, a very good purpose.

Thank you. In Discourse 10, you spoke of the plane of ozone and its great importance to life. Could you share your broader understanding of it and the effect of man's technology upon it?

In reference to the plane of ozone, of which we spoke some time ago, that encircles the entire planet of Earth, your scientists, for some time, have understood it to be composed of poisonous gases. In truth, this sphere or plane of ozone is the protective shield, without which life, as you know it this day, could not exist on your earth realm. Within the coming thirty years, your scientists will know more of the true purpose of the plane of ozone and, knowing more of its true purpose, shall gain great respect for the Intelligence that has placed it there in the first place, for the good of the Earth planet.

Thank you. Good night.

SEPTEMBER 25, 1975

CONSCIOUSNESS CLASS 97

Greetings, fellow students. This evening we should like to speak in keeping with broader horizons and ever expanding consciousness. We are speaking on evolution, universal consciousness, the gods and goddesses, and the cloak of creation.

Now, we have spoken before on the forty soul faculties and the forty sense functions and the one divine principle, which has been referred to, in the teachings already given, as the eighty-one levels of consciousness. We have also spoken with you in reference to the nine bodies in which your soul, in truth, is expressing.

In perhaps a further clarification of these functions and faculties, these levels of consciousness, and these bodies of expression, the nine bodies of which we have spoken are the nine spheres, known as the totality of expression. In each sphere of expression, there are nine planes of consciousness, which, in truth, are the eighty-one of rungs along the ladder of eternal progression. The forty functions and forty faculties are the expression through these spheres and planes of consciousness in your eternal moment in which your soul now resides.

Because you, many of you, are not aware of the dimensions in which you, in truth, are expressing, does not in any way free you from the expressing that you are doing in those dimensions. The reason that you are not yet aware of those levels of consciousness, those planes, and spheres of action is because your energy is directed so often to the one level or two levels of consciousness in your material, mundane world.

Now, the soul, as we have often spoken, is evolving in the sense that it is passing through a multitude of vehicles in this great sea of eternity. There has always been a few awakened souls on your earth realm who were aware that they did not come to earth from a nothingness and, not coming from a nothingness, they were not destined to enter a nothingness.

And so it is that in your world today you have many theories and many philosophies. You have a theory and philosophy commonly referred to as reincarnation. There is an essence of truth in the sense that the soul has experienced life prior to its present life. The illusion is that it experiences that life by returning to the plane of consciousness which you call earth that it resided on a century or so prior to its present experience. This evolutionary process, my friends, is not something in some far distant year or eternity. It is something that is taking place each and every moment in consciousness within you at this time.

It seems that some of my students are unaware of what the astral, spiritual, mental bodies truly are. And it is our purpose at this time to share with you our understanding of some of those bodies that you are in this very moment. As a point of clarification, we have stated before that the physical body is an effect of the mental body, which is an effect of the astral body, which is an effect of the other bodies. The astral body, my friends, is not *inside* the physical body: it surrounds the physical body. The physical body that you are aware of stands in the midst of what is referred to as an egg-shaped aura. This aura is an energy field, known as your astral body. This astral body permeates your physical body, your mental body, and etc.

When you permit yourselves to be controlled by levels of consciousness that are disturbing, you, in truth, are being controlled by other bodies of which your soul is striving to evolve through. We have often taught that self-control, the effect thereof is true freedom. Awareness, my friends, spiritual awareness—that you may evolve peacefully and harmoniously in the here and now.

So many people think, because they have not awakened themselves, that they will not experience an astral or spiritual world until so-called death or transition. We have stated many times that you cannot experience any plane of consciousness or any sphere that you do not have a vehicle of expression—an energy field—created to experience that sphere or plane of consciousness. And so it is that all earth children have an astral body. That this astral body, they are directing a great deal of energy to. Many times in sleep you experience the astral experience. Rarely is it pleasant; often is it a nightmare. That, of course, is dependent upon your individual efforts to place the light of eternal truth and freedom on the highest priority in your consciousness.

Everywhere you go and every thought you think is directing energy to one of the eighty-one levels of consciousness, to the nine spheres or bodies of expression. And so we see the earth realm, the effect, by far with the majority of souls residing upon it, the effect of astral stardust and astral sleep. We have stated before that a day's effort on earth to rise your soul consciousness to heaven, to God within, could save you a century in the other dimensions. For no matter how small the effort that you make each moment of each day, it saves you, my children, so many centuries in these other worlds, for you are creating, by placing your attention upon creation, you are creating the bondage of your own eternal soul.

Now, universal consciousness is a state of consciousness in which you become fully aware, not only of the spheres of action, but of the many, many centuries, the many, many, many centuries of your soul expressing in these various dimensions and bodies. We stated long ago that the body, the house, the temple of God, is a direct effect of your soul's evolution. You have all of the tools necessary to pass the test, which are the effect of the laws that you alone have set into motion. For there is no law, there is no law that is not, in time, fulfilled.

And so it is, my children, in universal consciousness you will know beyond a shadow of any doubt why you are where you are and what you are; that your soul has many, many times experienced the lessons, the difficulties, the adversities that you are experiencing this very day. So the greater the task before you, is a revelation, a revelation of your own evolution. So be indeed filled with gratitude in your heart if what you call your cross is heavy and a burden, for it is only a burden to the level of consciousness that for centuries has tried to learn its lesson.

We spoke at our last meeting on the handmaiden of responsibility, sanity, and surrender. But surrender is not the easiest thing for the mind to do, for the experience of surrender, to the mind, is a recognition of a greater power, a greater intelligence than the mind itself, a greater consciousness than all forms.

And it is the nature of form to hold. And though it seems unfair that the nature of form is to hold and to bind the eternal free spirit, it is, by the very process of the magnetic hold of form, that form herself is refined and evolved in time. That is the way through which form evolves. And so it is divine law and divine justice that he who holds to form, by form shall be bound. And he who surrenders form, by form shall be freed. You cannot, my good students—nor can anyone—stop the process of evolution, and evolution is the Law of Life.

Some of my students have asked, "How may I attain universal consciousness?" There is one way, and one way only, to attain universal consciousness. And that way is surrender. And when you face the soul faculty of surrender, which is inseparable from sanity or balance and responsibility, the handmaiden of faith, poise, and humility; duty, gratitude, and tolerance, you will need the support of those soul faculties. For it is those nine faculties, the trinity, that will grant you the strength to rise your eternal soul from the satisfaction of sleep that it lies in today.

And remember, my students, that courage is a soul faculty. And what is courage? Courage is the unwavering commitment of the eternal soul to principle. But deceive not yourselves. Principle, the essence of truth, is not known by the human mind. And remember, as you strive to evolve, which is the destiny of all souls, let the light of courage go before you, that you not stumble upon the stones of error and the cliffs of regret.

When we have had enough, indeed shall we pause to think. So let the struggle continue until you're truly ready. Then, my students, when you are truly ready, there will be nothing within your mind that you are not willing to surrender to God. And you will know when you have surrendered, for when you have truly surrendered, it will no longer entertain your thought. You will no longer be so impatient to see what the seed is producing before it has been given a chance to germinate. You will know when you have surrendered, for you will not be in turmoil. You will not be in constant complaint. You will not be in worry and fret. You will stop questioning God. You will stop blaming everything outside of your own mind for your frailties and weaknesses. For you will rise in courage and the lamp of truth will light your path and you will move on in consciousness and the dawn of happiness will flood your universe and the love of God will fill your heart and you will no longer need the trinkets of creation to entertain yourselves, for you will have the peace that passeth all understanding.

And now, my children, we will speak for a moment or two on the gods and goddesses of creation. You know from your own experiences that man is a law unto himself, that like attracts like and becomes the Law of Attachment. And so it is the Law of Creation that all things shall keep company with what they truly are. Now, all of creation is governed and controlled by what is known as the gods and goddesses of creation. For the true God, the Divine Light, the Divine Love, sustains all form and all creation everywhere.

The gods and goddesses, they are those in charge of the multitudes of workers in the earth, fire, water, and air elements—and there are more. Their duty, their responsibility is to maintain a balance between the electric and magnetic fields. And so it is that in many ancient religions you have heard of what is referred to as the nature spirits. These are the armies of workers that diligently work to maintain this balance in keeping with divine principle.

These workers are disturbed and affected by the vibratory waves emanating and polluting the universes from the levels of consciousness of greed and self-concern of the human mind. And so it is that you experience in your Earth planet so-called volcanic eruptions, hurricanes, floods, weather disasters, and so-called freak conditions of nature and imbalanced temperature changes. You experience these things because it is through your thoughts, your attitudes of mind, which are imbalanced by the directing of the divine energy to the magnetic field within your own universe, which, when multiplied by the millions of people, creates adverse conditions or so-called lack of energy for these nature spirits to do their job and bring about balance in the world of creation.

We are speaking to you about this subject that you may give more thought to your personal responsibility in the worlds in which you live. These nature spirits are also the workers of your physical body, for they are the ones that have the responsibility to maintain a balance of the elements and chemicals of your physical body. When you misuse and abuse, through the imbalance of your attitude of mind, this divine energy, the physical body and its deterioration is the effect. When this takes place, these little nature spirits of the elements become very disturbed. The fire spirits fight with the water spirits for energy to do their job. And the air spirits fight with the earth spirits and the other spirits. And the war goes on.

And so it is, my students, that we have shared with you over these years the laws of the universe that you may strive for greater balance, for the effect of this balance is the divinity, the birthright that is truly yours. But you *must* make much greater effort. What you do with your minds can no longer be considered for your own self-interest, for you are responsible, for God, the Divine Intelligence, has granted you superiority over all creation on the planet in which you reside. You can no longer afford to deny the Divine by misusing and abusing this divine energy, which belongs to God, for it is God. You can no longer afford to direct over 90 percent of God to a limited area of expression, for, in so doing, you are starving those nature spirits responsible to maintain balance in accordance with divine law.

And so it is that you are the microcosm of the macrocosm. The disturbing weather conditions are the direct effects of the imbalanced release of divine energy, that you, each and every one of you, are directly responsible to God, the Divine, for your abuse, for your errors of ignorance. For God has given you charge o'er all creation. And because of your abuses of that, you suffer, and sickness and death is the result.

Death, so-called, is not something designed by the Great Designer of all designers. It was not designed by the Architect of the universes. For the divine plan was, is, and shall always be, that you, your soul, may consciously choose to leave your body, to return to it, or to leave it and let it return to the elements of which it was composed. That is the divine plan. Death of anybody without conscious choice is the direct effect of the abuses and misuses of divine energy.

Would it not be better, my children, to see life as it truly is: grades of school of learning that you make your effort, study your lessons well, pass your test, and graduate from body to body in the spirit of joy in the freedom that is the design of the Divine? Would it not be better to have the conscious choice, rather than permit your conscious mind to be the effect of laws established that you lie asleep in error and in ignorance and question God because you suffer and because you die? That is not the way. You may live for as many centuries as you choose to live in keeping with the divine law. Each day you die from error and ignorance.

If only you would choose to surrender to God, you would live in the fullness of life as God intended it to be. You would no longer be concerned with age, for age you would not be. For you would consciously direct, in perfect balance, the Divine.

We all know that God, and God alone, is the physician, the power that healeth, for God, and God alone, brings harmony and balance. You know the way. You have the light and the truth. Your only step that is waiting is application. And when you make that first step to apply the infinite, eternal, immutable laws of life, when you, my children, make that first step, then you will know and go on harmoniously in the eternal moment, peacefully filled with the joy of living. And nothing, in truth, in all the centuries yet to be, will ever again rob you of that peace that passeth all understanding, for once the soul awakens to it by the divine Law of Application, it never loses it in all eternity unless it chooses to do so.

And so, my good students, remember, you are never alone, for a host of angels, either dark or light, entertain your thoughts twenty-four hours a day in your realm. Be they, by your own choice, angels of light, then harmony will be your reward. Be they angels of darkness, then discord and disaster shall be your reward, for that is the law. And if you find yourselves this moment disturbed, in bondage—for that's what disturbance truly is. *Dis-turb* is bondage, controlled by forces that seem beyond your own power. But remember, my students, those forces that seem to be beyond your power are beyond your power because *you* gave them your eternal soul. And when you give your eternal soul back to the source that it belongs to, then those forces of creation, of darkness, and disorder and disturbance will no longer have you as their victim.

Many times we have asked you to think, to think, to think more deeply, more deeply within, to go within and find yourself. You can always tell, my good students, when the forces of darkness have control of your soul, because the mind experiences it: it gets a hold of something that disturbs it and it will not let it go.

We find it advisable for students making great effort to be free to carry with them one of those new gadgets you have on earth, called a tape recorder. And each time you have a thought that disturbs you, speak it in your little tape recorder. And each time you talk to someone about you, which appears to be the most important subject to most people, when you find yourself talking about you and how difficult things are and how you suffer and how you struggle and you can't understand this and you can't understand that, speak it into your little tape recorder. And when you go home each day listen attentively, listen objectively. And ask yourself, "Do I have within me the tolerance necessary to have a friend like that: always gripping, always complaining, never understanding, filled with disturbance and suffering?" That reveals to you, my friends, who is controlling your soul.

If you will make that effort each day to record yourselves, you will be able to gauge the percentage of time, if any, that the angelic host from the realms of Light are able to penetrate and permeate your aura, your consciousness. If you find after nine days effort that the percentages reveal that you are over 50 percent into the forces of negativity and self-concern and self-importance and self-will, then, my good students, take hold quickly, for it only reveals that those forces, that drag your soul to depths of hell, have sufficient control of you and the centuries in those realms are often without number. For souls remain there to this day who have been there for over twenty centuries.

My students, we have striven in our way to speak as clearly, in keeping with the law, as we possibly can. If it means enough to you, you will flood your consciousness with encouragement and you will not feed God's beautiful divine love, light, life, and energy to things that disturb your world.

Many times we have stated, never leave a soul worse than you have found them, for, my students, there is one truth and one life. You are an inseparable part of that life. You cannot separate your consciousness from the consciousness of life. It is not possible, for it is contrary to God's law. You cannot, in truth, separate yourself from the Divine Consciousness that is the life of all form. And when you deny the right of expression of the forms, you become greater than God. And when that happens, you alone pay the price and learn the greatest truth ever given to the universes. And that is, love all life and know the Light.

Good night.

OCTOBER 2, 1975

CONSCIOUSNESS CLASS 98

Greetings, fellow students. In keeping with an ever-expanding consciousness, we should like to speak this evening on faith, the rainbow of which the soul must pass over to reach its fulfillment, its freedom, its eternal destiny.

We have spoken often before on the great importance of the lessons and the opportunities that your souls have merited in their experiences on your present Earth planet. You all know that the planet Earth is the fifth planet in your solar system, that five or fifth is the number of faith.

Faith is not something that you seek, for it is something that you demonstrate each moment of each day. It is not the seeking of faith: it is the direction of this power known as faith, the direction of it by the faculty of reason, for already all souls on your planet are using this great power known as faith. It is the misdirection, the abuse, of this power, called faith, that causes man so much of his turmoil and so much of his own grief. Because the mind has relied upon established patterns for its happiness and fulfillment and because those established patterns are created patterns—and created patterns are governed by the laws of creation, known as opposition or duality—the direction of this power called faith by the mind to established patterns causes great turmoil within the mind. And indeed is this turmoil, in truth, of great benefit, for sooner or later this power called faith gets redirected to the Source called God to free the human soul.

We have spoken about the elementals, the nature spirits, the created thought forms, all of those things are fed this great divine energy by the power of what is known as faith.

The souls on the Earth planet stand on the edge of freedom and bondage, equally distributed: the functions and the faculties. Man stands on this edge. If he wavers out of balance from lack of effort, sooner or later he is driven to balance, to reason, by the power that took him out of balance. And that power is called faith.

Our teaching is, and has always been, to keep faith with reason, for she will transfigure thee. You all know that reason is total consideration. And so it is that it is demonstrable that when one thought, one thought pattern, controls your mind, you are rest assured, my souls, you are not in reason, for reason is total consideration. It not only sees the left path, but it sees the right path. And seeing both paths, it is able, by reason and total consideration, to direct this great power known as faith. For this power, called faith, is a great amalgamation of the electromagnetic energies and will move, as it does, all mountains, all obstructions. And this is why we have taught you to place your attention—God's energy—upon what you want to become, to remove this divine energy from what you want to overcome. For the direction of this power to the obstacle, to the obstruction, creates an ever-increasing and greater obstruction. And so, my good students, try to think more often and try to think more deeply than the entertaining of your obstructions. For placing this divine energy to feed the obstructions denies your own divinity and your own godhood.

You stand in your universe, in your planetary system, at the halfway mark between the left path of yesterday and the right path of daylight and the morrow. What you are doing depends upon your true motivation. We have spoken before on motivation, on motive, and now perhaps we can expand a bit on the understanding of motive.

So often in our endeavors we deceive ourselves by saying to ourselves, "My motive was good. My motive was like anyone else's motive. I'm an average human being." You are here in this philosophy not as demonstrations of average human beings. If that were true, then there would be far more of you than I see at this time. By your efforts, you have already demonstrated an above average interest in life itself. And so it is we must ask the question, "How do I know if my motive in any endeavor is pure and right?"

My good students, the revelation is the experiences you encounter that follow the motive that you alone have established. If your motive was pure, just, and good, then the experience that follows the motivation is pure, just, and good. And if your motive is not such, then the experience is not so pleasant. However, you can change your motive at any time. You can establish a new motive, a new law governing any situation. And when the experiences in life become so distasteful, we start to think, we start to question, we start to ask ourselves, "What am I doing?" Not "What is the world doing?" But "What am I doing? If this is my reward, if this is the effect of my efforts, where am I in my motive? Not where I thought I was, but somewhere else."

Try, my good students, try harder to stop, to think, to free your souls from personality and bondage, to find your motive, to change your experiences in life, for you are in your solar system at the strongest point that you will be. You are on the Earth planet learning the lessons of faith. When you leave your planet, you will not have the gross, dense, physical body to protect you, to shield you from your own thoughts and your own motivations. The images will be with you, as they are already, as constant companions. May, in God's mercy, they be angels of light.

Truth is not something that the mind calls easy, but it is something that the soul knows is simple. Face the truth, my students. Be encouraged that things are better than yesterday, for they are better, if you choose to make them that way. If you choose to make greater effort to direct your faith, to control your mind, to control the thoughts of self, then things are better, and brighter tomorrows are already dawning.

You know what your motivation is, for you know what your experiences are. Let your experiences be pleasant and beautiful. Let your consciousness entertain heavenly realms by the purity of your motivation, by the strength of your character, by the principle of your eternal soul. Let your hearts rise to heaven's heights that your minds be freed from building the obstructions of selfishness and blame of everything. Rise in the surrender and beauty of heavenly heights. Ascend your consciousness. Enjoy the life that is your true right. Be filled with the happiness of God's love, which is yours, which is knocking at your door, if you, your minds, will step aside and let it in. Be not the obstruction forever.

My students, many words are given to your world. They are given freely as seeds cast upon the waters of time. God alone will move those seeds to fertile soil. We are not concerned with that. Our efforts are to bring to you a sharing of understanding of the eternal Light. What you do with it is your affair. May you do with it what your soul knows. May you be granted, through total surrender, the fullness of divine principle that you may stand up in the universe and be a witness for the mercy and goodness of the God of Gods, that never faileth a humble servant who bows in humility to the humblest servant of all.

May your thoughts be flooded with the Light, that your acts and activities may bring graciousness, kindness, and mercy to those who have been brought into your charge, that you may grant unto others what you seek so dearly to be granted unto you. May the mercy of the divine God of eternal truth rise in your consciousness as never before in your long journey through many, many, many lifetimes. For you are at the bridge of time on the fifth planet, weighing out between your soul and your created mind. Look only over the past years and see what freed you from any situation was never your mind. It was your soul.

Remember, my students, life is a school that you have created. Take control of your creations. Put them in order, in proper perspective. Take care of the children you have created, that they may serve the Divine. And let us never forget that like attracts like and becomes the Law of Attachment. Let us not forget that eternal truth that Life and all her experiences are the effects of our own mind. They are not the effects of someone else's mind: they are the effects of our mind. But we have the power within us to control our mind. We have the power within us to surrender the disturbances of our mind to God. We have that power. May we use it and stop abusing it.

May we rise our thoughts in consciousness to service to God. May we entertain in thought more godliness and less *self-ness*.

We know what brings us joy and we know what brings us goodness. We know it. May it be in order now that we do it. For to know a thing without application is a worthless, worthless entertainment in mind.

It has been said by some of my students that this is a very difficult and hard philosophy. My dear students, this philosophy is not difficult. This philosophy is not hard. This philosophy is the simplicity of truth. If we find it difficult, if we find it hard, it is the revelation of how great our self-will has become. That's the only hardness, the only difficulty with this simple philosophy. It is hard and difficult to our self-will. But it is not impossible for our self-will to bow to divine will.

We gave a class here awhile ago on the Law of Justification, of excuses. And it is most interesting to note the things we find in life to justify and to excuse ourselves from what our soul knows is our duty, from what our soul knows is our responsibility. It is so interesting to note the many devices, justifications, and excuses that our minds create, that we may not face the responsibility that we alone have incurred.

It is so interesting to note how badly we often feel when we look at life and we say, "This is the effect of the laws that I have set into motion. I am not happy with my effect. Now, what am I going to do about it?" If we sit around entertaining in thought, "I gave this law so much energy. It's going to take me this much energy and this much time to neutralize it," be rest assured our self-will, establishing that law, will take its full eye for an eye, its tooth for a tooth. But if we surrender it to God, if we declare the eternal truth that our soul evolving, destined to its freedom and fulfillment, has established certain laws that we consider today are not pleasant experiences, if we give it to God—that thought, that law—God, in his infinite mercy, will free us. Not in our way, perhaps, not in our time, perhaps, but in the right way on the right day in the right time.

When we find difficulty in giving a thought to God, the difficulty reveals the tenacity, the importance of our self-will declaring its great authority over the Divine. And if we feel badly because of the self-will that we have exercised, and continue to do so, then that is another revelation of self-will, for we are still entertaining thoughts of self. And so the merry-go-round spins and spins and spins. And someday man gets so dizzy, so weary, he falls off the merry-go-round. And when he does, it's called surrender.

Thank you.

You have some questions. You may feel free to ask.

Thank you. What is your understanding of the relationship between spirits presenting themselves in communication and the subconscious mind of the medium?

A most important question. I am very grateful that you have asked it.

It is a known truth to those who have awakened to some degree to the laws governing communication between the dimensions. In reference to your question concerning spirits from a spiritual world communicating with the earth realm, we have stated before that the spirit, directing through the powers of concentration, impinges a thought upon the conscious mind of the recipient or medium, and the subconscious reacts or speaks forth.

Now, I know that there are questions in the minds of the students present. How does a spirit impinge a thought upon the conscious mind of a medium who is in trance and does not have a conscious mind expressing itself? My good students, the conscious mind is not expressing in the mundane world of which you are aware. This thought impinged upon the conscious mind of the recipient or medium is then expressed by the subconscious of the medium. If there are subconscious patterns of restriction and denial, if there are limited patterns in the subconscious of the medium, then the message or communication from the spiritual realms is colored and it is known as colorization of communication.

Therefore, it behooves all students of truth to make great effort, great effort to face their own patterns that bind their soul to limitation, to prejudices, to rejections, and to denials, for the colorization of communications is the greatest problem or difficulty that faces the work between the dimensions—not only on your earth realm, but through the many dimensions in these other worlds.

Many people think that these spirit people appear in your mundane world. It is possible for those from the realms of light to descend, so to speak, down into certain dimensions. The higher planes of consciousness that the spirit has attained, the less degrees are they able to descend to reach the earth realm. Therefore, it is necessary for those souls encased in earth form to rise their consciousness to much higher levels than the earthly realm in order to receive from the realms of light. If that effort is not made by those souls still in earthly flesh, then what is received is not only colored and contaminated, but often distorted by the realms, the planes of consciousness, through which the communication must descend and, in descending, is interpreted and reinterpreted so very many, many, many times.

So often your world judges the so-called illumination of your mediums and prophets by the accuracy of predictions of your mundane, material interest and world. That, my good students, is not a criteria for the spiritual evolution of your prophets or your mediums. The criteria should be to judge, or weigh, the communication by the fruit that it bears. Is it demonstrable and beneficial to your soul? For your soul knows when your mind is still. If the communication pleases your mind, sooner or later it will not please it. If it is true, it is simple. It is easily understood. It is something that you can wisely use. With a little effort, it brings you freedom in keeping with your own efforts.

Thank you. How should one care for the physical body during spiritual unfoldment in order to maintain harmony and balance within the individual?

If one is caring for their spirit, their spiritual body, they need not be concerned with their physical body. For the effect of the spiritual body: the mental body, and the effect of the mental body is the physical body.

Thank you. Would you please share an understanding of the purpose of sentiment?

Indeed, the question concerning the word *sentiment* reveals, as all sentiment does, an attachment to things. And so we find that sentiment is a direction of the magnetic body and emotions in fondness, which is, in truth, desire hidden from view to a particular experience that the mind wishes to recapture. We spoke long ago: Hold not to form, for form shall pass. And though sentiment and sentimentality, we find, is an enjoyable thing to most earthlings, it only helps as a thread, or a chain, to bind your eternal, free soul to forms and things.

Thank you. Can the soul leave the form if the body is treated by the method called cryogenics immediately upon cessation of heartbeat? Is the form actually dead, as we know it, under these circumstances? Or is the soul imprisoned in this frozen form?

In reference to your question, whenever the Isle of Hist separates, the soul has left the body physical. It is possible for the body to have its temperature lowered in what you call freezing and for the soul to remain within the body in a state of hibernation for an unlimited time. This is something that is already in process. We spoke before that it is in the divine plan for man to choose consciously the time when he wishes to leave his physical body or other bodies.

Now, the question may well arise, "What about these poor souls being frozen in these bodies?" Why, those souls, in their evolution, have set those laws into motion and have the right to their lessons in life.

But when the Isle of Hist is separated, the soul has left. There is sensation within the body for seventy-two hours, for there are seventy-two gods and goddesses that control the form and it takes that time before all sensation ceases. We have, for many years, recommended what you call cremation after seventy-two hours. Our reasons for this recommendation to your world is for purification, that the astral body will not hover over the graveyards of your world and look at the decaying form, which is nothing more than an old shoe returning to the elements. But there is no way, once the soul has left the body, that the body can be frozen and the soul return.

Thank you. If scientists can create man in the laboratory by a process called cloning, it is said that a laboratory-created individual would be a duplicate of the person from whom the cell originated. However, would not the person created by cloning have the individual mind and soul of its own and not a replica of the parent?

No, absolutely not. In reference to the so-called new science that you are speaking of, which is a very ancient science, that you, your earth scientists, think they have discovered, the more proper word, instead of discovery, is "uncovered." The replica of the form created from the cells is exactly what it says: a replica, a duplicate. It does not have a separate, individualized soul. It has the soul which permeates the cells.

For example, this process, which is now in your world—you, in your creating, what you are doing, in truth, is simply duplicating nature's process scientifically, you call it. But the consciousness expressing—the consciousness is God expressing through what it is known as an individualized soul, not only permeates your physical body, it permeates each and every cell.

It permeates each and every thought. And so when you take a combination of those cells, it is the law of nature that they multiply. And so they do. Your soul is in each duplicate, for it is, in truth, a part of you. It is not something that man, in truth, has created. It is simply an expansion of your own form.

How does one protect himself from vibrations that disturb his serenity?

I am so very grateful to the soul of the student who has asked that question. How does one protect himself from disturbing vibrations that rob them of their serenity? One word, my student, one word: surrender. Each thought that disturbs your mind reveals your level of consciousness of self-will and self-interest. When that thought impinges upon your consciousness, if you are sincere in your efforts and you declare the eternal truth, "Surrender to God," then you will not dream of serenity, you will become serenity.

Good night.

OCTOBER 9, 1975

CONSCIOUSNESS CLASS 99

Greeting, students.

This evening we shall discuss the nine spheres, the nine planes, and the nine centers or energy spheres in the human being. These nine spheres or energy fields each have nine aspects of expression. They are directly related to the solar system in which your soul is at present expressing. We have always taught that self-control—its effect is what is known as freedom. As the thoughts of man are directly related with the nine centers of consciousness, which is directly related with the planets of your solar system, it behooves man to awaken within his consciousness these spheres and planes of expression that he may live within the eternal moment and not be controlled by the experiences of the soul on its evolutionary journey through so-called time and space.

The reason that this consciousness awakening has taken place in so few souls on your Earth planet is because of the magnetic identity that you have with your experiences in your short journey on your earth realm. The soul, in its evolution, passes through these nine spheres or planets of your solar system, garnering unto itself the multitude of experiences that it may free itself from creation and form while still expressing through form.

And so it is that your so-called science of astrology, though gravely misunderstood and gravely incorrectly presented to your world, is indicative of the influences and the experiences, revealing your soul in its evolutionary journey. What does this have to do with your present moment? It has everything to do with your present moment, for the center of consciousness on which you insist upon expressing is the revelation of the difficulties and struggles in eternal life that you have faced so many times before.

When you entertain in thought a disturbing attitude, you come under the influence of the untold multitude of experiences not only of your present earth life, but of those influences and experiences of eons of time ago. Without greater effort to surrender thought patterns, you cannot free yourself from that particular center of consciousness or energy field that controls you. If you will pause in your thought more often, you will become more aware that this great force, like an irresistible magnet that pulls your consciousness, is your greatest opportunity for growth and for freedom. It is only through a greater conscious effort by the electrical vibration of energy within your own universe that will free you from the magnetic pull of yesterday and centuries untold.

And so it is that we have taught that the lord of your universe is the will within your consciousness, granting you the right, the choice, to direct this energy to what you choose, in the eternal moment, to direct it to. The time has come for a greater broadening of horizons that you may free yourselves from the limited view that you have of life itself.

Long ago we stated that the soul can, and does, all things create, ever in accord to the laws that it alone has established and the evolution to return to the source from whence it has wandered.

And so, my good students, the greatest bondage the soul has ever known, the greatest bondage the soul will ever know, is known in your language as fascination. And so it is that man, placing his eternal free soul under the power and control of the mind's entertainment of thought, sooner or later guarantees, by the mental Law of Fascination, to place his eternal soul in the slumber and the sleep of satisfaction. Because truth is simple and is not fascinating to the mind, it is difficult for the soul, expressing through mind, to accept the simplicity of truth itself.

And so, my good students, when you reach that point in consciousness where you cross the bridge from fascination of the functions, created by mind stuff, to the eternal shores of light and freedom, where you awaken to life, to light, to love, which *is*—you cannot, and will not, free your soul until you alone decide to cross that bridge. The bridge is the bridge of reason. The power of the universes that takes you to that eternal crossing is known as faith. And so once again we state keep faith with reason; she will transfigure thee. But reason does not exist in the magnetic emotional body of the form. Reason does not exist in the glitter of fascination. Reason exists when man surrenders to the Infinite Intelligence of all. Then, at that moment in consciousness, by the power of faith, he crosses the bridge of reason and paradise, heaven in consciousness, is revealed.

These energy fields, through which your consciousness and eternal soul is expressing, are governed and controlled by the immutable laws of the universe. The expansion of consciousness is the redirection of divine energy to the wholeness, the totality, the omniscience of eternal and infinite Divine Intelligence, that, once accepted in the individualized minds of men, will guide your eternal soul across the bridge, where you will have the true joy of life, where you will be freed from the panorama of so-called creation, where the fullness and true purpose of your soul's journey is revealed.

And so, my students, it is the principle of effort that guarantees success. And the principle of effort is the lack of concern. It is only through the control of the mind that it may surrender to the great Intelligence that sustains it that you will have the freedom that you have sought for so very many, many centuries. Because it is the nature of the mind to attach in order to identify, it is difficult for those who insist upon the supremacy of mind to be free. It is much easier for those who know little, for those who know little, gain much.

And so in all your seeking, seek not for facts. Seek not for the letter of the law, for those things are the things that feed the mental substance that it may rise even higher in its supremacy and send your eternal soul even deeper into troubled, deep waters of the duality of the Law of Form, called creation. Until such time as you are willing to let go of the things you hold so dearly, until that time arrives in your consciousness, you can only continue on in the sphere of energy that you have been in for so very long.

The teaching of this philosophy is that like attracts like and becomes the very Law of Attachment. We know that attachment is the force of the magnetic energy field through which our consciousness expresses at any given moment. When you permit yourselves to tell yourselves how difficult things are for you, what a struggle you are having, you are feeding energy to the very thing that binds you. The law of the universes is very clear: direct the divine energy to that which you choose to become; remove the divine energy from that that you choose to overcome.

We have ofttimes emphasized the great importance of the spoken word. But because the eyes do not yet see, nor the ears hear, the immutable laws of the universe, the mind does not yet value the inevitability of the power of directed energy.

And so, my students, although the soul's evolution is dependent upon the surrender of the magnetic energy fields within your own consciousness, it is not beyond the realms of possibility to take the reins of your conscious mind moment by moment by moment and direct, through the sheer power of the lord, the law, of your universe, called will, it is not beyond—*[At this point, an electronic interference on the original recording prevents the teachings from being recorded or transcribed.]*—that you, your eternal soul, has the divine right to goodness, to godliness, to joy, to love, to peace, and to happiness. But only you alone can take that control and declare your divinity.

If you think, in being the recipient of negative projections, that you must dictate to something outside because of your inner experience, then you have forgotten the law that likes attracts likes and become the Law of Attachment. So when you have those experiences, which we find from our world are daily with earth children, take the reins on yourself before you speak. Take the reins on your own emotional body. Take control of yourself, for it is the revelation to you that you have lost control of yourself, that you are experiencing the projections of negativity from another.

And so it is that God helps those who help themselves. God frees the souls that make the effort to control the vehicles through which the soul is expressing.

I know that many of you have heard these teachings in seeming constant repetition, but only repetition guarantees the Law of Change. And you are here seeking change, change from the chains of bondage. And only through a constant repetition will you gain that control. You will not gain that control by the fascination of going here and there in the eternal hope that you will find a shortcut to happiness, a shortcut to truth. That is not the way to gain control. For it is from those very patterns that you lost control in the first place. It is from those patterns of constant fascination that you have chased through the universes and been left void, chasing outside for what exists inside. It is only by knocking at the door of reason within your own consciousness that you will start on the path. It is not by racing here and there in the universes that some teacher somewhere has such great power, has such great magnetism, great this or great that. My good students, the greatness that you are seeking is the greatness that you are denying yourselves by chasing over the universes ever seeking something better, when the better that you have, you refuse to accept, because you refuse to surrender.

Surely, my good students, the centuries wane long in your lives. Surely, surely, it is time. Surely, it is time to direct this divine, intelligent energy to freeing yourselves. Surely, it is time to help another soul along the path, for in helping another, you have helped yourself by the divine law that God helps those who help themselves and you help yourselves by considering another, for in that consideration, the divine law is fulfilled. When you see a soul struggling along the path, remember: that's God's invitation. For God is pleading with you to serve the Light, to come outside of your own self-interest long enough to consider another part of you is suffering, not the part you're thinking of: the part that is a part of God expressing through another form, another human being. And is it not long overdue that we make that little effort to consider the souls of the universes, to go out into the world and lift another, for we cannot be lifted any higher than we already are until we make that effort to help the rest of God's children.

You do not need to ask your minds for the opportunity. The opportunity knocks at your door every moment of every hour. You do not recognize it. You cannot recognize it when you are so active and so busy considering yourselves. You cannot see the need of the rest of God's children. And because you cannot see the need of the rest of God's children, your need cannot be seen by God. For you are so much in your brain that God cannot find room to enter. Always so busy with so many things, you cannot see the suffering, nor have the care for the rest of God's children. Then, my children, you cannot have the heaven that is justly and rightly yours when you let go of your self-related thoughts, when you let go of your self-related emotions, when you let go of your self-related interests. Surely, an expansion from the universe you now find yourself in is more than appealing, more than a hope, more than a dream, and certainly more than a wish. For it is eternal truth.

You are inseparably a part of one. And the longer you deny the inseparability of consciousness within you, as long as you do that, you will suffer. As long as you do that, you will sleep the sleep of satisfaction. As long as you do that, you will need trinkets to entertain your minds. You will need something, because what you have you are weary of looking at.

But the something greater is already within you. It is humbly waiting to do its job in life. It has been waiting for eons of time. It speaks to you in your conscience. Again and again, it whispers the eternal truth: "I am part of life. The part of which I am is the wholeness of life. It is my lack of acceptance that denies me from the fullness and the freedom, for I see variety in creation. I am not yet able to see principle, because I have not yet made the effort to get out of my head long enough to know that the God of Gods, in truth, is my humble spirit; that its tears of sadness for what I have done to my eternal life fills the oceans of many planets; that I have finally reached a state of consciousness to beg and pray for forgiveness for what I have done to the Divinity which is, in truth, my real and only life; that it has witnessed, as a judge, looking upon the changing panorama of time, it has witnessed the sadness of untold centuries; that it continues to witness until such time as I bow in the humbleness of all humbleness and do my duty and fulfill the eternal law of which I am in truth; that I do my duty in the here and the now; that I do not procrastinate to tomorrow, for that is what I have already done for eons of time; that I face my responsibilities in this moment, that my responsibilities are well known to my mind; that I face what I have set into motion in this moment; that I express the gratitude, the appreciation, and the humility to stand as a witness to the eternal Light that I may not forever, in this great eternity, bow my head in such a way as I can no longer see the true purpose of eternal life; that I have the courage and the strength of my conviction to serve God without self-interest, to serve God, for God, in service, is the only truth of life itself; that I am not the king of kings; that I have work to do; that I may be granted in consciousness the fullness of understanding to do what I have to do, to face the duty, to be positive, to speak the words of joy and cheer to the universe that God's heaven may manifest itself for all his children in the here and the now; that I turn my back no longer to the Light that ever begs me to face myself the way I really am, not to hide behind the cloak of creation that has deceived me for so very many, many centuries; that I respect the right of God to express itself through all forms, in all ways, at all times; that I not be so pompous in my attitude towards others that I feel a greater importance in life; that I am ready, willing, and able to become the humblest worm in the dust to serve the true purpose of life itself; that I no longer play the games of deception of my mental creations; that I begin to receive the goodness, the fullness of the Divine Life, Light, and Love direct in my consciousness as I serve to help a soul less fortunate than myself each moment of each day; that I make the effort to correct my thinking, that the thoughts may be thoughts of godliness, that they may lift my soul to encourage it to serve, which is its true destiny, that it may be the heaven on earth promised to all the children of the earth; that I face the principle of life; that I not fail to consider all God's children, whether they are the insects that crawl upon the ground or the eagles that soar in the heavens; that I know, in truth, that there is no difference between the ant of earth that crawls on the ground and the angels of heaven in the eternal light of truth; that I truly accept within my heart the divine right of all expression; that I truly accept in my heart that God, and God alone, sustains my thought, that God, the great humble servant, has granted me the right to direct and entertain thoughts of goodness, that he supports those thoughts of goodness, as well as supporting the negative thoughts of self-concern."

Let us not forget that forgiveness of oneself is the freedom of one soul and the lack of that forgiveness is the denial of one's own eternal freedom. Let us not forget the duty we have each moment. Let us not forget the principle of life itself. Let us not forget that license is bondage, that liberty exists because of divine law, not man's law.

And, my children, someday you will know the many expressions you have already been. And the only reason you do not already, in your conscious mind, know them is because your conscious mind is so filled with self-interest, there is no room, at present, for the universality of consciousness to enter.

Good night.

OCTOBER 16, 1975

CONSCIOUSNESS CLASS 100

Greetings, fellow students. On this, the one-hundredth class brought to your world, we wish to speak upon the principle of life and the idea, which, in truth, you call creation.

Long ago we mentioned that man is, in truth, an idea, that the universe is the law's meditation, that man is an idea of that meditation, and, whereas mind is ever one in substance, so man, the idea, the universe, and mind is, in truth, one and the same. And so it is that your philosophers have taught for ages the creation of so-called good and so-called evil.

The eternal soul enters creation, the idea, a positive vibration. It enters under a positive principle. It is formed and created under a negative aspect. And so the Law of Duality is established in the manifestation of the idea of an infinite, universal principle called Life.

And so it is when man entertains in mind substance what is known as negative thoughts and feelings, he creates forms in keeping with the Law of Negativity. You all know that faith is either directed through the soul faculties and known as positive or through the sense functions, known as negative. The principle of the soul faculties is surrender to an infinite, intelligent, divine Principle. As man literally broadcasts negative thought patterns, he creates in the atmosphere forms that return unto him, though he sees them not usually, that bring fear. For they are the created forms, created by the functions or negative faith, called fear.

The throne upon which so-called evil or Satan reigns supreme is the negative aspect or throne of fear. These entities that are created by your own minds from negative thoughts and feelings take on the necessary shape that, when you view and feel them, they will grant unto you the equal fear of the level of consciousness that gave them birth. And so it is that your religionists have taught in your world the paradise of heaven and the depths of so-called hell.

We have striven to bring to your world a balance between these two opposites, for in this balance, the divine Neutrality frees you in the perfect peace and joy of Life herself. Whenever you permit your minds to entertain and broadcast negative thoughts and feelings, you create these monsters that you alone are living with. The day is guaranteed that you will face them, for they, in truth, are your own children.

Now, the question must arise, How does man protect himself from the bombardment of his own negative emanations? Man cannot escape his own creations, but man has the divine choice of creating an angelic abode in which his soul may live throughout all eternity. Whenever we permit the mind to entertain thoughts of self-interest, of self-concern, of self-pity, we are broadcasting and emanating a negative aspect of consciousness, a direct denial of divine authority to care for its own children. Whenever you are in self-concern, self-interest, and self-pity, which from our view is most of your day and night, your denial of God's right must, in this great eternal law, receive its just due and payment.

When you permit your minds to blame yourself or others while entertaining negative patterns, which are self-concern, you, yourself, and those souls who you blame become the victims of the demons of the depths of hell. Now, the question must arise, "If a person was not, in truth, to blame for my negativity, how can that person then become the victim of this negative broadcasting of my own mind?" Because, my good children, there are eighty-one levels of consciousness: forty soul faculties and forty sense functions and one divine Neutrality, all souls expressing through form are receptive to the negative demons of hell, to the angelic forms of heaven.

We have repeatedly asked you to make greater effort each moment of your day and night to guard your thoughts that they be emanations of the lack of concern, for the lack of concern in any and everything is the open door to God's eternal heaven and peace in your universe. Because of a lack of understanding—and the lack of understanding is the lack of your own efforts to understand—this self-interest and self-concern has created within the universes what is known as the hand of greed. Now, we have stated that the hand of greed shall know her need when love supreme—divine love in your soul—sees life, her dream.

As you continue to feed the divine eternal love, called energy, to this hand of greed, which entertains your minds so frequently, denying you of divine love, total consideration, denying you of the balance granted through reason, denying you of understanding, denying you of wisdom, peace, love, and harmony, then you shall, ever in accord to the divine infinite laws, suffer the so-called consequences. Because these forms, known as hell, are created by mind stuff, because they are not the principle of infinite life, they demand for survival constant energy that they may maintain and sustain their grotesque and horrible forms. As we explained earlier, their grotesque features are created in keeping with the law of the fear that controls your thought as you entertain your own self-interest, self-concern, and self-pity.

You all know the principle of freeing yourselves from this hell of hell. You know that the principle that rises your soul through the soul faculties is surrender. You know that reason alone will transfigure you. You know that logic is a mind function, that it only has to balance what is already in your limited minds. You all know that reason has total consideration. And so, my children, now, not tomorrow and not some moment of the eternal future, is the time to free yourselves.

If you are not yet ready to make this great effort—great only to your minds—to think more often, to guard your feelings and thoughts, then it simply means that the suffering and grief and sorrow has not yet been sufficient for you to make that choice.

We do not believe that any soul is eternally lost, for in these many centuries we have seen, repeatedly, the saving grace of God's divine, eternal mercy. When, which is so often the case, you are plagued with the thoughts of yesterday's moments, when you are plagued with the fears created from your own minds—and the fear is only a denial of God—remember, you are not in the eternal moment: you are in the bondage of hell itself.

When you permit your minds to entertain discouragement, procrastination, and the so-called *mañana* vibration, then all you are doing is entertaining in mind stuff your personal desire to continue to suffer. And it simply reveals the importance that you have given to what you call your security, your individuality, your own self-importance. As long as you permit your minds to be greater than the eternal, humble God, then you will continue on your descent. As long as the only things that you can consider are negative levels of self-interest and pity, you will continue on your descent.

But be rest assured, my good students, the day is dawning when you will stop denying your divinity. The day is dawning when you will stop feeding the demons of the deep that you alone have created. The day is dawning when your cry in the universe will be the cry for the eternal God of mercy to free you. And then, if you are truly grateful for the crumb of crumbs, you will move your soul through the faculties and the dawn of paradise and eternal heaven will enter your consciousness and, once it does, you will never again cease to work to keep it there. You will have understanding, for the one blessing of the realms of darkness is that sooner or later in eternity you are freed from it.

Humility is not something that the mind learns. It is not within the power of the mind to learn a soul faculty. Humility, being a soul faculty, bows the mind, which opens the heavenly doors to God, to truth, and to freedom.

And so it is when you insist on your negative thought patterns, they are revealing to you the untold centuries of your own bondage and of your own victimization.

When you awaken within your consciousness and see the good in all things, then, and then alone, will you stand on the rock of understanding in the midst of creation as your heart rises to the eternal Light.

My students, in a million ways and a million days this, the Living Light philosophy, is given to the universes. And slowly, but surely, it moves from the minds of men into the hearts of men. For fear, the negative aspect of the idea called creation or form, does not exist in the heart, which is the expression of God through the individualized souls. It exists in the mind. But you have the power within your consciousness to still your mind. You have not been left void. You have not been left without the way. You have not been left without the angels from on high who work day and night without tiring, without ceasing, who's prayers are beyond the numbers of men's minds to help you to make the effort to free your eternal soul. It matters not to God that your mind cannot see the Light, for your mind was not designed to see the Light. God's light is in the heart, not in the head.

And so, my good children, once again we ask you in all humbleness to broaden your horizons to the universality of truth and consciousness, to make greater effort to free your soul from the hand of greed that feeds off of the energy in the error of ignorance, to make the effort to pray to God each day, each moment, to forgive you for your errors of ignorance, to forgive you from your own bondage, to forgive you for the transgressions of the divine, eternal laws, to remember that attachment to form is the bondage of hell—for the attachments to form are the denial of God's eternal principle—that, as your souls cry out for the freedom of the bondage that your minds have put you into, that it may be such a cry that you will bow the authority of your own brains. For it is a false authority, creating a false security, destined to die, as you gave it birth.

My good students, remember that truth is like a river: that it eternally flows from the Mountain of Aspiration, that freedom is not something that comes to the weak-hearted. It is something that comes to the humble who are courageous. It is something that comes to those who stand on principle.

It comes to those who are willing to work for principle and not tell principle what principle is.

My students, your journey on earth is numbered by the laws that you alone have established. Your days are not numbered by the mercy of God. They are numbered because the minds of men have created the numbers of years that the soul may express. That is how strong the minds of men on your Earth planet have become.

And so it is in the midst of hell man prays for God to free him from his earthly form and he is not freed. And the minds of men say, "God does not hear me." Be not deceived, my children. God hears the slightness thought you entertain in mind. God knows the number of every hair upon your head. God knows how it got there and God knows how it's going to go, for that intelligent Power is never sound asleep. It knows all your motives. It knows all your thoughts and activities. It knows all your denials and, yet, forgives you your own transgressions.

And so when you pray to God to free you and you, your mind says, are not free, be grateful, for the very process necessary to free you is being established within you. And so it is that man is freed in hell and saved in heaven.

No thought is ever lost: it is eternally recorded. And the day of all souls is guaranteed where you go before the judgment seat of conscience and you hear the verdict. That is not God who judges. That is the divine principle called conscience. And so, in truth, each moment of each day you are before the judgment seat, though you know it not in your conscious minds. You stand before the judge and each moment you choose. You choose between the eternal light of surrender and the darkness of self and self-concern. How just and how fair are the divine laws of the universes, for you are never left in any given moment without that divine choice.

And when you say to yourselves, "I know what is right, but I am too weak," that only reveals unto you, my students, a device of your minds, because you don't yet want to make the effort that you think is necessary. Someday you will, someday. But remember, when you permit your minds to say "Someday," you make the struggle within you more difficult. And how do you make it more difficult? You make it more difficult, because you alone have chosen to feed the energy, directed through the negative thought process of "someday" and procrastination, another negative aspect, to the demon you have created. For its only survival—and there are multitudes of them—is the energy that you direct through that negative aspect called fear and procrastination, which is born from that aspect called fear.

It is said by many that man fears what he does not understand. You all know how to understand: by freeing yourself from your own self-concern, you will understand. No other way, my students, is in keeping with the law. Man is capable of changing many things, but that which man will never change—for it is not within man's power to change—are the immutable, divine laws of God that are demonstrable to any and all humble souls who pause to view them.

Where you are reveals how much effort you have made. If you are not happy with where you are, truth is simple: make greater effort. And if, when you think about making greater effort, you choose to think you do not have sufficient desire to make greater effort, then all you're doing, all you have chosen to do, is play with your own mind. It's time, my friends, we all grew up. Surely, my students, do, in truth, aspire to become balanced. As their souls are expressing through adult bodies, I know they want adult emotional bodies, adult mental bodies, adult as their physical bodies reveal.

And so, my students, if you think I am taking much time and effort to reprimand you, be grateful. There are so few people on your planet so interested in your eternal soul. For they are so busy in their self-interest, they cannot be bothered.

And so, students of Light, encouragement is the soul faculty on which you ascend. To *en*courage, to be in courage, to think in what is known as positive principle—why do you think that your religions in your world have taught a father God? It does not mean that God is a male aspect. It means that God, the eternal Principle, is positive: that your soul entered form on a positive principle to bring balance to the negative aspect, called form. It is that balance, my students, that frees you. It is when your minds, filled with negative self-interest, are balanced with positive principles of surrender to God that you are freed. That is the law of life itself. Man cannot change that law. No matter what man does, he will not break the law, but be rest assured the law of God will bend the back of man, for the law of God has no emotion. The law of man is *all* emotion, for it is *all* negative. And that's the true suffering.

Balance is reason. And reason is: every time your mind has a self-thought, the divine law dictates it must be balanced with an equal God thought. Each self-thought must have equal energy of divine thought in order that you may be freed.

Students have asked if it is possible to have total freedom while yet in form. Not in your present forms does total freedom exist constantly. But there are moments of it. And those moments increase in keeping with your efforts. Those are those moments of joy. Those are those moments of peace. Don't say you don't have any. That's simply the authority of your ego demanding that it reign supreme, for we all know better. We all know that we have cherished moments of joy and cherished moments of happiness. If you cherish them enough, you will apply the Law of Appreciation, known as gratitude, and they will increase. You may, my students, be rest assured of that truth.

I believe there are a few questions that you have.

Yes, sir. Thank you. Can a person, while in physical form, ever be completely in divine will?

I believe we covered that question a few moments earlier in another way, called freedom. Yes, a person, any person, can, in moments, be in the fullness of divine will. Now, the student who asked the question may it be in order they know what divine will is. Divine will is total acceptance. And where does man have total acceptance? In his head? Impossible, my children, for that is a limited brain computer. Man has total acceptance in his heart. And so there are moments, oh, yes, indeed, when man, in form, is in divine will.

Thank you. In Discourse 10, you mentioned the use of the telephone and its effects. Could you please explain the principle involved in that statement?

In reference to that gadget that you people call the telephone, we have witnessed, since its invention upon your earth, whereas it is an instrument through which communication from soul to soul is made possible on your Earth planet, its abuses are such that we have recommended to the students to be brief that they may not be trapped into the negative vibratory waves creating demons of hell, when the angels of God work so hard to free your souls. For it is a rare telephone conversation that goes beyond nine minutes that is not filled with criticism, filled with complaints, filled with self-interest, filled with self-concern, filled with self-pity, and the total denial of God, the goodness of life.

Thank you. What is the cause and effect and remedy of auric pollution?

The cause of auric pollution is very simple: whenever a person, any person, permits themselves to be bombarded in conversation, or feeling, with negative self-pity emanations, then they are polluted. It is not necessary for the spoken word to be given for auric pollution to take place. If you permit yourselves to be exposed to anyone who is entertaining and feeling thoughts of self-pity, self-interest, and self-concern, then you are exposing yourself to the demons of hell, for that person, whether they speak or not, is denying God. And any man that denies God for himself is denying God for everyone else. For you cannot, in keeping with divine law, grant to another what you refuse to grant unto yourselves. And so we have taught our students here to choose wisely the company that you keep, for as you permit your eternal souls to be exposed to self-pity, which is the denial of God, then you, your soul, cannot help but descend, unless your prayers are moment by moment for God's forgiveness for the pollution that you are exposing yourselves to.

God's mercy sustains the right of man to deny him. But a wise man chooses wisely the company he keeps, knowing the eternal law that if he keeps company with any man that denies himself the goodness of life, that denies himself the right of God, the joy of life, then that person that he is exposed to cannot be granted the goodness of God, for one cannot grant to another what one has not granted unto oneself. And so, my good students, when you are exposed to the depths of hell, as you are exposed to the darkness of the demons of hell, remember, the mercy of God for all his children. And remember that in the midst of the Philistines, the God of Gods will deliver and free your beautiful soul.

Good night.

OCTOBER 23, 1975

CONSCIOUSNESS CLASS 101

Greetings, students. This evening we are discussing the river of consciousness, upon which the eternal soul is sailing ever homeward on the journey throughout life.

As the soul consciousness moves upon the river of life, it views many things of creation along the shores. As it views this multitude of variety, called creation, it identifies with those things with which it is interested and fascinated. As it identifies with creation and things of its own choosing, it becomes bound to them under what is known as the Law of Identity-Satisfaction and is freed by what is known as the Law of Regret. And so it is we find the soul moving on this river in a constant process of satisfaction and regret.

My good children, we have always taught that the way out of anything is the way that we got in, in the first place. And so it 'tis as man identifies, which is the Law of Self, man regrets, which is the Law of Self. And through the satisfaction and regret, man becomes irritated. And it is this Law of Irritation which awakens the soul, frees it from its own bondage to move along this eternal river of consciousness, the stream of life itself. And so, my good students, when you find things are not going your way, be rest assured they are going God's way in the sense that eternal progression, the Law of Evolution, is indeed the infallible law of God.

Long ago we asked you to hold not to form, for form shall pass. We were not speaking, in those days, about the form of what is outside. We were speaking, and continue to speak, about the form that is inside. The basic foundation of this, the Living Light philosophy, is the foundation of the eternal truth that whatever in all eternity happens to man is caused by man himself alone. Whenever we permit our mind to look outside to blame, to look outside to find cause, we are doing nothing more, and nothing less, than deceiving our eternal soul by what is known as the mind in its efforts to free itself.

There is no cure for any effect outside of our own consciousness. Every experience the mind encounters is an experience that takes place within our own mind by our own causes. God, the divine, neutral, infinite, intelligent Power, sustains whatever you choose to entertain in consciousness.

And so, my students, as you all know, these eighty-one levels of consciousness exist in all human minds. Any mind at anytime may, and does, experience, for the soul expresses through one, or many, of those levels of consciousness. Until as such time as you students are ready, willing, and able to accept God's eternal truth that all of your experiences take place and are caused by your own efforts in consciousness, until that day dawns within your consciousness and is accepted through the soul faculty of humility, which is inseparable from faith and poise, you cannot free your eternal soul.

Man was never left without choice in all of his evolutionary experiences. Because the experiences of life are not always pleasant in the growth process or the evolution of the eternal soul, the mind chooses to direct the blame for experiences that are not pleasant to something outside of itself. In many ways we have taught the eternal truth. We have taught that outward manifestations are revelations of inner attitudes of mind. But it is not easy, to say the least, to accept that we, and we alone, are the masters of our ship, that we, and we alone, are the captains of our destiny. My students, once that eternal truth is truly accepted, through the second soul faculty—and remember, the soul faculties open up in a progressive evolution. So you move from the foundation of understanding, total consideration, and total acceptance into the soul faculty of duty, gratitude, and tolerance and faith, poise, and humility.

We must, in some eternal day and moment, face ourselves. We must look at ourselves not the way we think we are: we must look at ourselves the way we truly are. And when we accept God's infinite divine right to sustain all expression, then we will not be disturbed at being honest with ourselves at looking at ourselves the way we truly are. When we look at one of our levels of consciousness that is not in keeping with our pride, that is not in keeping with what *we* think we are, look at it objectively and ask yourself the honest question, "Am I greater than God to deny God's divine right to sustain that level of consciousness?"

Whenever we decide what God's right is, we become a mental giant, greater than the true God of Gods. When that takes place, my students, we guarantee, by the law we have established—of becoming so important—we guarantee the law to reap understanding. And that understanding is not something that our mind can control, for understanding is a faculty of our eternal soul. It is not a conception of our temporal mind, which is identified with your present earthly experience of X number of years. Who, we must ask, is so great that they can decide for God what shall be? Who has risen in such illumination to know the eternal laws of life to dictate the rights of others?

Total consideration is the expression of divine love. It does not dictate within our consciousness which of the eighty-one levels has a right to express. It looks at all levels of consciousness. It sees the good in each and everyone, for he who does not see the good in all things loses the good within himself.

My students, inside is the way that it truly is. And if you will make the effort in all of your emotional frustrations and disturbances to quietly and peacefully say unto yourself, "This feeling and this experience is inside, inside my consciousness. The only thing this feeling, this thought, and this experience has to do with outside is simply viewing the mirror reflecting back unto my consciousness what I, in truth, am emanating." The law is eternal. The law is divine. The law is just. The law is like attracts like and becomes the Law of Attachment. The law is our adversities become our attachments. The law is our attachments become our adversities. The law is our rejections become our acceptances.

We cannot, my good students, change the immutable, the demonstrable, the living law of God. We can, and we do, transgress it and suffer the consequences. When we decide to truly accept the divine right of God's immutable laws, we will flow on the stream of consciousness. We will no longer be bound in the pits of bondage by the Law of Identity, guaranteeing satisfaction, regret, and irritation. My students, the law *is*. You cannot, and you will not, change it, for that that *is*, shall ever and forever be.

Whatever is necessary to awaken that truth in your consciousness is already in process. It is not something—that process—that is necessarily pleasing or satisfying to your mind. But if it was within the power of the human mind to grant you happiness, joy, and freedom, considering the time you spend in the human mind, then you would already be happy, joyous, and free. It is not within the power of the human mind to grant you that goodness.

And so we continue to teach: still the mind and free the soul. However, the stilling of mind takes as much effort as you have put into it to activate it. And if your struggle in life seems so great and if you judge your life by looking at other lives, then you deceive yourself and deny your eternal progression. The law of mind is the Law of Duality, the Law of Comparison. And as long as you continue, as students, to look outside of yourselves and then tell yourselves how much better everyone else is, then you are deceiving yourselves, for who knows so much that they know the eternal progression of another's own soul? Who knows the lessons that they have the right to learn?

Each soul knows, in truth, deep within itself what it must do in life. The only reason the soul is not doing what it knows it must do in life is because the mind has taken over the authority and the guidance of the eternal soul, that, in truth, is free when the mind is at peace or still.

And so, my students, look not in life for things. Look in life within, where God, in truth, reigns supreme. In the moment that you open the doors of surrender of your mind, that causes you the frustrations and sorrow and pity, that robs you of the love and joy of life in this moment, this moment inside is your truth. This moment, when you pause in consciousness and let yourself *be* what you be and not concern yourself with so many, many, many things. God, the Divine Intelligence, constantly reveals unto you—all souls—the immutable laws of life. You will view them when you stop deciding what they are.

The responsibility of each soul weighs heavy. And it weighs heavy because of the centuries that mind stuff has weighted it down. You all know the balance of the electromagnetic field is critical that you may remain free and at peace. But few students make the effort to move from the electrical conscious mind to the magnetic subconsciousness. And it is the imbalance of those two fields that causes *all* of your trauma and your frustrations. They are imbalanced because you do not make the effort to bring them into balance. And the reason that the effort is not made is because of your own decisions of what in life, in consciousness, you are willing to accept and reject.

We have taught you, as students, that the divine will, the divine will, the will of God, is total acceptance in consciousness. And yet in consciousness the multitude of rejections, which constitute the direct denial of God's eternal right of expression, continue to cause you great, great suffering. My good students, look objectively at your own rejections. When you look at them objectively and free them from the magnetic field that controls your soul—by its own imbalance—then, and then alone, will your eyes open and will you smile in the light of eternal truth—not the truth from outside. The truth that is deep inside.

The wall of rejection in your own consciousness is the realm of darkness between you and heaven. No one has placed it there, but yourselves. No one can remove it, but yourselves. God cannot remove what you have built. Until you surrender what you have built, then God, the Divine Law, will flow unobstructed. Because the Divine sustains your right to deny the Divine, the Divine does not transgress its own immutable laws.

And so, my students, indeed it is up to you to look in the mirror of life, which is all of your experiences, and ask yourselves the question, "This level, I do not appreciate. If I do not appreciate it, then I deny its right of expression in consciousness. Help me to trace my lack of appreciation for this level of consciousness deep within myself to see what walls I have built around me. And, once seeing those walls, the causes thereof, I shall free myself and move on the river of consciousness home, back home to paradise and to peace, no longer in the chains of bondage created by the imbalance of my own mind."

I know that you all know that like attracts like. I know that you all know whatever happens to us is caused by us. And I know that you all know you have the power within yourselves to free yourselves by surrendering the level of consciousness to God within you.

I believe there are a few questions.

Thank you, sir. Please discuss the green god of money and why the masses are controlled by it and how one can work to free oneself of money hang-ups.

Indeed, a most interesting question on the false god, the green god of money. Some time ago we spoke on the function of money, ego, and sex. Because man's magnetic field, emotional body—which the very nature of the magnetic field is to attract and to hold—has placed its security and its feeling of survival on what your world calls money, then man's emotional body has become controlled by it. The only way to free the magnetic field is by a perfect balancing of the electrical field.

And so we have taught when the electrical conscious mind faces the magnetic subconscious mind across the bridge known as kindness—kind to oneself—then you cast this electrical emanation, this light upon the dark recesses of the magnetic field. When that is balanced, the soul rises in its consciousness through the levels and you are freed from placing your emotional security upon money, ego, or sex. And that is done through what is known as surrender: a surrender of what you think you are to the eternal truth of what you really are.

Thank you. Greed manifests in many forms. Would you please explain how greed affects self-concern and self-pity?

Thank you very much for a most important question in reference to the law, man's law, called greed. It is the very nature of all souls, of all life, to express. The divine Life, the divine Love, the divine Light *is* the divine Energy. This divine Energy man has total free access to. Because of man's own rejections, he closes the doors to the flow and the freedom of God, the divine Energy, the divine Light. Therefore he becomes aware that he doesn't feel good, that he's lonely, that he is disturbed, that things are not right. It is the self-concern, which is the activity of the limited, accepted patterns of mind, that cause what is known as self-pity. Therefore the most destructive force known to man is self-concern.

As the mind activates its limited patterns and its rejections, his receptivity to the divine Light and Energy becomes very narrowed and very, very limited. When this takes place, as it does on your earth realm moment by moment, the mind, lacking in this rejuvenating energy, the soul, not freely expressing itself and finding itself imprisoned by the mind substance, seeks outside to gain this energy, which is God or good. The seeking of this goodness or God or energy is limited and directed by the patterns of man's own mind. We spoke once before on the needs of many people to receive this energy, this attention, in so-called negative ways. One of the easiest ways of receiving this energy or attention is by telling people how sick you are, how bad things are, and to blame everyone outside for your own weaknesses and frailties. And so we find in your world a constant effort, by earth men, of blaming everything outside for their own weaknesses and frailties. In so doing, they receive a feedback of energy and feel, temporarily, a little bit better.

You see, my good students, whenever we permit ourselves to entertain ourselves, which is known as mental gymnastics, we always feel a little better if we can get someone to support us in our blaming things outside for our weaknesses. But there is a much better way to receive the goodness, known as God. And that much better way, that positive way, is to surrender your self-interest and pity to the Infinite Power that will flood your consciousness with the angels from on high. Once you accept in consciousness that truth, you will no longer spend your time, your effort, and what little energy you have left in your pits of self-pity. You will no longer spend your time on blaming others for your own lack of effort to accept God, to accept his divine right of expression. And then you will know that feeling good is not a luxury: it is a necessity that grants you perfect balance and perfect health.

Thank you. Please speak on hypnosis—its use for good and its dangers.

In reference to what your world calls hypnosis, the control of the conscious mind by the subconscious mind—if you are speaking of self-hypnosis—the truth of the matter is the earth world is all in a state of hypnosis. I am sure you will all agree that hypnosis, in truth, is when the conscious mind is controlled by another person and your subconscious has risen and is open to all suggestion. And so it is that we find the children of earth, the children of king brain, are under a hypnotic state, for their subconscious patterns are controlling their minds most all of the time. If that were not true, then earth children would live in the eternal moment, would not live lives filled with rejections, addictions to past patterns, which are in the magnetic subconscious mind, not the conscious mind. They would not have the emotional frustrations and traumas that we view you to have most all of the time. So the truth of the matter is, the children of earth are 92 percent of the time under the control of what your world calls hypnosis.

Good night.

OCTOBER 30, 1975

CONSCIOUSNESS CLASS 102

Greetings, fellow students.

This evening the time has been spent to reveal to you the obstructions in consciousness that keep you from your joy, your peace, and your happiness. *[Prior to the beginning of this class, the students were asked to consider, during the meditation period, the level of consciousness that was causing them the most difficulty in their lives. After the students had considered that level, the Spirit revealed to each student the soul faculty necessary to express that will free them that level.]*

Many times we have spoken on the absolute necessity of balancing the soul faculties with the corresponding sense functions. I know that many of you would like a list of these faculties and functions, but a list will not benefit you, my students. What will benefit you is facing, in consciousness, the situation, the level of consciousness, in which you have trapped your eternal soul. Therefore it has been given to you, the corresponding soul faculty which governs the level of consciousness that you presently find your soul bound to.

And so, my good students, the light, the way, and the truth has indeed been revealed. We have spoken that when man takes the essence from any experience, the indispensable ingredient for the reeducation of the senses or functions, man will indeed free himself. Now, the essence of anything is the principle of the thing and the principle of a thing is the immutable law that governs it. And so it is when you make the effort to face your experiences, to accept them as revelations of the laws that you alone have established, then you will perceive the essence of the experience, the principle, the law that has governed it. This law, the immutable laws of life, no man can change, though many men have tried and continue to do so. But remember that God's laws are laws that man looks at in wonder, for they are infallible. They are the eternal principles of life itself. And so much time has been spent over these many years on the mind and the laws that man alone establishes.

When we face honestly, in our own consciousness, all experience, then what we, in truth, are doing is stepping upon the path of freedom, for we then view objectively the impartial, immutable laws of God. We look at them and we make the necessary changes in our own lives to flow harmoniously with God's natural divine law. And so, my good students, when you view life, your life, the way it truly is, not the way you think it is, but the way that it truly is, you will indeed perceive and begin to flow in perfect harmony with those natural, divine, eternal, immutable laws of life.

It has been stated that your Earth planet is a school. All life and all experience is a school. Your lessons in life continue to repeat themselves over and over and over and over, again and again and again. The question may well be asked, "How much repetition is necessary for a soul to awaken?" The repetition necessary is not something that has been limited to your present earth experiences, for you entered earth in keeping with the laws established. But you have never been left in all evolution without the right of divine choice.

Now, what is this right of choice, of so-called free will, that man has been granted? It is his will and right to look at the laws of God, to look at how he is either in accord with them or in discord with them. He has that choice to view them objectively. He has the divine right to look and to see that his experiences in life, in keeping with divine law, are repeating themselves not only year after year, but century after century after century.

And so, my good students, now is the time, for now is the moment in which you have power to look at your lives objectively. Not in sadness and disturbance and grief, for that will not free you, my good students, from your experiences, for that feeling emanates from the magnetic field of your consciousness—the magnetic field holds and attracts unto you. So that is not the way to be freed. The way to be freed is to balance these minds and fields, electric and magnetic. Then you will see the length of time involved in the fulfillment of the laws in your own lives. You will not have to worry, nor concern yourself, how long it's going to take any particular experience and its repetition thereof, for you can view, in the faculty of reason, when the lesson will indeed be perceived and when you, through your own efforts, will have fulfilled the law that you alone have established.

You will leave your present earth condition in a moment you know not in conscious mind. You will leave the dimension that you are in and enter those spheres and those planes of consciousness where you will continue in your schooling and in your lessons. For example, if you have spent much time in evolution dictating to your soul, by your mind, the way life, for you, will be, then you may be rest assured that your life, in its continuity, will grant unto you all the necessary experiences with all of its impact to help you to accept the divine right of infallible laws of God.

And so, my good students, though you may not think at times that your earth experiences and life are happy or pleasant, accept the divine right of God's laws, for the next expression is not necessarily one of beauty for millions upon millions of souls.

Many ways we have taught that self-will leads to the depths of hell, that divine will frees the eternal soul from all of these lessons. For what is the difficulty when man rises in consciousness and flows with the divine will and the divine right of all expression and all experience? What can possibly disturb your magnetic field, called your own emotions, when you accept God's rights? Then nothing will disturb you. You will no longer have the need to question why God does this and God does that. God is not a doer. God is the law, the principle that is. And when you accept that, you will indeed start upon your path of freedom. When you will look at all of life and you will say, "That is divine right. The divine right to be. The divine right of God." When you accept that in consciousness, you will no longer be dictating to God the way life shall be.

Many words have been used to help you to accept the right of law. The insistence upon the minds of men to break the law, the immutable law, is all of man's problems, all of his disasters. Again and again I hear students say, "I was in such a peaceful level and someone came up to me so disturbed and so emotional." My good students, they could not have come up to you so disturbed and so emotional if you had not established some law in consciousness to attract it. Do not forget that. For if you forget that, then you are forgetting the demonstrable law that like attracts like and becomes the Law of Attachment.

I don't honestly know what it will take to get you to finally accept that *you* alone are the cause of all your experiences, that *you* alone must face the eternal truth, that *you* alone view life from your own limited mind computer.

When the need within you to blame others ceases, when you no longer have that need to express your self-will in that way of blaming things and people outside, then you will start to flow in divine will. Acceptance, you know—for you can demonstrate it unto yourselves—is divine will. It is divine will that frees your soul. It is not your limited will of your mind. And divine will is total acceptance in consciousness.

My students, it is not in your best interest for us to go further into the universes revealing the many incarnations of your souls' journey until you face the effect of the untold centuries that got you to your present condition.

The need for expression is within all forms in all universes. How one chooses to express is dictated by their mind, which is dictated as an effect of their bondage of centuries. And so the law ever fulfills itself. Your adversities become your attachments and your attachments, your adversities until you alone rise in consciousness and free yourselves with divine will and divine love and divine light.

It seems that the basic, eternal truth repeatedly revealed to your world is entertained in thought and rejected immediately after. There is no simpler teaching of philosophy ever brought to your world than the one given to you eleven years ago: "Love all life and know the Light." But it seems, my students, that it's entertained in thought and never reaches application. Now, we must be honest with ourselves in life, for honesty is not only the best policy, honesty is the principle through which freedom is possible. You cannot be free in deception. You can only be free when you are honest with yourselves. For it is the truth that frees you and you cannot have the truth until you are honest with yourselves that you may see yourselves the way you truly are. No, my students, honesty is an indispensable principle through which truth and freedom flows.

Now, when a person starts to face themselves, they start to find many people inside of themselves. And if they keep looking and they are honest seekers, they are ofttimes amazed, frequently discouraged, and rarely encouraged in what they find inside of themselves. The reasons that they are discouraged, amazed, often disappointed is because the mind has decided what they are. You are not the mind, for if you were only the mind, then you would not evolve. You would not progress. And progression is the divine law of all form. Now, you may say that your mind progresses, that your mind is evolving, but it is not, my good students. The basic acceptances of your childhood have not changed. You have added unto yourselves bigger words than when you were babies and many more words. Your basic feelings and the principles established have not changed, do not change, and will not change.

It is the nature of the magnetic field, called mind computer, to attract its kind. You do not change the basic foundation of mind. You broaden your horizons by the control of the mind, not by its expression. This is a truth that all honest seekers, in time, have always found. If it were possible for you to transgress this principle, then the basic magnetic field, which is known as your security and self-preservation, would be destroyed.

And so a person says, "Change is the Law of Form. Progression is guaranteed. Evolution is my destiny. How do I change?" Ah, my good students, you change in the sense that you rise your soul consciousness. And when you rise your soul consciousness, you become freed from the bondage of identity with childhood experiences, which are the effect of your evolving soul in the school of life.

So do not deceive yourselves that you can change your mind. You only *think* you change your mind. Your soul rises to different levels of consciousness. And this is why you speak to a person one day and they tell you they are going to do this and that's what they want to do. The next day they tell you the direct opposite, because they do not yet have control of their soul consciousness. They have not yet, in evolution, made sufficient effort, through the power of will within, the lord, the law of their universe, to choose a level of consciousness and by the power of will to make the effort to stay upon it, that level of consciousness.

And so the teaching is irritation wakes the soul and satisfaction lets it sleep. The soul within the temple of God, your human body, may be viewed like a barometer. It rises and falls. It takes determination, will, effort, and suffering to rise it. As long as you, as students, insist upon living in yesterday, then you will be controlled by the mind and the experiences of yesterday. If you choose to be happy, then you will make the effort to rise out of yesterday, for it has gone and is of no benefit to the eternal moment unless you view it not from your magnetic field—for viewing it magnetically is permitting it to control you.

And so when the hindsight, viewed through the faculty of reason, becomes the foresight, you gain the insight necessary to make a wise choice and be on the level of consciousness that you enjoy. As long as you permit your minds to dictate that you have never been happy, you never will be happy. No matter how many centuries it takes, you never will be happy. For the moment that you speak the life-giving energy of God that you have never been happy, in keeping with that impartial law of God that sustains all things, your soul, in that moment, lowers to the level of consciousness where all experiences and emotions that cause you unhappiness exist. So if you want to be happy, then declare the truth: "This is my moment. This moment I am happy. This moment I am free. This moment I am fulfilled." For that's a law. You cannot change that law. You can only be the victim of it if you insist upon living in yesterday.

No man can ever be free, no man can ever be filled with the joy of life, with peace and prosperity, as long as he establishes the law that is contrary to it. And the law is the spoken word.

When so many words are spoken that are negative, controlled by past experiences, so many words are spoken that drive our soul into pity, those words, my students, are established laws. There is an old saying: if you're not happy where you are, then move. If you are not happy where you are in your feelings and experiences, then move in consciousness. Speak the words of happiness. Speak the words of joy. Speak the words of fulfillment and free yourselves and begin to live.

I believe there are a few questions.

Thank you, sir. I am trying to obtain a more complete understanding of principle, its uses and abuses. Would you please help me?

Thank you very much for that question on principle, its uses and abuses. Whenever the mind entertains the effect of any experience and the entertainment thereof is dictated by the magnetic field of emotion, which is dictated by past experiences, then you have abuse of principle. For principle is the essence of the experience itself or the law. When you view the experiences without emotion, objectively, when you are not controlled by your own past experiences in viewing the present experience, you look at it through the faculty of reason, you know that it took place in your own consciousness, that it had absolutely nothing to do with anything outside of yourself, then you find the law and you are freed.

Thank you. We know that our entities are our children, our creations and therefore our responsibilities. Once we become aware of our responsibilities, how do we meet them?

There is one word to meet anything in life and it's called *honesty*. By becoming honest with yourself, you face your personal responsibilities. Honesty opens up freedom, truth, illumination, and the great beauty of heaven, which is here and now.

Thank you. Should one attempt to free himself from all attachments, including the strong ties of family?

Sooner or later, all attachment, the soul is freed from. For attachment is the magnetic field in creation. Man is not creation. Man is expressing *through* creation. And so it is that whether your attachments are to family and friends or things—for it all takes place within your own mind—you will follow the eternal, immutable laws and be freed. Therefore it is advisable to surrender all attachments, to surrender them to God. And if you truly surrender them to God, you will no longer be concerned about an attempt to free yourself.

Thank you. Would you please speak on staying in your own vibration and protecting your vibration by keeping others out of your aura?

When you make the effort, by facing yourselves, to know yourselves, then you will know which is yours and which is not. But until you make the effort to know yourself, you cannot discern which is which.

And it is a most interesting question and should be clarified a bit further. When we truly accept the right of God, then we will face ourselves, know that our soul expresses on eighty-one levels of consciousness, that we are a part, an inseparable part of a so-called human race, that what is possible to one is possible to all, that levels expressed in others that are distasteful to us are simply distasteful because we have not faced that level in our own consciousness. That level exists, but our ego, controlling our lives, will not permit our soul to view that that level exists within us. Therefore, not being willing to face it within, we find it distasteful when expressed in another. And so in time, we establish the divine law. We flow with the established divine law—correction—and that that we cannot tolerate befalls us. That that we fear descends upon us. For we fear by the functions, not the soul faculties. And it is the functions that fear, because the functions do not have understanding. Understanding is the rock upon which the soul faculties rise.

And so it is when the functions control our soul, we know fear, or what is called negative faith. When the faculties are expressed of our soul, we have faith. It's called positive.

And so, my good students, as Job said long ago, "The thing I fear the most has befallen me." For the fear is the revelation that the functions are not balanced with the soul faculties. When the functions are balanced with the corresponding soul faculties, man is freed from fear, for man then rises in consciousness to the divine neutrality of reason—perfect balance—and is transfigured. Fear, it is not within its domain, for it is not within the domain of the mind to have understanding. I do hope that's helped with your question.

Thank you. Would you expand upon the teaching that the sense to pause is the lion's strength?

The sense to pause is the lion's strength. The sense to pause, my good students, the sense to pause grants your soul the opportunity, in that pause, to rise to levels of consciousness that are not controlled by baby-childhood tapes of your own mind. That is the lion's strength. The lion represents the soul faculty of courage. And so the sense to pause grants you, your soul, the opportunity to rise to the soul faculty of courage and the strength of God flows and directs your life.

Good night.

NOVEMBER 6, 1975

CONSCIOUSNESS CLASS 103

Greetings, fellow students. For several years of your earth time, we have often discussed soul, its evolution, its journey, and its purpose of expression in form. And so it is at this time that we wish to broaden your horizons in reference to the laws established that govern your eternal soul journey.

As you all know, the form in which your soul is this moment expressing is an effect of established laws, established by your soul in its own evolution. All of the lessons attracted to you by this law are the effects of that law established. And so it is that the eternal soul identifies through what is called intelligence or mind substance.

Now, the soul itself is a consciousness, and consciousness *is* God. As the soul identifies, through what is known as mind substance, it establishes law. The established law attracts unto itself the direct effect, that man's true purpose of expression may be the freedom and the fulfillment of his own eternal soul, which is, in truth, the only part of man that is eternal.

How does this soul consciousness express itself through the mind that it has earned in keeping with the divine Law of Evolution? The minds' of men reveal to men the laws that they alone have established. And so it is that the soul, knowing the lessons in life that it must learn, knowing the way to learn them, impinges upon the conscious mind of man what, in truth, must be done that it may be free in its evolution and harmoniously flow with divine natural law that is immutable.

We have given unto you the great demonstrable truth that total acceptance in consciousness is the divine will. And so it is that the only obstruction to the freedom and the eternal progression of the soul is what is known as the self-will of the limited identity of your present earth experiences. If it were true that these limited experiences that you have, and recall, could free you, they certainly would have done so by now. It reveals that identity is the Law of Bondage, that total acceptance is the Law of Freedom.

Why is it that man identifies with some things and does not identify with others, reveals to man the lesson in life, in eternity, that he must learn in order to be freed. The difficulty with the mind is the Law of Identity.

And so it is that people ask the question so often, "What is principle?" We have revealed unto you that principle is the essence of the law, that the law *is* the truth. We have also given unto you the eternal truth that one experience in life calls forth another experience of like kind unless the essence of the experience is taken, which is the indispensable ingredient for the reeducation of the senses or mind. And so it is that man, not truly being aware of his own motivations in life, cannot perceive principle, because he has not yet qualified himself to demonstrate it. He cannot demonstrate it until he perceives it and he cannot perceive it until he becomes honest with himself and looks at his true motive for his own thoughts, acts, and deeds.

We have spoken on the Law of Adversity and Attachment. We have also spoken on the law of like attracts like and becomes the Law of Attachment. We have also spoken on the necessity of broadening your horizons of expanding your consciousness. Without an expansion of consciousness, there is no freedom from bondage, for expanding consciousness is indispensable to the freedom that is your souls' eternal destiny. That cannot come until you free yourselves—your eternal souls—from the limited identity of your limited mind of earth experiences.

And this is not possible until you demonstrate the law, through application, of total acceptance, of total consideration, of total surrender of your limited identity. The law established guarantees your freedom in time.

There are many detours on the path of evolution. And when we awaken to the dead ends—which we do awaken to, as we continue and insist upon having the way in life that is dictated by our limited mind of earth experience—when we free ourselves from those dead-end detours, then we will know beyond a shadow of any doubt and we will apply the freedom and the fullness of life itself.

There is no escape from established law. It is the eternal destiny of the individualized soul to follow the divine Law of Freedom. And so it is, my good children, that we have given unto you a key that opens a door of eternal truth: when you ask in humbleness and honesty in all of your experiences, "Why this and why now?" When you search your consciousness for principle, remember, it cannot rise until you bow in the soul faculty of humility and become honest with your hidden motivations that you alone know what you, in truth, are doing.

We have also stated that man always gets what he really wants in life. He always gets what he really wants in life because he establishes that law. How he gets what he wants in life is not always the way that his mind decided he should have it, but it is ever in keeping with the laws in evolution that he has, in truth, established.

The promise of God is the fulfillment of God's laws. And what is the simplest of all of God's laws? We spoke to you many, many times on that law and we repeat it for you once again, knowing, in truth, that repetition is the Law of Change. The law again stated: Love all life and know the Light, the Light of eternal Truth. Ask yourselves the honest question, Why, after so much teaching and so much truth revealed, you deny God the right to love all life and know the Light? You must ask yourselves in all honesty why you insist upon denying God's right to love all his children. Is it because, the question must be asked, is it because you continue to rely upon your limited minds, of limited experiences, that you deny God's right?

Only when you become honest with yourselves will you rise in consciousness, will you truly live the life that is your right. But to rise in consciousness means a surrender of what you are relying upon. When negative faith, known as fear, the king of the house of the functions, called ego, has greater authority over your eternal soul than faith, poise, and humility, the faculties of your soul, then you cannot, and you will not, find happiness—only in fleeting moments when, seemingly by accident, you have surrendered and are, in that moment, relying upon the divine law. And that is called positive faith.

When you have a job in life to do—and all souls have a job to do. I never met a soul that had a position, only souls who have jobs to do. When you have, as you all have your jobs to do, and you rely upon the limited identity of your mind for the fulfillment, then the Law of Negative Faith, the Law of Fear, controls your soul and controls the experiences that are to return unto you. When you dictate to God how things shall be, relying upon your limited intellect, then you shall live by the letter of the law that killeth. For the letter of the law is the law of the mind, through the identity that you have established in keeping with your evolution to free yourselves. And so it is the letter of the law, the law of man's will, killeth. The spirit of the law, the law of the eternal soul, giveth life.

Once you awaken your souls, that is, you surrender your self-will to divine will, called total acceptance in consciousness, once you do that, you will rely, in truth—not in word, but in truth—upon God's law for your sustenance, for your joy, for your success in life. You need not to question God whether or not you are relying upon the law of your mind or the law of God. You already know what you are relying upon. Again and again and again life's experiences reveal unto you in every moment of your life the reliance that you have upon mental, self law. And in so doing, the chains of bondage wrap closer around your neck.

The teaching has always been: Not my way, but thy way, O God, is the path of true life. But how does man make the change to reliance upon divine spiritual law, when he has spent so many, many centuries relying upon mind-identity law? The words are given in many ways. They all mean one thing: surrender. It is not easy for the mind to bow. And because it is not easy, it reveals the false king controlling your own true being. "Least ye become as little children, ye shall not enter the kingdom of heaven." Little children do not have all these established mind-identity laws.

Acceptance is such a simple thing, but man does not accept unless the mind, in its identity, sees the possibility of something better. And what does that, in truth, reveal? It reveals another truth that states, Truth is taught through indirection, demonstration, and example. Unless you become the example of freedom and joy, unless you become the example of reliance upon God's laws, divine law, you cannot expect a soul to follow. Let us not be hypocrites in the world. Let us not speak the words of truth and, when it comes to application, demonstrate the opposite and be a poor example of eternal truth. Let us not give unto another theory and facts. Let us become the example of truth. Let us not tell another they are in self-will unless we are qualified in freeing ourselves from self-will. Let us awaken in consciousness that we may not only think of another's eternal journey, let us awaken that we may feel, in soul compassion, their struggle in evolution. Let us not question what principle is until we become honest with our soul and perceive our motives.

And so, my children, the journey is without ending, for the journey, in truth, is without beginning. As you pause in consciousness to truly think and think more deeply, you will see the wonder and the beauty of God's eternal, infallible law. You will no longer bind your souls in guilt, which is nothing more, nor less, than rejected desire. You will not bind your eternal soul in guilt, because of the lessons that you have had in life. You will no longer seek outside support for the guilt feelings that you are entertaining in consciousness, for you will accept the eternal truth that that is the law that you have established. But because you have established it, *you* can change it. You can return to divine law and flow in the freedom of principle. That has been granted, in all eternity, to all of God's children. And remember, as you look outside in life, what you see, in truth, is what you are inside. And as you see the opposite of harmony, be rest assured that's where you are.

When the soul views life, as it does at all times, there is a sadness, like a cloud, that comes over it. And that cloud of sadness is known, in truth, as the lack of effort. All souls know what they should be doing. And what they should be doing and they are not doing is the true struggle of life. But the day comes to all souls when the battle is over. And when the battle is over, the war is about to be won. That is known as victory, victory of eternity over the delusion of time and form. That victory is not in some distant future waiting for you unless your mind, establishing its own laws, places it there.

Your evolution, your experiences of today are the constant reminders and revelations telling your mind repeatedly the way to let go and let God in. When you leave your earthly bodies, the effect of those laws will be much more vivid. Now, my good students, is the moment to make the great effort to step forward. Search your conscious. Ask yourselves the honest question, "O Lord, what are my adversities in life? What are my true attachments?" Write them down on a piece of paper and ask yourself, "Is this God's law or is this a law created by my own mind?" And if it is a law created by your mind, trace it in consciousness, through the deep recesses of your mind, and find its true cause that you may be freed from it.

For laws of creation, based upon your limited acceptances, are the laws of bondage. And when you say you don't understand a principle, be rest assured you are not in a level of consciousness to perceive it, for you are not willing to face your own motives, be rest assured. And now, my students, make your daily list of your adversities. Make your daily list of your attachments. Then you will see more clearly the laws you have established that your soul consciousness is moving according to your established laws and you are destined to live your adversities and free yourselves by loss of your attachments.

It is the nature of the mind to wonder what will happen next. It is the nature of the mind to wonder what is going to be in five months or five years. Do you know why the mind, its nature is to wonder? Its nature is to wonder because it establishes so many laws, called mind laws, it doesn't know which law is coming to pass. And so it wonders.

Do your daily duty. Mark down what we have mentioned to you and you won't have to wonder anymore. You won't have to wonder why your automobiles break down. You won't have to wonder why something doesn't work. You won't have to wonder about tomorrow, for you will know the laws that you alone are establishing, and have established.

But it is a great beauty to free yourselves in time from all those mental self laws and totally rely upon the great simplicity of life: the laws of the Divine.

I believe you have a few questions.

Yes, sir. Please define the difference between spiritual understanding and superstition.

Spiritual understanding has nothing whatsoever to do with mind gymnastics, called superstition, given birth in the functions, which are controlled by the king of fear. *[After a short pause, the Teacher continues.]* You have another question.

Yes, sir.

The answer is complete.

Thank you. Is taking life to sustain life a transgression of spiritual evolution?

Absolutely and positively not. If that were the case, there would be no survival of the form. It is the law that form shall survive, called self-preservation, in order that the soul may express in the temple of God, called body or form. And it is the Law of Evolution and the refining of the species that one species feeds off of another species, for there is one God, one law that sustains all. If it were contrary to spiritual law in the present state of evolution on your planet, man would not long survive, for there is life, there *is* life—the blade of grass, the carrot, or the potato.

And so it is in reference to that question that there are some people who consider themselves highly spiritually evolved because they have become vegetarians. Because they think they are more spiritually evolved because they are vegetarians reveals, in truth, the low state of their own soul evolution, for it is their mind which takes glory and pride in their so-called spiritual evolution. And because the mind has taken it, reveals they have not yet started, in truth, upon the path.

Now, my good students, when the soul impresses you to certain things for what you believe is in the best interests of your spiritual awakening, stop in consciousness and ask yourselves, "If this is true and right for me, then let me do it. If I have the need to try to change everyone else, to tell them what I am doing, then something's wrong inside of me, for I need support for what I am about to do." And that reveals the fear, and the feeling has entered the functions and is not the soul faculties.

Thank you. I have been aware for some time of the statement, this is the Age of Aquarius. I don't know if we are in that age at present or if it is very soon approaching. Can you give us your understanding of the statement and whether it applies to a spiritual, cultural, or social renewal of the physical plane of evolution? Do those souls who have entered the physical world under that sign have any specific responsibility as to its effectiveness?

Thank you so very much for your question. And it most certainly does apply to the spiritual, the cultural, the social, and the political states of your world. The Age of Aquarius has already begun. That age is in reference to the element known as air. You have been in the Age of the Piscean, which is the Age of Water. And during that age, the waters, the element water was explored and conquered. During the Age of Aquarius, all things dealing with the element air shall be revealed. Not only travel through air, but so-called spiritual awakening—an awakening that the spirit moves through the element known as air. That God breathed into the nostrils the breath of life and man became a living soul. The soul travels through this so-called element known as air. In this element air, are the electromagnetic energies. And so it is as man awakens in the Aquarian Age, in which you have already entered, man will learn the great importance and value of proper breathing. Man will learn how to travel through this element through other bodies than the physical.

Those souls who have entered earth under this symbol of Aquarius are souls who have entered, by laws established, and merited a responsibility to the awakening of this element air in the Age of Aquarius. That does not mean, however, that other souls entering through other zodiacal signs do not have a great spiritual duty to do on your planet. It does mean that the souls under the Aquarian sign have merited the job in life, their present life, to help other souls awaken to this spiritual truth that there is more than a physical body, more than a mental body: there is the eternal spirit. And their jobs are to demonstrate, through example, this eternal spirit.

It is said that man does not value that which he does not make an effort to attain. And so it is that greater effort is required of all souls. We stated before that your Earth planet is the fifth planet in your solar system. Your souls have come to earth to learn the lesson of faith. And the souls who permit their minds to demonstrate fear, negative faith, the opposite of true faith, are denying themselves the lesson, the primary lesson that your planet has to offer your evolving soul. And when your permit yourselves to be governed by those mind laws, your lessons, yet to be, become even greater burdens than what you think you now have.

Thank you. How do you distinguish between the faculty of reason and the function of the mind? I find it sometimes confusing.

Because the questioner has found it confusing, reveals the struggle for the supremacy of mind and the surrender necessary to express the soul faculty of reason. We stated before that knowledge knows much, which is the mind, but reason knows better. We also stated that reason has total consideration. Knowledge is based upon limited acceptance of your own experiences. Now, when you have confusion in mind—that's the only place where confusion exists—it reveals to you that you are in mind. Being in mind, you have no light of reason. And so, as you find yourself confused, stop, take control of your mind, and pray for surrender. It's like a man who says, "This is principle." He says it's principle, because the mind dictates it, not principle.

And so, my good students, when you are truly in reason, you are not confused and, not being confused, you are not concerned and, not being concerned, you are free, for you have surrendered: your faith and your reliance is upon God's immutable law. Therefore you have total consideration, divine love; you have divine will, total acceptance. You are free and reason transfigures thee.

Thank you. Good night.

NOVEMBER 13, 1975

CONSCIOUSNESS CLASS 104

Greetings, students. This evening, in concluding the final class of this semester, we should like to speak on the king of man's law and its children: fear, frustration, and fascination.

Now, you all are well aware that fear, in truth, is negative faith, negative in the sense that it controls the minds of men and establishes what is commonly known as the laws of ego. The divine eternal laws, through which man's soul is, in truth, evolving, are obstructed by the continuity of what is called man's law. Now, this fear or negative faith, which is the true authority of the mind and mental patterns, establishes laws in accordance to the faith and reliance that we have placed upon our own accepted experiences in a short span of so-called life.

And so it is that man, relying and depending upon the superiority of his limited mind, becomes what is known as a frustrated person, because frustration, in truth, is the mind's control and expression of what is known as indecision or dual decision. This indecision or dual decision causes a state of confusion within the mind, called frustration, the obstruction to the release of the divine energy emanating from the eternal soul.

As man continues on with his patterns of frustration, he seeks release from this confusion and disturbance within his own being. Because he is not able to make a decision—because he has not risen the soul faculty of courage to do so—he releases this divine energy in what is referred to as fascination. Now, fascination is a process of the mind that is, in truth, a type of entrancement. The mind dreams its dreams of fulfillment in accordance to patterns that it alone has established. It is, in truth, a total lack of soul fulfillment and leaves the person in a state of emptiness, loneliness, and void.

And so, my children, look clearly at your minds, look clearly at the bondage that you are supporting by fascinating in mental dream worlds that lack soul expression, that create a prison of walls around your eternal being. Because we have such reliance and dependence upon our mind, we establish these mental laws and are ever left in a state of frustration.

How does man free himself from these patterns that are contradictory, from these patterns that he has made into a king, known as the king of fear? It is not within the realm of possibility for man to believe that he can step aside from his own creations. It is within the realms of possibility and probability to work his way gently, but surely, through his own mental maze, which, in truth, is a concentration camp for his own true being.

We have stated before that we find on earth the souls are encased in forms, in mental bodies, that are more properly known as walking time bombs. They are known as time bombs because at any moment a certain button, so to speak, is pushed in their own computer and their frustrations, their anger, and all of their functions are seemingly exploded in a split second. This clearly reveals the lack of control over the mind. It clearly reveals the state of frustration that the mental emotional body is truly, truly in.

Knowledge, we have stated, is worthless without application. And so it is we find, in truth, a lack of application. And without that application, there will be no freedom from your frustrations, your fascinations, and your own fears. As the soul strives to rise in the consciousness, it must move through these established, contradictory patterns. It must move through the emotional body, the mental body, and all of the other bodies that it may see clearly what, in truth, is happening to it. As the soul rises in its consciousness, the emotional body, which is the magnetic field, goes into what is commonly called a state of trauma. This experience of trauma is one of the early signs that the soul, in truth, is ascending to its own freedom of expression. The degree of trauma experienced by any individual reveals the degree of reliance upon the established patterns of the past. The Law of Evolution is the Law of Eternal Progression.

And so it is that each soul must face its own rejections. Each soul must face its own prejudices. Each soul must face its own restrictions and its own so-called emotional trauma. And it is indeed interesting to note that when the soul in its ascendancy, experiencing the emotion and trauma of its own addictions to patterns of past, insists at that time on blaming the cause outside in someone else, totally disregarding the demonstrable eternal law that whatever, in truth, happens to us has, in truth, been caused by us. We have repeated that truth many, many, many times. For not until the soul faculty of courage and humility is opened can we, in consciousness, accept God's eternal law that all experiences take place within our own mind.

If people in the world do not do what we think they should, then we must accept the truth that the law we alone have established is reflecting back to us. If we insist upon disregarding that eternal law, then what we are, in truth, insisting upon is our own bondage. We are insisting upon keeping patterns that are no longer—nor were they ever, in truth—any value to us.

When the mind is so filled with what is taking place outside, it cannot see what is going on inside. However, let us look at the world from levels of consciousness that see the light of eternal peace, that see clearly the games that we play. Let us look from a level of truth that sees clearly how we are victimizing ourselves. And when we look from that level of consciousness, the soul faculties will begin to awaken. And when that moment comes, we will gain understanding and each experience in life that we encounter we will be able to trace in consciousness to the true cause to the level deep within ourselves that established the law that set it into motion.

When we permit our minds to dictate, as we do, that this can only be accomplished this way, that that can only be attained that way, then we reveal to ourselves our total reliance, our total dependence, our total fear, upon the laws established by our own minds. In that moment of declaration, we deny the supremacy of the Divine. We deny the power of God. We deny our faith in anything greater than our own intellect.

When that is truly faced, we will know beyond a shadow of any doubt why we are where we are. We cannot permit the lips to praise God, while the heart denies him. And that, in truth, is what we're doing as we build greater and greater reliance upon the supremacy of our own mind.

Let us not forget, my students, that this great, humble God sustains whatever we choose to think. This great God sustains whatever we choose to believe in. A God so humble, such a great servant, supports your right of your intellect to deny him. But in so doing, granting unto you the false and limited glory of the human brain, this Divine Intelligence knows someday, someday the king will bow to the king of kings.

And so, my students, in concluding this class of this semester and during your semester break, may it be in the divine plan, in keeping with the laws that you alone have established, may it be within that divine plan that you truly will begin to apply, for we have asked you for many years to think, to think, and think more deeply. And the time surely has come to apply what you have been thinking about for so very, very long. For without the application, you cannot have the revelation, the demonstration of the divine laws in your life. And not having the demonstration, you cannot become the living example of eternal truth and freedom. And not becoming the living example of truth and freedom, you have not the right to speak it to another. And not having that right, by the Law of Example, you are transgressing immutable law and will pay the price that it extracts.

For no man can grant unto another what he has not made the effort to grant unto himself. And to speak the words of truth without having gained, through your personal efforts, the demonstration and become the example, you feed the law, man's law, called deception. That Law of Deception leaves your universe, goes out into the world, gathers up its like kind, and returns unto you. And it's known as becoming the victim of the games the minds of men play.

So think, my children, stand up for the principle of truth and become the living light of truth. No man can expect any other to follow him if he does not first demonstrate the law and follow an authority greater than his own mind. It is a waste of time, a waste of energy to expect anything different. And so it comes to this: "Does it mean enough to me to make the constant effort to become the example?" If it does not yet mean enough to you to become the example, then pause and take whatever vacation your mind dictates.

Freedom comes at the price of redirecting your attention from the mind to the soul. And when that redirection takes place, the faculties begin to open. And when the faculties begin to open—the very first one: duty, gratitude, and tolerance—call forth from the universe all of the experiences necessary to keep them open. And that is called the beginning of understanding. To deny your soul by blaming everything outside for your experiences is to establish mental law to close your own awakening soul faculties. It is not practical, my children, to make such a grave, grave error.

It has taken, through centuries of evolution, already great effort to bring you to this point in consciousness. Now is the time to go forward as examples. Now is the time to stop the mental gymnastics of theorization. Now is the time to apply. And so the minds question, "To apply what?" To apply reliance upon a greater authority than your brain. For if you, in truth, were fulfilled and happy with what your brains have already granted you, then you would never have entered these philosophy classes in the first place. Separate, through your own efforts, your limited law that you may see clearly divine law.

It is stated that the children, the little children shall enter the kingdom of heaven, a state of consciousness we grow to within this moment. They will enter the kingdom of heaven because they do not yet have total dependence upon their limited mental patterns. And that is how they enter heaven.

And so in keeping with the basic principle established in bringing this teaching to your world—the principle of personal responsibility—it is our responsibility to impress upon your consciousness the grave responsibility that you have incurred by exposing yourselves to eternal truth, for the law is that blessings shall be shared, not sheltered. And the blessings involved are the blessings of the awakening of your own eternal soul that it may follow the Light and the path of peace and joy. And having gained that blessing, the Law of Personal Responsibility demands that you share to the world in need not by word alone, but by deed. And so, my dear students, we have impressed upon your consciousness as firmly and as strongly as has been permitted in keeping with the laws established.

You may ask your questions.

Thank you. Please discuss how service frees one of fear tapes.

In reference to your question so appropriate for this evening's class—Please discuss how service frees one from their own mental tapes—service to God directs God's energy back to the source from whence it comes. In so doing, we become a free channel, freed in the sense that we no longer depend upon mental, limited so-called tapes of the mind for our sustenance, for our freedom, and for our joy. And so it is when man chooses to serve God, he is no longer dependent upon how, when, why he will serve God. For if man, in his motive of choosing to serve God, stops to think about the ways in which he will serve God, he is not serving God: he is serving his own brain ego.

And so when we speak of service—that service, in truth, is the only path to illumination—we are speaking of service to God. We are not speaking of service to what will bring back to mental mind tapes a little more glory, a little more satisfaction. I do hope that's helped with your question.

Thank you. Would you please give your understanding of inspiration?

In reference to the question on inspiration, when man experiences what is called inspiration, a soul faculty, there is no reference to the mind and what it has already accepted. Inspiration is not related to the limited patterns of one's mind. Therefore, to know thyself is the greatest law in the universe. To know thyself grants unto man the truth that he may discern between what is called inspiration, a soul faculty, and perspiration, a sense function.

Thank you. What is the relationship between self-concern and inspiration?

In reference to the so-called relationship between inspiration and self-concern, we stated earlier they are as different as day and night. If you are inspired, you cannot be in self-concern. And so there is, in truth, no relationship between inspiration and self-concern. However, a person may be inspired and, being inspired, permit the inspiration to enter the brain computer. When that happens, self-concern almost always rises, because the inspiration is not something that is already existent in the mental computer.

Thank you. Please elaborate on the saying, Exposure frees the soul.

In reference to the question on the statement in this philosophy that exposure frees the soul, we must pause to think. What do we, in truth, mean by the word *exposure*? We mean, in that word, "light upon the darkness, freedom upon the bondage."

And so it is that the mind has created an exclusive, so to speak, domain of its own. It rules its domain by the king of fear. Whenever the light of reason is cast upon the domain that the king of fear is controlling, it's known as exposure. That light, exposing the limited patterns of mind, the domain that the king of fear rules, permits the eternal soul to rise. When the soul rises and faces the king of fear that controls the minds of men, the soul, being eternal and being the authority in life, in truth, is stronger and greater than the limited fears of man of his form. Therefore, this king of fear slowly, but surely, begins to bow. In that process, the emotional body, which is totally dependent upon the king of fear for its sustenance—because it has not depended upon the eternal soul for its sustenance—goes into what is known as a traumatic experience and experiences. And so it is as this light of reason, called exposure, is cast upon the king of fear of the human mind, the soul ascends and becomes freed.

We have stated long ago that confession frees the soul. And, in truth, it does. Confession is the soul rising, permitting, by its own light, the confessing of the limited restrictions of the mind and its fears. As you rise and become stronger, you are grateful, your eternal soul, for the exposure of the games and the deception that your mind has been playing upon you, for it is those games of the mind that cause you all your sorrow, all your suffering, and all your grief.

We have stated that harmony and peace is perfect health. The soul does not, *does not* create poor health. The mind, the king of fear, creates the discord and the disturbance. And so it is when exposure, the light of reason, is cast upon the mind, there is a harmony that rises and the soul is at peace with the mind, and the mind is at peace with the soul. And then, the joy and the true purpose of life is experienced by all your nine bodies.

Thank you. Can you enlighten us on the transmission of energy called affection and attention between ourselves and our children, pets, and spouse?

It is the divine Law of Love, of Light, of Energy. It is the eternal, divine law that God expresses through all forms. We understand that God is Light, that God is Life, that God is Love, that God is Energy. This Energy, called God, expresses through all forms: children, animals, minerals, plants, all people, and all things. When the minds of men take control, they limit this God, this divine Light, Life, Love, and Energy, in the ways that they will permit God to express through themselves. When they do that, they establish the superiority of mind law over God's law. That is when man's problems truly begin.

Now, why does man, his mind, establish such an authority of how he will permit God to express through him? He establishes this authority by education. Now, education is what the minds of men believe is right or wrong. And so the more educated our minds become, the more restricted, the more limited, we become in how we will permit God to express through us. And so it is we have stated that primitive cultures and people, they have joy, peace, and freedom, because they do not have the education that so-called civilization has taken such great pride in. The primitive cultures don't know any better. And, not knowing any better, they, in truth, are free instruments for the expression of their own eternal, evolving soul. For the soul has freedom of expression in the lessons that it has to learn in its evolution. It is not obstructed by such great knowledge that reigns in the minds of men. Therefore it is more difficult for an educated man to enter the gates of heaven than for a humble soul who has not had the simple education that your so-called civilization offers to your world with such great pride.

Now, we have stated many, many times that it is not what you need to put into your mind to free your soul: it is what you need to take out of your mind to free your soul. Of what benefit is all the scientific material knowledge of your Earth planet, if it deprives and robs you of your happiness? It is not within the power of the educated mind to grant the experience of happiness. It is not within the power of the educated mind to grant freedom, joy, or love. That power is the power of God, expressing through an open heart, and reveals a free soul.

Good night.

NOVEMBER 20, 1975

CONSCIOUSNESS CLASS 105

Greetings, students, and welcome to another step along the way. This evening we are discussing the business of common sense and how it works in your life each moment and each way.

We brought to you some time ago that simple affirmation of common sense, which states, "It is the principle of effort that guarantees success and the principle of effort is the lack of concern." Now, the question must arise within our consciousness, "Why is success the lack of concern?" and "Why is the principle of effort success?"

We all know from classes that have already been given that man is a receiving and transmitting vehicle of electromagnetic energy, that this energy is directed by man. And when directed by man, with conscious choice, then man awakens to all experiences in his life that are yet to be. Therefore he places himself in a position to know himself and to know consciously the laws that he is establishing and can choose at any given moment with reason and, in so doing, live a life of joy, of beauty, of happiness, and success. However, man, through his transgressions of natural law, concerns himself with himself—it's called self-concern—and, in so doing, denies for himself, by that transgression of self-concern, the success and fullness and joy of his own life.

How does this work and how can we make the change in order that we may flow freely and have this happiness? When man, consciously choosing, as he does, to concern himself with himself, he directs this divine, neutral energy into what is called his magnetic field or computer of his own subconscious. And, in so doing, he reaffirms the supremacy and the authority of laws established in yesterday, governing his life of today. For example, through the laws of self-concern, this energy, entering the inner computer on any given subject, is controlled by all experiences of yesterday that are associated with it. Each success that has been, each so-called failure that has been, is called forth, broadcasting energy along those wavelengths and patterns into the universe, magnetically pulling the experience to him.

And so the business of common sense is the lack of self-concern. It's like a person who speaks forth a law of negativity, declaring that they wish they could control, for example, their temper, but they are unable to do so. What, in truth, does that reveal to the impartial laws of God? It simply reveals that the experiences the person is gaining from the lack of control of their temper are, in truth, more valuable to their mind than the effort they believe it would take to exercise that control.

And so it is that, in truth, we always get what we really want. It's like a person that says, "I have so much compulsion. I have such need for power. I have such need to control things around and about me." What does that, in truth, reveal? It's known in this philosophy as reflections from within. The revelation is that a person who decides that they cannot control their compulsions, that they have great need for power and need to control everyone else, has an unbelievable need to control themselves, that they have a great need to control their own mind, a great need to control their own emotions, that they have an insatiable need for recognition.

Now think, my good students, whenever we permit our minds to become the obstructions to the free expression of our evolving soul, then our minds register need, for it is our minds, and our minds alone, that are the obstructions to the lessons that the soul, in its evolution, has the divine right to learn.

We have stated before that all men, in truth, are successful. They are successful in being a success in life by applying the positive laws of God and they are successful in life by applying the negative laws of man, which man calls failure. And so it is the soul, encased in form, has experiences with what we call the success of failing, as it has experiences in the success of winning.

The world in which you live offers to all souls the lessons necessary to free them. The very things that we need to remove our mental obstructions are brought to us in keeping with law established. If we refuse to face honestly the many experiences of life, if we turn our back on the law, then we guarantee the strengthening and the continuity of the law to return unto us another day, another way, through another person.

If in our evolution we are obstructing the soul faculty of duty, gratitude, and tolerance, we call forth from the universes everything necessary to help us to bow to infinite, infallible law. And if we do not bow today to the immutable laws of God, we only guarantee the continuity of ever-increasing experiences in life until someday in eternity we surrender. If we are in question as to whether or not we are bowing to infinite law, all we need to do is to view our life. If we are spending our time, our efforts in directing energy outside of our consciousness, seemingly, to blame others for our difficulties and struggles, then we are not yet accepting in consciousness eternal, demonstrable truth.

It takes courage and strength of character to work on the areas of our consciousness that are still so weak and feeble that they direct God's energy to blaming things outside for our success and happiness. It takes courage and absolute conviction that the laws of the Divine are impartial, ever-working, and never failing.

Self-concern is a reliance upon yesterday's experiences accepted in consciousness and that reliance upon yesterday is a total denial of today. And so man, looking backward, cannot see clearly where he is, let alone seeing clearly where he's going. And so, as the consciousness, directed, through the vehicle of mind, backward to the multitude of experiences of yesterday, having no light or true perspective of the eternal moment, can only guarantee in that delusion a repetition of yesterday's experiences, wearing perhaps new garments, but old, very old principles.

Now, how does man, having spent an earth life in self-concern or looking backwards, how does man redirect his consciousness to looking clearly at the eternal moment in which he has God's power to do something constructive and beneficial for himself? Only through a firm decision, only through a continuous effort to stand firmly: guardian at the portal of his own thought. And there, and there alone, is the door of man's true freedom, for there, and there alone, does he have the power of the Divine to choose which way he will permit that great energy to flow. And standing there, a constant vigil, he will know what is yet to be, for he is awakened at the portal of truth and he sees the flowing of neutral energy and there he chooses where he will direct it. And, in so doing, he establishes the laws that govern all his experiences.

That is not an impossible or improbable task. In truth, it is not a task at all. It is the joy of growing up and becoming a human being.

Now, we must—in that—perhaps clarify the difference between a human being and the other beings of your planet: namely, those souls evolving in animal forms. The great principle of seeming difference between the evolving souls now encased in human form and the evolving souls encased in so-called animal forms, that seeming difference, that principle involved, is known as the principle of choice. The animal, in its evolution, does not have yet the conscious choice of standing guard at the portal of truth and directing God's neutral energy to establish new laws and change. The animal has control by the patterns established. Man has control by the establishing of new patterns and new experiences.

Now, it may be said that all animals have experiences. In truth, they do, but they do not have the conscious choice that man has to establish firmly and clearly new laws that he himself can choose, that he himself can clearly see the effects thereof. And so it is when man permits himself to look backward by self-concern, he is placing himself in what is known as the animal vibration of cause and effect. It is referred to in some philosophies as the karmic wheel.

Man has the only form on your planet that has 10 percent free will: a 10 percent choice to redirect God's energy into the eternal moment and make a change in his own life. However, the 10 percent opportunity granted unto man takes great will, for man, by his very form, is attracted to the pull, the magnetic pull of creation, granting unto him the dual law of joy and sadness, the dual law of pain and pleasure.

And let us, in speaking of the dual laws of creation, look clearly at what they really are. Man cuts his finger and has sensation. The mind registers sensation. We alone choose to call it pain or pleasure. Man alone chooses to call an experience good or bad. Man alone chooses to call sensation pleasure or pain. Now, we must ask the question, How does man choose to call pain in his mind from a sensation of cutting his finger? He chooses that by hindsight, by self-concern, for when he cuts his finger, he looks backwards into his computer and by the laws of his own acceptances says it's painful or it is pleasurable.

Now think, my good students, how your minds really work. For if you won't think more deeply how they really work, you will not be able to use them wisely. We have a teaching in this philosophy that clearly states when the tools no longer serve the worker, the worker begins to serve the tools. What we mean to say by that is, when the vehicle through which the eternal life is expressing no longer serves as a vehicle for the eternal life to express by its own choice, then the eternal life begins to serve the created life or the tool.

When we no longer make the effort to choose what happens to us, we begin to serve the created tool known as our own subconscious mind. And it begins, as it has for all, to dictate what our eternal soul must do. And so we have what some people call compulsion, power, and control needs. And that, my good children, is where the souls of earth in their evolution now stand. The minds are deluded by thinking they are making conscious choices. But when they are honest with themselves and they look at their lives, they clearly see the ever-repeating patterns of yesterday. That is the personal revelation of how much effort you, as individualized souls, are really making to change yesterday's experiences and patterns that continue to hold your souls in the bondage and the duality of your earth lives. You know the way: by making the effort to remain free from the concern of yourselves, for to remain free from that concern is instrumental in helping you to establish new laws, rather than repeat worn and tired old patterns.

And so, my students, in beginning again this semester, let us pause in consciousness before we speak. Let us look clearly and have greater value for the spoken word, which is the establishment of man's laws. Let us look to see how much a greater life, a fuller life really means to us. Let us take control of ourselves, for only in so doing can we know not only where we are going, but where we are, in truth, this very moment.

We have, over these years, striven to bring to you a philosophy that is simple, that is demonstrable, that can easily be applied to those who have value for its living demonstration.

And so it is that we begin this new semester with a vibratory wave of cheer and encouragement that life, in truth, means much to you and that its meaning will ever expand your consciousness, for in such an expansion is the true wonder and beauty revealed unto you; that you may be ever the living demonstration of brotherhood, which is, in truth, personal responsibility; that you will ever remember and demonstrate that to knock another is to knock yourself; that you will demonstrate the path of eternal Light by becoming that light unto the world; that you have entered these classes in keeping with laws established; that you may know beyond any shadows of doubt that our interest is not in quantity of numbers; that our work is in quality and sincerity with souls that they may grant to another what they have granted unto themselves; that as the Light ever increases in your world that those who are not ready shall go along their ways and that those who are ready will carry their share of the responsibilities that they have incurred to the very Light that is freeing them; that they will demonstrate unto themselves that efforts made to divide a house only divide oneself; that in so doing the house divided, in keeping with God's law, is sure to fail.

And in speaking with division, may we take a few moments to speak once again, as we did in your year of '64, on the realms of satisfaction and regret. For we have found in viewing the students on earth that many have read that truth and have entertained the belief that its only existence is after you leave your earth body. And because that is a falsehood, we wish to speak at this time upon it. The realms of satisfaction and regret exist in consciousness whether you are out of the earth body or you are in it.

And so it is in a world of variety that man establishes his laws and he has his experiences and he is satisfied. But in the satisfaction, he wonders, and in the wondering, he seeks other experiences of like kind in order that he may compare. And in comparison, he has regret. And so the wheel of illusion is established: satisfaction and wonder and regret. And in that wheel, the very hub that turns it, is the Law of Fascination. And so man, the dreamer that he is, instead of dreaming a life of beauty, he dreams in what is called fascination. But you can be rest assured, my students, no one, no mind entertains fascination that the mind who entertains it is not always the king of the roost. And so man spins his own web, becomes the victim of his own drives, because he will not accept yet the laws that govern, in truth, his own life. When we spoke to you some time ago on dreamer dream a life of beauty, we did not intend to imply in any way that the dreaming was not the effect of laws that you alone established.

Good night.

JANUARY 8, 1976

CONSCIOUSNESS CLASS 106

Greetings, fellow students. This evening we are discussing auric pollution and the Law of Disassociation.

We spoke with you in our last class on the value of the lack of self-concern in order that you may free yourselves from the repetition of law established by yourselves, granting to you a continuity of bondage and frustration. And so we will continue on with the expansion of those laws and how man, in his need for attention and recognition, permits himself to be polluted through his own associations with those souls who are not making sufficient effort to free themselves from their own bondage. And so it is through these laws of association and through these needs of personal self-importance, recognition, and attention, we deceive ourselves in the illusion that we, and we alone, are so important in life that we can save a human soul. Let us first clearly understand demonstrable truth. Let us accept the common sense and reason that is in our consciousness: that we are not, in truth, in a position to dictate to divine law who shall be saved—if saved you wish to call it—and who shall not. That process is the right, and the only right, of God, the infinite Law.

We must honestly ask ourselves the question, when we feel we must do this or that to change another person, "Are we thinking with reason or are we in the delusion and need of our own self-importance, the deception of our so-called need for recognition and attention?" For if we, in truth, are flowing in divine law, then we need not be concerned with auric pollution and the effort necessary for disassociation.

However, we have found, and continue to find, on your planet that that is not the case: that the motives that prompt most earth people are motives of need for attention. And because of that, there are laws that govern the pollution and the freedom from it, called the Law of Disassociation in consciousness.

We can easily determine whether or not we are acting in the divine law, for if we are so doing, then we have no interest and no concern whether or not the person that we think we are helping is helped or is not helped. We are not concerned, nor interested, in their reactions: what they have done with what we think we have given them. If that is our true feeling, then there is no need for concern, whether or not our motive is pure or selfish.

And so it is, as you go out in your world and you see people stumbling along the way, ask yourself the question, "What is the law—or laws—they are transgressing?" For their experiences are nothing more and nothing less than an effect of transgression of immutable law. If we have, in truth, granted unto ourselves the great freedom of personal responsibility for all our thoughts, acts, deeds, and experiences, if we have, in truth, granted that to ourselves, then, of course, we are then qualified to grant that to another. However, if we have not granted that unto ourselves, then we look at another person with sympathy and we say to ourselves, "I, God—not your immutable laws—but *I* can help that person to change and to be free." With that type of a motivation, we guarantee the pollution of that level of consciousness to control us, regardless of what we think and regardless of what we do. For we have, in that very motive, established a law that shall fulfill itself in our own consciousness. And having established that selfish man-law, we guarantee the fullness of its effects for ourselves.

And so it is that you hear so many people say, "I was doing fine and felt wonderful until someone spoke to me." That reveals the law that you have, in truth, established. Now, my good friends, how does one go out into your mundane world with the many diverse laws constantly being established by the minds of men and remain free? Only through this conscious effort of disassociation in consciousness: through a declaration and an affirmation of God's immutable law that, "Whatever is happening to me is indeed, in truth, caused by me."

My good students, you have received, over these many years, several affirmations. These affirmations are a declaration and an establishment of divine law in consciousness. But the law cannot be established unless you direct the energy through your own attention and effort to the law that is infallible. When you make this greater effort to affirm the truth in your consciousness, to affirm it again, again, and again—"Nothing happens to me that is not caused by me"—you will start on the path of freedom and success.

We all know that there are no accidents in any universe; that an accident is a lack of understanding natural law. The bondage of man is the ego's insistence upon blaming things outside of its domain—things that it does not, in its mind, appreciate. This delusion has been fed so much energy for so many years it takes constant affirming of truth to be freed from it. Only the law established by the minds of men has put man's soul in bondage. Only the divine immutable law of God can put it in freedom. And so, my good students, again and again we repeat to you the law that is. We have given unto you all of the mechanics, so to speak, that are necessary, but you must make the effort to think more deeply and more often.

The world in which you live is governed and controlled by the laws that you have established in your yesterdays. But you are not without the way to free yourself. Each time you speak, law is established. Each time you think, law is established. We gave to you that great truth—that man is a law unto himself—and we asked you the question, "What are you doing with the law that you are?"

When we continue upon the merry-go-round of delusion and we continue to speak and establish negative laws in our life, we will only have negative experiences. For each word, feeling, and thought is the vehicle through which the law is established in your lives. Here, where you are today on your Earth planet, is your greatest opportunity to free yourselves. But, my students, it's going to take more effort than has already been directed. It's going to take greater effort to control the mind, for the mind has been out of control for so many—very, very many of your earthly years.

When, in consciousness, you affirm the Law of Personal Responsibility, when you truly accept it, you will indeed become the masters of your ship and the captains of your destiny.

I am aware that some of you declare that you have great struggle and great difficulty in opening the soul faculty of duty, gratitude, and tolerance. When we speak forth the word that we have great difficulty or great struggle to do anything in life, it simply reveals that the tapes of our own subconscious mind have used that declaration as a device to keep us where we are. And so, as the teaching goes, he who insists upon seeing the obstruction shall never find the way.

When we declare that "God, and God alone, is guiding my ship in keeping with evolutionary law established, that the sole purpose of that law that is guiding my little ship is to free my eternal being," when we declare that truth, we will begin to see the stepping stones we're walking upon are, in truth, ever leading upward, that we need not be concerned with so many trivialities that flood our little minds.

And so, my good students, we want to speak to you once again on what is known in this philosophy as the forces of frustration and emotionalism. Whenever in our daily experiences we do not have what we think is our way, we react. We react emotionally. And to the degree of our emotional reactions, when things don't go the way we think they should be going, reveals the lack of discipline in our lives, the lack of control that we indeed are expressing.

Whenever a thought is introduced into the mind and the mind, receiving the thought, has no compatible reference tape of association with the thought, the mind records that thought as a threat to its emotional security. For example, when you speak to a person who has accepted that their life is a struggle, that they are not successful, to a person who has flooded their consciousness with negativity and you speak the truth to that person and you tell them, "Whatever happens to you is alone caused by you," the person records that truth as a threat to its security. And the subconscious mind, the great magnetic computer—the king of that computer is called fear or negative faith. And so in working with another we are, in truth, working with ourselves. For what is taking place in the mind of another, that we are speaking to, is a revelation of what is going on inside our own consciousness.

And so it is that misery demands company for its own survival. And so it is that we must look more clearly where we are spending our time, so to speak, in mind. A person may say, "Well, I spend my time doing this and I spend my time doing that." My good students, be not so interested in where your physical body is moving. Be so interested in where your mental body, in attitude, in level of consciousness, is moving. Go deep inside and face the delusion in your minds that you call needs. Face them honestly, for they reveal unto you your denials.

I know that it is difficult for many to understand that a need recorded in mind is denial. For a person says to themselves, "I need a sufficient supply in my life that I can live happily without worry or concern." The truth is they already have it. Because they cannot see it, reveals to them their denial of it. Now, how does a man who declares his needs are such awaken in consciousness to the truth that he has it and does not yet recognize it, therefore, in truth, is denying it, which continues the law of the delusion, called need? This philosophy reveals to you that gratitude is not only the first soul faculty, but that it is also the divine Law of Supply. Therefore, when the mind declares need, it denies what it has, transgresses the divine Law of Supply, called gratitude, and the delusion increases and controls the being.

If a person says, "O Lord, I have a need for one thousand dollars," and that person, declaring that law, does not take a look at the principle—for example, does not take one dollar and say, "I am grateful, O God, for this represents your divine law"—we know that gratitude is *applied* appreciation. When we appreciate, we apply that appreciation to the crumbs of life, we establish the Law of Acceptance. And the establishment of the Law of Acceptance is continuous supply in principle.

However, this divine immutable law, called gratitude, is inseparable from duty and tolerance. My friends, people on your planet do not become success: they *are* success when they accept it. Now, a person says, "I've worked for thirty or forty years and now I am successful. But it took thirty or forty years for me to be that way." What they mean to say is, it took them thirty to forty years to demonstrate the immutable law.

And so when you permit yourselves to listen to transgression of natural law you are permitting yourself to be polluted with delusion and limitation. For what you, in truth, are doing unto yourselves is to deny the natural law for yourselves.

We all know that our minds demand recognition. The sadness is that they use the deception and negative laws to gain it. When this acceptance of this Law of Fullness and Supply awakens within your consciousness, you will live a life of fullness, for you will live in the light of reason.

We have stated before that reason has total consideration. You cannot deceive reason. She is the power that transfigures your very being. Look more closely at the laws that you have received. Apply them wisely. Remember that which is yours knows your face and is already on its way to your heart. Know that success in life is not dependent upon the mental gymnastics of your mind. The Law of Success is the Law of Gratitude. For then, you're freed from yesterday's experiences. You're freed from chasing the rainbow of promise, for you become the rainbow of promise, for it is the effect of the law, and we are that effect. So let our promise be a rainbow that stretches across the universes, that we may see life eternal, that this passing moment is indeed passing, that it has been necessary to bring us to the level of consciousness upon which we now stand, that these eternal laws have not yet failed and because they have never yet failed, it is more than indicative that they are not about to fail.

Let us place our reliance upon something worthwhile in life. Let us rely upon a reliable source for the goodness we claim to seek. Let us stop the seeking and start the fulfilling by a simple acceptance of demonstrable truth. Let us refrain from being so concerned about tomorrow, for in that concern we're denying the fullness of today. Let us take hold of the reigns in the moment that we hold them. Let us steer the ship wisely in the eternal moment. Then, all concern we shall be freed from.

And when opportunity knocks at our door, like the hands of the clock, meeting every so often, let us grasp that opportunity in consciousness, for it has come to us in keeping with law established. Let us use the opportunity wisely, considering not only the momentary experience, called opportunity, but the law in that moment that we are establishing. Let us look in simplicity at the consciousness which we are in truth. Let us rise above the so-called delusion, called need. Let us rise above the petty personality of created tapes in our mind. For we are not those things in truth. We are not the tapes of ingratitude, called complaining. We are not, in truth, the tapes of ingratitude, called griping. We are not, in truth, the tapes of blaming others for our frailties. We are not, in truth, those things, for we are, in truth, far above those created disturbances of mind stuff.

Remember, each gripe, each complaint, each blaming others for our frailties establishes the Law of Ingratitude. And the establishment of that law causes us to be deprived and record, in consciousness, need.

And so I'm sure now that you have a greater understanding of that truth, which states: mans needs are divinity's denials. We stated once before that the minds of men spend twenty-four hours a day and night striving to commit suicide. Doing all in their power to destroy you. There's no power outside in the universes that works to destroy you. That power is the energy, the attention, that you have given to patterns of mind. And its sole purpose—the mind—is to preserve whatever you choose to feed into it. And so it is the mind's own effort at preserving certain rigid tapes, patterns, attitudes that you make great effort—those mental patterns—to preserve themselves. And so perhaps now you can understand when new ideas, new thoughts are revealed to your minds, what a threat it is to those patterns that have bound you.

But there is a way and the way has been revealed: stop your complaining, your gripping, and your blaming and you will free yourself through the first soul faculty. And you will have all of the success, all the fullness, all the happiness that you could possibly imagine or dream and, yea, even more, for the mind knows much, but the divine law knows better.

You may ask your questions.

I understand that the condition known as asthma is often the result of emotional disturbances. Is there any connection between the solar plexus and asthma? Please give us your understanding.

In reference to your question concerning asthma, it is an emotional reaction of the subconscious in very early, early childhood. In reference to its relationship to the solar plexus, there is no direct relationship in that respect. First, you must examine and analyze what this so-called word *asthma,* what it affects, what part of the body. Knowing the meaning of the different parts of your anatomy, you will know the slow, but sure, process for its cure.

Thank you. We have been taught to find our birth number using the Christian calendar as a delineator. Would one arrive at the same number using another calendar, such as a Chinese or Hebrew?

You students have been given the process through which you may find your particular birth number, which should be your only interest. However, if you are interested in the what Chinese and its calendar would reveal, then grant to the Chinaman his right to his calendar, for it will reveal the truth unto him. Thank you.

Thank you. Would you speak on the incurrence of spiritual debt?

Repeat the question for the benefit of the class, please.

Would you speak on the incurrence of spiritual debt?

First, I would like to know what the questioner means by the word *incurrence*.

I'm not the questioner and I have no idea.

The questioner is present. They may feel free to explain the word to the class.

The taking upon oneself of an obligation spiritually.

Thank you very much for the clarification of the word for the benefit and consideration of all. Man, in truth, takes nothing upon himself that he, in truth, has not merited in keeping with law established. If man feels or records the need to take unto himself what he alone decides is a spiritual debt, then he has declared that he has a need: he has a need to take on a spiritual debt. Because man, in that type of thinking in the declaration of need, which is the denial of divine law, which is spiritual law, man, in that type of thinking, is not in a spiritual level of consciousness. For if he were at that time, then he would not have what he calls need. For need is the denial of the Divine. I do hope that's helped with your question.

Thank you. Is it right to indulge in automatic writing?

What does the questioner mean by the words, "Is it right?" For what is right to one is so often wrong to another. That, of course, is dependent upon the level of consciousness, the laws established by the individual. In reference to automatic writing, it is no more dangerous than electricity. However, electricity is used to electrocute or to illumine. And so it is dependent upon the motivation of the questioner.

Thank you. Would you please discuss application through communication?

The question, in reference to application through communication, is very clear. To communicate is to apply. The question is, To apply what? To apply energy to the establishment of law. And so when man communicates and he speaks to another or to others, he is, in the very process in those moments, applying energy to establish law. Man's awakening to the laws he alone establishes in his communication, thoughts, acts, and deeds is ever revealed in the experiences that he encounters in life.

Thank you. Would you please clarify the difference between laws established by the mind and laws established by the soul? How can one discern the difference?

That's a wonderful question. And it should take a few moments of ponder to all of us. How can man discern between laws established by the mind and laws established by the soul? My good friends, the soul, in its evolution, has established many laws. Many of them have been fulfilled, many of them are in the process of fulfillment, and many of them are yet to begin the process of fulfillment. Now, the discernment between a mind law, created in your present earth experience, and an evolutionary soul law is very clear and can be easily be summed up in this way: The stone the builder rejects becomes the cornerstone.

Man, when he gets what is pleasing to his mind, is reflecting back unto himself the mental laws established in his present incarnation. The experiences returning unto man that the mind records as adversities and intolerable conditions are the revelation of the soul's evolutionary laws, for the laws—the evolutionary laws of the soul are the laws that free the soul. And so it is that the mental laws bind us and the soul laws free us.

And so, my good students, as you look out into life, you know, and I know, there is no mind that does not desire the things that please it. And the things that please the mind are the things that the mind has accepted in this short life. But the things that our mind has accepted in this short life have already proven unto us they are not the things that free us. It is those things that are intolerable to us, it is those things that we reject and want nothing to do with, it is those great barriers of prejudice, which is the denial of God's right of expression, that we don't want to face in life.

And so it is the soul, which is the eternal consciousness, the true you, by the very law, brings unto you everything necessary to free you, but it is not pleasing to your mind. But when you look over life, when you look from the forty years to the hindsight of what you have done, then you can say, "Oh mind, yes. Yes, I have had many experiences that are pleasing, but they certainly didn't free me, for had they done so, I would not be where I am today."

Now, the laws of evolution established in the many incarnations of you entering in and out of form is a greater law than the temporal mind laws of your present incarnation. And so the awareness and application and reliance upon the immutable law that is freeing your soul is the greater law. And the attachments that you have permitted your minds to have in this incarnation are guaranteeing the adversity that the soul may free itself from the bondage of limited thought and acceptance. And the very thing that our minds say no to are the very things that our soul is rising and will demand, by the greater law, a yes to. And so we have stated many times in our classes, look well at your adversities. Make friends with them, for soon, very soon, they will be your attachments. And look objectivity at your attachments, for soon, very soon, they will be your adversities.

And, my good students, you know what happens to a reformer. The pendulum swings, the intolerance rises, but they're only intolerant with themselves. It's only the minds of men that say, "I made a fool out of myself for a lifetime. Now, I will not tolerate anyone else to do the same." That's not the soul that speaks: it's the retaliation of the mind working against itself. So, my students, remember, God is a law—*the* law: the divine Neutrality. And neutrality is the perfect balance between attachment and adversity, for only then do we perceive the beauty and immutability of the Law of Life itself.

Everything necessary is taking place in consciousness to guarantee that no man shall be eternally bound by a limited computer. All of the experiences already are taking place, for when man, the mind, judges God, the Law, balance is demanded by all eternity. No man can change it. He only tries to side step it. The destiny of the eternal soul is the home from whence it has wondered. That home is not a place in centuries yet to be. It is a total surrender of the mind, that eternal consciousness shall arise within. There's the home of the soul. It's waiting for you to knock at its door this moment, not tomorrow.

And so it is the beauty of life that our great adversities we welcome with open arms, as we rise to other levels of consciousness. But we must never forget: the adversity becomes the attachment until we free ourselves in consciousness and grant unto God that which is God's.

Good night.

JANUARY 15, 1976

CONSCIOUSNESS CLASS 107

Greetings, students. At our class this evening, we shall discuss energy, the source, and how it works for you.

Man, in truth, is a receiver of pure, high-frequency energy which emanates from the Source called, by man, God. Man receives this pure energy and by his choice directs it to the levels of consciousness which are, in truth, varied frequencies that he broadcasts continuously, while he, the true self, the pure energy, is in form.

Now, we have discussed several times that man is a law unto himself. And now we shall discuss how man, through his own error of ignorance, has chosen to direct this pure energy on the downward path into the delusion of so-called form or creation. As this pure energy enters into the mind of man, man directs it to one of the eighty-one levels of consciousness or frequency bands. As he does so, he emanates from his aura, from his own universe these particular frequencies. In so doing, as the law states, they return unto him and cause him either his joy or his sadness.

However, if this pure energy was not directed downward, then man would not have the identity that he has in his present form. You all know that all the physical world is the effect, or lower frequencies, of the mental world and that the mental world is lower frequencies than the spiritual world.

The purpose of this evening's discussion is to help you to become aware of this energy field, that, in becoming aware of it, you will demonstrate to your own satisfaction how it is, in truth, controlling your life and all of your experiences. The Law of Division is the Law of Delusion. And the Law of Multiplication is the Law of Complexity. And the Law of Addition is the Law of God. And the Law of Subtraction is the Law of Evolution.

Now, my good students, let us pause to think. For when we pause to think, we can see clearly the demonstration of the laws established. Unto those who have, more shall be added. And to those who have not, even that shall be taken from them, in keeping with the Law of Gratitude. And so it is in keeping with these divine laws, we see, in truth, these emanations, from our own being, broadcast out into the universes on different frequency bands and then, through error of ignorance, we question the experiences that return unto us.

All of life, in truth, is this pure energy. And therefore separation, which is, in truth, division, is the delusion created by the low frequency bands of our own mind. When man makes the effort to unite in his own consciousness to pull all things together within himself, then he will demonstrate the great power of this uncontaminated Energy or God, which he is the receiver and the transmitter of.

We do not value, in life, whatever is easy to attain. And we do not value it because it does not stimulate the lower frequencies, called the human ego. And because we do not value what is easily attainable to our minds, we guarantee, in time, in consciousness, to lose it. Man, in the delusion of division or separation of consciousness—which it is, in truth—considers that which is difficult to attain in life must, in truth, be the most desirable and the most valuable to him.

When, in truth, the things the mind says are difficult to attain, is a lack of accepting divine law. When, in the small, seemingly unimportant experiences of life, we look clearly to see that they are, in truth, an expression of one inseparable energy of which we, in truth, are part, when we make that little effort with the small things in life, the seeming big or important things will no longer be difficult to attain. For the difficultly, which is the delusion of attainment, is the refusal of our mind to accept the inseparability of consciousness or pure energy. Man communicates with man, he thinks. But it is the divine Energy or God which, in truth, is flowing.

We think that we give, but we do not. We think that we gain, but we do not. Only to the minds who are yet deluded in life does duality exist, for it is a low frequency vibration. It is a division and multiplication process. And for those who remain in that delusion, the highs and lows of life are guaranteed to continue. But for those souls who are ready and willing and able to rise in thought within themselves to view life as life truly is, those souls no longer live in denial, in need, in lack, for those souls have risen, by their choice and laws established, to a state of consciousness where all is one and one is all. That state of consciousness is the eternal destiny of all people in all places. But that evolutionary process is a process of subtracting the multitude of things that man holds to in mind.

When we, in truth, are ready to give all that we, in truth, have considered ours, then we shall be free. It is not the things of physical, created substance that man must learn to give. It is all of the things within himself that he considers his, he must, in time, give. For those things that he considers are his are the obstructions, by error of ignorance, denying the true Source, called Life, to flow unobstructed in his own universe. And it is those things of mind substance that cause the pure energy to be redirected on the downward path. Those obstructions are called identities, denying the source that sustains them.

We have spoken to you before on a little affirmation, "To put God in it or to forget it." But the minds of men have strange views of what they call "God." We understand this neutral, pure, intelligent Energy *is*. We do not attempt to define beyond that: that it is neutral, eternal, intelligent; that it has always been and will always be. It is the Source. And all other things are the effect of the Law of Identity, caused by mind substance. And so, my good students, remember, the moment that you put God in it, you free yourself from the Law of Creation, you free yourself from the Law of Duality, for you put divine Neutrality, the Source, in it.

You no longer put the created vehicle of duality into your endeavors. And when you do that, there is no concern for effect. You are freed from the lower frequencies of consciousness. You are peaceful. And joy in life is, in truth, the expression of peace.

All people, all places, rise and fall, for that is the Law of Division and Delusion. And a man of reason knows that immutable law and does not attach, by the Law of Identify, his free eternal consciousness to it. But he sees the forms of delusion for what they truly are: a puff of smoke that comes and goes. He frees himself from all those dual disasters, called experiences. For he knows that he has always been. He knows he will always be; that the experiences the soul has already encountered cannot be counted, for they are beyond the numbers the minds of men can record.

And so, my good students, in keeping with these divine laws and this source of eternal Light, called Energy, let that Source, which is flowing through you, let it free you, for it is—its very nature—freedom and joy. It is uncontaminated by the changing thoughts in the minds of men. There is no room within its wave bands for pity, concern, sadness, and all other negative expression. What does it behoove the soul, in its evolution, to dictate the path, to dictate by the mind that says go or stop? We have already spent untold centuries on the roller coaster of creation. It is not intended by any intelligent source for any soul to remain in that type of delusion.

Whenever we entertain this concern with our form, whenever we do that, we enter the lowest of frequencies, known, on our side of life, as diabolical delusion. And so it is that the dual experiences on your Earth planet, sooner or later, will drive your consciousness to neutrality through divine will, called total acceptance.

I believe there are a few questions waiting to be asked.

Thank you. Would you please give us an example of principle, showing how principle is the essence of truth and law?

In reference to your question on principle, how it is the essence of truth and the essence of law, immutable law, God's divine law—which are the immutable laws and principles—are an expression or emanation that goes out from its source into all universes. This emanation of energy going from God, the divine Source, returns unto God, the divine Source. Therefore, there is no place, nor person, nor thing, expressing, that God, in truth, is not there. This is a demonstrable law of what you call life. It is the principle which demonstrates that which emanates from any source returns unto the source that it has originally emanated from.

And so in keeping with the demonstration of that law, we have already stated that addition is the law of God. Now, addition is the law of God is a demonstrable principle. It *is*. No one can change it. And so it is that this energy, emanating from its source, travels out into the universes, adds unto itself, and returns and goes out again. As this divine principle, this essence and energy, expresses through a multitude of forms, as the forms evolve, they go through a process known as subtraction. As the forms are refined, unto this divine energy is added, each step of the way, a return of the energy that it has emanated through the forms through which it is expressing.

And so our teaching is that like attracts like and becomes the Law of Attachment. And so when man, as he does so frequently, considers himself the source, he adds unto himself and, in so doing, guarantees the evolutionary process, called the Law of Subtraction. When man no longer entertains the delusion that he does this and he does that, that he alone is *the* source, then man will be freed from the payment of the delusion. I am sure you have found the principle.

Thank you. What is the meaning of "revelation" in the understanding of the Living Light philosophy?

In reference to the word *revelation,* it is used in this philosophy in conjunction with the word *illumination.* For exposure frees the soul, for it reveals unto the soul what is in the way of the soul and that, in truth, is illumination.

Thank you. Please explain how medication temporarily alleviates pain. Does a chemical change take place in the physical body, which then assists the mind to change its level of consciousness?

No, my friends. Acceptance wrought the change. The mind accepts that this will alleviate pain and the moment that is accepted, pain is alleviated. There are chemical changes taking place within the physical body dependent upon the acceptance in the magnetic field or subconsciousness mind of the recipient. And so it is that man, in truth, alleviates pain by a thought in consciousness, but that thought must first be accepted. Now, how does mind accept a thought in consciousness and alleviate pain when there are so many contradictory thoughts that will not accept the thought? That, my good students, takes knowing thyself and the effort to free thyself from the limited patterns of yesterday.

Thank you. Does the food we eat reflect our spiritual evolution?

You might say, in a way, that it does, but only in the sense the minds of men have programmed experiences which dictate to them which food is good and which food is bad for them. This, of course, has taken place within their mind at a very early, early age. Now, if a person has accepted that certain foods help them to be more spiritually evolved, then by that very acceptance they may, in time, become more spiritually evolved, but not because they have dictated that those foods have made them so. No. They become more spiritually evolved by the discipline that they exert upon their own temptations in keeping with what they have accepted is right for them.

Now, there is much discussion in your world in reference to vegetarianism and the lack of eating meat. All things, in truth, are placed upon your planet for final—in speaking of forms—eventual return to your planet. And so man slaughters the animal, as he slaughters the carrot. And, in so doing, he is destined for his own slaughter, for there is no man on your planet who can remain in the physical flesh forever. But he is slaughtered by something that is greater than he, as the animal is slaughtered by something that is greater than the animal. And that is known as man. And the trees are slaughtered and the blades of grass are slaughtered. But that is the Law of Division. That is the Law of Delusion, called creation.

And so it is that man, in his lower levels of consciousness, makes great effort to divide and conquer, for his soul, eternal and beautiful, is trapped in the delusion of division. And we have spoken unto you concerning this great delusion and we have stated to you to complain, to blame, to grip, and to gossip is division. To entertain those levels of consciousness is to divide yourself against yourself and sink deeper in despair and darkness. And so each word you speak, each thought you entertain is building your heavenly paradise in the eternal moment within you or it is building its opposite. To accept the law of life is to flow on a stream of consciousness back to the Source from which we have all wandered. To spend thought and time releasing pure energy into division is to destroy oneself, their forms, in time.

Thank you. Does the smoking of cigarettes in any way desecrate the holy temple of the evolving soul?

In reference to your questions, it no more, nor no less, desecrates—if that's the word you choose to use—the temple through which the soul is expressing—it does it no more and far less, if at all, depending on your thought, than the judgment seat of the human ego. It is the judgment of man, when God alone is not a judge, that destroys the holy temple of God, which your eternal soul is residing in at this moment. It is the judgment seat, called the great king brain of his realm of delusion, that looks out in the world and says, "God, you have no right to express in that way, for when you, God, express through form in that way, you, O God, repulse me." And so it is that those souls trapped in the importance of their self and their limited views suffer so greatly in God's universes.

Thank you. How may we expand our thought energy positively without stifling our reasoning processes?

In reference to the question, the questioner has stifled his own reasoning processes by the very form of the question. Now, please reread the question for the benefit and awakening of the students.

How may we expand our thought energy positively without stifling our reasoning processes?

The question is asked, How may we expand our thought energy without stifling the soul faculty of reason? My good students, God is the expanding consciousness in the sense that man is the receiver of that consciousness and, in truth, the transmitter. If man permits a question in his mind to dictate to the Infinite Consciousness the possibility of stifling the soul faculty of reason because of an expanded consciousness, then, my good students, we have yet to view truth and freedom. What I do believe the questioner, in truth, is saying: "How may I expand my thought, my view, and *still* maintain my identity and superiority of my limited acceptances of God's eternal right of expression?"

Good night.

JANUARY 22, 1976

CONSCIOUSNESS CLASS 108

Greetings, students. This evening, for our class, we shall discuss the function of decision, denial, and destiny—its corresponding faculty of acceptance, consideration, and expression.

We have discussed many times the varied ways and the intricate mechanisms of what you call the human mind. And so it is at this time we will discuss this function which establishes the mental laws, which, in turn, create your destiny. Whenever the mind entertains the thought of decision—and it entertains thought of decision constantly—the question arises within the mind, "Which shall I do and what shall I not do?" This question, arising within the consciousness of the human mind, opens the door, so to speak, to what we call our sense of values and priorities of the moment. These values and priorities rise from the deep recesses of our own mind in keeping with patterns that have long been established.

And so it is when man strives to make a decision, there is a contradiction that takes place in consciousness and he ofttimes is confused. This contradiction is, in truth, a struggle, so to speak, of the different values and priorities that exist within the mind governing any particular situation. From a lack of control of one's mind, this confusion causes man to rely upon the strongest mental pattern established within his own subconscious.

And so it is that these decisions—and so many they are—are, in truth, based upon what is known as negative faith or fear. For the patterns of mind, demanding the continuity of their own expression, cause the mind to go into a type of self-defense in order that the patterns of old, longest established, fed the most energy by attention, shall rise supreme. And therefore man follows those patterns—those laws established—and is victimized by the denial of his own mind of the possibility of other avenues of expression. Consequently, these denials become, in keeping with these mental laws, his own destiny. This is the balance that is intricate and indispensable to the very purpose for which the mind was designed in the first place.

And so man is the living demonstration of the ancient truth that states, "The thing I fear the most has, in truth, has befallen me." That truth is the demonstration of the infallibility of the divine law working through the instrument called the human mind. Now, negative faith, in truth, is fear. And it is called "negative" because it *is* the magnetic law. Being the magnetic law, it pulls forth unto itself all things that it fears.

Man awakens in consciousness to the immutability of those magnetic laws by viewing his daily and moment-by-moment experiences. That is the principle of the Law of Bondage or, what you may prefer to call, the Law of Form. The counterbalance to this law, this mental Law of Bondage, is the infinite, divine positive law, the Law of the Soul, which is the Law of Freedom. The soul faculty of acceptance, consideration, and expression is not governed by negative law, called fear. It is governed by positive law, called faith. And so it is that man, his eternal soul, when expressing through the soul faculty of acceptance, consideration, and expression, does not experience what you call fear, for that is not within the domain of the soul or its attributes, called the faculties.

The path called joy is the expression of peace. And the expression of peace, when shared, is known as the happiness of life. The separation, so-called, between truth and creation is an awakening to infinite, divine law governing the soul. This awakening and acceptance is what, in truth, is freeing man, in spite of his own mind.

Many times our students, in your world and in this world, have asked the question, "Why must man learn so many laws in order to enjoy the fullness of life?" It is not a matter of learning laws. It is a matter of unlearning the complexity that the mind places over the simplicity of infinite law. How can man, in the world of complexity, see clearly the effects of these denials that he, repeatedly and constantly, is establishing in mental consciousness? Each move that you make, each physical move of your physical body, each word that you speak, each and every experience that you encounter is effect.

And so we have, and continue to do, a constant expression in a multitude of ways, knowing, in keeping with law, one of those ways will enter your consciousness with sufficient impact upon it that you will begin to think more deeply than you have done before. For if a lesson is not perceived, compassion dictates that it be repeated; reason dictates that it shall be given in another way.

And so, my good students, the separation of truth from creation, the path of freedom, is an acceptance, consideration, and expression in consciousness that you may free yourselves from negative law, which is the bondage that you, in truth, your soul, the true you, is striving to free itself from.

We have spoken to you in reference to the realms of diabolical delusion and we do not mean to imply that they are some dimensions in a distant future. They are dimensions in consciousness in this moment, in the moment in which you, in truth, are aware.

We stated several times before that gratitude was, and is, the first soul faculty. We all know, in truth, what the opposite of gratitude is: it's commonly referred to as greed. It dictates that we don't have enough of what we desire. And because the function of greed dictates to our consciousness that way, we work through the realms of delusion of negative laws, ever chasing more, never seeing what we already have, what we already are, in truth.

And so, my friends, let us pause again. Let us review in consciousness, for a moment, our yesterdays. It is interesting to note the tendency of the human mind whenever a pattern of long ago, well established, wishes to express itself: the mind always says how wonderful it was in yesteryear. But let us ask the self the question, "If yesteryear was so wonderful, then why did we ever change from it?" Yesteryear was greater than today when the mind is in the delusion and division of comparison, striving to express, once again, old patterns that bound us and that we made great effort to free ourselves from. No one, in truth, can live in that which has passed, for it, in truth, has come and gone as experience. It is the chains of bondage demanding their continuous hold upon us that dictate that all our yesterdays were the greatest. And that delusion, which is a division in consciousness—dividing the consciousness of your eternal moment and, in so doing, robbing you of the fullness of the here and the now.

Because we have not made a conscious choice in reason to review the past objectively—and the reviewing of past experiences objectively means a freeing of your consciousness from the magnetic field in which those laws were established in the first place.

We move on a stream of life in spite of our efforts to hold to the shores of creation. Whether or not we desire to hold to those shores, our ship, our soul, moves onward. And so it is not only a waste of energy, but, in truth, a lack, a complete lack of reason to look backward in so-called time. He who chooses in the eternal moment to take the fullness that life offers to him is preparing and building the joy which, in truth, is the effect of peace. And peace, as you all know, is the control of yesterday's experiences by placing them where they belong: in yesterday.

And yet, to be born again is the opportunity offered by divine law, for acceptance is the miracle of transformation: to declare, by application, your divine right of happiness, to declare it through application of the control of your mind and then to flow in the stream of life unhampered and unobstructed by what, in truth, has already gone. To entertain in mind regrets of past experiences is to deny the right of your soul to whatever experiences were, and are, necessary for its own evolution. And the evolution of your eternal soul is a greater law than the temporal, negative laws of your mind.

And so it is, my friends, that destiny and truth is at your command. And that destiny is the effect of your denials, and your denials are the effects of your decisions. For the decisions are based upon yesterday, from whence cometh the throne of judgment. For man's judgment is based upon yesterday's experiences. We have taught in this philosophy, and continue to teach in this philosophy, that God is a neutral, infinite, intelligent, energy, freed from judgment, for judgment is never based upon the eternal moment. It can, and is, based solely upon the experiences and denials of yesterday.

Now, I know the question is rising within the minds of some of our students, "Without judgment, how can society and a social structure on earth exist?" And in the present evolution of the souls on earth, the mental laws, being the supreme laws of society, judgment, in that way, is necessary. But it is not necessary to entertain that bondage in your own consciousness, for the longer it is entertained, the more you are bound and destined to your own denials.

When the soul views life from the lower frequency bands of expression, it is governed and controlled by yesterday. When it makes the effort to rise to higher frequencies, it views the eternal moment. And the eternal moment is eternal. It views beyond the illusion and delusion of time and so-called creation. And in so viewing, it is home, in truth. And being home, it does not rely upon passing patterns of mind for its security. And not relying upon that for its security, it has no fear and no longer establishes laws of bondage and continuity of yesterday's negative experiences.

I know there are many questions that are waiting to be asked. And you may feel free to ask them at this time.

Thank you. How does the conscience differ from the conscience-conscious mind, referred to in The Living Light [Discourse 24], *example belief?*

In reference to the question of the conscious-conscience mind and the conscious mind, let us perhaps speak in this way: When the conscience, the spiritual sensibility with the dual capacity, knowing so-called right and wrong, in respect to the laws that it alone has established—it knows the difference between mental laws of bondage for itself and soul laws of evolution for itself—when this becomes a conscious awareness, then man is no longer controlled by the subconscious educated conscience, which is the negative laws of bondage. And so man, in his beliefs, frees himself, instead of binding himself to that which has already, in truth, gone.

Thank you. How responsible are we for others, as an example for their happiness and welfare, etc., when they attempt to block our right to pursue our studies?

In reference to the Law of Personal Responsibility, if we are having experiences attracted to us that we decide are caused by someone or something outside of ourselves, then we are, our soul, expressing through the lower frequencies of delusion, for we have denied the Law of Personal Responsibility by looking for the cause for something, which is an experience in our own consciousness, by looking for the cause outside of ourselves. And so in reference to that question on happiness and another person interfering with our right to our studies, we must ask ourselves the question, "What law, what negative law in my mind is attracting unto me a person who is striving to rob me of my freedom to study?"

The blame does not exist outside. That is the delusion in order that the patterns of mind that we are addicted to may perpetuate themselves. For the moment that the mind accepts the truth—that it is a law unto itself, that personal responsibility *is* the law of life and that the cause for the experience—and all experiences—exist within ourselves—when that acceptance enters the mind, then the patterns must bow, for that *is* the law.

Thank you. The climb is never higher than the fall. But the fall seems so much faster and the pull of gravity downward is so strong. Is there a pull upward as strong? When we climb, we can stop climbing. But when we fall, doesn't gravity take us all the way down?

There is no all the way. For if there were, there would not be infinity. There is no all the way up, no more than there is any all the way down. In reference to the pull upward to the realms supernal in consciousness, there is a pull as great as the pull downward into delusion and bondage. And it may be clearly stated in this way: Judgment is the gravitational pull of the magnetic field and the negative laws, known as fear. Acceptance is the positive pull of the Divine to free us that we may live in peace and joy and the great wonder of life itself.

Thank you very much. How does man know when he is freed from his brain?

Fine question. How does man know when he is free from his brain? It is not within the power of the brain, which is a vehicle through which negative magnetic laws are established. The brain is an instrument of duality, creation. And the brain does not have within its power the great peace that passeth all understanding. Peace is the divine neutrality. It is the perfect balance. And so when man experiences within himself peace, he's freed from all thought, all contradiction, all division. He is then truly aware of being an inseparable part of a united whole. He no longer acts, because he no longer reacts. He just *is*. And that is the home of the soul.

Thank you. We are taught there are nine spheres and eighty-one levels of consciousness. Would you please tell us just how we know what level we are on at a particular time? And would you clarify this?

In reference to these nine spheres and nine planes of consciousness on each sphere, these eighty-one levels of awareness, How does man know on which level of consciousness he is at any given moment? Man has the experiences of many levels and he fluctuates from moment to moment, ofttimes, from one level to another. In order that man may perceive these forty functions and forty faculties, the door that must be opened is the door of wisdom. Now, the door of wisdom is opened with the key of understanding. And the key of understanding is made from the substance of personal responsibility. And the substance of personal responsibility is garnered up from the efforts that are made to accept the eternal truth that all cause is within. And so to the questioner, who is viewing the effects of levels of consciousness, find the cause by stepping upon the path that will grant it to you.

Thank you. If one aspires to become a healer or medium, is it wise for him to associate with people who are in harmony with him? It seems to me that one should. Otherwise, his energy would be depleted for work or service of this kind.

Well, in reference to the question, it is true and in keeping with the law that one should spend some time, if they want to be a golfer, on the golf course and should associate with those who are proficient in that particular sport. However, if one spends all of his time on the golf course or conversing with golfers, then one will not long remain in balance. For they are denying the expression of other levels of consciousness within themselves.

And so it is in keeping with the demonstrable law, revealed in golf, that man must consider, in reference to spiritual endeavors—if you can call them that—that one may associate with other healers and certainly enter the so-called ballpark where the healing is expressed. But if one does so at the expense and the denial of all the other levels of consciousness, then one will not long remain in balance. And a good healer—if you can call it good—a person proficient in being a channel for the healing energies must be a person who is well balanced. And "well balanced" does not mean exclusive to one level of consciousness.

Thank you. When we do not accept or sink into others problems, especially those of family, is it probable, as we become more detached, that the Law of Attraction is being demonstrated?

Well, in reference to the question, as we become more attached—did you say?

"Detached," it says.

All experiences reveal—and we state this truth again and again, again and again and again—all experiences—family, business, and otherwise—are effects. In time, we learn to be in the world and not a part of the world. In time, we learn to be with a thing and not a part of the thing. We learn that when we demonstrate by application the Law of Personal Responsibility. The acceptance and the response—the ability to respond in all experience, the ability to respond in consciousness to the infinite truth that we alone are the cause of the experience, no matter what the mind chooses to delude us with—to respond to that truth within us that we alone can change the experience that is taking place in our consciousness, that it is our consciousness, that we are personally responsible for its action and reaction. And being personally responsible for its action and reaction, we can consciously choose whatever we choose to choose.

Thank you. How can you best learn to concentrate on the now, when the mind has the tendency to project in the future?

The mind has the tendency to project—if you wish to call it that—to the past. Now, it is an interesting delusion of the mind: it thinks many things and imagines many things and it tells itself, "Well, my future I am working towards and it is going to be this way or that way." Now, what is really speaking are the strongest patterns of yesterday. They rise in new garments, more subtle, more refined. They rise that way when man decides that he is going to make changes, that life, for him, is going to be better. And so he makes this decision from a level of mind. And making it from a mind level, which is governed by negative faith, which is based upon the acceptance and rejections of yesterday, he finds, in time, he's made this effort and it hasn't happened the way he decided that it should happen. But it did happen in keeping with accepted patterns of the past.

Now, how does man free himself from this very refined and subtle delusion of these patterns? He does so by placing his consciousness in the eternal moment and living the fullness of that moment and accepting. And this is the key that opens the door of eternity: by accepting a divine Authority that is guiding, in keeping with the laws of his acceptances, that is guiding his eternal soul to the fullness of life. That acceptance is something that man must ever keep as a banner before his conscious awareness. That does not mean that man, in keeping before his view the banner of acceptance, called divine will, that he has become weak. For no man could call God weak. You may call God many things, but weak, the Divine Intelligence cannot be called. For the demonstration of that Intelligence upholds all universes and everything in it. That's not weakness. And so, my good friends, "Acceptance—something good is happening" is an eternal declaration that frees you, that you may flow in divine will throughout eternity, which is the moment of now.

Thank you. Would you please share your understanding of color meditation?

In reference to your question on what you call color meditation, it is not something that we have discussed in our classes. If you mean by those words "vibration of color," then we are happy to discuss with you vibration, color, sound, and its effect upon us. However, we recommend and suggest that the questioner who is asking the question concerning so-called color meditation kindly clarify their question at our next class. Thank you.

Thank you. Have we not been visited by beings from so-called outer space who are of a higher degree of intelligence? Please clarify.

In the first place, if we believe we have had an experience with intelligences from so-called outer space, it would take a degree of higher intelligence to get in rapport with them. It would take higher intelligence to record the experience and higher intelligence to use the wisdom and the reason of how we wish to express it, if at all. Thank you.

Thank you. Where do you draw the line between the responsibility of sharing the Light and the presumption of trying to change another human soul?

How beautifully put. If the motivation is pure, from your soul, there is no thought, let alone concern, that you are presumptuous, which is the Law of Descent. All souls know what to do, how to do it, when to do it. It is the minds, and the minds alone, that dictate the contradictions and the concern of whether or not they're in humility or ego and presumption. Thank you.

Thank you. I understand the lungs represent harmony. Please explain what the rest of the respiratory system, such as the bronchial tubes, represent.

Well, in reference to the lungs that represent harmony—and the questioner has a personal reason for asking the question in reference to the bronchial tubes. When reason, the divine light of perfect balance, descends over the magnetic field of self-concern, we begin to flow in harmony and in unity. For then, we demonstrate "The Law of Harmony is my thought *[See the "Total Consideration" affirmation in the appendix.]*."

Now, the bronchial tubes themselves are representative of a soul faculty, which is unity. When we make effort to put our house in order before confusion sets in—that means to unite ourselves in thought, to be not filled with guilt, to be not controlled by yesterday, but to unite, to unite the several bodies that we are, for, in so uniting, we make the first effort to bring balance and reason into our lives. Thank you.

Thank you. What is the true meaning of the statement, "The meek shall inherit the earth"? Is it a divine law that we are our brother's keeper?

Divine law of truth *is*. There is no separation in consciousness. The meek shall inherit the earth, for the meek already have it. It is those active in the magnetic mental fields that are constantly denying what they already have. The meek do not chase after something that they already stand upon, for they have accepted and, in so doing, all, in truth, is theirs.

Thank you. Please expand on why selfless service is the only path to illumination. How can we tell when selfless service is truly selfless?

We know when selfless service is selfless when we no longer ask the question. Thank you.

Thank you. If the neck represents the will and the shoulders courage, what does the lower back represent?

In reference to the back, it represents strength.

Thank you. How does the mind recognize a greater authority than itself?

In a thousand million ways we have given the answer. And once again we will give it to you: Acceptance—something good is happening. When you accept that and the mind no longer says, "What?" and the mind no longer says, "When?" and the mind no longer says, "How?" and the mind no longer says, "Why?" then, my good students, you have it.

Good night.

JANUARY 29, 1976

CONSCIOUSNESS CLASS 109

Greetings, students. This evening we shall dedicate our class to a response to the many questions that you, as students, have been asking. For we know that in this exchange the opportunity is granted to you to perceive the true motives and levels of consciousness that are revealed in the class this evening. And so it is that we shall begin our class with the questions that you have presented to us.

Thank you. I can't remember ever hearing you laugh. Are you beyond earth-plane type humor?

It is indeed most interesting to note that the questioner has decided, first, how humor shall be expressed, has also decided that there are, evidently, various types of humor. And so in reference to the question concerning humor, which is, in truth, the salvation of the soul, we must, in this question, ask ourselves the question, "What is humor? Is humor expressed in one way or many ways? And is humor classified into such things as Earth type? And if so, does that in the question mean such a thing as Martian type, Saturnian type, Juperterian type, etc. through your universe?"

My good students, often we have heard your minds speak forth that certain people have what you call dry humor. Now, we must ask ourselves the question, "If humor is dry at times, does that not imply that humor may also, also be wet? And if so, why is it the mind only refers to dry humor and not to wet humor?" What do we truly mean by the word *humor*? We mean, by that word, the willingness and the ability to accept in all things good, which, in truth, is God. And in so accepting in all things goodness, we accept peace in our consciousness. And when that peace within us is expressed, we experience joy. Now, the expression of this peace, called joy, is, in truth, what is known as humor.

If we decide, and judge, that humor is this and is not that, that humor, in truth, may be expressed in this way and not in that way, that humor is either dry or humor is wet, that humor may be classified into different types, then, in truth, we are not discussing humor. We are discussing, however, what our minds, by their limited acceptances and experiences of the past, have judged, by its own decision, what humor is.

It is a wise soul who laughs on the inside that they may sincerely smile on the outside. It is a sad soul, in truth, that forces laughter on the outside while the soul weeps in weakness for its sadness on the inside.

And so, my good students, if you do not find humor where humor, in truth, is, then remember, you have decided. And in so deciding, you have bound your consciousness to how life truly is. And in so doing, the horizons cannot be broadened for your greater fullness and joy of life itself. Thank you.

Thank you. Would you please offer some practical suggestions to parents on how to effectively discipline their children? And, in giving your understanding, would you please comment upon why parents sometimes neglect to discipline their children and what effect such neglect has upon the evolution of the soul of the child?

In reference to the question, we must first go to the principle, the essence of the Law of Happiness. Without discipline, there is no happiness. For without discipline, there is no control. Without control, the effect of which is freedom, there is only bondage for the evolving soul. And so it is in reference to the guidance of what you call children on your Earth planet.

The view of the souls which are in the smaller forms, that you call children, is not a view of the soul, but a view of the form. Viewing its size and being controlled by the mind's limited education, man deceives himself in reference to what he calls proper guidance and discipline for what the mind calls children. When you look at the soul—and you must first look at your own soul within in order to view a soul without—then you will see that the soul has been expressing for untold centuries. That soul responds to understanding, to kindness, to love, for love, in truth, is the language of the eternal soul.

When you reach in your consciousness that perspective, then you will take a child in their guidance and you will converse with them. You will not permit your mind to say to you, "That this child is so young, they cannot understand." For you will go beyond your limited, mental acceptances. And going beyond that, you will become the instrument of eternal truth. You will speak to the child whether or not they are in physical age three or thirty. You will speak to them with reason. You will explain to them why this is the way things shall be and why that is not the way they shall be. And in so doing you will grant unto the evolving soul that which is in truth its divine right: the right of discipline of the mind, which is the vehicle through which the soul, evolving, is striving to express itself.

Now, the mind, as you all know, is a creation. And creation it be is governed and controlled by the Law of Duality. And so you grant to the mind the discipline that is the right of the soul to have. You clearly speak without emotion and you make it very clear: "This is what you do and this is the reason that you do it. If you do not do it, then you will experience what is your soul's divine right and your mind will call that discipline."

Now, just how does this discipline work? The mind, controlled by negative faith, called fear, responds to that which it is, in truth, controlled by. And so when the child does not do what it has been told to do, you deprive the child of the desires that it has value for. Now, there is no child, there is no mind, that does not have desire. And there is no mind that does not have value for its desires. For the nature of the mind is to garner unto itself. And its process of garnering unto itself is through the divine principle of expression called desire.

In the guidance of children, one does not, one does not take hours to express principle. The word is spoken. The so-called penalty is enforced without emotion. And it is enforced repeatedly. And the mind, in turn, responds. Without that type of discipline, the mind gains control over the evolving soul. And when that happens—as it has happened to most all souls on your planet today—there is emotional immaturity in so-called adulthood. The body and the intellect matures in keeping with the physical age, but the emotional body remains the child, untrained, undisciplined and, in so being, controls the soul by its own darkness of license.

In truth, it becomes the greatest deceiver the soul ever knows, because it has not been properly trained to express itself in the areas of which it has rightful domain. And so man experiences in his earth life, from the lack of childhood discipline, he experiences frustration, the bondage of fascination, the lack of continuity, the lack of control, failure, depression, and the negative results that are given birth by the greatest deceiver the soul ever, ever knows.

However, in properly guiding and disciplining the vehicle through which the eternal soul is striving to express, one must never forget any expression of so-called discipline from the emotional body of the disciplinarian, in truth, is not discipline at all. But one must care enough for their children to make the effort—and effort it does take—to grant to them, their own children, that which is, in truth, the divine right of the evolving soul. If a parent does not grant that divine right of the discipline and the balancing of their own mind, then they cannot, in truth, grant that to anyone, especially their own children, who are the effects of laws that the parents have set into motion. Unless that is granted to the children, there is a regret that knocks eternally at the door of the parents true conscience.

Usually those who have earned the charge of little souls—little only in the view of what we call children—usually those people are far more interested in reliving their own childhood. And because that selfish motivation, in truth, is their prime objective, they play the mental games that they were not allowed to play in their own childhood. And the child is only granted what the parent, in their own selfish motivation to relive their youth, decides to grant to them. However, it is true that the evolving soul through the child has established laws in evolution to merit that type of parent or parents. That does not, however, exempt the parent from the transgressions of those immutable laws.

We look at children and we decide how we can express ourselves through them. We do not view them from the soul faculty of reason. Because of our emotional attachments and selfish interest, we do not grant unto them the balance which is the effect of discipline, which is their right. And so we view in this great eternity the untold millions of souls that habitate the realms of satisfaction and regret. For the guilt, which is rejected desire, floods the consciousness of those souls until such time, from their efforts, they discipline themselves and grant that great freedom to another soul. It takes so little effort to grant that right, but it does take the continuity of that little effort. And that continuity, the minds are not willing to grant unto themselves until such time as they awaken and view the bondage of license that their own dear children are moving into.

Thank you. It seems some spiritual aspirants have some difficulty resolving and balancing their spirituality with their sexuality. Would you please share your wisdom with us?

In reference to that question, it is necessary for the students to rise in consciousness to the principle involved in the question and not to fascinate themselves with their minds and mental gymnastics concerning a simple principle which belongs wholly, solely, and completely to the Divine.

We stated some time ago in your study book [*The Living Light* and also *The Living Light Dialogue Volume 1*] that the sole purpose of what you call sex is for the procreation of the species. Looking from the spiritual view of this divine principle, we see that the soul enters form through that divine principle of exchange of energy. The difficulties and problems in your world are because the mind has taken control of that which it has, in truth, no business in. Because the minds have taken that control, they have bound themselves to the mental world of division. The mental world of division is, in truth, delusion.

The nature of the mind is to create images ever in response to stimuli. Once, having created the image, it continues to expand it into what you call variety. This is the great delusion: when the intellect, the mind, tries to control divine infinite principle.

Therefore, the mind's attention upon that which is divine causes an obstruction in consciousness. And causing this obstruction in consciousness, the fullness of the divine exchange of energy does not take place in a way that joy and happiness may be the result. In time, because of the mind and its nature, finally it bows in disgust and what you call repulsion. However, there is good in all things. And when the mind—and it usually takes many years—bows in disgust and repulsion, when that happens, usually there is no longer an expression or an exchange of energy in that respect. This is the greatest transgression of God's divine right and law that we witness in the lunatic fringe, called earth.

Because, in truth, all is an exchange of energy, whether or not it is speaking with a person, touching a person, or the sexual act. Because there is such grave transgression, man loses sight and wanders in the dark recesses of his own delusion.

The principle through which the soul enters form is infinite and immutable and infallible. It has nothing whatsoever to do, in truth, with your minds. But your minds, desiring to control everything, including the divine right of God, have placed a titanic mountain of insanity upon the truth of simplicity.

The soul entering form under this divine principle has the potential to exit from form by the same principle. But it cannot do that as long as you insist upon controlling that which is, in truth, impossible for your minds to control, for principle is beyond the duality of your minds.

The exchange of energy is divine law. It shall, and is exchanged at all times by all souls expressing through all forms. The only thing your minds can do is to limit in respect to how *you* will permit God's divine energy to express through your mental body, of which your physical body is an effect.

When this energy is blocked by your minds, there is discord, disharmony within your being. You have already chosen in which way you will permit God, the divine Energy, to express through you. You have not only decided how, but you have decided when. And because you, your minds, have made those decisions and judgments, the transgressions are, in truth, your own discord, your own discontent. For you are no longer united within yourselves.

And so, my good students, look from spiritual view at the simplicity of divine principle and immutable law. Do not take this understanding to mean the bondage of license and promiscuity. But look objectively at the ways in which you have limited the right of the Divine and your own evolving soul. That takes an honest view of oneself.

We are spending much time on this question, for your world is revealing in the ethereal waves a great interest in what you on earth have made a great problem. For had you not made it such a great problem, then your minds would not spend so much energy and interest in it.

Truth is such a simple thing. But you will never find it through division. You will never find that simplicity in your minds, for it cannot live in your minds: it exists in your soul. And it is experienced by you when your minds are still. And so, lacking the principle for what it truly is, you find yourselves void of the fullness of life, for you do not recognize God moving through all forms. You limit God to what you choose. And in so doing, your denials become your eternal destinies. And that's not, my good students, a far-off tomorrow. It is when you pause and take an honest view of your life this very moment.

Thank you. Would you please dissertate on Adam and Eve, the symbolic tree of knowledge, and what the apple represents?

In reference to the allegorical story and the garden of paradise and in reference to Adam and Eve, we can share with you at this time a bit. And the serpent beguiled Eve. She was overcome by fascination, which is, in truth, the great deceiver called the human brain. And she went against or transgressed divine law in the sense she permitted herself to be controlled by mental law and, curiosity and fascination controlling her mind, plucked the apple from the tree of knowledge.

Now, you all know that curiosity is the father of frustration and that fascination is, in truth, its mother. And so Eve plucked from the tree of knowledge its fruit. Now, what, in truth, is the fruit of knowledge? The fruit of knowledge is an awareness of the Law of Division, which, in truth, is the delusion of the mind.

And so they ate the fruit. They experienced the Law of Division, which is the fruit of knowledge or mental supremacy over the eternal, evolving soul. And having accepted and experienced the Law of Division, their soul sank into division and they became aware of what the mind calls form. In their awareness, they experienced what your world calls sin. And what, in truth, is sin, but the error of ignorance? And what, in truth, is the error of ignorance, but the view of duality, of division, which guarantees the complexity and multiplication that keeps the soul in a constant state of bondage?

Man cannot view neutrality until he becomes neutrality. And man cannot become neutrality until he makes the effort to balance his own universe. And man cannot balance his own universe until his soul is permitted to flow through the faculty of reason.

Now, reason, we know, is total consideration. It is not limited consideration of one or two levels of consciousness within. And so when the Law of Division, delusion, rose supreme, the soul began to sink. Now, this is not something that took place thousands of years ago and has not happened since. For that is the delusion of delusions. It is a process that is taking place within you each and every moment. Each and every moment, you stand between Hades and heaven. Each and every moment, you experience the garden of Eden or the so-called pits of hell. That process is within your power each moment to control.

I know that this evening's class has seemed to be a bit difficult for some of my students. And the difficulty that you are experiencing—some of you—is the revelation of the very thing that binds you. Accept it in consciousness and work with it objectively, using the eternal light of reason, and you will, my good friends, free yourselves.

Good night.

FEBRUARY 5, 1976

CONSCIOUSNESS CLASS 110

Greetings, students. This evening we shall discuss, for a time, the Law of Delusion that governs the human mind.

Some time ago we revealed this to you in the statement, "When of thy mind thou seekest to know the truth, / On the wheel of delusion thou shalt traverse [Discourse 1]." Now, the nature of the mind is to identify. And that which the mind identifies with, the mind, within itself, controls. And the very nature of the human mind is to control what it identifies with or it cannot, in truth, accept. For if the mind, controlled by the Law of Identification, could not control within itself that which it identifies with, then it would lose the very principle for which the mind was designed.

Now, this may seem contrary to some of you. And so we will continue on, sharing our understanding of the very nature of the mind and how it works in its identification processes. When the soul enters the form at the moment of conception, there are, at that time, so-called ethereal bodies that are already formed. And the physical processes, or the physical growth of form, is in keeping with the mold established by the ethereal form. That ethereal form is in keeping with the laws governing the evolution of the evolving soul. Those laws of evolution are the effects of what is known as identity or identification.

Now, we identify with those things that our minds have accepted, that they can, to the satisfaction of the mind, control.

The minds of men speak in this way, "I identify with the world. I identify with people. I identify with the sky, the water, and the trees. But I do not, and cannot, control them." That, my friends, is the great delusion of delusions. For we identify in keeping with our own perspective, with our own minds.

An ancient truth was given long ago to your world and that is: Beauty is in the eye of the beholder. And so it is that each mind identifies in its own way, but that is what you call reality. The reality known by the mind is its own limited identification and, consequently, it establishes those laws of control within itself.

It has often been stated here that the world is ever as we are within, that inner attitudes of mind—that outward manifestations are the revelations of those inner attitudes of mind. We have also stated that the effect of self-control is known as freedom; that is the controlling of the duality within man's own mind. For the mind, for every yes guarantees a no. And for every no, the mind guarantees a yes. This is because the mind, a created instrument through which the soul expresses, is governed by the laws of duality, which are the laws of creation.

And so it is a very natural and normal feeling for the mind to desire to control. That feeling and desire for control reveals the great need within the mind to control itself.

We have stated that energy follows your own attention. It follows your own thought. We have stated that which you give thought to, you give power over you. For, my good friends, you identify by the very process of thought. And, as you identify by that infallible law, through the process of thought, you are controlled, for that is the very nature and the very purpose of the mind.

To still the mind takes a great deal—for most people—a great deal of effort. It takes great effort because there has been little, if any, effort demonstrated before. The importance of understanding the very nature of the human mind cannot be over emphasized. And so it is when we awaken within to the Law of Identity—which is taking place, in truth, all of the time, whether we are so-called awake or asleep. We must never forget that the true you, the eternal being, called soul, never, ever sleeps. It is in a constant process, day and night, throughout eternity, striving to express itself and to evolve.

This seeming great need for sleep is, in truth, a revelation that we, as evolving eternal souls, are not yet fully ready to face the infinite eternal Law of Personal Responsibility: the ability to respond to the effects of laws we alone establish. Now, many people believe they are tired and require what they call sleep. They do not believe they are tired and require sleep when they are sufficiently interested in whatever their minds are identifying with. It is when the mind, in its own identification processes, becomes bored and does not want to face what it alone has established. And so, in truth, so-called sleep is what you may term an escape mechanism to hide and to run away from the effects of personal, established laws.

However, what takes place, in truth, though the conscious mind is not aware ofttimes, is a moving in consciousness through the desire body into areas of fascination of things that interest the mind.

My good students, the path of peace, joy, and freedom was never termed by anyone of reason as the easiest path for any soul. But let us look more clearly at the very nature of the human mind. Let us view it a bit more objectively and see its true purpose and its true nature that we may gain a clearer, a fuller understanding of why the mind cannot, and shall not, know eternal truth.

It identifies and controls within itself all things that it identifies with. That is its very nature: to preserve. And so how does man, the eternal being, know freedom and truth and the joy of living when his true consciousness is expressing through what is called a human mind? He knows the joy of living and eternal truth when he takes control of the controls and he stills the mind. And when he stills the mind, he experiences that which is beyond the mind. And in so experiencing that which is beyond the mind, he knows beyond a shadow of any doubt that life is eternal, that there are laws greater than what his mind can entertain, for they are the principles of divine law. They are not separated and divided into the dualities of creation.

"Is it possible," the question must be asked, "to be aware of that beyond the mind, while still in the mind?" It is possible to experience truth and have some degree of conscious awareness, for that is known as being in the mind and not a part of the mind. For that is the way that the divine Architect truly designed the vehicles through which the eternal life is expressing. But because of what could be called overidentification— and overidentification simply means that our soul, expressing through the mind, has become the mind and, having become it, it knows no different. Therefore, it behooves us to use the arm or the foot without becoming it; to use the thoughts of the mind and yet be not a part of it.

We have stated, "When the tools no longer serve the worker, the worker begins to serve the tools." And so it has become that the mind, a tool of the eternal soul, has stopped serving the eternal soul and is serving the tool of the human mind. Many ways have been shown to you to free yourselves from this situation, but it is within your hands to make that simple effort. We have stated, "To give it to the Divine," to surrender the thought or thoughts. But it takes a little effort to permit the peace of your own soul to rise to give up the things that entertain the human mind.

In many ways for many, many centuries we have taught, and continue to teach, the simple truth. And we shall continue to teach the simplicity of truth, though it must wear many, many different garments in order that the many levels of consciousness may someday accept a little.

Remember, my friends, there is one law. It is the minds, which is their nature of division, that have made so many laws. And because so many divisions of the simple law, the oneness of truth, is controlling the human beings, they must learn to pull back into themselves and find that great simplicity, returning home unto themselves, for there, and there alone, is the true joy of life.

And now, we will spend some time with the questions you have asked.

Thank you. What is the difference, if any, between freedom and salvation?

In reference to your question, "What is the difference, if any, between freedom and salvation?" the word *salvation* implies the need to save. The word *freedom* does not. When man speaks, in your world, of salvation, he usually means the making of effort to a power or authority that he does not understand, that will, by its very grace or nature, through one's effort, save him from his own transgressions of law, which are, in truth, errors of ignorance. Freedom is that which man, in truth, already is. He is able to recognize what he is—that freedom—when he demonstrates what is known in your world as self-control.

Thank you. Will man be able to cross the time barrier through hypnosis or other forms of psychic power? That is to say, will he be able to step out of his home in 1976 and into the real physical world of 1876 or 2076?

In reference to the question concerning what you call hypnosis, which is, in truth, permitting the magnetic field to take control of the electrical field or conscious mind, the subconscious rising in supremacy, has nothing to do, in truth, with crossing so-called time barriers. It is interesting to note that your world considers that there are barriers in time, for time, in truth, is illusion and in that respect a great barrier indeed.

Thank you. Would you please explain how curiosity leads to frustration?

The question is, How does curiosity lead to frustration? Man becomes curious with many things. And the curiosity is an instrument through which the mind, by its nature, identifies. It identifies with those things that it is curious about. When it identifies with those things, the nature of the mind is to control them, for that is the very purpose of the mind. And so the mind, in its efforts to control that which it has identified with, by the Law of Curiosity, battles with its many other identities in its own consciousness, in its own mind. And so man, in that process, becomes frustrated.

And so you have a process of curiosity, identification, frustration, and fascination. Because of the frustration created by these multitudes of things that the mind has already identified with and because of its nature to control, it then moves into fascination. For there, it can reign supreme. It can create in the mental imagery the way it wants things to be, the way that it is for them and therefore be in keeping with the things that it has already identified with.

Now, we have spoken many times on the bondage of fascination. And the bondage is very simple: we identify through mental imagery. And we are always, in our fascination, in control. And so it is that man moves on his wheels of disappointment, for he always makes, in his mind, the experience to be under his full control, for that is the nature of mind.

And ofttimes, when the experience is truly expressed, it just never seems to come up to his own requirements. And so the wheels of curiosity, the wheels of frustration, the wheels of delusion, fascination, identification, and all those things move his mind ever faster until there comes that moment when man has had enough. And he surrenders it all. For it's just too much to keep spinning, year after year, and century after century, upon the wheel.

Thank you. Would you please tell us if Light is synonymous with God?

Indeed, it is, for it is energy. And God is intelligent Energy, intelligently expressed. It is one and the same.

Thank you. Could you please tell us why you take the form of an older man?

A most interesting question. I could take the form of a child, if, in so doing, it would serve the purpose for which my life was long ago dedicated. I take on the appearance of that which will best serve the purpose to which I have dedicated my life.

Thank you. Some teachings indicate that the earth is entering the golden Age of Aquarius. And that avatar, one not born of the union of male and female, will appear to help rise the vibratory level of the planet by example and teachings. Is such a high being now in form? And, if so, is that form female?

In reference to the question, it is indeed most interesting to note that the minds of men ever look to so-called virginity as the divine incarnation of God himself. The reason that the minds of men create these fantasies is because, to the minds of men, that which is divine and beyond the mind must be contrary to what the mind has accepted as natural law. Otherwise, the minds of men could not worship it as a greater and higher authority.

God, the Divine, is flowing through all levels of consciousness, be they mental or spiritual or physical, astral, ethereal, celestial.

And so man looks for something or someone to usher in a golden age. The golden age, which means the age of wisdom, is not something outside that is being ushered in by any soul entering creation contrary to the very laws of creation. It is true that the minds of men do not fully understand the natural laws of life. But the golden age, which is already taking place on your planet, is an age of consciousness of wisdom.

And we stated before, in all your getting, get understanding. And in all your giving, give wisdom. Wisdom flows like a gentle breeze from your soul and expresses across your mind, but is not within the mind. And that is taking place in many places on your earth. You can view it when you listen attentively. And the words of wisdom flow from the very fountain of God. And the vehicles through which they flow are not concerned, nor interested, in what the recipient is doing with what they are receiving.

Thank you. Would you please give us your understanding of how one might truly apply or unfold the soul faculty of strength and, in the process, effect self-healing of back disorders?

Yes, yes, indeed. How may one unfold the soul faculty of strength? Man cannot unfold the soul faculty of strength without consideration and the application of what the Law of Consideration dictates. And what does the Law of Total Consideration dictate? It dictates: grant unto another what you have granted unto yourself, for that is the Law of Unity. And without the Law of Unity, flowing unobstructed through the consciousness, there is no true strength, for the house is divided and cannot stand.

And so, in referring to the question, I can only say, the body, being effect of laws established—and each part of the holy temple, representing a soul faculty and sense function—that those seeking greater strength make effort for greater consideration. And in so doing, the revelation of personal responsibility will awaken more fully within. And when it does, the seeming problem concerning that part of the holy house will disappear into the nothingness.

Thank you. Would you please explain through which avenue or technique the emotional body is brought under control and why this control is so critical to the spiritual progression?

Well, in reference to the emotional body, which is an effect of one's own accepted experiences, through the Law of Identification, How does one bring it under control? By first becoming aware of it and not reacting spontaneously to it. Through making the effort to know oneself, one will know their own emotional body. They will know what causes it to act and react.

And, in knowing that, they have the key to open the door of reason and no longer, no longer pride themselves with their spontaneous so-called tempers. The only thing spontaneous about the volcanic eruption of the emotional body is the ignorance of the very laws established that cause it to explode in the first place. Only a fool takes pride in the discord and disease of their emotional body. It is there to serve a purpose. And its very purpose is to preserve what it has identified with. But the preservation of it is not controlling other human souls. If you wish to be upset because something does not go your way, it is your divine right to be upset. But it is not within your right to be the instrument to help others to be upset, for that is contrary to the Law of Personal Responsibility: the responding, within yourself, to your own laws and not to direct them outward in the delusion that the experience, in truth, came from someone else.

When man moves in consciousness and uses the mind and its part which is the emotional body as the tool for which it was, in truth, designed, then man will have no need to be concerned about techniques, for he already knows the laws that govern those bodies.

Thank you. Can you please explain the process of exactly what happens when we send somebody a thought, a good thought or a so-called bad thought?

The question—I might advise the questioner to study the philosophy that has been given. I know that the questioner has our study book, *The Living Light*, and Discourse 61 clearly and simply explains the Law of Thought. And if the students will make that microscopic effort, I know, in truth, their question is well answered. But we must make the effort, my good students. We sincerely pray that you be encouraged in your spiritual endeavors.

Our needs of our minds are the needs to control them. To use them wisely, for the purpose for which they have been designed:

to truly do unto others as you choose to do unto yourselves, to look beyond the illusion to see the great beauty and purpose of eternal life, to truly open your eyes and see beyond the limits of your mind, to go into the realms of eternal peace in this moment and not some far off distant future.

Though the minds of men have established many laws, the law of God is the greater law. And when, in time of greatest need, though you have transgressed a multitude of mental laws, what little effort you may have made in evolution to serving God, the Light, is deposited in eternal consciousness. And so in your darkest hour, though your errors and transgressions are many and count far more than the hairs upon your head, there is a greater law, greater than all law. And it's known as the one Law of the Light, called God.

And how does man flow in the purity and beauty of the one Law, called God? He does that, my good children, when he surrenders what he calls his mind.

Thank you. That is all the questions I have this evening.
Good night.

FEBRUARY 12, 1976

CONSCIOUSNESS CLASS 111

Good evening, students. We have been with our class this evening in discussion of the magnetic principle of life, also known as the power of believing.

Now, it is commonly understood by most people that one only questions what one does not believe. However, the direct contrary is true. For man, in truth, only questions what, in truth, he believes. For what man does not believe does not exist in consciousness for him. And therefore man cannot question what, for him, does not already exist.

We find with the human mind and its great intricate system, designed for the good of man, so misunderstood and ill-directed, because of a lack of understanding its true purpose, its understanding of the soul, standing between the power so-called of light and the forces so-called of darkness. For man, this divine spark, stands between an electric field of consciousness, which purpose it is to question, and a magnetic field, which purpose it is to believe.

All people already believe many, many things. And the mind is in a constant process of refining or, perhaps better stated, expanding the beliefs that it already has. This believing process is a law known as the magnetic principle of life. Without it, there is no identity. Without it, there is no individualization or delusion of separation. And so it serves—properly used, it can serve a very good and useful purpose. This believing magnetic field, once accepting a thought into it, once believing it, becomes the law on which your soul must travel.

And so many times we have spoken on becoming aware of your thoughts and of your own beliefs. We have stressed, over the years, the great importance of affirmations: to affirm the good that you may believe the good, for in your believing is the law established that you may experience what it is you say that you are seeking. And so again we emphasize the great power of belief, the great necessity for those who are still struggling along the path. And remember, my good students, the struggle never ends as long as you have what you call identity, individualization. It cannot end until you, your eternal soul, the spark of Divinity that is expressing through it, rises in its consciousness, which is within your power any moment, to the peace that passeth all understanding. And it passeth all understanding, for it is beyond things to understand.

Now, my good students, with so much that has been given to you in so very many different ways, we know that sometimes the so-called mountains of obstruction seem indeed insurmountable. But if you believe that, then that is the law that you shall experience, for whatever it is that you are choosing to believe, that, in truth, is where you shall be. There is nothing that can change that law, for that is your right and the law is ever fulfilled.

We have repeatedly stated not to place your attention, your belief, upon the obstructions of life, for there you shall make them even greater. When the mind dictates that something is difficult, be rest assured that it believes accordingly and, for you, it then becomes difficult. If the mind is permitted to say that it is almost impossible to surrender the things that disturb you, then, for you, it shall be.

The philosophy that we offer to your world over these years, and shall continue to offer, is the simplicity and common sense, for that's what it is in truth. We have listened attentively to our students sharing their understanding of the Living Light philosophy and we are grateful for the efforts being made. However, we should also like to caution those who share so readily that through demonstration is the truth about us revealed. It is not what we say in life, but what we do with life that reveals our true motives and is, in truth, the Living Light philosophy.

It is easy to intellectually conceive these simple laws of life that demonstrate themselves to those who have eyes to see and ears to hear each moment. But it is the demonstration of what you do in life that is, in truth, the expression of the laws revealed within the philosophy. And so, my good students, give greater thought to the power of believing, for that power of believing, that principle of the magnetic field of life itself, already, and forever, controls the lives of so-called forms.

And so as you continue on your journey through what is known as life, which is, in truth, consciousness, remember that it is your divine and eternal right for the happiness to be expressed through you and 'round and about you. Wise are those who speak less of their struggles and speak more of their joys. Wise indeed are those who speak less of their failures and more of their successes. Wise are those indeed who choose who and what and why to speak at all.

For life is the dream of dreams. It is its very nature. No one shall, or can, change it. However, because it is, in truth, a dream and because, in truth, you are the dreamer of your dream, which you call a life, it places you in a position, as the dreamer, of personal responsibility to all the things that you, by your own choosing, are dreaming in the eternal moment.

Ofttimes I have heard the question asked, "How can I free myself from some of these levels of consciousness that trap me?" We are trapped by what we believe and those beliefs exist in consciousness. But it takes a little effort of conscious thought to know when we are descending, so to speak, and to take corrective measures. There is no soul in any universe who does not know how to take corrective measures to stay in higher levels of consciousness. For that is the inner knowing that is with us at all times.

And now, for a few moments, in keeping with this evening's discussion, I would like to share with you an experience or two of long, long ago, some of which I have already given to you in your little book [*The Living Light* and also in *The Living Light Dialogue Volume 1*].

I had entered on this side of life and, as I had stated, wandered so very long upon the barren desert. For you see, it was the effect of my own beliefs. Gradually, slowly but surely, with the help of what you may term an angel that came unto me, seemingly a dream, the gentle voice sang a song that reached the very strings of my heart. And as it did so, she beckoned me onward and I crawled along the desert for what surely, as I look back in time, must have been a thousand miles or more. However, the voice never failed to encourage me, no matter how long, and how thirsty I got.

And one day after seeming a great eternity, I lifted my head as I crawled along that desert floor. I lifted my head and saw a great body of water. And the very sense of its moisture filled my nostrils with the joy of life itself. And as I crawled closer to that great body of water, the voice said to me, "Pause, my child. Do not drink, though you are thirsty. Do not wash, though your very heart cries for the moisture and coolness of the water. Do not do those things until you have asked yourself, Are you willing, my friend, to give all that you think you have? Are you willing to give it without question, without hope, and without any knowledge of an ending or a beginning? Are you willing to give what you think you have?"

And I looked at that beautiful water and I had to think, "What did I truly have?" I had a body and a rag upon me for clothes. What did I have that I could possibly desire to hold on to? And I thought and I pondered. It wasn't what I called my clothes on my back. It wasn't my body, for it was weary, tired, and sick. What was it, I had to ask myself, that didn't want to end? For I had no guarantee that it wouldn't. What was it? I thought and I thought and I thought. And the more I thought, even my thoughts, I thought I was willing to surrender. And finally, as the days became the nights, and the nights became the days for three months and more I thought. And one day I reached what I know today was my final thought. And that is what I was not willing to give up. And that, my good children, is called the greatest magnet of all: it is the thought of I.

You may ask your questions.

Thank you. Would you please tell us what is the derivation of the word Amen? *What does it mean and why is it used at the end of a prayer?*

In reference to your question concerning the soul's expression and recognition of a divine authority, to which, in truth, it is eternally responsible, has come unto your world what is called "Amen." It has gone through many changes over the centuries. And in the Eastern, Far Eastern part of your earth, they call it "Ah Um." However, the proper expression—and I will leave its understanding for your own efforts for your soul to perceive—the proper expression was always, and, to those who know, still is, "Ou Ah Mm." You may ask your next question.

Thank you. Would you please clarify the statement, "Presence is the Law of Solicitation," which appears on a card in the Serenity Game?

The question concerning, "Presence is the Law of Solicitation"—the presence of a person's consciousness and body is the effect of directed thought. As we stated earlier, thought, entering the magnetic field, becomes belief, which, in truth, is the principle of the magnetic field and the law of life. And so, directed by that law, man's presence, by his presence, is solicitation, the effect of the law that he alone has established.

Thank you. What is the origin of species?

Species are under the Law of Evolution. We stated some time ago that the so-called missing link of the human would not be found on your Earth planet. And it would behoove the questioner to concern themselves in this respect with the origin of thought, for, in so doing, they will know the origin of species.

Thank you. What is the nature of claustrophobia and how does one control it?

If one is afflicted with the disease known in your world as claustrophobia, then one has great need to make the daily effort to become aware of the thoughts and patterns that they have suppressed within their own consciousness. For the disease known as claustrophobia is revealing that they feel smothered or suppressed, which, in truth, that is the way that they feel emotionally in their magnetic field. For they have suppressed and smothered their own inner feelings at the expense of the expression of their soul and have done so under the delusion and guise of what man calls his pride.

Thank you. What is the difference between illusion and delusion?

A person making the effort, as man does, to take illusion and use it for his personal self-gain is known as delusion.

Thank you. What law does one transgress when they themselves—correction—when they find themselves in self-will? How can a person stay out of self-will?

Many times we have discussed self-will and divine will. And each time, in the final analysis, it simply means making a little effort to control oneself. Self-will is an expression based upon the beliefs and limited patterns of the individual. It doesn't have total consideration, for it is not within the realm of the magnetic field of individualization and identity to have total consideration. For total consideration only exists, and flows through, the soul faculty of reason.

And so man finds himself frequently in what he calls self-will and rarely in what he calls divine will. But because man's mind decides what is self-will and what is divine will, then it is highly questionable which is divine will and which is self-will. We must rise in consciousness beyond this mental gymnastics of the mind. Make that little effort to be as little children: to believe in the goodness of life; to believe that God, in truth, is expressing through all life; to believe that we alone are the effects of our own efforts; to believe, for in believing, the law is established in the magnetic field of life.

Man can think many things and man can think about God each moment of each day. But the thinking will not grant him the experience, for the thinking is in the electrical field and the feeling is in the magnetic field. And so when man says that he struggles, he believes it and experiences it. When man says he can't find God, he believes it and cannot find him. When man says that's the way life is, he believes it and experiences it. And so, my good students, begin to choose today in the light of reason what you believe. Look first at what is already in your magnetic field of beliefs, expand them, for your own good, and watch the seeming miracle of life transform you, for it is your right today.

Thank you. Will planet Earth ever evolve from that of faith to that of divine love?

Indeed, all things evolve and all things return to the source from whence they came, be they an ant, an angel, or a planet.

Thank you. What is humility? How should I surrender to be free? On a daily basis, how can I practice greater acceptance in my life?

Because the mind has questioned, reveals to the questioner the refusal of the mind to simply surrender that they may accept something greater. And the refusal by the mind is known as the lack of the soul faculty of humility. However, because the mind was also prompted to ask the question, also reveals something deeper, something greater, that knows beyond a shadow of any doubt that is the way to freedom. Only by taking, through effort, control of the mind firmly, but kindly, placing it back in perspective to do the things that it was designed to do—no more and no less—can the soul arise and the faculty of humility express itself.

It is interesting—the human mind and how it works. And for centuries we've spent much time with it, because it is such, because man has made it an obstruction to the soul's free expression. If you want to help your mind, then learn the principle of discipline, for the mind responds to what is known as give and take. Learn what it is you value most. And if you want discipline, which is the happiness of life, and you tell your mind what it is to do and your mind does not do it as you tell it, then take away the things that it desires the most. You will soon find that your mind will begin to bow, for the mind does not enjoy being deprived of its desires.

And it is most interesting for the minds of men are trained in the same way, in truth, and the same principle as the minds of dogs. When they do what they're told, they get something they enjoy. And when they do not do what they are told, that is taken from them. And if they continue to do what they are told not to do, yea, even that is taken from them. Now, that's the way the mind works—so-called human and so-called animal. Learn the Law of Balance. That is known as reason.

And when you don't do what you know you should do, then deprive yourself accordingly of the things you desire the most. And soon, if you are firm and strict with yourselves, you will be transformed, for it is known as keeping faith with reason, for she will transfigure thee. Reason is known as balance. And balancing the mind is freedom of the soul.

Good night.

FEBRUARY 19, 1976

CONSCIOUSNESS CLASS 112

Greetings, students. This evening we will continue on with our discussion of the experiences encountered so long ago on this side of life.

As you will recall, I lay there on the burning sand by that cool and beautiful body of water. I had been warned by the angel that guided me there not to enter the water until I had surrendered the thought of I. I pondered and pondered. And the days became months and time no longer seemed of any import, for my mind could not, at that time, understand the possibility of surrendering the thought of I. And so, as I continued to ponder upon that question—how to surrender—the thoughts entered my mind of what I thought the I, in truth, really was. It awakened within my consciousness, after much pondering, that I had been asked to surrender the thought of I. I had not been asked to surrender the I.

And so my mind with great effort tried to reach a decision on what was I and what was the thought of I. As I continued with what I now know to be mental gymnastics, a great weariness descended upon me and in that weariness the feeling and sensing of my parched body to the cool moist breeze coming over that great body of water increased within me a great desire, a desire for its coolness and its comfort. And as that desire increased within my consciousness, the weariness finally overtook me and the angel once again appeared before me. And she said to me, "That which you desire is what you believe you do not have. And because you believe you do not have it, you desire it. And you desire it, believing what you do not have, you are. And because you believe what you desire and do not have is what you are, you are bound to the thought of I."

I drifted off into realms I do not recall, but I know, upon my awakening, there was a great throbbing within me. It seemed like I had become the heart of the universe and everything within it. For I had, without conscious effort, surrendered what I thought was I and I had become that great body of water, the desert, the sky, all things unseen, unknown and yet to be known. That, in truth, is the surrender of the thought of I.

As I looked across that great ocean, I saw a glittering on the horizon. And as I continued to look, it seemed like a great ship was coming towards me. As it got closer, I saw that it was such a beautiful ship—all purple and gold. And I felt a great joy coming over my being, for somehow it meant to me there was someone coming. And that, indeed, was great joy to me. Although my consciousness, in truth, had expanded and become what it is in essence, that essence still could recognize what is known as joy.

At that moment the angel again appeared to me and said, "Your ship has come from the far off land of the double serpent. It will take you to the realms that you, through your journey in life, have earned. Be grateful it has arrived, for many souls wait much longer than you for its arrival."

And as the ship came closer to the shore, I looked in vain: I could not see a single soul upon it. And finally, as I embarked upon my ship of destiny, I searched in vain to find another soul. There was no captain that I could see. There was no crew that I could hear. And slowly, but surely, the ship turned and off across the ocean we sailed. Somehow I knew I was not alone, though I could not see, nor hear, another soul. I sensed that someone or something was watching my every thought, my every act, my every deed.

The years passed from ten to twenty, from fifty to century and century and I sailed and sailed and sailed. And one day I looked out o'er the horizon and I saw land. And upon that land were many, many people. As the ship came closer, with me upon it, to that shore, the angel once again came to me and spoke, "You are home: the home that you have earned from your own thoughts, acts, and deeds. You will recognize each person in the realm that you are entering, for each person you have shared your thoughts, your acts, and your deeds." And I looked at the many people on the shore and indeed did I recognize each and every one. And I looked across the land and somehow knew that a few were not present.

As I got off the ship, I was greeted by what I was told was the Council of Justice, the guardians of the realms of regret. It was their duty to see that the souls who entered those realms would receive their just dues. But I was so overcome with seeing other people after all those many years and centuries that the feeling of joy was greater than my thought of justice or regret. But slowly and surely, as I lived in that realm, without even the possibility of escape, I experienced the deepest regret possible to the human heart. For through my desire for considering other souls, those who I now lived with were the victims of my own hand while yet on earth.

They had not yet evolved to forgiveness and their vengeance, from lack of understanding, was almost unbearable to me. However, I had to serve whatever their desires of the moment were. I was their total victim. And their desires were many and varied and seemingly without ending. For was it not my desire to do my duty while yet on earth? Was my desire not so great? It was so great. And because it was so great, it denied me of the light of reason and consideration for other souls.

And so I lived in those realms of regret. And I worked and worked and worked. My job was but the effect of those hundreds of hundreds of souls, the effect of their ever-changing desires. Yet somehow I knew, when my duty to reason was truly fulfilled, somehow, someway I would be able to leave those realms of vengeance, of satisfaction and regret.

The angel who had guided me along the paths did not forsake me in my time of greatest need. Although she did not deny me my suffering or regret, there were those moments of encouragement that someday it would come to an end. There, in those realms, I gained and learned much. For it is there that I learned a little about the human mind. It is there I learned something about the freedom of forgiving. It is there that I learned a little about the tenacity of the human mind. And for the many things that I learned in those realms I am eternally grateful. For there, I truly surrendered.

I had had the experience upon the shore of surrender, but it was a spiritual experience. I was not in the midst of the living hell of vengeance. And there in the realms of regret was born into that realm what you children have today: the Living Light philosophy. For there, within my consciousness, it was given birth by the encouragement of one of God's angels of light.

The evolution of the soul records all experiences. And each time the soul enters form, it pays the so-called price of the things it has chosen not to face. The birth of this philosophy, in truth, was a rebirth for what had been done with it in untold centuries past.

One morning at dawn, they came for me, for the souls in that realm had permitted me to dig a hole in the ground four feet square and four feet deep. That was my home in the realms of regret. The days were hot and dry. The nights were cold and wet. But that so-called suffering was, in truth, my greatest blessing. And one morning at dawn they came and said I was to leave. My job had been finished. And I was to be taken to the next realm that I had earned. I could not help but wonder, if it was the next realm I had earned, hopefully it was better, but it could, in truth, be worse. And so it was with mixed emotion that I followed them to the water's edge where the ship that had brought me to their land was waiting to take me away.

I believe you have a few questions.

Thank you. Is it ever possible to change a commitment without setting negative laws into motion?

The question—"Is it ever possible to change a commitment without setting negative laws into motion?" When man commits as a united being—soul, mind, and body—there is no need to change the commitment. It is when there are halfway commitments that man experiences a need to change them. And because they are not full commitments—man is not united within himself when he commits—then he experiences in life what he calls the Law of Duality: positive and negative.

Thank you. How do we close the heel, as suggested in The Living Light?

Through the soul faculty of humility.

Thank you. Is it true that a pulsating or a pulsing sensation in the forehead between the eyes indicates a developing spiritual eye?

Not necessarily so, no. There are many things that cause pulsations within the body. There is no guarantee that a sensation of pulsation between the eyebrows of your body is definitely an awakening of the spiritual sight. However, there are those who have had experiences of that kind where that was true. It is not advisable, however, to place the duality of mind upon the divine, united, neutrality of spiritual essence.

Thank you. Would you please explain how the ego is created in fear and also how, through fear, it is educated?

It is through the Law of Identity—the ego's creation and control by what is known as fear. Man identifies and, so identifying, denies his oneness with all. In so denying his oneness, he declares the supremacy of his so-called separatism from all the universes. In that denial, fear is given birth. That is the power of the mind when it identifies. For by identifying, it denies. And by denying, it fears. And so in truth in keeping with the laws already revealed to you, our denials become our destinies as the things we fear befall us. And so it behooves man to expand his consciousness to free himself from his so-called identity, for his identity is dependent upon a multitude of denials and those denials are a multitude of fears.

Thank you. Is the attitude of resignation the same as acceptance? And if not, how does it differ?

Absolutely and positively not. When man says, "I resign myself to circumstances. I resign myself to this or to that," he declares a mental law. "I did what I could and now I resign myself." That is definitely and positively not the expression of divine will. Acceptance is an expression, through the soul faculty of reason, that sees the light of eternity and knows that it is the light and that the light is inseparable; that there is only one light and one truth; that there is only one eye; that the eye is the eye of eternity. That is acceptance, not the mental, dual expression of the function of resignation.

Thank you. Is it true that where we are and with whom really does not matter, as it is what we are becoming within that is important for our soul's growth?

My good students, what we are becoming within is revealed by what we are expressing without. Indeed, are we known by the company that we keep. And the experiences that we are having are the direct revelations of what we are becoming within ourselves. For inner attitudes of mind are revealed by outward manifestations. And so if we want to know what we are becoming, all we need to do is take a look at our associations.

Thank you. Would you please give us some deeper understanding of alcoholic addiction patterns? How beings relate to the self-pity level and what immediate gratification the ego expects from such self-destructive behavior?

It is indeed like any habit or pattern of mind that is suicidal and self-destructive: a sad day for any soul who, unable from the lack of directing their will, unable to control their mind.

We have taught for many years when the desire is the greatest, take control for five short minutes. But don't make that five-minute control a new habit pattern.

All of life, as we have stated many times, is the expression of one God, one Energy, one Light, one Life, one Truth. And when the mind, in its dual expression, does not find within itself the fulfillment that is craved by it, it does many diverse things.

It is the basic teaching of this philosophy to surrender. And when the soul is speaking, surrender is not only a beautiful word, it is a simple way. It is not difficult. It is not a struggle. It is peaceful. It is joyful. It is wisdom. It is good. But when the mind and the so-called self-will and uneducated ego are in control, the word *surrender* to a higher power, a greater intelligence that exists in flowing through you, then it's a great struggle. For the mind takes it as a direct threat to its security, for the mind truly believes it is it. This is the greatest of all delusions that the soul experiences.

And so the more we rely upon the patterns of mind for our security and our joy, the more disappointed we become, the more frustrated we become, the more discouraged we become. And yet those very things are the stepping stones upon which the soul must trod to free itself from its own mental concentration camp.

And so in the final analysis, the good, in truth, fulfills us. This is not something—these stepping stones of suffering and discouragement and failure—is not something that you trod once and it's over. It's something that we trod each moment of each day. We choose the left path of darkness and authority of the so-called human mind, which is based upon yesterday's experiences, or we choose the right path of light and peace and freedom that has the banner of truth upon it. And the banner reads, "Surrender. God is the power that never faileth." Only God can bring you what your soul is crying for.

Thank you. Would you please tell us the most effective approach to use in working with an alcoholic, drug, or food addict?

In reference to the questions on addiction, the mind responds to what *it* thinks is satisfaction and fulfilling, and deprivation and pain. For it is a dual instrument that responds to loss and gain. And so it is in one's effort to help a soul to be freed from the prison of duality, one must use the laws that govern the prison house. And those laws are very clear: Give and gain; effort and reward. That is the law of the mind. It's very nature is get, get, get, get, get. It is the nature of the mind. And so it responds to what is called temptation.

Now, we all know what temptation is. And we all know that ancient, ancient prophets granted to us that great prayer that the law, called the law—called the Lord, may deliver us from temptation: to deliver us from our own mind, to put our mind in proper perspective. Man cannot be delivered from temptation until man makes the effort to free his soul from his own limited mind. For temptation is an indispensable part of the human mind.

Thank you. Good night.

FEBRUARY 26, 1976

CONSCIOUSNESS CLASS 113

Greetings, students. At our last visit, we were recalling the journey of long ago and were speaking of the realms of satisfaction, regret, and revenge.

And the journey had taken me to those many years in that realm and I stood at the shore waiting to embark upon the ship that had come for me, hoping that it would bring me brighter horizons than I had already experienced. However, as the ship came nearer the shore, a deep inner sense of fear began to overtake me. For that is the way that it is. No matter how great the suffering may seem and the mind may wish for better things, it does have some type of security with that with which it has become familiar. And though my experience, in those years on the realms of regret, was something that my very heart cried out to leave, I could not control the fear that began to overtake me, for I had no assurance that the next voyage would be better and I feared it could be worse.

However, I did embark upon the ship, for those were the orders that were given to me. And I had become accustomed, in those realms, to taking orders. And I left that realm. And many months passed, as my ship journeyed on across that great seemingly endless ocean of time. And as I voyaged on and on and on, twenty-three months had passed when I sighted a small island on the starboard side of that ship. And for a moment an excitement overcame me and then a fear and then a feeling of resignation. And as the land became closer, I saw there were other islands. There were eight islands and I wondered upon which one of those islands would the ship dock. Or would it stop at those islands? And many thoughts went through my mind.

Finally, we came to the largest of all of those islands. And a strange site appeared before my eyes. It was a very mountainous type of island and the cliffs and the hills seemed covered with moving things. And I was not yet close enough to be sure of my vision. But the hours passed and the ship came closer and I was able to discern that those moving things that I thought possibly were animals, were people—thousands upon thousands upon thousands of souls crawling down those mountain sides and over the hills and vales on their hands and knees. And as the ship came to dock, these thousands of souls crawled onto the shore. And I disembarked.

I cried out, "Would someone please answer?" But no one spoke. I wondered why they did not look up. And all of those thousands of souls, all crawling along the ground. And so I stood there and several times I cried for someone to speak, but no one spoke. After a great time had passed, it seemed to me, but it was only a matter of a few hours, a strange sight appeared o'er one of the hills. And as it got closer, I realized that it was a large number of people stacked one upon the other on their hands and knees, like stones of a great pyramid. And high on the pyramid sat a figure, all bejeweled and in glittering robes. He sat on that pyramid of human bodies. And it came closer and closer.

And then, my guiding angel appeared to me and said, "Do not question in this realm. Obey without thought, for you have entered the realms of pride and pity. Your stay will depend upon your unshakable faith in God and your complete and total obedience to the rulers of this realm." In that moment I thought, "O God, this realm, indeed, is worse than what I have left." For that's the way it is when you experience something that the mind feels it cannot bear. The experiences of yesteryear are not as great, in memory, as the frightening experience of the moment.

And high on that pyramid a voice boomed out and ordered me to follow. And so I followed up the mountain. And the day passed and the night passed. Another day dawned. Another night passed and on and on I walked. And on the third day, the eleventh hour of morn, we appeared before a great temple—a temple of eight—all built of human bodies. I looked and saw the bodies were alive, yet they were motionless, for they were the very structures upon which sat the rulers of the throne of pride and pity.

And then, another voice spoke to me and said, "Because you have not crawled to our temple and because your pride is so great, we have a special duty in our realms for you, pitiful souls, who entertain the thoughts of rule and by your very expression of pride by not crawling to our temple, you shall learn, as the days become months and the months become years."

You may ask your questions, if you wish.

Thank you. We understand that the Serenity Game has been in design for centuries in the spirit world. Would you please share with us your hopes and aspirations for its success on the earth plane and what you see as the deep, true value in playing the game?

In respect to your question, we are not concerned, nor interested, in success, as we are not concerned, nor interested, in failure. However, in reference to the other part of your question, what is known in your world as the philosophy game of Serenity was designed over a number of centuries in our realm and designed in this way: that each word contained in one card would be so placed within the structure known as sentence that it would be instrumental in awakening within the consciousness of men on earth, and in other realms, the soul and its true potential.

And so it was a number of centuries in the study and in the application of what is called the human mind. For it took great thought, a great pondering by many, many, many souls dedicated to the eternal Light to bring about a philosophy of living truth that would awaken the souls, that would psychologically remove from the depths of the subconscious the obstructions that were standing in the way of the soul's expression, freedom, and peace. And that is what took so many, many years.

For no matter what language is spoken or used, no matter what education the player has had, the so-called game is so designed that certain mental and emotional levels of consciousness are guaranteed to rise and, in so rising, help the individual to face themselves to work with their own mind and remove their own obstructions.

Thank you. Why do people insist upon allowing the ego to obstruct the divine flow of peace and happiness?

My good students, it is only a error of ignorance. But it is indeed a great, great error. For the minds of men can be told many things. But out of the many things the mind receives, there are so few that are applied. Because the effort is not made by the conscious mind, moment by moment, to stay free from the magnetic control of the subconscious and its past experiences, this error of ignorance takes the souls of multitudes into realms of regret and into realms that their little souls cry out for centuries.

It is interesting—about the human mind—that it likes to concern itself only with the continuity of its limited patterns, regardless where those patterns of mind have already lead the soul in yesteryear. But there is a great magnetic power called familiarity. It's a delusion in the mind of false security. And so it is easier to swim, so to speak, with the tide than to make the effort to swim against it. The tides being the acceptances of yesteryear. And so the bondage and the grief and the sorrow continue to perpetrate themselves not only in your world, but in other worlds beyond number.

Thank you. Would you please give us your understanding of the term spiritual psychology, *differentiating it from the limited view of our psychology we commonly refer to?*

In reference to the term *spiritual psychology*, we are referring to an acceptance in the mind of an intelligence beyond, that supersedes the limited mental intelligence of the human mind. And so the term means to us, "spiritual psychology" or "to spiritualize your present psychology," which is limited to mind planes of consciousness. It is the introducing into the limited mind of demonstrable laws, that, once having been accepted by the mind, will become the very instruments used by the mind to free itself from its own limitation. For that is the very nature of the mind: to use whatever it grasps ahold of for its own benefit.

And so a mind that grasps ahold of demonstrable law becomes the recipient of the effect of that law. And it is a known truth that the human mind, when it reaches a certain point, called saturation, will pause in the expression of its limited patterns. And it is in those moments of pause of the mind that spiritual truth may enter.

For many years we have stated one truth. In its expression it has worn, and continues to wear, untold thousands of different garments, for that is what is necessary that it may enter the consciousness of man. For in those rare moments when the mind, the human mind, has a moment of pause, you must consider the level of consciousness being entertained prior to the pause. And if truth does not wear many garments, the garment worn by truth may or may not be able to enter the pause that is in one mind, for that pause is a bit different than in another mind, dependent upon the level when the pause was made.

Thank you. Would you please explain how the goddess game operates and how the ego may be educated to no longer need to play it?

In reference to the question concerning the uneducated ego, the eternal soul knows its own home. The eternal soul knows that it indeed is a part of God, the so-called Allsoul. The soul, its expression is known as the faculties of your being. The mind, in its expression, is known as the functions of your being. The soul looks at the mind in which it is imprisoned in form and does everything within its power in keeping with its own attributes, called soul faculties, to express itself.

Let us, for example, take the soul faculty of humility. When the soul strives to express that attribute, that faculty, the mind views it. And the mind knows that humility could cause a loss of something that the mind cherishes as its own. Therefore, the mind will not permit the soul to express that faculty unless the mind, in the searching of its own experiences that it has accepted, can find some gain in permitting that particular faculty to express itself. If the mind finds and decides that by permitting an expression of the faculty of humility, it may gain what it considers is a gain for one of its—or many of its—personal desires, then, you see, that someone, you say, is a very humble person. Be not deceived, my good students, for that is the mind and how it uses the known and unknown attributes of your eternal soul.

One of the ways of perceiving whether or not the soul attribute of humility is truly expressing or a false humility, which the mind permits to sift through, is expressing is to look at the demonstrable law known as continuity. If you do not find the living demonstration of the Law of Continuity, then you can be rest assured that those attributes are being censored by the mind for its own personal gain and interest.

Now, what does that have to do with what the questioner asked, in reference to the ego and the so-called goddess complex? It has everything to do with that. For the mind, viewing the attributes of your eternal soul, also views the many other things of your eternal soul. Not your spirit, formless and free, for that is known by spirit; not your soul, per se, for that is known by soul, but the expression of your soul. And it looks at the soul's expression and it senses its great power. And it senses that that power is so great that it wants it for itself, for the mind. It does not consider the expression of the soul in its humble faculties as necessary, for it can only consider what it can do with what it senses is the power behind what it calls the throne. And that, it wants for its mind, for its mental world. And that is known as the god or goddess complex.

Thank you. Frequently, during interdimensional communication, a person may be encouraged by the spirit friends to sing or to play a particular musical instrument. Would you therefore please share with us your understanding of the importance to the soul of pursuing such training?

If what is known as a soul talent is given to any soul, then it is of soul benefit. Because the question of the advisability of pursuing that which is revealed as a soul talent, because of the need of questioning the advisability to pursue it, reveals unto the questioner that their mind, not their soul, is speaking and that doubt, the servant of the power of fear, the force of fear—for fear is the expression of the mind. Because the questioner, by the demonstration of the question, is controlled by doubt, in respect to it, reveals the need for bowing to the God of Gods within and there, know for themselves beyond a shadow of any doubt the eternal truth: That which is mine knows my face and is already on its way to my heart. That law is not dependent upon the gymnastics of the human mind.

Thank you. Given the previous understanding that middle C on the piano is the color white, would you further elaborate the other notes with colors?

I thank you for your question and answer in the only way that it could be answered. Middle C is the balance of the scale. Its color, to you, has been revealed, known as white. White is the combination of all colors in the universe. And when the effort to maintain and sustain balance, which, in truth, is reason, is made by the questioner, there will no longer be the question, for they will perceive the truth for themselves, which is the effect of the efforts they will have made.

Thank you. In what way do the vibrations of the soul faculties correspond to the keys or strings of a musical instrument?

The soul faculties—there are forty faculties and forty functions and one God. Their correspondence with any man-made musical instrument is most difficult to perceive or discern, for man has created those instruments. However, there is an indication of his soul's expression—the faculties—as he, his own soul, responds to different tones. That inner knowing is something that all souls have. There are certain tones that your soul responds to and there are certain so-called tones that it does not. So find your note by finding first yourself.

Thank you. A student has asked the question, "Why am I bored by the questions?"

Indeed, the soul of the questioner has great, great, great need. We must first ask ourselves what we mean by the word *bored*. I believe it is evident that we mean, "we are disinterested," for if we had interest, we could not be bored. And so we must look at the great need of the soul, as the mind of the student is prompted to ask such a question.

We accept, as a demonstration, that boredom does not mean interest. We also accept that it does mean the lack of interest. And so the question reveals that the questioner has no interest in any question asked by any student. And because there is no interest in any question asked by anyone else, it reveals there is no interest for any mind outside of their own. For the question could not have been asked, if the questioner did not have some interest in their own question. And because there is no interest in any mind outside of the questioner's, it follows, in truth, that there is no interest in any soul outside of the questioner's. And because there is no interest in any soul outside of the questioner, then God, the Allsoul, the divine, infinite, eternal Spirit of love becomes very, very microscopic for the questioner.

And when that happens to any soul, there is a great loneliness that descends over the consciousness. I should know, for I spent many, many, many centuries on an empty desert of so-called time. And that is why I say, pray for the soul that it may look this moment and save untold centuries of sorrow and grief.

Good night.

MARCH 4, 1976

CONSCIOUSNESS CLASS 114

Greetings, students. Before going on with our classes, we should like to spend a few moments in discussing the purpose for revealing to you my personal experiences of yesteryear.

We should like you to know that these many and varied experiences that were ofttimes so painful to me are being brought forth in the hopes that they may be instrumental, by their revelation of immutable law, to help you to think more deeply and to consider wisely the Law of Identity. These experiences are not something that are fantasy of the mind or allegorical, so to speak, unless you consider your thoughts, your acts, and your deeds of your own mind to be fantasies and allegorical. Remember that man becomes that which he identifies with and becomes the living experience thereof. And so it is that this history of my many centuries is revealed in bits and pieces to you.

I am well aware that many of the students find it difficult, distasteful, and something that they personally would rather not hear. We have looked into the basic vibrations established by the class and in keeping with those laws of sincere interest of your soul to learn more of life, to learn the laws and hopefully gain a greater dedication to the freedom of your eternal soul, this experience is being revealed to you.

I want to assure you that in my many centuries of moving from one realm to another not once did I ever encounter physical violence or physical cruelty. Although I experienced much concerning my own mind and emotions, you must remember that I was not a physically cruel or violent person while yet in your earth realm.

And so it is this evening that we will continue on with these experiences in the realm of pride and pity.

As you recall from our last class, I was patiently waiting before the rulers of the realm who had stated to me a special duty I had earned because of my great pride. And so it was that I was there on the ground. And as I heard that statement from the ruler, I began to shake within my body. It seemed that a great fear was overtaking me. I could not, in all honesty, know what was the cause of my great fear, for I had already had much experience in the realm before that one. And so I tried to calm my emotions, but the fear persisted. And then the order came from the ruler: "Send him across the land. There is a special place where he will learn and, in learning, bow his great pride and become a humble soul."

And so they sent me on my hands and knees to crawl over the hills and vales to the other, far side of the island. I dared not to question what was to come. I dared not to ask what that special place had to offer. And no one told me. And so I crawled a day, two days, three, four, five, a week, I thought. And then somehow I lost count, because I had lost interest. And the weeks, as I review back to that experience, became months. I continued to crawl and after five months had passed, they told me to stop.

You must realize, my good students, I had only one place that I was allowed to look and that was down. I did not see the sky or anything around me, only that which was beneath me. And I stopped, so seemingly weary and even, it seemed to me, without hope, without interest, and without care.

It is interesting to note at this time what the human mind, in truth, can endure. For when a soul has earned the realms that I had earned, when, within the very being, the drive is so great, somehow endurance becomes your very lifeline.

And those who had taken me over to the other side of the island said to me, "Now you may look around and about you, for there you must learn and become the very thing that you see." And I looked to my left and there was every nature of crawling thing, from snakes to lizards. And I looked to my right and there were many more. And then they said to me, "Now lie flat on the ground and learn to crawl as the lowest of creatures crawls around and about you."

And there I lived not for days or weeks, but for many, many, many months. But from that realm of the lowest of creatures, a light within me dawned. And you may recall it as a truth brought to your world centuries later that states in part, O God, I love the roses, the weeds, and thistles too. O God, the snakes that crawl are you. [See "God We Love" in the appendix.] For there, my good students, from those many months of experience, the light within me began to dawn. And I knew beyond a shadow of any doubt, no matter whatever happens there is an infinite, divine Light of truth and love that never, ever fails.

And so I became an expert, so to speak, in crawling, like the lowest creatures on the ground. And after so very many months, there was a type of communication established between those creatures and myself. Beyond the seeming repulsive and fearful form lies an eternal, infinite Love. And I began to communicate with those thousands of creatures. And they became my greatest and lasting friends, even to this day. And to deny God anywhere is to deny God everywhere. From that realm and that experience came the dawning of the truth that was to free my soul.

And so they came for me, after those many, many months. And I crawled, like the snake and the lizard, back to the realm, to the throne where the rulers waited that I may demonstrate the bowing of my great pride. And I lived on that realm for over two and a half centuries. And when the time came for me to leave, I was called before the throne and the ruler spoke to me and said, "You have learned your lessons well. You have become a living example of humbleness. And because you have done your duty so well, your ship of destiny is waiting at the shore."

How interesting the mind is. I began to feel within my being a great loss, for once again, having made friends with myself—for that, my good students, is what outward experiences are: an extension of one's own self. And I had made friends with those experiences over those centuries and now I was to leave what I had made friends with. And that loss came over me—such a deep, inner sorrow. And after a time that feeling passed and a great fear rose within my being.

And so it is, my students, that as you face the known and unknown experiences of life, you face them with fear. You face them with loss, with anxiety, with expectation and turmoil. But in time, as the centuries pass, you will learn to face them with courage and the true spirit of joy.

And so there I lie at the shore, waiting for the order to go aboard, once again, my little ship. And finally the word was spoken and I boarded the ship. And I sailed on and on and on. And so much time passed that I began to wonder. Had the angel that had guided me through so much forsaken me? And more time passed. And then one day just before dawn the angel appeared and said, "You have done well so far, but you must call forth from the depths of your being for the courage of the universes. For each step becomes more difficult, for the pull of the old and the drive of the new is the battle between the mind and the soul."

I believe you have some questions.

Thank you. Would you please discuss the meaning of power and force as in the statement given in church, Faith is the power of the soul over the force of the mind, and also as used in the healing power?

In reference to your question in respect to the power of the soul, which is an inseparable part of the Allsoul, the expression of God, and the force of the dual creation of what you call the human mind, we're most happy to discuss. In respect to your healing prayer, which contains great good, it is not from the philosophy that we understand.

And so let us consider the mind and what force really and truly is. It has long ago been stated that a house divided cannot long stand. And so that's the way the mind truly is: a house divided. For every yes, it has a no. And for every answer, it has a question. For every good, it has its bad. For that *is* the mind, which is an inseparable part of the dual law of created substance.

When the soul, expressing through the mind that is waiting to be disciplined—which, in truth, means educated. And without that education or discipline, then what you call insanity is the manifest experience. For insanity is nothing more, nor less, than an undisciplined mind. Because of the nature of mind—to divide and conquer—the expression of that division, which is its basic nature, is known as force.

Now, a person may well ask the question, If that is the true nature of the mind—divide and conquer—then of what benefit is the mind? The mind is of great benefit, for it is a vehicle through which the eternal soul is expressing in the duality of creation. When the mind, more properly referred to as the self-image or ego, is educated or disciplined, then this division process is brought into balance. For example, in reference to any question, a disciplined or educated ego, having said yes, will also say no with equal intensity and, in so doing, neutralize the force of the mind. And in that neutralization process, the soul will express itself fully.

Now, my good students, try to understand what usually happens with the force of the mind. It drives itself, imbalanced, in a total force of expression in a particular direction. And in so doing, it attaches itself, by the Law of Identity, to its own drive or desire. In so attaching and identifying, it becomes a victim of its own natural, neutralizing process. We have stated this in many ways. One of which is: all attachments are guaranteed adversities and all adversities are guaranteed attachments.

For man to find true peace, he must make the effort to neutralize the so-called duality of his own mind. Then, the power of God, infallible, infinite, eternal, never failing, will guide the soul through what is commonly referred to as the concentration camp of the uneducated ego.

Thank you. Please tell us what brings about high blood pressure and by what faculty and/or function can it be controlled?

Frustration. The direct effect of it is so-called high blood pressure. When the effort of the questioner or anyone experiencing that so-called condition, when the effort is truly made to free the mind from the attachment to its acts and activities, there will be no need for further concern of the condition, for the condition will no longer exist.

Thank you. Are the tapes that are playing in our minds actually in the subconscious or are they really in the conscious mind, but unrecognized because we choose, for whatever personal reason, not to focus upon them?

How wisely put. These so-called tapes exist in the subconscious mind and express through the conscious mind. Man chooses, for varying reasons, not to face them. But man wisely should face them, for man is permitting them, constantly, to express themselves.

And so it is here in your school, called Serenity, great effort is made by the many teachers and helpers in our realms to constantly place before your conscious awareness these multitude of so-called tapes to bring an awareness of them, to consciously discuss them with you. The experiences of the mind, though varied, are governed and controlled by the same principle and that is called self-preservation. And so it is, as the effort continues to be made to discuss these many tapes of the mind, we see how irritated the students in the school become. Our responsibility is to grant the Light ever in keeping with the Law Of What Can Be Borne. And so it is, as you find yourselves irritated with the exposure of these many levels of consciousness, this irritation that you experience is an indispensable ingredient to freeing your soul from its own bondage.

It is true that the undisciplined mind does not wish, nor desire, to be freed, for freedom to the undisciplined or uneducated ego means an annihilation of its tapes of bondage. And so it is when you find yourselves irritated or disturbed, pause for a moment. And in that moment you have the golden opportunity to view the true cause of your irritation. If you are peaceful, a vision will come into your consciousness. And the vision will reveal to you how that particular tape experience first was introduced to your mind. Sometimes, when you have that experience of review, you will smile to yourself, because it goes back to when you were little children. And you will smile because it seems so silly to be upset over such a trivial matter. Sometimes you will be very hurt emotionally, for in the review in consciousness you will reexperience the true cause and all of the emotional trauma associated with that particular tape. And so, my good students, irritation wakes the soul; exposure frees it.

Thank you. Is it possible to explain how the pursuit of one's soul talent frees the soul of the bondage of fear, resentment, jealousy, or hatred?

Yes, indeed. The expression of the soul—and what you call its talents—is simply the experience, the continuity of the experience of service well earned by the evolving soul. There are many talents for many souls. The talent simply reveals the untold centuries of effort made by the soul to perfect a particular so-called expression. Now, when the soul is doing that that is, to it, natural, from centuries of expression, then it is freed from the trauma and the turmoil of identifying with the petty and trivial experiences of one short—so very short—life experience of one incarnation.

And so I know the question is rising, "How do I know my soul talent?" All souls know their soul talent. Some souls have earned being reminded of their soul talent, but even the souls who have not earned being reminded of their soul talent, they also know when they still their own mind.

Thank you. Much has been given on testing the spirit with regard to experiences encountered through the vehicle of one's own mind. How may we test the spirit that speaks to us through another, as in communications within and without a spiritual sanctuary?

By testing, if you need to use, the word one's own motive. When we make the effort to become aware of our own motive in life, then we will begin to know ourselves. And he who knows himself, knows not only his mind, for that is only one of the vehicles of expression, but he knows his soul. He knows his infinite eternal spirit. And so we first must become aware of our own motives and then become aware of our true self. Then, there'll be no interest about what's going on outside, for we will know what's going on inside. And when we know what's going on inside, we then become the captains of our ship and the masters of our destiny.

Thank you. Is true principle or only the form of principle expressed in the sayings relating to the limitation or bondage of creation, for example, "License is bondage because it is the child of desire [a saying from the Serenity Game]"?

My good students, principle is principle. When the mind, through its efforts, decides that this is principle because of that and that is personality because of this, the mind is simply accepting, in its own way, what it chooses to permit to enter its own mind. Principle *is*. It's like truth *is*.

We so often cloud principle because our mind insists upon putting it into form. Now, the question has been asked—license, it is stated, is bondage because it is the child of desire. Then the question rises, Is the child of desire the bondage of license? Now, let us think for a moment. The statement made does not say that license is bondage because it is desire. That is not what was stated. We all know that desire is the divine expression. Now we come to principle. And we must discern, through our inner perception, what is the child of desire. It is so clearly stated. The child of desire is not desire, but the effect thereof.

Thank you. Could you please comment upon the statement one should never grant the right of difference at the sacrifice of principle?

One should never grant the right of difference at the sacrifice of principle. Any soul, expressing principle, knows the difference between fear and faith. And whenever the mind, which views multiplicity and division, accepts the right of difference or variety over the divine principle of unity, then that soul descends into the dark pits of fear, which are controlled by form or personality. Principle *is*. Unity is the law of the Divine, demonstrated throughout all the universes. There is one God, one Truth, one Light, one Love, one Law. And any soul that stands on the rock of principle will act accordingly, by demonstrating the continuity, which is the principle of effort, will not be swayed by the fluctuating desires of the human mind, will be dedicated to the eternal Light regardless of the mind's justification to change, will treat each and every soul that it encounters in keeping with the impartial law, which is known as merit, and will not permit their mind to dictate what merit is, for the living demonstration is the revelation of merit. And a soul that stands on the rock of principle regardless of all temptation is dedicated to the eternal Light, regardless what people do with it.

Thank you. Would you please give your understanding of the statement, "The caution of reason is the joy of understanding and the wisdom of consideration"?

"The caution of reason is the joy of understanding and the wisdom of consideration." How beautifully stated, this eternal truth. We have also stated it in other ways: to keep faith with reason, for she will transfigure thee. The caution of reason, the joy of understanding, the wisdom of consideration. Reason stills the mind. It brings balance: the negative, the positive, become neutralized. There God, the infinite intelligence, flows unobstructed and the individualized soul flies to heaven on the wings of reason. There, in that moment, caution, the caution of reason—that moment to still the mind and then you, the true you, freed from all duality, truth eternal is separated from creation, which is the constant change. And being creation, a constant change, there is nothing there the soul can rely upon.

And so, my students, the caution of reason brings the joy of understanding and the wisdom of consideration. Ponder well that great truth. And in your pondering, a new light will dawn within you. And that new light of eternal truth will guide you gently to heavenly realms.

Good night.

MARCH 11, 1976

CONSCIOUSNESS CLASS 115

Greetings, students. We shall continue on with our classes and the journey of the soul.

As you will recall from our last meeting, I had, once again, embarked upon my ship of destiny. And with mixed emotions I stood on the deck of that ship and looked back at the land that I had left. For the mind easily attaches to that that it becomes familiar with and in the attachment it finds its own security. And so it was that time passed and my thoughts drifted ever backwards in so-called time, for each effort that I made to look forward brought a great fear over my mind, for I could only recall what the angel had said to me: that great courage, the courage of the universes, would be required to face my next destination.

And time passed on. One day the waters were so peaceful and calm and the sun was high in the heavens, when I spotted land. It seemed like a land so great, so very, very, big, for as the ship moved on, the land took on the entire horizon. And as I got closer, I saw the beauty of its lush mountains, the beautiful forest, and I thought, "What did the guiding angel mean when she said courage of the universes?"

Again my heart began to beat ever faster, as the ship came closer to the shore. And I wished that I had some power within me to steer the ship away and yet I knew from the experiences of the past that the ship on which I was traveling was guided and steered and controlled by some unseen force that I could not hear, that I could not see, let alone command. For I was not yet awakened within my consciousness that this ship of destiny was controlled by laws that I alone had already established.

And so the ship came unto the shore and there I stood on the deck, looking at the beautiful forest and waiting, waiting for what I did not know. And I looked in vain and saw no movement, not even a breeze was in the air. And then a voice from out of nowhere spoke and said, "Welcome to our realm. We have waited so very long for your arrival." But I could see no one and though the voice, which seemed to rise from the very earth below, seemed kind and compassionate and seemed to have a sincere welcome, somehow I sensed a sinister note concealed within it. And my fear rose even greater and I stood there. Fear alone kept me from disembarking.

It seemed like an hour had passed, yet, in truth, it was but a minute. And once again this voice that rose from the earth below spoke. This time a bit more firm and it said, "Disembark now." And I started to move. I dared not to do anything else. And as I walked onto that land, looking everywhere for someone, I saw no one. And I walked and walked and walked. And as dusk began to fall, it came—a thought—into my mind: "I have not seen, nor heard, a bird in the sky. I've heard no noises of insects, nor animals. What kind of land, so beautiful, must this be?" And again fear rose within me.

And I walked and walked and walked. And then night fell and I began to think, "Am I on this land alone? But then, how could that be, for I heard a voice that ordered me to come ashore? And that voice must have come from someone, somewhere, for twice it spoke to me, seemingly kind, but firm, yet something very sinister. Why do they hide from me? They must be here. Or is that voice something within my own mind that is deceiving me?" And my thoughts began to move quickly within myself. And finally I fell asleep. I recall awakening from a seeming sleep of nothingness to hearing a voice that said, "Awake and walk on. Your journey is about to be begin."

I believe there are some questions.

Thank you. What is the spiritual significance of the so-called sacraments of communion and baptism?

Well, in respect to the spiritual significance of baptism, spiritually, means "cleansing." And the so-called sacraments—we must discern between what the minds of men have done with spiritual purposes of helping the soul to be freed from the mental processes of mind substance, known as creation, and the evolution of the eternal soul. And so the spiritual significance of what you call baptism is the cleansing of, or washing away of, creation that the soul has entered that it may, through that spiritual cleansing, remain awakened and not be blinded by the creation of the life that it has entered in form.

And so it is that man, having taken a simple, spiritual experience of cleansing, man has placed it into his mind in such a way that he now believes that baptism is a process by which some higher authority descends over the form and purifies it. That is not, and was not, the spiritual intent of baptism. However, some good comes to many souls, ever in keeping with their own faith, which, of course, is dependent upon their own beliefs. And baptism in your world today, though distorted in many ways, is serving a beneficial purpose to many, many, many people.

The so-called religious sacraments, which vary according to the limited, mental acceptances of those who perform them, are done more for a type of dramatic expression and type of celebration than it is for true spiritual benefit or awakening. Whenever the minds of men entertain the thought that they are so superior that they can dictate to the Divine Infinite Intelligence that by doing certain acts that they can remove the so-called sins, which are nothing more than transgressions of natural law, from the souls that these things are being performed over, then deception, mental deception, becomes the ruling force.

However, we must look and see the good in all things, for there is good that does exist in all things. And, as I stated earlier, the beliefs of the people, ever in keeping with their own beliefs and acceptances—it does serve as a strengthening for their faith in times of greatest need. But it does not, it does not in any way free the soul from its own transgressions of divine, natural law.

Thank you. When we speak of the evolutionary—correction— the evolution of a soul talent, does this mean the talent had a definite beginning with one person in order to start it all in motion?

Well, if you wish to call the Divine Infinite Intelligence, God, one person, then you may do so. However, remember that all talent and all things, in truth, emanate from the one, infinite, eternal Light, called Divine Intelligence. What the mind does in directing this infinite power and light, of course, is ever in keeping with the mind. And the mind, in truth, is what does the transgressing and the mind, in truth, is what reaps the harvest.

A soul talent is something that comes directly from the source, as all things, in truth, do. But it means that the soul has expressed energy in a particular area of expression over many, many centuries. And so, having directed energy into a particular area, they have become proficient in that area. And because they have become proficient in it and because so much of the soul's energy has been expressed in that area, it is a responsibility unto their own evolving soul that they use that talent or expression not only for the benefit of their minds, but for the benefit of their evolving soul and the souls of others 'round and about them.

And so, my friends, remember that it is the mental body, known as the great decision maker, that establishes these mental laws and, in turn, is the recipient of the effects of those laws. The eternal soul, coming from the Allsoul, has the capabilities and potentialities of the whole. It is the mental vehicle that the soul in its evolution has merited, that is the limiter of the soul's eternal expression.

Thank you. In Discourse 62 we learned that there are nine states of consciousness and you mentioned six of them. Would you please give us the other three?

Whereas the six states of consciousness that have already been given are yet to be applied under the Law of Continuity and the faculty of reason, we are waiting for a student to rise to make the application under the Law of Continuity and reason. When that takes place, we will be more than happy to reveal the other three states of consciousness.

Thank you. Very often children's fairy tales contain great underlying truths. Many of these tales deal with elves, fairies, and other little mysterious people. Are these such beings in another vibration that is not visible to our physical eyes? And if so, what are their functions?

There are many forms, of course, in many dimensions. And in reference to elves and fairy tales and things of that nature, they are nothing more, and nothing less, than what is called and known as the nature spirits. Their job and their responsibility is to care for the forms of nature. And that is exactly what they do. Ofttimes little children will see them as playmates. They will see them as the little people, which, in truth, they are little people. They are different from the evolving individualized soul of what you call the human in the sense that they are the forms through which the Divine expresses itself in order to form the many multitudes of forms of so-called creation or nature.

Thank you. Where does one draw the line in giving attention to details so that one is not drawn into the bondage of fascination?

By not being concerned about details. The moment that we permit the mind to be concerned, then what we do is bind ourselves to the authority of the mind. Now, the question may well arise, "Then how do I define where my personal responsibility meets my desires, for a thin line of reason must exist?"

Now, we have spoken in many ways and in many, many days one simple and pure eternal truth and we have spoken it in a multitude of different ways. And yet we have found over these many centuries that that very simple truth is the very last thing the human mind will accept. The reason that the simple truth, about to be spoken again, is the very last thing that the human mind will accept is because the human mind knows once it accepts and applies this great, simple truth that its authority over the eternal, evolving soul will no longer exist. This is the very thing that all souls are striving to rise to be free. And so once again we reveal that great, simple truth: Everything that you experience in life is an effect of what is going on within your own mind. Everything is inside.

When the soul is ready, when it is strong enough, then the mind is forced to bow to the truth that frees it. Now, this takes place in many different ways. And we have repeatedly spoken on the need of the mind to control itself—to gain control over the mind. It is reason that we must permit to rise in order that there may be a gaining of control over the mind. Now, reason dictates this eternal truth. And reason clearly states all of your experiences, you have willed into action; it is a subtle law. All of the experiences you encounter are revelations of your own mind and its many levels of expression. This is the Law of Personal Responsibility, the ability to personally respond, to personally respond to your own experiences, to respond to them in the light of eternal reason.

When that happens this mental need for concern about detail, this mental need for attention—because, in truth, you feel so very lonely, which is the effect of the mind entertaining thoughts of itself, therefore throwing the mental vehicle out of balance. Those needs which reveal an imbalanced mind will no longer exist.

When the effort is truly made each moment, each moment, to stop, to pause, to think, and to say unto oneself, "I am not happy with the way people talk to me. I am not happy with my experiences in life. I am not happy with the way people act and think and seemingly judge," then, my friends, we stop and we say to ourselves, "Oh mind, you great deceiver, how is it that you keep this cloud and this veil in front of me?" Ask the Divine that great eternal question and you will hear a still small voice whisper from the depths of your own soul, which says, "What are you doing to demonstrate through your own acts the divine, natural, immutable law of life, the Law of Continuity with whatever it is that you alone have chosen? What, oh mind, are you doing?" In what way are you granting discipline unto yourself, that through discipline and control of the diverse levels of consciousness within that you have gained control of the duality of creation called the mental substance or mind? What are you, in truth, doing to bring balance into your own consciousness that your soul may rise, through that perfect balance into the paradise called heaven, which is in the eternal moment when you make the effort to gain control of the negative-positive poles of your own being?

Reason, the pure, simple truth, reveals repeatedly unto us, it, in truth, is inside. To entertain any thought—a single thought—in mind that the cause of any single experience in your life, that the cause is outside is to drive your eternal soul into the very depths of diabolical delusion.

And so, my good students, again and again and again we speak on the truth that frees the soul. And remember that each time you permit one single thought to be entertained within your mental consciousness that the cause of one single experience in your life is outside of your own mind and your own domain, you create, each time, a form, an entity that is, in truth, a part of yourself. And, in so doing, you alone must live with it. And you alone must face it, face-to-face.

In the density of your earthly bodies, you are, in one way, blessed, for it acts as a buffer, so to speak, of the multitudes of mental forms created by the minds of men. But stop and think, my good students, how you feel. When you entertain these thoughts that the cause of your experience lies outside your domain, outside your own mind, you don't feel too well. When you start to feed that thought the life-giving energy of the spoken word, you feel worse for a time. And then the moments pass and if you have someone agreeing with you, you begin to feel better. Now, what, in truth, takes place at those times? The spoken word, speaking forth and feeding the forms of deception by declaring that the cause of our experiences is outside, finding a sympathetic listening ear, they move from your aura into the aura of the person who is listening to you. At this time the person who has been speaking this deception feels better for a short time. The person who has been listening, someone else has to pick up a few hours later, the next day, the next week, or the next month. This is dependent, of course, upon the laws that they have established for themselves and dependent on their receptivity and the rapport established with you. That is one of the ways that these forms grow and control for a time. And "for a time" ofttimes means centuries, not days.

Then there is another experience that takes place. A person locked in the delusion of causes being outside of their power and outside of their own domain talks to another person and the person speaks forth kindly the truth that it is created by their own mind and that's the only place, in truth, that it does exist.

They don't like that, but if there is some rapport established on some other level of consciousness, they continue to discuss their delusion and deception. Now, if they leave the discussion feeling better—and sometimes they do—it simply reveals that they have temporarily freed themselves from those deceiving entities that they have created. If they return—and they 99 percent of the time do return—then it reveals that no effort, in truth, is being made in accepting truth: personal responsibility.

And so, as that book on your earth teaches you, cast not your pearls before the swine. For in so casting, the swine not only consumes your pearls of wisdom, but takes your eternal soul into darkness, because you have not used wisdom in casting forth the pearls of eternal peace, truth, and joy.

And so, my good students, the wheel progresses. And ofttimes it seems in spite of ourselves we do awaken. Not because our minds want to, but because in the final analysis our eternal soul is greater than our temporal, mental vehicle through which it is expressing in the one lifetime that the temporal mind is aware of, called earth.

And so the question arises in the atmosphere, "How should I guide myself in reference to doing the work of the Divine?" That, my good students, is in keeping with putting your house into order before confusion sets in. And that means each moment of awakening. And so it has been given to you in order to start your day in a vibratory wave of balance, it has been given unto you discipline: awaken and turn your thoughts to the source of all life! And we call it the morning meditation.

But we have looked and we have seen that the minds of some have decided they don't need that. And how true. The mind, surely, doesn't need it, for that represents discipline to the mind and that is the one thing the mind does not desire. And the mind does not desire it because the mind knows if it has discipline, it will have to bow to the light of eternal reason.

A faculty of the eternal, evolving soul will become supreme in your life and the fluctuating desires, the nature of the human mind, will have to bow. And that's the one thing the mind says it doesn't need.

And so, my good students, think. If truth and freedom does not yet mean enough to awaken in the morn and spend a few moments of effort—just a few—on discipline and continuity, its handmaiden, then, my friends, it only reveals that the soul is not yet quite ready. But in time it will be. It means that the mind has not yet suffered sufficiently and is not yet ready to bow to the truth of eternity. For a mind that cannot bow to an eternal, evolving soul cannot possibly bow to eternal truth.

And so we must learn to cultivate our own garden, to take care of our own little home first and the many departments that are within it. And when we begin to do that, then we will be able to grant that, the understanding thereof, to another human soul. But we cannot speak of continuity and discipline and success in life until we become the example, for to do so without first becoming the living example is to expose oneself to a world that can see what gross deception. We cannot speak of freedom and joy and love and life if we are not making the efforts to become it.

Look clearly in life at the very things that the mind says it doesn't want to do. Look at the things that it cannot tolerate. Look at the things that aggravate it. Those, my friends, are the precious jewels that, properly used, will free you in life. For they are the very instruments that your own mind is using against you to hold you captive. And there is no mind that does not know the things it does not want to do. But ask your mind the question, "Why don't you, oh mind, want to do these things? Why are you so intolerant of this and that and that?" And then, through your efforts, your mind will expose itself and, in so exposing itself to yourself, you then have those precious keys, called the jewels of life, to turn in the lock that holds you the victim in bondage, that makes life not the beauty and joy that it truly is.

Good night.

MARCH 18, 1976

CONSCIOUSNESS CLASS 116

Greetings, students. We shall continue on this evening with our journey on the continent of conscience.

As you will recall, I was wandering on that continent and the weeks became the months and the months turned into years. And those years rolled on into centuries. And I looked and looked in vain everywhere for some sign of life. And as I wondered, "Could this possibly be my final journey?" I began to become more weary as each day passed. It was the weariness of my own mind, of my own wonder and suspicion, and my thoughts began to be my greatest cross of life. And for many years I had not heard the voice of the angel that had guided me this far. And I wondered if she had forsaken me. And the voice that had risen from the depths below, I had not heard now for many, many years.

And so, as I became totally bound by the weariness of my own mind, I found myself with an ever-increasing desire to sleep. And one day about midday, as I was lying on the ground in the meadow, I fell asleep, which had become my daily pattern. For it had seemed that there could not possibly be life on this planet and in this realm, for had I not searched the centuries over and found not even a breeze, nor a bird in the sky, nor an animal, or anything that moved. No wind, no breeze to move the leaves of the trees. And they stood so stately, like silent witnesses that watched my every move. It seemed to me they even watched my thoughts that were passing through my mind.

And so I lay, that day, in a sleepless, yet sound sleep. Sleepless in the sense that some sensation was in, and on, my hand. I could not, in my sleepless sleep, understand what was happening to me. Was I dreaming once again, as had become my pattern over those centuries of sleeping so very much? And if it was a dream, why did this strange sensation move up and down my hand? Finally, I awoke and by some inner instinct I looked at my hand. I could not believe my sight. And then the shock turned into a spirit of joy within the depths of my heart, for truly what I saw was an angel direct from God. For I had come over those years and centuries to finally believe in the possibility of some intelligence greater than my mind. And so I looked at what was, to me, a heavenly angel crawl back and forth on my hand. It was the tiniest little creature: a little insect known as an ant. And from that moment to this very day, I see no difference between ant and angel, for that little insect became my lifelong friend.

And as many years passed, I learned to communicate with that tiny, little insect. I learned what work—the value of it—was on that realm that I now was in. For that little insect I cherished with all my love and all my heart. I watched it each day from early morn till dusk. And I prayed and hoped that it would lead me to others, but I was never ungrateful because only that one did I ever find.

And from watching that ant work so very hard for its food, work to build its little castles, I became inspired. And a thought arose from the depths of my being and I began to work to make what you might call in your world an axe of stone to fell those giant trees. I well recall that it took me over twenty years to fell one tree, for I had a thought that had arisen within my mind: I would go to the highest hill on that realm and I would build a great tower. And from the heights of that great tower perhaps some other life could find me.

You may ask your questions if you wish.

Thank you. What is the spiritual significance of Christ's crucifixion?

The spiritual significance of crucifixion—which, in truth, is simply an accepted means of transition at that time and period in your history. And so the spiritual significance of what you call crucifixion is the revelation to all who have eyes to see, to all who have ears to hear, that that which is created is governed by dual opposing law, that that law will take that which is its own, and that the Law of the Divine will ever sustain itself.

And so it is that each moment man, in truth, is crucified—crucified by his self-inflicted suffering. For suffering, or so-called crucifixion, is, in truth, the revelation of the payment that we shall ever make by entertaining the diabolical delusion of the supremacy of our own mind over the infinite authority of the Divine Intelligence. And so it is through suffering that man, in truth, frees himself from the delusion of his so-called self-importance and authority over life.

We have spoken many times on the subject of life. And we have stated that the mind is capable of creating many things, but the divine, infinite life force is not within the power of dual creation. That is within the power of the Divine Intelligence. And so man, crucifying himself with his own delusions of authority over his life, in time, from the ever-increasing and intensity of suffering, bows, in the final analysis, to the soul faculty of humility. And in that surrender, the crucifixion serves a good purpose.

Thank you. Why do those in the spirit worlds wear clothes?

Because of the minds of men in the lower realms of insanity. For if they did not wear garments in their appearances to you earthly souls, your fascination, the bondage of hell, would control your souls and, instead of being spiritually uplifted, you would descend farther down into the dungeons of hell as an effect of your own fascinations and lack of discipline of your minds.

Thank you. We understand that the Earth is the fifth planet, the planet of faith. Does this necessarily infer that our souls evolve through each planet through numerical order, that we have already passed through four prior planets? Or is the soul designated to specific planets for the individual lessons required?

The soul does not evolve in numerical order, for no man establishes laws in numerical order. And his journey is dependent upon the laws that he alone has established and is establishing. And so we find on the planets a great diversity of minds, but beyond this great diversity and variety of minds is a higher law, known as the Law of the Evolving Soul, for that law is the supreme law. And so it is that all souls presently incarnated on the Earth planet are learning the lessons of what the planet has to offer. And the principle lesson of the earth realm is the lesson of faith.

When, in giving forth these simple truths that have arisen from many centuries of effort to be free, we sincerely pray that we may so give them that they will touch the thirsty soul. We are not concerned with what *you* do with them, but we do pray that our efforts in expressing them may be instrumental in reaching the living soul.

Thank you. If the ego of the four-legged animal is far less tenacious than that of man, does this mean that spiritual progression is usually more rapid for the animal than for man? Would you please describe the animal realms?

The so-called ego of the four-legged forms is the ego of simplicity. Its purpose—to preserve the form for the expression of the evolving soul. The difference between the so-called ego of the human mind and the animal mind is a difference between simplicity and complexity. And so it is as the effect of self-consciousness in the human form without the guiding light of reason, the effect of discipline, the ego within the human mind becomes most complex from its own awareness. And the awareness, in turn, feeds the complexity of self-importance through self-awareness and man's complexity becomes the Law of Division. And the Law of Division divides the house, the temple of his eternal soul, from his eternal soul. And in so doing, the ego becomes the supreme authority and the soul descends into bondage.

Thank you. Would you please discuss male chauvinism? Is it an aspect of universal motherhood?

Well, the word *male chauvinism* is an expression by the ego for its supremacy and authority not only over its own soul, but over any soul that it becomes in rapport with. Now, the uneducated ego wears many garments of deception. Recognize that the sole purpose, the *sole purpose* of the ego is preservation of the form through which the eternal soul is striving to evolve. There is no other spiritual purpose for the design of the so-called ego. Its complete, whole, and total purpose and duty is the preservation of the form to keep it in balance, in working order for the soul's expression. However, we have not kept the reins of reason, the effect of discipline, over the human ego. And because we have not done that and do not make the effort to do that, the human ego does not serve its true purpose: preservation of the form in a balanced expression for the freedom of the soul.

Thank you. When one has a weakness, should one court temptation in order to strengthen one's character or should one avoid exposure to temptation altogether?

A most interesting question and statement. If one has a weakness, should they court temptation? My good students, the recognition of the weakness should be the recognition of the temptation. No effort consciously needs to be made for the weakness is the effect of temptation. It is not the cause of temptation: it is the effect of temptation. For it is temptation that has caused the weakness. It is not the weakness that has caused temptation. I do hope that you will ponder well in reference to the Law of Temptation.

Thank you. It has been given that fascination is the mind's way of covering up or cloaking one's true motive, that they may not reveal themselves to their own mind. Is deception, therefore, synonymous with fascination or is it just one aspect of fascination?

It is synonymous with fascination.

Thank you. Would you please explain the deception game the mind plays by taking so many, many words to get to the point and how we can free ourselves from such bondage of fascination?

Whenever we find it necessary to speak a hundred words in reference to any subject, when ten words or one would reveal the particular subject to the listening ear—and we are speaking now in reference to the mundane conversations that flood your consciousness on earth—then what we are doing, in truth, is feeding the level of consciousness called self-importance, that we have an ear waiting, waiting, and waiting upon us. And this is the true cause of what is known as going around the world to get to the world. And so you will find in the conversations on your earthly planet, many, many millions upon millions of souls who do not get to what you call the point, because if they got to the point, they would not have that feeling of self- importance of someone waiting for them to finally get there. This is the effect of playing with one's own mind. And in so doing, someone, some soul, must wait upon them.

And so it ever proves the divine demonstrable law that like attracts like and becomes the Law of Attachment. We cannot grant to another what we have not granted unto ourselves. And so when we, in our efforts, want to get something done and we have spent a life of thinking about it and dreaming about it and doubting it and questioning it and not being sure and having no faith in a power that would not fail us, then that is what we grant to another by going 'round and 'round the so-called mulberry bush.

Thank you. It has been given that commitment without total consideration is not total commitment, for if it was, bondage, not freedom, would be the law of life. Would you please give your understanding of this?

For anyone to commit themselves to anything without total consideration of their eighty-one levels of consciousness is not only foolhardy, but it reveals the unwillingness of the person who commits themselves—it reveals the unwillingness to make the effort to know themselves. And so we find those who commit themselves and do not demonstrate the divine Law of Continuity, which leads to success, are the minds who have not made the effort to know themselves. They are the minds which have made great effort to place all cause outside of themselves—to blame the world and the people around and about them for their joy and for their sadness.

And so prior to making any commitment, one should make great effort to consider their personal responsibility and, having made the effort of total consideration of what their personal responsibility in life is—the ability to respond to the authority of God, for the good of all. Once having done that, you have no broken commitments and therefore do not suffer the transgression of God's immutable laws.

Thank you. We are taught to control rather than to try to annihilate desire. How can we best do this?

Man can best control his desires by becoming aware of the level of consciousness on which they have been given birth. Becoming aware of the level of consciousness on which they have been given birth, then he will become aware of more than one or two or five or ten levels of consciousness. He will then consider and weigh within his mind the advisability of which level he should express on in any given situation.

Man gains control through his efforts to respond to God's infinite laws. And when man makes that effort, he not only knows the motivating, true motivating force and power—for it is a power. Desire is the divine expression. It becomes a force when the mind takes over. When man truly traces to the cause what man calls desire, then he sees, in truth, it is God's infinite divine expression and he has the power within him to guide it in the light of reason.

Thank you. How can we learn to use greater reason?

By greater effort to control our own mind. Man cannot view the soul faculty of reason until he is able to control the multitudes of thought that blind him from the infinite Law of Balance and Good. We can talk a multitude of words, but they will be of no value unless your heart, the instrument of your eternal soul, is ready to receive them.

Thank you. Why is it that seekers of truth are often those who are misfits within the society in that they are unable to conform to expectations placed upon them?

It's a most interesting question and statement—to declare that seekers of truth are the misfits of society. We do not find that, in truth, to be an accurate statement. It is true that many seekers of truth, expressing that inner truth through the limited conditioned minds of men, are mistaken in some societies as a revolutionary. But it is not an accurate statement to say that seekers of truth are the misfits of society. For in so making such a statement, we are looking from a view and judging according to that limited view what fits and what does not fit into society.

We must make the effort to rise our level of consciousness to be more interested in what we are doing in the world, our world, within our own mind. For if we are doing that, then we will become a light in the world. And we will have no need to be concerned about fitting or misfitting. For our responsibility in life is to be fitted, if you wish to use that word, for the job in life that we have earned through untold centuries of evolution. So let us take care of the house we're living in. Let us view the effects within ourselves and, in so viewing those effects, we will know if we are, in truth, as a vehicle for our soul, fitted or unfitted.

Thank you. Those who enforce the law often seem to be very much like those who break the law. Can you please explain this?

It is obvious and evident that the questioner is referring to the law of man and the enforcement and breaking thereof. And the questioner has made the statement that those who enforce the law of man are frequently the ones most prone to breaking it. And unfortunately in your world, it is indeed frequently true.

However, my good students, all your world knows that there is no greater enforcer than a reformer. Look at the souls—the minds of those who have reformed themselves. Whether it be alcohol or smoking or anything else, the first thing that a reformer does is, with a vengeance of hell itself, demand that the world be reformed. And are they not well qualified? Having spent years as the offender and transgressor, are they not qualified in their minds to now be the enforcer?

But it is not true that all souls who enforce your mental laws are reformers or that all of them are the greatest transgressors.

Now, why does a reformer use such vengeance to enforce their new will upon the souls of others? It reveals, my good students, that it has taken great will within their being to reform, that they have reformed against their own patterns of a lifetime and they did not accept the change within them graciously. This is why you see so-called reformers expressing with such vengeance. For they have not accepted yet that God is the law and that vengeance does not belong to the minds of men. But surrender, the gentle voice of reason that whispers to the minds of men—and it whispers ceaselessly each moment, "Surrender to God, the law that frees you. Surrender your thought. Surrender your feeling." And in so doing, you will be eternally freed from fear that now binds you to years of yesterday.

Thank you. Are there dreams from the soul as well as dreams from the past or taped experiences? And if so, how can we perceive the differentiation?

Life, as you know life, is a dream. And you, your mind, is the dreamer. The soul, in its evolution, has what is known as an indispensable part of its own expression—what is called conscience. Not the educated conscience of the mind of which you are now aware, but the conscience of knowing right from wrong, of knowing positive and negative. This is a soul conscience. It knows its own responsibility. And as it evolves throughout the centuries, it garners unto itself a multitude of experiences, known as the effects of the dreams that it has dreamed. Now, those effects or dreams establish laws in a mental world. And so each soul knows, in truth, its own journey.

Now, how does man discern between the present dreams of one soul incarnation and the untold centuries of dreams recorded in what we call the memory par excellence, the soul conscience? Man discerns the difference when man pauses in his daily meditation, when he pauses in his acts and activities in the course of a day and he prays for the light of reason to rise within his consciousness. And slowly, but surely, as your earth years pass, this light of reason begins to dawn within you. And as it does, you become aware. You become aware of why you are who you are, of why life's experiences for you are the way they are. You become freed from the identity of your short, little earth life. And in so becoming aware, your consciousness begins to expand until the day dawns for you that you arrive in consciousness in the realms within you known as universal consciousness.

There, you're aware that you, in truth, are an inseparable part of Allsoul, that what happens to one soul is also happening to you. For the tuning fork is affected by that to which it is attuned. And so when you become attuned to the universality of God, then your feelings, your hopes, your desires, your aspirations become universalized and you become free from the petty disturbances of microscopic identities. You no longer identify with personality, for you have risen in consciousness above personality. You are no longer interested in playing the little, childlike games of the mind. You are no longer interested in manipulating the souls of others, for you have become aware that manipulation is the deception you are placing over your own eternal soul, that it is a blight upon the light of your soul, a great, dark shadow.

And so your mind becomes more still. And the peace that's known as passing all understanding becomes your precious jewel in life. And you no longer become the victim of the games the minds play, for you now have freed yourself in acceptance of divine will. And that divine will, known as acceptance, grants unto you total consideration. Beyond the little identities and beliefs of your mind, your soul has risen. And that rising places you in the heaven here and now.

You not only feel the universality of your eternal soul, but you see it, you know it, and you hear it. Then, eternity becomes the moment of the now. There is no longer separation between you and God. And remember, my students, he who entertains separation between himself and any living creature is separating a part of himself from God. For you cannot entertain thoughts of separatism and be in God. We have stated many times, "Love all life and know the Light," for the Light is God. And not until man rises in consciousness to love all life will man ever know God.

Good night.

MARCH 25, 1976

CONSCIOUSNESS CLASS 117

Greetings, students. We shall continue on for a few moments with this journey of which we spoke in our last meeting with you.

As you will recall, I had begun to build a tower. And surely to my mind it seemed that eternity upon eternity had passed. Yet the day finally dawned when my tower was completed. And one morning, during my daily vigil on the tower, I saw far off in the distance what I thought must surely be some type of a bird in the sky. I was so filled with so many mixed emotions that my mind began to play tricks upon me. And I began to doubt in my own mind if what I thought I saw I really did see. And seemingly hours passed that day when, as this bird came closer and closer to my tower, I was finally convinced that it was really true.

And my heart, overwhelmed with the spirit of joy, rejoiced as the bird flew and circled my tower. And I saw that that bird was a great bird. It was an eagle, a golden eagle. And as I watched it soar in the sky, I prayed and prayed that it would come closer that I may have another friend with me. But it seemed that was not to be for me, not, at least, at that time. For finally that beautiful bird flew on and disappeared from my view. However, we must remember in life: when all seems lost, it is but the beginning of the new. And so it is in our evolution, we must always let go that we may move graciously forward, though our minds know not what is yet to be.

You may feel free at this time to ask your questions.

Thank you. Would you please give us your understanding of why the ego equates time with money?

Thank you for your most interesting question. The mind equates security, which is represented in your world by what is called money, with time, for the mind views the passing of time as a losing of its own security. For the mind views the world of time, the delusion of creation, as a passing thing. For example, the mind accepts that you are youthful for a certain number of years, that you are, for a certain number of years, in your prime of life and middle age, that you are, for a certain number of years, in your older age span. And then, for your mind, the light goes out. And so it is that the mind views time as security and it views material substance or money as security. And that is the reason that the minds of men equate money and time as one and the same.

Thank you. Would you please discuss so-called time and money pressures in relation to desire fulfillment and frustration of desires?

Whenever the mind has accepted that it is not, and has not, fulfilled its many desires, then the mind registers in its own consciousness what is called pressure. It is the very nature of desire to ever fulfill itself. And if the mind, entertaining thoughts of desire, which it does—for that is, in truth, the purpose of the human mind—and the will is not sufficiently expressed that it may make, so to speak, the necessary payment for the attainment of its chosen desire, then those desires become multiplied and what you call pressure begins to register within the mind.

For the mind, by its very nature, places the blame for the lack of the fulfillment of its desires on circumstances and conditions outside of its domain and beyond its own power to control. For if it did not do that, then the mind would become totally discouraged and defeat its own purpose. It is the very workings of the mind to ever strive for a balance in its own duality. For every disappointment, it must register somewhere in some area an encouragement. For every acceptance, it must register an equal rejection in some area. And this is why we have often stated, "When of thy mind thou seekest to know the truth, / On the wheel of delusion thou shalt traverse [Discourse 1]."

Thank you. When the ego computes it has had a very image-shattering experience earlier in life, how may one free oneself of the emotional and guilt-ridden tapes connected with the experience?

The ego, so-called, of the human mind, which is an instrument to preserve the mind—for without the preservation of the mind, the soul has no vehicle through which to express on your planet. When in life we experience a shattering of our ego image—and we experience those shatterings more often than we consciously realize. It is only through viewing the experience for what it truly is—When the mind decides how life is to be, then the mind, a dual instrument, calls forth unto itself all the opposing experiences that it may, through its own negative-positive balancing, be the instrument through which the eternal soul may rise and be free. Only by an objectification of the image-shattering experience—that is, through an honest and open discussion—can the mind be freed from its own destruction.

Thank you. Is it possible that we could so censure ourselves for a supposed wrongdoing that we believe others are talking about us and blame them for broadcasting that is actually going on in our own heads?

That indeed, my good students, is a most frequent justification of the human mind. Whenever in life we have experiences that are traumatic, that is, extremely emotionally disturbing to us, we suppress the experience by forcing it down into our subconscious mind, where we no longer are consciously aware of it. However, the law established, that Law of Suppression, feeds energy to the very experience. And so in keeping with the law that our adversities become our attachments, suppression is an adverse reaction of the mind. And we force this experience, whatever it may be, out of our conscious awareness by the very Law of Adversity.

Now, we all know that to be adverse to anything is to direct energy to it. And that that man chooses to direct energy to becomes his child for he, and he alone—not God or someone else—has created the form. And because he—man—has created it, it goes out into the universe. It gathers like vibrations around and about it. And it returns someday to its own creator. It is indeed a freedom for man to make greater effort to expose to himself the very things that are causing him emotional disturbance. For without exposure, which frees the soul, man does not honestly and truthfully face himself, his mind, his levels of consciousness. And when we do not face that which we have, in truth, created, we become the slave and not the master of the mind.

Thank you. One of the Wise One's sayings is, "Gossip is the worst enemy in your camp [A saying from the Serenity Game].*" How can one refrain from gossip? What effect does this have on the soul?*

First of all, we must consider what *we* mean by the word *gossip?* For what that word means to one mind, an hour or so later it means something entirely different, dependent upon the level of consciousness that the person, their soul, is expressing through at the time. For example, a person might consider their discussion of politics and those responsible for their governments as gossip. Another person may consider that to be a dutiful citizen. Another person may consider gossip as a person who discusses another person by name and directs their attention to what they judge to be the frailties of that particular individual. And so it is that that word must be honestly faced within each mind that they may, in their understanding, accept or reject its meaning and its use.

If, in discussion, there is a beneficial upliftment for the human soul, then the discussion, in truth, is worthwhile. If the effect is not, in truth, an upliftment to higher levels of consciousness for the eternal evolving soul, then, of course, it can only be detrimental.

The student has asked, How, in truth, may one control themselves from what they call a gossip? They must first find what they mean by the word and then they must also accept whether or not their discussions are proving to be constructive and worthwhile, first for their own good—for they cannot grant to another what they have not first granted unto themselves. However, the interest in the word expressed by the questioner reveals within it a conflict in their consciousness concerning what they have decided is judgment.

Thank you. Is the mind or the soul—correction—Is it the mind or the soul that is susceptible to praise and criticism?

What affects the mind affects the soul. And what affects the soul affects the mind. For what affects the mind, in truth, affects the body. And what affects the body, in truth, affects the mind. Therefore you cannot separate truth to find truth. A house divided cannot stand.

And it brings an interesting question with the question, for it implies that the questioner has accepted a separation, a separation—a lack of relationship—between the eternal soul and the temporal mind and the temporal body. Without the mind, the soul could not express in a mental world. And without the physical body, the mind could not express in a physical world. And so these vehicles through which the eternal being is expressing itself at this time are necessary vehicles for the evolution of the eternal soul.

The soul, the mind, and the physical body respond or react to encouragement. Like a healing balm, the bodies respond to being encouraged if the encouragement is true encouragement, if within it is contained the sincerity of one's own heart, which is a vehicle for the soul's pure expression. And so the mind responds—also the other bodies and the soul—to criticism. And so, my friends, remember the great eternal truth: "What today I criticize, tomorrow I shall idolize *[A saying from the Serenity Game]*." For that is the beauty of divine law.

Thank you. On page 82 in The Living Light *book [Discourse 31] the first line states, "For in truth, my children, there is no time. It is the created illusion of your functions." Since there is no time in truth, are all of our incarnations into form happening simultaneously? If so, explain please.*

In reference to your question concerning the illusion and delusion called time, time, created by the illusion and the delusion of mental substance, and being the vehicle through which the soul in your earth realm must express, and due to the eternal truth that that which is expressed through mental substance guarantees its own duality, explanation of that which is timeless and truth is beyond the power of the human mind. For it is not possible to explain with mental vehicles the eternal truth of timelessness. However, we have often spoken of the eternal moment. We have stated many, many, many times that the eternal moment, the moment of eternity—and think, my students, eternity is the moment of which you are consciously aware. That is the moment in which you have the fullness of the power of the Divinity itself.

And so because I know, as students, you are not yet happy, let alone pleased, with the discussion concerning your question, then I shall in my way attempt to give what I can concerning the many incarnations of the evolving soul. Because the eternal moment is the moment of the fullness of the Divine, in the eternal moment is the possibility, the possibility of the awareness of the eternal, evolving soul and its multitude of expression in so-called prior time, which is, in truth, the illusion of mental substance.

Thank you. Would you please give us your understanding of the saying in the Serenity Game, "Freedom in creation ever seeks to find that part of self that loves, the joy with which to bind"?

Oh yes, my students, indeed. "Freedom in creation ever seeks to find the part of self that loves, the joy with which to bind." In discussing that question, let us speak of the relationship of another affirmation which is inseparable from that. And it states, "I am spirit formless and free, whatever I think that will I be." And so it is that the free, formless, eternal Spirit ever seeks to find in creation the part of self—the magnetic part of self—the love with which to bind. For love is the great magnet. And if the divine, free Spirit does not seek this love, this magnet in which to bind to creation, then it does not have a vehicle of form through which it may express itself. And without that form or vehicle through which the Divinity may expand and express itself—that is the only time that the formless, free

Spirit becomes aware of itself. I do hope you will ponder well the great truth of that. For in so pondering, it will dawn within your consciousness—another truth which states, "When of my God I seek to know / The purpose of my life, / The answer comes, / The pain to grow / And willingness to strife *[Another saying from the Serenity Game]*."

And so it is that in this binding process, the form, the vehicle through which the free Spirit is expressing itself, the vehicle becomes the master, for it forgets the formless, free Spirit that sustains it. And when the formless, free Spirit leaves the vehicle of form, the form returns to the elements from which it was created, only to rise again a bit more evolved, a bit more aware.

And so, my good students, remember that the mind identifies and forgets its own true source, through which the identification process has been made possible. And in so forgetting, we lose our divinity of the peace that passeth all understanding.

Thank you. Would you please give us some words of wisdom regarding the conscious nature of our fellowship with the spirit helpers in order that their inspiration may flow more freely through us to do God's work?

In reference to being more receptive and in rapport with the angels that surround us for the good and upliftment of the eternal souls, man needs but one word, one simple word, called *surrender*. For through surrender comes great good. When man truly surrenders, in the moment of surrender he enters what is called divine will. For in that moment he is a vehicle of total acceptance, divine will, the will of the Divinity for the good of all, seen and unseen, expresses itself fully. Divine love becomes the great magnet fully lighting the world and then, truly, you experience what is known as divine life.

And when the minds of men must ask the question, "How do I surrender?" then the mind is yet not ready to do it.

Thank you. Would you please speak on the importance of concentration? How does it work—correction—how does it relate to disassociation and why is it so important to the unfoldment—correction—the unfolding medium?

We have stated many times that concentration is the key to all power. Concentration is placing the mind pointedly and fixedly upon the object of your choice until only the essence remains. Without concentration, you cannot pierce the veil of delusion, called the duality of creation. You cannot enter the very essence of life itself without the use of concentration. For concentration is oneness, and oneness is godness. And so, my good students, remember, that which you place your attention upon you, in truth, become. And so we are this moment this day what we have directed God's energy to. Does it not behoove us to direct God's energy, through these vehicles, to God? For that is the very law of life: that that which comes from a thing shall return to the very thing from whence it came. And so our very life is the divine expression called God. And it is our duty, our personal responsibility to direct, through these many vehicles of bodies, that energy back to its source.

He who does not make this simple effort—to direct this divine energy back to its true source—becomes the obstruction to this divine energy. And so it may be likened unto a cable that contains a voltage of high-powered electricity. If you insist upon being the obstruction to the flow of that current, in time you will indeed burn out. And this is the great lesson of life. We have stated that the first soul faculty is duty, gratitude, and tolerance. And indeed it takes that soul faculty to permit God's energy to flow through us and to return unto its source.

And so do you not now see the great value and absolute necessity of surrendering the thoughts of mind that disturb you, that this energy, which you have temporarily directed into mental substance and obstruction, may return unto its source and, in so doing, cleanse your universe that you may be the instrument through which the river of life may harmoniously flow to the Mountain of Aspiration?

Thank you. Would you please clarify the meaning of the line in the Lord's Prayer which says, "Lead us not into temptation, but deliver us from evil"?

For the law shall lead us into whatever *we* have chosen. And so the prayer clearly states, "Lead us not into temptation, but deliver us from evil, for thy namesake." Man is the law unto himself. And the question rises, What are we doing with the law that we are? When we choose the path of temptation, we establish the Law of Temptation and therefore we are tempted, for the law is just and returns unto the sender. And so the voice of the divine, eternal, free Spirit speaks to the created form and says, "Lead me not into temptation." And it says to the eternal God, "But deliver me from evil for thy namesake." Now, what does it mean, "for thy namesake"? It means the identity that the mind can accept of the eternal Divinity, for the mind must identify.

Millions of words are given to your world. If you use them, if you make the effort to apply a few of them, then the philosophy shared with you will be of great benefit in the here and the now. If your soul is not yet ready to apply that which is demonstrable, then it is recorded in your memory par excellence and will serve you well in the centuries yet to be.

Good night.

MAY 6, 1976

CONSCIOUSNESS CLASS 118

Greetings, students. This evening we should like to spend some time in discussion of the many experiences and the purposes and benefits of the evolving soul as it passes through the forms called creation.

As the soul in its eternal destiny of movement through the various levels of consciousness finds itself so often in great struggle, great suffering, and pain, through certain levels, we must view, in the struggle and suffering, the true benefits that are taking place at those times. For as the soul in its evolving, finding itself in the great struggles of creation, releases from itself a greater degree of purifying energy into those levels and, in turn, is instrumental in rising the vibratory waves of those levels of consciousness, demonstrating the eternal truth that man indeed is an inseparable part of the united whole. And so it is that regardless of what we think or do, in the final analysis, the eternal journey continues on for all souls at all times. It is ever in keeping with the laws established by the individualized souls to be the instruments of benefit to those who are attracted by the law unto them.

And so, my good students, as often has been stated, be not discouraged in your struggle, for regardless of it, you will, in time, be freed from it. The Law of Payment and Attainment is an impartial law that is applicable to all souls, to all forms everywhere. And so the true being, the true self, is shedding the many garments of creation each and every moment of its expression. The garments that are being shed, recorded in the mind of mental substance, by a losing, a feeling of loss—for it is the nature of mind substance to attract and to hold.

And yet the greater Law of Freedom, moving through the magnetic field of creation, is the supreme law. And so regardless of the thoughts of the mind, that supreme law, the Law of Change, the Law of Evolving, takes place. And it is only in the recognition and the acceptance of that supreme law, that man is able to use the faculty of reason and let go of the many things that he has garnered unto himself. And the seeming difficulty in letting go is a revelation of the temporary efforts of supremacy by our own magnetic field, commonly referred to as emotion.

Wise indeed are those who recognize the true purpose of emotion, who are not deceived by its many devious ways of expression, for then they are able to use it and not permit it to use them. It is the recognition and the acceptance of separating the truth from creation.

Many exercises of breathing and etc. and affirmations have already been given. And their proper use, as a preventive measure to keep the souls from being trapped in those magnetic fields—but they must be used not after the fact, but before. For in their use, you, as individualized souls, will gain a greater objectivity and find that true purpose for being on your earth realm at this so-called time.

Many, many philosophies have revealed truth to the world. The reason that man finds such difficulty in his acceptance of it is because of the fear of change. Our affirmation states, "Be ever ready and willing to change *[A saying in the Serenity Game]*." For it is only in your willingness and in your readiness that you will flow harmoniously with the supreme law, which dictates a constant state of change for the form called identity. Accept the changes with a gracious spirit and a joyous heart and a sincere mind. And then you will experience that great freedom, that fresh air, the gentle cool breeze of happiness and joy.

For as you ponder in your moments of your experiences, you look at life and its constant flux and flow, its positive law of constant change, and flow with it, that the goodness that awaits you may enter your consciousness sooner. A man of common sense does not hold to that which is destined by law—greater law than he, his mind—does not hold to that which is destined to pass. And it is indeed a foolish mind that attempts to hold to what is passing down the stream of consciousness called the river of life. Let it all go from your mind in this eternal moment, for if you will do that, those doors of fresh air will open in the moment of the now.

The only thing that stands between you and the fulfillment of all that you, your minds, could possibly desire is your own unwillingness to let go of what you thought you had.

And so, my good students, though it has taken me many, many, many centuries to learn that simple truth, once having awakened to it, I stand guardian at the threshold of my consciousness that I may not be deceived by my own mind, whose very nature it is to hold and to secure that which enters it.

For when that awakening dawns and is applied in your lives, you will, in that moment, find the true security of being. For man is not being until he removes, by the Law of Application, all thought held in the domain of the human mind. Let thoughts flow freely, for only in permitting them to do so can you move freely. The thoughts that you hold become the laws of rejection, for in the holding of the thought, you reject all others from entering. And that, in truth, is the way that concentration truly works. That is the positive aspect.

But it is the negative aspect of that simple truth that is demonstrated by the supremacy, so-called, of the human mind. For man, in placing his thought pointedly and fixedly upon the object of his choice until only the essence remains, becomes the essence itself. And that is the reason that we have taught for so very long to choose wisely what you place your attention upon, for you become, through the power of concentration, the thing itself. And this is why it has been taught that concentration is the key to all power.

But man has a strange understanding of that word *concentration*. He thinks that it is a conscious thought that he thinks of something and blots out, so to speak, everything else. My good students, Life herself is revealing unto you how concentrated certain patterns of your mind really are. And when those patterns rise within your consciousness, through that power of concentration, you become the essence of the attitude of mind and then believe that that is you. And through that process is man truly deceived: a house divided against itself. The climb up the Mountain of Aspiration, the soul's true expression, will always be as easy or as difficult as you alone permit it to be.

When the exercises that have already been given are religiously applied and the student, in their application thereof, does not permit the deceiving mind to dictate how long it will take and does not permit the deceiving mind to dictate what the results should be, but gradually and surely gains control over their magnetic field, that it may be brought into balance with their electrical expression, then the reason that transforms the universes will express itself, known as the symphony of the spheres. For the symphony of the spheres is a perfect balance in all eighty-one levels of consciousness. That is then known in our world as the cathedral of the eternal soul.

Some time ago we stated that C, middle C, was the note of perfect balance. We also stated at that time, for you, as eternal evolving souls, to find your note. For when you find your note, you then will see beyond the shadows of doubt and will have that perfect balance or symphony of the spheres as your eternal expression. Now, there is a door through which the soul must pass in order to find their perfect note of balance. That door is known as the door of honesty and it is awaiting all souls. It is awaiting for them to enter. But we all know that we cannot be honest with ourselves until we are willing to face ourselves. And we cannot be willing to face ourselves until we open within our consciousness the first two soul faculties: duty, gratitude, and tolerance; faith, poise, and humility.

When those two soul faculties are sufficiently open, a willingness will rise from the very depths of our being. And as it does so, there will an interest within the human consciousness to face life, ourselves, the way we are. Not the way that our minds want everyone else to think we are—for that is not honesty—but the way we are. And in so doing, we will gain the courage of our convictions. For it is our divine right to have our convictions in life.

We will no longer spend our time in playing the games of pleasing that we may temporarily gain. For our eyes will have opened and we will know that the game of pleasing for the sense of gain is a high payment that does not have lasting value. And in the courage of our convictions we enter the door of honesty and we grant, graciously, to our eternal being, what is the right of our eternal being. We no longer, in entering that door, are interested or concerned about the passing things of creation. We recognize and know that they are there as tools, to be used for the purpose for which they have been designed. We no longer try to hold them, nor to horde them. We permit an unobstructed flow through our universe and the law demonstrates herself: as freely as we give, do we, in truth, receive.

And therefore the question no longer rises within our mind of need, for we know when our mind says we have need, that we have become the obstruction to the divine flow and we have need for we have blocked the flow of givingness and, therefore, are not receiving and the mind is registering so-called need. Opportunity presents itself each moment to our consciousness: the opportunity to be a free channel, that the Law of Receiving may be as free as the Law of Giving. And he who has problems with his receiving reveals unto himself—and those who know the law—that that mind has problems in their giving.

The teachings of old clearly state that the gift without the giver is worthless. And that truth means just exactly what it says. If your heart, your joy, your soul, your goodness, is not in your giving in life, then it cannot be in your receiving in life. If, in the givingness, which is nothing more, nor less, than your efforts to be a free channel that the divine intelligent Energy may flow unobstructed, if, in your giving in life, a part of you— your true being—is not there, then it is hollow and has no lasting value. The most precious so-called thing that a man can possibly give is the giving of his obstructions that God may flow freely through him as an instrument and clear channel of the goodness of life itself.

For if we give a word, or anything, with reservation, we have not given: we have loaned. And the loan will return unto us as a debt that we alone must pay. It is not the easiest thing for most minds to give what their minds have accepted is their security. And so the most difficult thing to give is whatever the mind dictates is a part of its security and that, my good students, is the very thing necessary for those types of minds to give that they may free themselves and receive the divine intelligent Energy, called God, as their true and only security.

When the deceiving mind dictates to the eternal soul what receiving and giving is, when it dictates what balance is, when it places value priority of temporal things above the eternal value of your true being, then man experiences the struggles of dual creation.

When we speak the word, we must, in that moment, stand firmly on the rock of principle, for whatever we are the instrument of, we are, in truth, responsible for.

And in keeping with this discussion, let us not view the Law of Commitment lightly. For man commits himself with verbal energy to many things. And those commitments are created forms of which he is the mother or father. And those children shall return. They will first gently knock at the door of your conscience, requesting a reentrance home, where they were born. And if you do not permit your conscience to answer the door, then they will knock louder and louder. And the day will finally come when the knocking will cease, for they will have broken down the door to enter your conscience and demand their just right to live in the home in which they were created.

My good students, let us make a little more, perhaps, effort to face life as life truly is. Let us stop the war of the emotions within. Let us cease the battle of the mind and let us live the way the design and plan of the Infinite has brought it to be. Let us put the reins on the deception of so-called accidents. Let us take hold of blame. Let us stop, truly stop, in this moment and go inside, where it really is. Let us truly pause more frequently in each day's experiences and see that, in truth, it's the effect of our own mental laws. For only in that pausing can honesty rise and only in being honest can we truly be ourselves.

It is not our purpose in life, nor your purpose in life, to be someone else, for you cannot have your fulfillment in that desire. The purpose of life is to be you, not the dual, deceiving mind, but the true you that is forever and ever and ever. Let value rise in consciousness to heavenly heights in the moment of now. For in being your true self, you will have all the beauty and fullness that life has to offer.

There is no lack in God's givingness to his children. And therefore an acceptance of lack in your mind is a denial of your right to receive the Fullness, the Goodness, called God.

Good night.

MAY 13, 1976

CONSCIOUSNESS CLASS 119

Greetings, students. Once again we are pleased to be with you in class. And this evening we shall spend some time on the relationship of mental patterns and physical disturbances and corrective measures in redirecting this electromagnetic flow through the temple of God, called the human body.

As you all experience these dual emotions, these so-called highs and lows, and ever seeking some peace from the ebb and flow of the mind, several exercises having already been given to you, this evening we shall give to you some of the pressure points through which a redirection of the energy may be accomplished. All of you have experienced, at different times, so-called pressure in the mind until you felt you, yourselves, would explode, so to speak. Through a proper application on the area just below the earlobe, you may, by rhythmic breath and proper applied pressure on the exhale of the breath, redirect the energy from that pattern of mind that the soul is experiencing at that time.

As you often experience what you call temper, a proper application of pressure upon the temples will relieve the condition. As you find yourselves directing your energy to patterns of mind in which you are blaming conditions and people and circumstances beyond your control for the state of your affairs and are sinking into the so-called failure, discouragement, and self-pity levels of consciousness, an application of pressure upon the side areas of the neck where it joins the body will redirect the energy from that mental subconscious pattern.

These are not cure-all methods, my good students, but they do bring a temporary relief from these conditions until you are able, through the directed power that is flowing through you, to surrender the condition to the Divine and, at that time, it will sprout its wings, so to speak, and leave your universes.

This peace and harmony, which is your divine right, is so infrequently, we find, experienced during your earthly journey. The mind is such a clever instrument and uses so much justification to preserve its old patterns. But it is through your attitude of mind of encouragement, through your attitude of mind of ever looking beyond in the eternal moment, viewing not the obstruction in life—for when we permit ourselves to view obstruction, we are bowing as a servant to our mind which has created it.

And so it is that he who views the obstruction never finds the way. For in the viewing of obstruction, we not only recognize and accept, but we declare to God that our mind is superior to the Divine, for our minds have created the obstruction and only our minds, in truth, can view it. Therefore, my good students, man cannot see his own success, his own accomplishment, as long as he permits his own mind to view the obstruction to it.

It seems to be, for many, difficult to let go, because for those who find difficulty in letting go, in surrendering, it simply means the mind demands its own authority over the Divine. It's like a person that says, "How do I know that God is? How do I know?" It's a good sign to ask the question, because it means, in truth, that the God the mind has created no longer exists. And the mind is now questioning, "How do I know there is a God?" The mind does not know there is a God unless the mind creates a God. It is that which is beyond the mind that knows.

The automobile does not know there is a driver until the driver moves the automobile and the driver has the power and the automobile moves. And so it is with the human mind: something moves it. And the mind knows that something moves it, but the mind searches for that something inside of its own domain, the human mind. It's first reaction to that search is to create in its domain what it can call "God." In time, because what it has created as "God" exists under dual law of mental substance, the mind is disappointed and, in time, dethrones its created god or gods.

After having done so, once again a search in the human mind takes place. And this time it searches and does not create another god. And then it rises and asks the question, "How do I know there is a God?" And when the minds of men ask that question, they begin to step upon a path that has a forked way in front of them. And at that fork, they choose the left path of mental supremacy or the right path of surrender and eternal peace and happiness.

We all must face that crossroad in our own way, our own day. But be rest assured, my good students, we are, in truth, facing it. And each and every thought that your mind entertains, each and every desire that rises within it, and each and every decision that you entertain, if you surrender, you may be rest assured, you are on the path of Light, guided by the divine hand of reason, and wisdom, which lives in the faculty of patience, will be your eternal handmaiden.

There are only two paths in all of life: the path of the Divine Spirit and the path of the created mind. All of the realms through which your soul is passing—and has yet many to pass through—are created by mental substance. They are heavenly or its opposite. And there is no ending to that which is the true you, for there was no beginning.

So the thoughts that you have garnered up unto yourselves are not, in truth, the real you. In time, they all shall go, as you, by divine law, are moving back home to return to your true source, that, in truth, is as distant from you as your willingness to surrender to that which sustains you.

It is true that there is an inner knowing within the soul, recorded as a drive, an urge, by the mind, to find its other so-called half. You will find it, my good students, when you give it, in truth, to God, for your minds cannot conceive it, let alone attain it.

May you in your efforts rise your soul ever upward each moment of each and every day. For all of the things in mind you try to hold will battle within you and leave you in time. There is nothing in all the universes that can be called your own, for that which calls for possession is possession, known as creation or mental substance. The desires within your consciousness are beyond the numbers of hair upon your head, for that is the divine expression.

And so, my students, waste not and want not is a demonstration of enjoyment. Waste not your energy with that which reaps such poor harvest. Use a bit of common sense and enjoy what is rightfully yours to enjoy. Accept the true source from whence it cometh. Do not permit yourselves to dictate its length of stay. Let it enter your consciousness joyously and freely that it may leave it as it came. You do not think about your breathing until you have created an obstruction to it, for you have accepted breathing as your divine right. When you accept joy, peace, and happiness, the fullness of life, the totality of all, the limitless supply, as you have accepted your breathing, you will then be the demonstration and the light of God's care for his children.

But when you permit the mind to question and to judge whether or not you should be breathing fast or slow and how many breaths you should be taking in a minute, then you have placed the superiority of mental substance, known as self-concern, you have placed that as an obstruction to infinite divine flow through your being.

My good students, take hold and do not permit your minds to continue to view the obstructions that you alone insist upon creating.

Be rest assured in life that you shall, in spite of the mind, surrender the mind to God. Is it not foolhardy, to say the least, to waste so much effort in postponement? Let us face the inevitable in this moment, that we may refrain from what our mind calls suffering. Why struggle up a mountain called success, when you can fly over it above and beyond it, feeling the freedom that is your right?

Somehow, someway the simple light is entering your consciousness.

The centuries, for me, have been many. And compassion, my ship of destiny, has brought me to your world and to many other worlds. For I know if you do not accept in your moments of now a surrender of the delusion of supremacy of your mind, then your payments are heavy, your payments are great. For I have walked those paths of judgment and I have lived my life in realms that my heart cries out you may be saved from.

Take a different view of what you call self-reliance. Take a different view of what you call individuality. Take a different view of what you think you are, that you may save yourselves from these created realms that are not pleasant to view, that are truly hells to live in. There is no escape, my children, from these mental realms without your surrender to God.

It was not in my evolution to have merited, in my years on your planet, someone to show me the way. Do not take lightly the simplicity of truth, for it is only that simplicity that will free your souls.

Make your decision and rise with the soul faculty of courage to carry it through. Your earthly realm offers nothing that can come close to the value of your peace of your eternal being. Each soul is moving at its own speed and in its own way. But each soul within the sound of my voice is touching the light of reason. I am only urging you and striving to encourage you to use what is entering your consciousness, to use it for your own good.

A life without meaning is hollow as brass. And the meaning of life is the return to that which, through delusion, you have separated yourselves from. Lift the veil, so thin, between you and that which is your true home. Lift the veil now, before it grows so thick and heavy that the centuries untold will pass before it can be passed through.

My job in life is a sharing with the souls who show the slightest interest, a sharing of my experiences along the river of consciousness called life. And I strive to share those experiences in many different ways that it will reach an untold number of souls who are listening.

And as you will recall, I had viewed this beautiful golden eagle who had flown away. And my heart was heavy and sad. And the days and the weeks passed me by, but I kept up my constant vigil. And one morning early at dawn that beautiful bird I viewed the second time on the horizon. And as I viewed it in the far distance, I began to pray that I may be, somehow, humble in my spirit and soul that that bird would come closer and somehow, possibly, I prayed, might become my friend. As you will recall, I had my little friend, the ant. But as you know, the mind, though the heart is grateful, the mind ever seeks more. And there I knelt in prayer, the best I knew how. And I looked up as that golden eagle descended and landed on the tower. I looked into the eyes of that beautiful bird. I saw the strength of character. I saw great determination and a total absence of fear.

Somehow that bird had come to me to show me the very things I needed to rise within myself.

Good night.

MAY 20, 1976

CONSCIOUSNESS CLASS 120

Greetings, students. Once again we come to speak with you on the experiences and paths of life itself.

Though you may feel you are small in number, you are never alone in your times of need, of trials and tribulations. For we have walked the path of these many levels of consciousness and because we have walked them, we do know what lies ahead. For some time now we have come to share our understanding with you and some of you have been aware that the other teachers from our school are working with those students on earth who demonstrate their value by their own efforts to be in attendance at class.

That, in life, that is difficult has great value once you have made decision of reason. And in keeping with decision of reason, I would like to continue on at this time with another bit of my personal history. The eagle had visited me again and time passed. And it began to visit with me on the tower each and every dawn. Such a joyous experience for me—that that beautiful bird would come to be with me for a few moments that I may begin my days with hope and courage and cheer, for somehow, to me, that eagle represented a great and broad horizon of joyous and new experiences, though I knew not what.

And as the many months came and went, one day at dawn, as the bird came close to the tower, I noticed a strange object in the bird's claws. It flew over the tower and dropped the object and perched itself along the side. I picked up this strange looking object. It seemed to be made of some type of stone. I examined it and found strange symbols upon it. And I studied, I studied, and I studied. I prayed and I studied again. And the months turned into years. What did those strange symbols mean? And late one afternoon, after many years of examining that stone object and the strange symbols upon it, somehow I felt a strange sensation well-up within me and I was propelled to start walking. And I walked until night fell and I fell asleep. At dawn my eyes opened to view my beautiful golden eagle. Yet, I had walked far from my tower. And the bird circled over me several times and I started to walk again. And somehow I knew I was to follow the eagle. Somehow I knew it was guiding me to what I knew not. Yet, I felt a great peace and goodness in the depths of my being.

You may feel free to ask your questions.

Thank you. Please tell us how to balance compassion with reason.

The question of balance between compassion and reason can only be experienced by an effort to control the emotions and the patterns of our own subconscious. For it is within all minds, an experience of what you call compassion. Compassion is a soul faculty expressing through a mental body and expresses through the magnetic field of the mental body. Reason, a soul expression, expresses through an electrical portion of the mental body. And the day will dawn when the soul faculties and how they express through the magnetic or the electrical field takes place.

Now, when you feel compassion, what you call compassion, for a soul and you do not, in that feeling, make the effort to be at peace to see the demonstration of natural law to see that the experience the person is having is an effect of laws they have established and if you do not make that effort, then you cannot find the cause, nor be the instrument through which the cure can be revealed. Therefore, what is known as soul compassion becomes the blindness of sympathy, which sends the soul deeper into the pity of self. Therefore, my good students, if you are having difficulty with balancing soul compassion with reason, which will transfigure the individual, then learn to pause before you speak. Learn to look more deeply beyond appearance that you may view the error of ignorance created by the mind of the person you are striving to be an instrument of the Divine to help.

To encourage is to lift the soul. And man, using reason and compassion, never leaves a soul worse than they have found them. For to do so is to be an instrument of darkness and not an instrument of light. Look beneath the seeming appearances of the transgressions and find the error of ignorance that drives and propels the mind to do such things that cause such suffering. Then, you will have the light of reason, the love of God, known as compassion.

Thank you. Would you please speak to us on the dangers of indiscriminate sittings? What are the physical dangers, as well as the spiritual?

When man makes the effort to discipline himself, to organize himself, to demonstrate the Law of Continuity, the Law of Respect, the Law of Consideration, then man does his meditation and daily sitting at a proper hour and in a proper way. The law clearly states that like attracts like and becomes the Law of Attachment. If man does not use consideration and respect, then man attracts unto himself entities from the so-called invisible realms that have no consideration and no respect. And then you souls on earth become the puppets of indiscriminate entities bound in their own licenses to do what they want to do, when they want to do it, and how they want to do it. They are not organized, because you are not organized. They have no respect, because you have no respect. They do what they want when they want, because you do what you want when you want.

And it is like adding an army of a thousand entities upon your own path upon your own struggle. It is indeed not only foolhardy and an error of ignorance not to organize oneself spiritually before opening the doors to other dimensions, but it is extremely detrimental. If you think you have a weakness that you are striving to overcome and you are indiscriminate and promiscuous with your spiritual efforts and you will not make the minor effort to organize at a set time each day, then be rest assured what you considered a little weakness will grow into a momentous one because you have opened the door to armies of souls from the lower levels of consciousness and your struggle only becomes greater.

It is of no value for man to pray for organization and discipline while he demonstrates its opposite. It is of no value for man to pray for illumination and freedom while he demonstrates bondage and darkness. Your guides and teachers and helpers cannot enter your consciousness on any level that is not in keeping with their own. So what does it behoove a man to sit in meditation to see forms from other dimensions unless they are beneficial? And they cannot be beneficial unless you are being beneficial to your own soul.

Thank you. Would you expand upon the statement, "O compassion of my soul gratitude has shown life's goal" [A saying from the Serenity Game]*?*

The soul compassion, the love of God, is experienced through the soul faculty of gratitude. When man demonstrates gratitude, applied appreciation, your goal in life is revealed unto you. The only reason that man, so many men, are not yet consciously aware of their goal in life is because the faculty of gratitude is not sufficiently open for the love of God, expressing through the faculty called compassion, to be experienced by the whole being. The obstruction is the mind and its limited acceptances and its multitude of rejections. Therefore this beautiful flow of gratitude cannot be experienced. And because it is not experienced in its fullness, man wanders and cannot find his true goal.

Thank you. Please give us your understanding of what is meant by, "The sins of the fathers are visited upon the third generation."

Yes, we have discussed that in one of our other classes some time ago. The errors of the parents are invested unto the third generation, the manifestation and completion of the law established. Now, each law established by the minds of men is governed by the Law of the Trinity. And so what happens is, a thought entertained by the minds of men goes out into the universe. That's one point of the triangle. It meets its kind—the second point of the triangle. And it returns unto the sender—the third point of the trinity. And so these errors, or laws established by people, are invested unto their children through the third generation, ever in keeping with the divine Law of the Trinity of truth.

Thank you. You have spoken of many centuries it has taken to bring the philosophy of the Living Light to our earth realm. Over that period did you evolve to other incarnations or forms or are spirit teachers guides still connected, so to speak, with our earth realm?

The question concerning dimensions of timelessness is indeed more than difficult to bring into a time-conscious dimension. As the soul evolves into the higher levels of consciousness, which is within the power of one at this time in your earth world, then you will understand that that which has been and that which is yet to be, in the delusion of time, is taking place in the eternal moment. In order that this truth may enter your time-consciousness dimension, we must use what you call reference, for without reference, you could not possibly comprehend. The evolution through these dimensions is not controlled or governed by time consciousness. Time consciousness is dependent upon the Law of Identity. Without the Law of Identity, there is no time consciousness. Without time consciousness, there is no reference. Without reference, there is no form and you experience the freedom of the divine formless Spirit in the eternal moment, which is ever your divine right to capture.

Thank you. Can you please explain the statement, "I am that I am"?

I am that I am because I am. "I am" is the right, the undeniable right of identity, which is the Law of Form. And so the formless free Spirit—Divine Intelligence, Neutrality, God—I am what I am because I am is the divine right of choice to identify.

Thank you. Will man's thought someday enable him to travel physically? That is to say, will man be able to send out a thought of going to a destination and will that thought transfer him instantly to that destination?

It already does on many planets and in many dimensions. Yes.

Thank you. How many levels of consciousness are on this plane?

The plane in which your soul is presently experiencing contains eighty-one levels of consciousness.

Thank you. Would you please give your understanding of how we may clearly see through the delusion of lack of money so that we may free ourselves of this self-imposed limitation?

Only through the processes of surrender. The benefit of surrender cannot be over estimated. The only difficulty that man has, in demonstrating the freedom and fullness of the divine principle of surrender, is the Law of Identity. What man identifies with, he believes he is. And when he believes he is what he has identified with, then he has entered the veil of delusion. To free man from the veil of delusion takes the power of concentration. When man in his efforts of his concentration frees himself into the peace that passeth all understanding, he has, in truth, surrendered. He is, therefore, free from the veil of delusion created by the Law of Identity and sustained by a belief.

When we, in our daily activities and thoughts, slowly, but surely, begin to realize that we are not the thought that is passing through our mind, that we are not the feeling, that we are not the many obstructions, that we are only the creator of those things in the veil of delusion called creation—now, man, in order that he may become aware and experience what you call creation and its opposing forces, must identify and believe. As long as you permit your mind to believe that you are the duality of expression, then the duality of expression will control your eternal soul. You are not the duality of expression. You are the neutrality of divinity. It is only through your identity, which creates your belief, that you are deluded to *believe* that you are such and such and so and so.

When man, viewing his created delusion, adds up his created assets, he dictates to the Divine that that *is* what *he* has. This is the authority that man gains by the Law of Identity. When man, surrendering this Law of Identity and separatism, when he surrenders that separatism, he becomes the whole. And when he becomes the whole, he no longer has the delusion of limitation. But man cannot become the whole until man surrenders. And surrender, to man, is total acceptance. And total acceptance is freeing the soul from the Law of Identity and the delusion of self.

Thank you. Would you please explain how to use, not abuse, God's natural laws in order to bring an adequate money supply into our lives, adequate in the sense of a balance between taking care of spiritual responsibilities, mental desires, and physical needs?

Because the questioner has dictated to the divine Principle what adequate is, then the questioner cannot experience the fullness of the Divine in respect to their material supply. For the delusion is this: what we call adequate one moment becomes inadequate the next moment. And so, my students, do you not now see the great value of surrender?

It is not your soul that makes surrender such a struggle and difficultly. It is the delusion of the mind and your identity with these opposing forces, called creation, that cause the difficulty that you experience. A person, being in the mind, ofttimes says,

"I surrender my need to God," and experiences what they call a God that doesn't listen. It is only through pure concentration, the path of peace, that the freedom, the direct effect of this control of the mind and its duality, that you can experience the fullness, the joy, the love, the prosperity, the goodness, the wholeness, which is your true being.

As man places mental conditions on his faith in the Divine, the mental conditions, not the Divine, become his god or gods. It is the false gods of creation that we are striving to free our eternal beings from. We must learn to choose more wisely our use of the Law of Identity.

It is the very nature of the mind to identify. And each thought you think establishes the Law of Identity. And as you identify with limitation, you become limitation. As you continue to speak forth your lack and your limit, you become the thing you speak. Use the Law of Identity in a constructive and beneficial way. You identify by the mental thought. You identify by the spoken word. Identify with that that you truly, truly want to be: whole, complete perfect, and free. Identify with the neutrality of the Divinity, then you will no longer experience separatism and so-called lack and limitation, for you will have demonstrated your divine right.

As long as you identify with a job that pays you a limited amount of money, you will be controlled by that very experience, for you, in consciousness, have identified with it. It's like a person that wants a promotion or they want to move to another job. And the mind says, "I'd like to have more money. I would like to have this. I would like to have that." They keep dreaming and thinking about it while their consciousness is identifying with the thing they want to grow out of.

We have given this teaching in so many different ways, my good students. We have often stated that, He who sees the obstruction never finds the way. So a man who views the obstruction is identifying and demonstrating the Law of Identity.

Therefore, because he identifies with the obstruction, he becomes the obstruction. Therefore, he then becomes his own worst enemy.

Let us be at peace within our being. Let us identify with the goodness of life. But to identify with the goodness of life does not mean permitting the mind to dictate what the goodness of life is, for that is an opposing law and will guarantee its own destruction, which, in turn, will balance the electromagnetic fields and free your soul in neutrality. That is not the goodness of life. The goodness of life is the God of life. And the God of life is the identity with the neutrality and the peace that is the God of Gods.

When you permit your minds to identify with what your minds have decided is good for you, you establish the Law of Delusion of creation. Therefore, a little good comes and a little of its opposite. And by the time it gets to you, you have usually moved on in consciousness and it no longer has value. Only through identifying with the wholeness, which is the true life itself, can man be freed from the delusions of a world of duality. Let the mountain be the beauty of your life and not the obstruction in your consciousness.

Man says, "How can I identify with the fullness of life, when I'm experiencing the lack and limitation of life?" Man cannot identify with the fullness of life as long as he permits his mind to entertain the delusion of life. My students, the Divine sustains any thought you think. Does it not behoove us, as instruments of the Divine, to entertain thoughts of the Divine? Then we become the free, clear and open channels. I assure you, for it only takes the unity of two minds or more, united in the divinity and the neutrality of God, to move the mountain of mountains. But we must first identify with that Divinity to express its wholeness, its goodness, and its fullness.

Be of good cheer, my students, for each and every painful growth step you are making is necessary that you may grab ahold of your eternal right. And identify by your thought, by your act, and by your deed, identify with the goodness and ye shall become it.

Good night.

MAY 27, 1976

CONSCIOUSNESS CLASS 121

Greetings, fellow students. This evening, we shall continue on with this journey of my personal history of so long ago.

As you recall from our other class, I was following the golden eagle each day as it appeared to me in the morning. And I walked and walked and walked. The many days turned into months and, then, to many years. And as I traveled on, I noticed a great, huge mountain before me and it did seem that towards that mountain is where we indeed were going. And so finally, one dawn, at the very break of dawn, I noticed before me at the foot of that great mountain an immense stone wall. And as I came closer to it, I perceived upon that wall many strange symbols. And soon it dawned in my consciousness that those symbols were the same symbols that were on that little piece of stone in my hand that the golden eagle had brought me some time ago. As I got closer and began to examine the wall, my good friend, the eagle, perched upon one of the symbols of the wall and insisted upon staying there.

It seemed to me that some intelligence was trying to direct me to that particular portion and symbol of the wall. And so I began to examine it very, very closely. And as I did so, I began to wonder what, if anything, could be behind that wall. And as I continued to wonder and to examine, I began to be a bit disturbed, for something inside of me knew somehow that I was to pass through that wall, but I couldn't seem to find a way. And night fell and I slept and awoke at dawn to examine and try again to find some way through the wall. The nights and the days, they came and they went.

And after nine months of effort, one day, as I was examining that particular symbol that the eagle continued to perch upon, I finally, *finally* surrendered my thoughts and my efforts and my desires to get through that wall. When that feeling overcame my entire being, an opening appeared before my very eyes, an opening through the wall. It was many, many years later that I learned, from my total and complete surrender, the door of objectivity to the realms of self-preservation had opened for me and my evolving soul.

You may ask your questions at this time.

Thank you. Please give us your understanding of how to be practical in what we view as our needs.

As the minds of men view and decide that they have need for anything, they place themselves under the authority and the control of the temporal mind and its limited experiences of yesterday. In so doing, great difficulty arises within their being, for the moment that they seek, with their minds, to be practical, practicality is dictated by priority value, which, in turn, is dictated by the various desires of the mind and their constant fluctuations. A person seeking, truly, to be practical learns the first law of practicality. And the first law of practicality is to rely upon that which brings a perfect balance, which is, in truth, light and reason. For to rely upon the mind to be practical is to defeat the divine plan of perfect balance for the nine bodies through which the soul consciousness is striving to express.

So man, in one of his bodies, cries out to be practical, because his so-called needs are crying for their expression. Only through a peace, brought about by a surrender of the thought, can man lift his soul to higher levels of consciousness and view life as it truly is. For to view life from the dual expression of mental substance is to become the victim of gain and loss, the delusion of mental substance. It is to become a victim of success and failure, a victim of all that disturbs and robs the true being of its beauty and its fullness of life itself. However, in your seeking to be practical, sooner or later, the mind will grant unto the seeker the necessary ingredient for the soul to free itself and experience true practicality.

Thank you. Would you please give your understanding of generosity and what it truly takes to unfold this faculty?

The question on generosity is one of the most important questions that can be asked by any evolving soul. Some time ago we stated, When you have given all, what then is left? When you become the instruments of givingness, then you become the givingness itself. To believe in the possibility of a divine, supreme Intelligence that is not the epitome of generosity is to be a very foolhardy person. To view a world of creation and not to observe the impartiality and the divine principle and fullness of generosity from an Infinite Intelligence is to be indeed blinded in delusion.

And so it is whoever strives to become generous, in truth, is striving to become selfless and to rise their consciousness to the Divinity of allness, of fullness, of goodness, which, in truth, is God. It is, in striving to rise to that level of consciousness where you may truly be free, it is difficult only for the minds of men who have relied upon the mind for its sustenance. And in so doing, in this self-reliance, a fear rises from the depths of our own being. And that fear dictates, "There is so much. And there will be no more unless I take corrective measures, which I choose not to take at this time." Therefore, the soul experiences a great struggle in rising through those lower frequencies, for it reveals unto us that our mind, not our soul, is still in control of our lives.

We aspire to go home in consciousness each moment of each day and night. The aspiration for that freedom and that fullness and completeness is a very strong, but subtle and delicate, feeling within our heart. And slowly, but surely, as the years turn into centuries, we will indeed rise through those lower frequencies of consciousness. And when we do, we will wonder why we have waited so very, very long.

Remember that fear is the force and the control of our mind over our eternal being. But faith is the light of eternal truth and will never fail the soul that rises to demonstrate it.

Thank you. Would you please explain the true meaning of poise, *as in the second soul faculty of faith, poise, and humility?*

Poise, the triune soul faculty, is the perfect balance between faith and humility. As man gains faith—and gains it in the sense that he permits his eternal being to express and to demonstrate a greater authority over his life than his temporal mind—as man, in that sense, gains more faith, the mind experiences what is called humiliation. But humiliation to the mind is the expression of the soul faculty of humility.

And so as man experiencing by his mental being humiliation upon humiliation, it is the degree expressed of faith that will keep him in balance and in the light of reason. That expression is known as poise. For as we awaken in evolution, we become very aware and alert to the low frequency expressions of the mental body. We know beyond a shadow of any doubt that the expressions from the lower consciousness are temporal, that they are not, in truth, the eternal soul. And as we, in our knowing of that great truth, demonstrate an equal balance of our faith in God as our minds experience the humiliation of the errors of ignorance, we have poise, reason, balance, and the freedom through our own forgiveness for those ignorant levels that, in truth, exist somewhere in ourselves.

Thank you. Could you share a guideline in discerning the difference between indirection and deception in our own expression?

Speaking on the question of indirection, the path that truth takes in expression—for truth is taught through indirection, demonstration, and example. When the minds of men take the time to decide how they will speak in the using of indirection that truth may flow freely, when the mind makes that decision, man is in deception, not the instrument for the path of peace and truth. Indirection does not require the conscious effort of the human mind in order that truth may be expressed. And when the human mind believes that it does, then you may be rest assured the deception, born in the realms of duality, has come forth.

Thank you. Why do we sometimes have precognitive experiences when it seems that we cannot do anything about them, the ones that are seemingly of illness or accidents?

The question on precognitive experiences is most important in how we view it. A person says that, "I have an awareness of an illness yet to befall an individual. I have an awareness of a seeming so-called accident to take place and, yet, I cannot speak to the person, nor do anything about it." To permit the mind to decide that it cannot do anything about anything is to bind the eternal being to the limitation of the mental sphere and planes of consciousness.

What can man, in truth, do about experiences that are to take place for another soul without directly, in the mental realms, speaking or trying to divert the experience when that door is not opened to him? My good students, we have often spoken on the universality of consciousness. For the truth is the truth. We are one mind. We are one consciousness. We are an inseparable part of one consciousness.

When we make the effort to surrender the multitude of identities that we entertain in mind stuff, our soul will rise above the limitations of form and we will experience our formless, free being. In so experiencing this true being, free, above and beyond all bondage, wants, needs, and desires, when we truly experience that level of consciousness known as the universal mind, we will look at all form, including our own, and we will know beyond any doubts that we are, in truth, the oneness and the wholeness of everything. At that moment and from that level of consciousness, we are free to choose and to identify with anything that exists in any dimension. And through this Law of Identity we may become the instruments of lifting a human soul to higher levels of consciousness. And in that way, we can be the free instruments for the goodness of God.

Thank you. Would you please elaborate on the reason why the lack of concern is the principle of effort?

The lack of concern is the principle of effort and guarantees success. The only thing that is capable of concern is the limited mind of man. Beyond the mind of men, there is no concern. Concern is born on the throne of fear, and the king of fear rules the mind of man. Faith exists in the heart and fear exists in the mind.

Whenever man permits himself to be concerned over anything, he becomes the instrument through which the Law of Duality is established. And because the Law of Duality is an opposing force, he seeks success to experience failure, because he is the Law of Concern.

True success does not come from the concern and effort of the human mind. When man permits himself to be the authority over his true being, then man, having concern, or better stated, fear of his possession, then man has attainment and man has payment. And the attainment is ever equal to the payment. And so man has varying degrees of success in some areas and equally varying degrees of failure in some areas, for man has established the law of man and man is concerned.

The minds of men are quick to say, "If I wasn't concerned and made the effort, then everything would fall apart in my universe." In the mental realms are the laws of effort and reward. In the spiritual realm is the divine law and principle of neutrality, known as joy. And so if man will permit, through the second soul faculty of faith, poise, and humility, if man will permit that little light of joy to enter into his consciousness, then man will do what he has to do and not be concerned what the world does with it. And man, in that moment, accepts the wisdom and the will of the Divine.

Thank you. We are taught that the circle of logic is balanced by credulity and suspicion. How can we best question without being overly suspicious or lacking in faith and acceptance?

The question on credulity, suspicion, and the circle of logic is in the realms that we have just discussed: the realms of mental substance. And so man bases his suspicions, a mental experience, upon the experiences that he has encountered in his short earth life. This circle of logic within the mental body ever strives to balance out his suspicion with his credulity and this system of logic is controlled by what is called the self-preservation level of consciousness.

The mind, in order that it may ever strive to keep its own stability, requires a certain degree of energy to pass through it at all given moments. Whenever the mind does not experience sufficient energy flowing through it, it begins to lose its so-called balance or stability. The only time that the mind does not have sufficient energy passing through is when the mind becomes grounded by self-interest, self-concern, and self-pity. When that takes place, the human mind goes to work to once again achieve the necessary energy balance for its own preservation and its own stability. These are the experiences in life that you encounter with people who will do anything, it seems, and everything, it seems, to receive the necessary energy required by their mind and emotional body for its own preservation.

As we've stated long ago, the only path to spiritual illumination is through selfless service. When we permit our minds to dictate what is selfless service, then selfless service, for us, does not exist. It is not only therapeutic, but it is for our own preservation and good health that we redirect our thoughts, that we become instruments through which sufficient energy is permitted to flow through our mental-emotional bodies. And through selfless service, we become those free channels and instruments in order that a balance may once again be attained for our own good mental and physical health.

If we made the effort to become more aware of our thoughts, we would find that we are spending 97 percent of the energy on personal, self-related thoughts and self-interest and self-concern. And because our minds have run wild, so to speak, with that, we find that things don't go too well in our universe. My good students, it is for our own good that we become the instruments to free ourselves from ourselves.

Good night.

JUNE 3, 1976

CONSCIOUSNESS CLASS 122

Greetings, students. This evening we shall continue on with our journey of long, long ago.

As you recall from our last meeting, I was standing before this great wall and an opening had finally appeared in the wall and I looked through that opening. And I began to wonder and then I moved through that wall. As I did so, my eyes viewed so many multitudes of forms all around and about me. I could not help but experience feelings of fear and disturbance, for many of those forms that I was now viewing, to me, seemed to be hideous and grotesque. However, they did not appear to have life or movement of any kind. I walked along through that strange and mysterious realm, viewing the millions upon millions of forms, for, in truth, their numbers were so many.

And as I walked along I saw to my left a form that appeared to me to be quite beautiful. And as time passed, more and more beautiful forms appeared amongst the grotesque. I wondered what strange realm I could have entered. And as I continued to wonder, a voice rose from the seeming nothingness and spoke to me and said, "You have entered the realms of self-preservation. You have been enabled to enter them because you have surrendered them. And, in so doing, you have the view of objectivity, for you are no longer a part of them as long as you remember to separate your eternal being from all these things your mind, in its evolution, has created. But should you forget and once again believe that they are a part of you, then a part of them you shall once again become."

I continued to view these many forms and wondered, "How could I have possibly created such diverse forms in my mind?" And as I continued to wonder and to ponder and to think, I noticed a movement around and about me. Fear rose from the depths of my being. A hand moved out to clutch my throat. And in that instant I knew I had lost my own salvation. For a moment I had forgotten and became concerned.

You may ask your questions at this time.

Thank you. This philosophy provides much food for thought, lending a seriousness to all acts and deeds. How can this seriousness best be balanced with humor, the salvation of the soul?

In acceptance within the consciousness that all things, in truth, are serving the purpose for which they have been designed. In viewing life from a level of consciousness that sees the basic good in the depths of all expression, man then may enjoy life for what life truly has to offer. It is in making a constant effort to entertain the beauty that is the divinity of one's true being—the loss of that beauty is when we give that divinity to so-called creation. And the giving of that divinity to so-called creation takes place when man does not make the constant effort to entertain thoughts of peace, to put the brakes on, so to speak, to the constant creating processes of mind substance.

Thank you. We are taught never to leave a soul worse off than when we found him and irritation wakes the soul. Can this irritation sometimes have the opposite effect and leave the irritated soul worse off than we have found him?

In reference to the teachings of never to leave a soul worse than you found them, the awakening within one's own being, known as discernment, is absolutely necessary to perceive the difference between the mind and the eternal soul. If, in your efforts to be an instrument of peace and light, you are called forth to help another soul to help itself, you must, in discernment, become aware of your motivation. You must become aware of whether or not you are moving from a level of consciousness known as judgment or whether or not you are moving from a level of consciousness known as unity.

This awareness comes from within your being: a feeling rises and that feeling you may perceive as a hurt within your own being, for, in truth, be ye on a soul level of consciousness, you will feel as your own the suffering of another. If that feeling and perception is not with you at the moment of your so-called decision, then you are moving from mental levels of consciousness and are moving in judgment. And in moving in those mental levels of consciousness, there are dangerous waters before you, as an evolving soul. For you lose the divine principle, known as unity, and you move in separation and judgment. Consequently, the final result is leaving a soul worse than you have found them.

To leave a soul better than you have found them does not mean that the vehicle through which the soul is expressing is necessarily happier than you found it. But it does mean that the soul is at peace, that principle, once again, has been reestablished in their consciousness, that they know beyond a shadow of any doubt that their experience was indeed an effect of their own transgressions. They are then stronger to lift up their own soul when a similar experience, they encounter.

And so, my good students, let us move in unity, in the universality of consciousness, for what affects one soul, in truth, is affecting all souls. And when our consideration is limited to certain areas in consciousness, we are not only hurting ourselves, but we are hurting others and, in so doing, we suffer greatly our own transgressions.

Let us not speak from levels of judgment. But let us not be deceived by mental substance. Let us look at life as life truly is: the way we make it and the way we alone take it.

Souls who have evolved in consciousness to step upon the path of spiritual freedom, in truth, are well aware of the need of change in the vehicles through which their eternal soul is expressing. And so it is they are aware of the need for change within themselves. When they enter into certain schools of spiritual thought and consideration, unless they accept wholly and completely the divine eternal truth—that man alone is responsible for his acts and activities, that all experience, in truth, is taking place within the consciousness, that everything, in truth, is inside—unless that truth is fully accepted, the vehicle through which the eternal soul is expressing demands and dictates that changes be made outside. But the soul knows. The changes necessary to be made are inside. And when those changes are made inside, they will view a different world outside.

And so, my good students, remember, change is the eternal Law of Progression, but it is a change inside. Man must learn to direct his attention inside for change, that he may free himself from the delusion that changes must be made outside by other people and places.

Thank you. Would you please further explain the teaching that divine desire is expression?

Yes, indeed, my students, divine expression is known as desire. Without desire, there is no expression in form. And because expression does not exist without form, when of no desire, there is no form. Therefore it is the very nature of form to desire. When man in consciousness, through total consideration, through total acceptance, enters divine will and divine love, then his soul, on that level of consciousness known as the universal being, is freed, for he is then formless and free—freed from all desire. In that instant, truth is separated from creation. That is known as being in the world and not a part of the world. However, those moments of consciousness are fleeting moments. But they are indeed most valuable moments, for it is in those fleeting moments of truth that man knows it's all worthwhile.

Without desire, there's no expression. But in the desire, man forgets that desire is an instrument, a vehicle, through which the Divinity is expressing itself. And because man forgets that desire is a vehicle through which Infinite Intelligence expresses, man becomes the desire and denies the Divinity. And because man becomes the desire, forgetting its true sustenance and source, man falls into the so-called pits and dungeons of created substance.

It is our view of the divine expression that we must make effort to educate. It is not the divine expression that needs change, for the divine expression—its principle—is changeless. We forget that which sustains us. And in our forgetting, we pay the price, known as refinement—that which man calls suffering—that we may not eternally descend into darkness.

And so the climb is never, in truth, higher than the fall, for the eternal soul is still expressing through a created vehicle. And as long as the soul expresses, it must face and experience the duality of creation. When man, through total acceptance, rises to that level of consciousness where peace passeth all understanding—that is man's heaven, for that is where reason reigns supreme.

Thank you. How can we balance pride in what God has given us with gratitude for what he has given us?

As you all know as students, pride is a function that, in truth, denies the true eternal Source. We have never taught that man should strive to annihilate the functions. And therefore, in keeping with our philosophy, we do not teach that man should strive to annihilate pride.

Gratitude is a soul faculty through which there is an ever-increasing abundant flow of all good into man's universe.

Whenever man permits himself to make statements of spoken word and thought that he is limited and lacks so many things, in that spoken word man denies the divine right and fullness of God. For what man, in truth, is saying, what he, in truth, is dictating in his consciousness is that he, his mind, is greater and more reliable than the divine Infinite Intelligence, known as God.

So, my good students, whenever we say, "I must do this and I must do that in order that I may have this and I may have that," we are rising to the epitome of pride, dictating and declaring that our minds, a created substance, is greater than the Divine. And because we are rising in the function of pride by such a declaration, we close the door of the soul faculty of gratitude through which all good may flow through our universe. For what we have done, in truth, is declare and dictate to God our total reliance upon mental substance, which limits the free flow of goodness in our life.

And so it is that man suffers the consequences and swims in the sea of deception and delusion, known as lack and limitation, and further deceives his own eternal soul by another deception when he says, "Those things never bother me."

Let us look at life, my friends, and be free through the soul faculty of gratitude. And when we face our daily activities, let us recognize and accept the fullness of God. That acceptance comes through a surrender of our function called pride. But without that surrender, we continue on in our own delusions in our own deceptions in our own lack and limitation and our life becomes the demonstration of our own fear, the demonstration of our own reliance upon our own limited mind.

And so, my good students, man constantly battles with his own being, with his own thoughts, with his own reliance. Man constantly dictates what is right and what is wrong, what is good and what is bad, and deprives himself, from those constant contradictions, of the peace and joy and beauty—the true purpose of the soul's expression.

Thank you. Can desire ever originate from the soul?

Desire is the divine expression. And the divine expression flows through the soul. Flowing through the soul, it's called "aspiration." As it enters into the vehicles and functions, it's called "desire."

Thank you. Why is it advisable for a person to meditate each day and what are the benefits of meditation?

The benefits of meditation have been discussed many, many times. Without discipline, there is no control of the wanderings of the mind and its multitude of thoughts, which, in turn, create so many forms. The true benefit of meditation, we speak forth once again: to rise the soul consciousness to realms supernal of peace and beauty while still expressing through the forms of creation.

As the soul enters these realms supernal in the here and the now, there is a great peace that enters and transforms the vehicles through which the soul is expressing. The effects of this transformation are known as perfect peace and perfect harmony and perfect health. A disturbed soul is disturbed by the vehicles of form through which it is expressing. The disturbance is a revelation, revealing to all people that the vehicle through which the soul is expressing has become the superior authority over the eternal soul that the vehicles, the mind and the body, have become the king rulers and there is no peace or joy left at that time.

Thank you. Please expand the meaning of faculties and functions.

In reference to the expansion of the meaning of faculties and functions, I do feel that it has been well covered in many, many, many classes that have already been given. Functions are the expression of the vehicles through which the soul is expressing through form. The faculties are the expression of the eternal soul. The functions rely upon created substance for their sustenance. The faculties rely upon the divine eternal being for their sustenance. Faculties have total consideration. Functions have total consideration for themselves. The expression of a soul faculty is from a universality of consciousness. The expression of a sense function is from individualized self-consciousness.

Thank you. Please expand on the meaning of the power in the spoken word.

The power of the spoken word: when the soul, united with all the forms through which it is expressing, united in perfect harmony, when that divine principle freely flows, man speaks the word. His heart, the vehicle through which that eternal soul is expressing, is in the word. And being in the word, the word is the law. And that law is infallible, for that is the spoken word, direct from the infinite Source itself. And so man should make greater effort to unite his being before he speaks the word, for the word is the law and the law never, ever faileth.

Let us remember, my good students, that the Divinity expresses through all forms. Let us have our faith directed to that which is infallible. And the only thing that is infallible is the divine law. Let us accept the infallibility of the divine law and, in accepting that infallibility, let us become the living being that we may be the true instruments of goodness, which is godness in the worlds.

Thank you. Would you please tell us something about sex and sexual relationships?

In reference to that question, man has placed his mind in that expression to such an extent that he truly believes that he is the sole owner and expression. And because the minds of men have taken it for their own, they have paid the price of prices for it. Instead of viewing it as an expression of the Divinity, which, in truth, it is, they have become it. And because they have become it, they have established the mental law. And that mental law dictates: that which man thinks he possesses, he guarantees to lose. For that is the payment to all men who entertain the delusion that they own or possess. Instead of being free instruments of the divine expression, they have deluded themselves and therefore they pay the price. And the price of that we think we possess is its own loss.

Let us direct our thought and our attention and our energy to the impartiality of God. Let us not rise in such bloated nothingness that we are the kings of the world. Let us view all creation. Let us look at the animals and let us look at the plants. They are not so interested, nor concerned over a simple expression. Let us take some simple examples from the rest of God's kingdom. Then we will not have such troubled thought over a simple, natural expression.

Thank you. What are the reasons you feel Serenity has a church or rather is a church?

The question is a most interesting question. We had requested, some time ago, that a center be opened in your world that our school on this side of life, and the centuries that it has spent already in bringing about a philosophy, known as the Living Light philosophy, may be brought into your world that it may reach as many souls who were seeking it as possible.

In your world, you have many organizations. And in bringing forth this philosophy to your world, we are working through an organization that you call a church. You could call it many things.

But what is truly important is that this simple truth be shared with those who are seeking it. Without an organization, you, as students, would not be blessed with the golden opportunity of growing through your various levels of consciousness by being exposed to other students who are growing through their various levels of consciousness and at the same time receiving the demonstrable truth: that everyone has the same levels of consciousness. If they still believe they do not have the same levels of consciousness, it simply reveals they, for themselves, have not found that level in themselves, for they have not yet demonstrated total consideration of themselves.

It would have been perhaps easier, for some, for us to bring this philosophy through our channel without an organization, such as a church and school that you have. We know, and have always known, for our own channel, it would have been much easier and certainly more appreciated by our channel not to have an organization to contend with, so to speak. However, the fullness of the demonstration of the philosophy would have been denied him. For it is in experiencing these many levels of consciousness with students in a group that our channel becomes more receptive to more teachings and grows, through the process of duty, gratitude, and tolerance; that our channel may not lose sight of the divine principle and true purpose of the philosophy; that you, as individualized students, may look more deeply into yourselves by facing the mirror of yourselves, known as your own co-students. And therefore the true purpose, the fullness thereof, is being demonstrated in the Serenity school each moment of each hour of each day.

There are few, and only few, whose souls have risen to levels of consciousness that they will be in this humble school in the many years yet to come. But those who have come to the well thirsty and to drink will have benefited and have gone on their way to rise in consciousness in another time, in another day, to once again start their journey all over again.

That, my friends, that disturbs us reveals the attachment that we have to our own opinions, decisions, and judgments. And so you see the true beauty of the Serenity school and church, for in that school that you are presently in, is the golden opportunity to unfold your soul faculties and to gain, as you never have gained before, a greater understanding of the true purpose of life itself. For what you cannot tolerate in another is yet to be educated within yourself. And when everything is wrong outside, it is simply directing you, your eternal being, to accepting the divine truth that everything is wrong inside. And as the changes are made inside your own being, all of harmony, beauty, and love will start to manifest around, about you and through you.

Although there are many schools on your earth realm, there are few schools that take the personal interest and make the personal effort day after day after day to help you in your evolving through the levels of consciousness that have bound you to creation. There are few schools, my children, in your world that make such effort. And though you think the price is high, it is high only to the very things that are your obstructions: the things that stand in the path of your own joy.

And so the Serenity school has come to your world. It will remain in your world long after I have moved on to other areas in the universe. But that which has been given shall remain on your earth and it shall grow as the seeds, this day, are planted. And the harvest shall be reaped in the realm in which it can be reaped: it's known as the realms of the Divine Spirit.

So be of good cheer for those early years of your schooling, for they are the years that are building the foundation upon which you may firmly stand in principle, that you may free your being and rely on that which will never fail you, that you may be freed from the fears that exist in your own mind. Then, my children, the day shall dawn when you shall stand in the universe and, though you think you may be alone, you will look towards heaven's heights and see the angels of infinite love who have guided your little souls to this day, for they are working for that which never faileth. And because they are instruments of that Light, the light inside of you, though flickering like a small and delicate candle, shall not fail you, for the gentle breezes of heaven are ever with you. And as you descend into the dungeons of your own mental bondage, that which is, is ever with you. For each and every student within the Serenity school is never alone, for our teachers are ever amongst you to help you, to guide you, to inspire you, to encourage you when you sink to the depths of self-pity.

Our doors of principle are never closed, for, my good students, they have never opened, for they do not, in truth, exist. Principle is principle. And those souls who make the slightest effort, the slightest effort to flow in that stream of consciousness known as Divine Principle shall ever be in that stream. And though there are many experiences in your world of creation, those experiences that cause your distress, your disturbance and trauma are not greater than the humble light of principle.

Be grateful for that your souls have earned. And in that ounce of gratitude, the fullness of your life shall manifest itself. Although things are not often the way you would like them to be, they are the way that is right for you in your present moments of growth. They are ever in keeping with the principle and that principle, my good students, will never fail you in this school or any school once you truly have it.

Good night.

JUNE 10, 1976

CONSCIOUSNESS CLASS 123

Greetings, students.

In the many years of my wanderings through creation, I had finally come to accept that life indeed was the way I had chosen to make it. But that acceptance and awareness did not dawn within my consciousness until after many, many centuries of experience in a world of mental bondage. And so in keeping with those experiences of so very long ago, you will recall at our last meeting, I was wandering through the realm of self-preservation.

I had paused to wonder in my curiosity at the many forms and, having been attracted to one of those lifeless forms of beauty amongst so much and so many forms that distressed me, a hand had moved and clutched my throat. In that moment, a fear overcame my entire being. Yet, with the fear rose a small flickering light of what I know now to be reason. And that little flickering light spoke softly within my consciousness and it said, "My son, move in your consciousness to faith, poise, and humility, and you shall be free." And in that moment, I surrendered that great fear. The hand that was clutching my throat disappeared before my very view and returned to the hideous form from whence it had come.

In this great land of self-preservation, I got to view the many objects and forms which were the direct effect of my own emotions in years long, long past. But they lived on because of my own errors of ignorance: I had continued to feed them energy.

And so it is, as I passed on through that realm, mile after mile after mile, I asked in all humbleness, "How could all of this, which, in truth, was my family, how could they be transformed—all of those hideous forms—into forms of beauty, into joy, into happiness and move with a purpose that would do good, not only to myself, but to the world?" And out of the seeming nowhere the voice spoke to me and said, "In the ways that you have entered through the wall, on that path and on that path alone can your family be transformed and your soul rise to heavenly heights."

And I asked the question, "I surrendered the thought and the desire to pass through the wall and the wall opened. But how can I surrender that which is a part of me—forms created from long, long ago? How can I move backwards in time to free them, to transform them, that I may not forever live with that which is so unpleasant to me?" And the voice spoke again and said, "Move through the soul faculties." And I said, "I do not know what you mean." For at that time in my evolution, I did not know what the voice meant. I had been told within to have faith, poise, and humility, in a moment of great fear, but I did not then know that that was a soul faculty. And so I asked the question and received a still, a stillness that not only perplexed me, but disturbed me. For in that stillness and a lack of response to my pleading, I felt a loneliness overcome me. And as that feeling strengthened within my mind, hundreds, yea, thousands of forms began to move towards me. And as they moved, the greatest fear I had ever experienced overcame me.

You may ask your questions at this time.

Thank you. What, in truth, is teasing? Does teasing someone else deprive that person of energy when they are seriously trying to accomplish a task and another person teases them?

The question on teasing, though seemingly an innocent word, is dependent upon the motivation of the individual who, in truth, is tempting another. For to tease is to tempt and those who tempt are as guilty as the ones who are tempted. Teasing and tempting is a childish game of the mind. The mind feels a slight degree of self-importance and temporary power over another soul.

I know in your world that many times a person says, "Well, I didn't mean to get them angry. I was just teasing. I didn't mean to upset them. I was only teasing them." The truth of the matter is, the person who is doing the teasing already knows what will upset the person and so they do it that they may have a false and temporary power and control over another soul. The sadness perhaps, but the beauty of the law, the impartial divine law, is that those who make the effort to tempt and tease others become the victims, in time, of what they call circumstances. And when the teaser becomes the victim, you see a different side of the coin. And they're not so happy and they blame others for their condition, for they have not yet evolved, their souls, from those low frequency vibrations and their need is yet so great.

Thank you. How may one help another who is locked into desire for revenge?

The only thing that casts light upon the level of consciousness known as vengeance is the light of reason and understanding of the natural, divine laws of life. When man truly understands the great doors of suffering and distress that he, in truth, is opening the moment he entertains thoughts of vengeance, revenge, and getting even, once that light enters into his consciousness, he will not seek vengeance, for he will know beyond a shadow of any doubt that to seek vengeance is to have that very Law of Vengeance befall you.

And so it is, in truth, that man always gets what he really wants. And when we view life with that humble light of truth, we can look at our experiences, though ofttimes unpleasant and distasteful, and we can say, "Thank you, God, for the revelation of truth that I am viewing. For I am, in truth, viewing an impartial law, an infallible law. And those so-called chickens that I have sent out into the universe to play their little games have all come home now to roost. Let me bow in humbleness, O Divine Spirit, that I may face myself the way I really am, knowing, in truth, that I can become something much better, much greater, for that is the potential that is truly mine."

Thank you. Would you please tell us something about minerals and their effect upon the body and the role of the alchemist?

The question on minerals and the role of the alchemist is a question that bears much thought and much consideration, for your world looks at alchemy as a pseudoscience filled with magic, occultism, and strange and mysterious workings. When, in truth, the science of alchemy is a clean, pure, and simple science that strives to understand the laws that govern formation. And in that understanding, those scientists who have perfected themselves are able to make changes in the chemical formations of minerals, of plants, of all types of forms. Because the science is such a simple science, the minds of men have shrouded it over with mystery, with things supernatural, and that is a sadness for the good and the progression of the human soul.

Many, many times in our classes we have stated how attitudes, thoughts, cause chemical reactions and chemical changes within the physical body. If it is true—and truth is taught through indirection, demonstration, and example—that the attitude, which is the effect of thoughts, causes a physical, chemical change in the human body, then it follows, and is demonstrably true, that the thought and attitude of any person directed to any individual and especially to the so-called lower kingdoms can, and does, cause a chemical change within their bodies.

And so it is that the alchemists who are true alchemists are able, by their attitude of mind, by the control of their own thoughts, they are able to change the shape and the sizes of various forms. They are able to heal, for they lift their soul consciousness to a level known as divine neutrality. There, the transformation takes place. So let us give more thought, let us give more consideration to our thoughts, for we are, in truth, my students, the effect not only of our thoughts, but we are the effect of those with whom we come into rapport and, therefore, become the effect of their thoughts.

And so it is that man, being the effect of his thoughts, has within his power the divine right of making life, his life, the way he chooses. Man is already making life, his life, the way he chooses, but he is ignorant and blind to his own choices. It is when we make the effort that we see the living demonstration of the law—and how beautiful and how impartial the law truly is.

It is the nature of the mind to ever strive to be what people want us to be. This is the very nature of the human mind. If you, being in rapport with anyone, tell the person that you are in rapport with that they're a terrible person, that they are weak, that they will never learn, you project an image to that individual. And because they are in rapport with you, their subconscious goes to work to be a failure, because that is the image that you have directed to them. You see, good students, we are, in truth, our brother's keeper. We are our brother's keeper, you see, because we are creators. We create images in our consciousness and those images are broadcast out into the universes. It is within our power to be the constructor of good in the universe or the destroyer. And we are doing this each and every moment, whether we are consciously awake or asleep.

The soul, we have often spoken, responds to encouragement. Let us take on the responsibility that is truly ours: it's called personal responsibility. Let us believe in the goodness and, in so believing, we shall become it. Let us unite, for, in truth, we are inseparable, for we are the effects of one divine Intelligence. And being the effect of one divine Intelligence, we are personally responsible to that one divine Intelligence. Let us not only recognize, but let us accept, the demonstrable truth that the minds of men, including our own, have many experiences, that those experiences are recorded in our memory. They are not the true "I." They are only the effects of yesterday. Let us, when we communicate with the rest of God's children, be they two- or four-legged or the plant or mineral kingdom, let us communicate soul to soul, for, in so doing, we will become the instruments of the divine, evolutionary plan.

We have entered Earth to be those instruments of the evolution of goodness in the world. The Earth planet has been viewed by many intelligences for many, many, many untold centuries. It stands, in evolution, at a crossroad, the Earth planet. And it, the planet, is affected by the thoughts of man. And everything on your planet is affected by the thoughts of man. In turn, the other planets in the solar system and the solar systems beyond your solar system are, in turn, affected. It's like an apple that has rotted in a bushel of good ones. Either the rotten apple is removed or the entire bushel has to be destroyed.

And so in facing personal responsibility in life, you must consider your responsibility for every thought you entertain, for it goes out into the universe and it lowers the vibratory frequencies which are necessary—these frequencies—for balance in nature. You become the instruments of darkness by the thoughts you entertain. You lower the frequencies. Or you become the instruments of light from your own soul and you raise those vibratory frequencies.

Each soul faces its own creations. Each soul lives with them until it makes the effort to raise them to higher levels of consciousness.

All of nature is responding, and has been responding, to the polluted thoughts from the minds of men. And the response that we have viewed, especially in these last five centuries, has not been the most beautiful.

As man, in his physical suit, journeys farther out into so-called space, he will encounter certain intelligences. Those intelligences, I assure you, are of a much higher evolved consciousness than man's present state of evolution. You may be rest assured that man who continues to pollute his own planet, known as Earth, shall not be permitted to directly pollute the solar system and the rest of God's universes.

We must come to that step in evolution where we are willing to separate truth from creation, where we are willing to let go of recorded experiences, known as tapes in our own mind. For each moment that we spend in entertaining experiences of yesteryear deprives us from the duty and the job that we came to earth to do. Now, that effort, that we have lacked in, will have to be made up. And it is not something that we can decide how long we'll wait before we make it up.

The separation of the true being from the entangled tapes of the mind and experiences of yesterday must take place in the moment of the now. And in so doing, you will rise to the peace that you have yearned for.

I know that I have spoken thousands upon thousands of words to my classes concerning the human mind. But, you see, my good students, it was the human mind—my mind—that caused me to spend so many, many centuries in distressing, to say the least, realms of consciousness. I know that it is my compassion that dictates to me to continue on. I also know that it is a light, a little light perhaps of reason, that requests the lessons be presented in so many different ways. If I believed for one moment that there would be a lasting and beneficial effort on your part to make greater effort to separate truth from creation, to make greater effort to control, through education, these taped experiences that have you victimized with a chain around your necks, if I thought or believed for one moment that my physical appearance to your physical world would make the necessary changes in your consciousness, I would have requested that long, long ago. But I have viewed much such phenomena in my life's experiences and I have found it to be such a temporary and passing experience, without a lasting or enduring value to the human mind.

And so I have chosen, by laws established, to bring to you, to your world, a philosophy that has proven itself to untold millions of souls in many realms of consciousness. It is this very philosophy that has taught that repetition is the Law of Change.

My good students, it is repetition of experience that has caused tapes in your mind to control you. And it is only through repetition of the divine truth that you will be freed from those chains of bondage. It is through this very philosophy that you have learned that irritation wakes the soul. And I can assure you, my good students, that sufficient repetition does, in time, guarantee irritation, which does, in time, permit the soul to rise. For the mind, when sufficiently irritated, it tries to run away. It tries to block out and, in so doing, it becomes so immersed in the contradictions existing within its own mind that it surrenders for the sake of preservation. And that is the process of the soul's rising.

So when you feel irritated and when you feel bored and when you feel all of these things, stop in that moment. For in that moment, your chances of the mind's surrender is excellent. And when you find the need to yawn and when you find the need to run away and when you find the need to do all those things, stop. For, my good students, in that moment you stand at the gates of victory—victory for your eternal being.

Over and over and over again, but the light is dawning, slowly but surely. And for that, we are, in our school, indeed grateful. Although your minds may think the change is microscopic, so to speak, the principle has been established. You do know the way. No longer can your minds say, "I didn't know." For now, my students, you do know. And in your knowing, deep in your being, changes have been taking place. And they continue to take place for you are indeed awakening. And each day you awaken just a bit more. Many times you try to run away. You're not running away from school. You are running away from yourself. But you won't be able to run away as often as you used to run away, for now you know why you do it. And knowing why you do things is a gaining of understanding. And that gaining of understanding is increasing each and every moment.

It does not mean that you do not continue to slip, so to speak. But you do not stumble or slip as often as you used to. And as the days turn into weeks and the weeks into months and the months into years, your stumbling will not be as frequent, nor will it be as hard. And you will pick yourself up, each time, a little quicker, a little more graciously. And each time a little more dignity will manifest itself in your being. A little more understanding, a little more consideration, a little more divine love will express itself.

And so we are indeed joyous and grateful for the progress that is, in truth, being made. But because some progress is being made does not mean it's time to take a vacation. For you know what it took to get where you are and you know you didn't get where you are by all those vacations you used to take.

Thank you. Good night.

JUNE 17, 1976

CONSCIOUSNESS CLASS 124

Greetings, students. We shall continue on with my wanderings in the realms of self-preservation.

As these many thousands of forms were snarling and clutching and attacking me and as this great fear of fears rose supreme in my mind and I, my humble body, was wrenched and torn and bitten by these many creatures, that wonderful, gentle voice of my guardian angel once again spoke to me.

And the voice said, "All that you are experiencing is necessary for your eternal soul and its evolution that you, your mind, may learn the greatest lesson of all: that attachment guarantees its own adversity and adversity guarantees its own attachment. And so these children, which are, in truth, the effects of your own attachments of yesteryear, are only trying in their way to survive and to preserve themselves. And if you, in your fear, continue to direct energy in adverse ways towards these forms, which are, in truth, your children, then they shall remain with you. If you, in your mind, pray without ceasing to let go of all mental thought, then you shall be freed from them. You entered the doors of self-preservation as you rose in consciousness to surrender. You will free yourself from this realm when you begin to rely on something that is above and beyond all thought of your mind. When you place your eternal being in that home of true reliance, then you shall be freed.

"For life in form is called the pendulum of time: it takes the soul from shore to shore. And so you must learn someday to accept the laws of life, to accept the nature of form. And in so in accepting, you shall use it and not abuse it. You will accept the sunshine as you accept the rain. You will accept the sadness as you accept the joy, for that acceptance is a recognition of the divine right of the Infinite Intelligence to express its just laws without the interference of the minds of men. And so as you, in your mind, let go, then that which sustains you, the true eternal Source, will bring the great peace and love and freedom that is your right."

I remained in those realms for many, many years after my angel had spoken to me, for to hear and to know does not guarantee the Law of Change. To know is only a simple part, a step to final and total acceptance. For as we, in our efforts to let go of that which we believe is ours, there is a part of ourselves that suffers. And that part of ourselves that suffers in letting go is the part of our mind that believes that we have.

And so out of those realms of self-preservation dawn the awareness of the divine truth of the five steps of creation. So in all of life the payment ever precedes the attainment. And though the centuries, to me, in those days were long and eternal in themselves, I would gladly in my heart go back in the illusion of time and relive those centuries, for what was gained in the living and experiences of those realms was the gaining of the truth, that has not only freed my soul, but is instrumental in freeing the souls of millions in so many realms of darkness.

And if you will honestly study those five principle steps of creation and you will honestly and sincerely study the diagram that was given to you in these classes several semesters ago that was drawn out and explained to you, you will not have to spend those centuries that I have spent in those realms. [The creative principle diagram is in Consciousness Class 29, which is in *The Living Light Dialogue, Volume 2* on page 177.] For you, my good children, have been given, in keeping with the law of your seeking, you have been given the light, the path, and the way.

It is not this philosophy, as difficult as your minds would like you to think—and when the mind thinks it is so difficult, be rest assured it is the level of consciousness striving to preserve itself that is convincing you of the struggle and the difficultly. For that is how self-preservation truly works. But those levels that are striving to preserve themselves are not you, your soul eternal. But they are the beliefs that you alone have created. They are the thoughts that you alone are entertaining. To rely in consciousness upon anything except the divine Intelligence is to bind oneself to the dual law and suffering of so-called creation.

You may ask your questions at this time.

Thank you. Why is it that a variety of diseases can affect the same organ of the body?

Because each organ of the body has the totality of consciousness within the organ. And the totality of consciousness is eighty-one levels of expression.

Thank you. Would you please describe the animal realms and the kind of training that takes place to help the animals evolve?

The animal realms are realms of compassionate discipline. For we have found, over these centuries, that it is so much easier to communicate with our four-legged friends than it is with our two-legged friends. And so in the compassionate discipline, where these animals are trained—and their training is through understanding—understanding the needs of their little minds and guiding them gently, but firmly, to face their responsibilities.

As man has personal responsibility, so does animal, plant, and mineral life. And it is the duty and the responsibility of those teachers in our realms that have earned the teaching of these four-legged friends to have the patience, the understanding, to share with them an awakening of their responsibility. There is no animal, nor plant, that is expressing that does not have a duty and a responsibility in its evolution. This is the simple message that we share with the animal kingdom and those little souls who have earned that sharing.

When our friends, the four-legged ones, graduate from our schools, most of them, willingly and joyously, go down to the lower realms, known as earth, to stand guardian as the souls pass over into our realms, to help those souls to follow those animals to the various schools and halls of learning that are available for all souls who are seeking something better. And we are so filled with gratitude at the demonstration of the soul faculty of loyalty that these four-legged friends demonstrate day after day, year after year, and century after century. For as these friends go down to these lower realms, they are tempted by the souls trapped in those lower realms not to do their spiritual duty and bring those souls passing over into the halls of learning. And those entities in the lower realms are well and fully aware of the so-called weaknesses of our animal friends. And so very often do those lower entities tempt our guides with food and various pleasures. But we can say, for the good of humanity, these four-legged friends have an expression of the soul faculty of loyalty that far exceeds the masses of earth men.

Thank you. Would you please explain the old saying, Fools rush in where angels fear to tread?

Yes, fools rush in where angels fear to tread. An angel, so to speak, represents the embodiment—an unobstructed flow of the divine love of God through the soul faculties. "Angel" means, to us, the totality of consideration. And so, being the totality of consideration, angels have considered where they may walk and serve the purpose of love without entrapment. For they, being the embodiment of service to God, have not the need, want, and desire of the human mind.

And so man walks in, guided and controlled by his need for superiority, by his need for so-called glory and power, man, controlled by those entities, walks into hell and becomes a part of hell. But angels know, when man is first, all is hell, and when God is first, all is well.

The revelation of the soul's evolution is demonstrated by the degree of self-control that is being expressed at any given moment and in any given circumstance. Man's tools, the human mind, are designed by the Infinite Intelligence—not created, but designed—to serve the purpose of the soul's evolution. When man, not using the tools wisely, becomes controlled by the tools, then man demonstrates, from his own lack of control over the tools, known as his human mind, his own grade of evolution.

Thank you. Would you please discuss the predicament of people who, because of their psychic experiences and lack of understanding of them and lack of control of them, have been labeled by society as mentally ill?

Society labels anything it does not understand and, not understanding, does not accept. If man relies upon society and controls his life according to the fluctuating desires of society, then man has earned that enslavement.

The most difficult thing for the human mind is to accept anything that does not already exist within the domain of the mind or is, at least, in rapport with the new experience through the Law of Association. And so it is that these various entities, being created by our minds, know our minds. And so we find ourselves in what we call a lack of control, which, more properly stated, would be the victim of our own circumstances. For what we are, in truth—until we make the effort to gain control—is the victim not only of our own uncontrollable desires, but the victim of all the other uncontrollable desires that are attracted to us in keeping with the law that like attracts like and becomes the Law of Attachment. This victimization, which is, in truth, within our own power to stop at any moment, moves our little soul in circles, so to speak, on the merry-go-round of ever decreasing in fulfillment of so-called desires.

Because these desires are no longer serving us, we are, in truth, serving them. And because we are, in truth, the victims serving them, we no longer have the fullness of the desire experience and expression, which reveals, in truth, to any man of common sense, that we have given up our own control and we have to do what those entities want us to do, when they want us to do it, and how they want us to do it.

Now, think, my children, if we have entered that sad state of affairs in the here and now—and the only thing that stands between us is the buffer of your physical body to view those multitude of forms and their demands—think, it is so much easier for you, children, while yet in the buffer of physical form, where you do not yet hear and do not yet see these creatures who have control of you. Think how much easier it is for you to declare and demand your right to freedom, which is the direct effect of self-control, of these entities that order you, like a little puppet, to do what they order you to do. They cause you blindness and your eyes no longer serve the purpose of awareness. They cause you deafness and your ears no longer serve the purpose of perception. They cause your tongue dumbness and your tongue no longer serves the purpose of truth. They cause you deception and your lips no longer serve the purpose of aspiration.

Think and think more deeply. You have the opportunity in the eternal moment, called now, to make your changes, yea, even more. For even the smallest change you make this moment will save you years hereafter.

Good night.

JUNE 24, 1976

CONSCIOUSNESS CLASS 125

Greetings, students.

In my many, many years in the realms of self-preservation and through the multitudes of experiences that I was having, there arose within my mind a strong and intense desire to be free from the many forms that were around and about me, that were clutching and crying for their needs and attention.

As this desire, ever strengthening, rose even higher in my consciousness, I began to experience a seemingly strange, yet distant, attitude of mind. I later learned that this experience was the effect of my gradual, but sure, ignoring of that which was around and about me. And that ignoring of the forms around me was the effect of this intense desire that I had, slowly, but surely, placed my thought upon.

In those realms of self-preservation, indeed I had gained much, for I had gained what those realms, in truth, have to offer all souls. For all souls must evolve through that level of consciousness. And those realms granted unto me the law that freed me: To be in creation and not a part of creation; to ever be with a thing and not a part of the thing. It also granted to me the power and demonstrable truth of the Law of Concentration.

Although, in my experiences in those realms, my mind cried and questioned and, in so doing, granted a further attachment to the experience, it surely, in the final analysis, freed me from them.

And so in those realms I also learned that freedom indeed was the direct effect of self-control. As this control of my mind came into a fullness and completion, I found myself leaving those realms. On through the many levels of darkness, I seemed to rise higher and higher, as if floating in space itself. And one day, I found myself sitting quietly and peacefully on a little mountaintop. And there, quiet, peaceful, and filled with an inner joy, a new horizon had opened for me and my angel spoke and said, "You have now qualified yourself to serve. And all that you have experienced has been necessary for you that you may serve the Light fully, wholly, and completely, that, as an instrument through which the divine Energy flows, the obstructions have been removed, for the obstruction is only the attachment to forms. And now that those attachments have been removed from you by your own efforts, you are now free to serve. And serve you shall."

You may ask your questions at this time.

Thank you. When a medium is in trance, what effect does movement of the sitters have on the physical condition of the medium?

The question, important to all seriously-minded students, must be answered in consideration of more than one vehicle of expression. We all know that no part of the body, the physical body, can move without directed energy through the mental body. Now, energy, flowing through the mental body, creates what is known in your world as thought forms. For it is thought that is the vehicle through which energy is expressed. And so each movement that is made by the physical body reveals to you a thought form. This thought form, though invisible to those who have yet to open their vision, is indeed visible to the workers from our world who, by directed energy, are able to speak with you in this way.

Each created thought form must be neutralized in order that we may continue to work and bring you this understanding in this way. The more energy that must be utilized by us to neutralize the thought forms created by the sitters, leaves, so to speak, less energy for us to give unto you these teachings.

For it is our responsibility not to permit the diminishing of the energy level to such a state that it is detrimental to our channel. Although that has happened on some occasions, we make great effort not to permit it to take place. And so the effects upon any medium serving as a channel in this way is extremely detrimental to the health of the channel if we continue to use the channel where there is a lack of energy for the sustenance and balance, which is health, for the channel.

If the neutralization of the thought forms created by the movement of the sitters did not take place—those thought forms have one great desire: the desire to express. And because they are a created form, the vehicle of energy, they are intelligent, for they have the intelligence of their creator. And, seeking to express, they bombard the channel and try to express through our channel, rather than hover in the atmosphere. For it is the very nature and the principle of the creation of the thought form to express. And this is one of the great misunderstandings in your world of communication. For it is easier for any human, becoming receptive to these other dimensions, to be the victim of thought form entities than to be the free and clear channel of the spirit. The reason that it is easier for a channel, a medium, to be the victim of thought forms is because it is more difficult and takes a great deal more dedication to rise above the mental levels of consciousness to serve the Light of eternal truth.

And so, my good students, because you have asked the question at last, you now bear even a greater responsibility: a responsibility that comes with awareness, a responsibility to the Light that you may do your part, through a greater effort of self-control, knowing the divine truth and knowing beyond a shadow of any doubt that your bodies cannot move without the vehicle of thought through which energy moves them.

Now, a person may think, "Well, I just moved my foot," or "I just moved my hand." But in order to move the hand, you must create a form. And you do not create a form of moving the hand. You create the forms related to the movement of hand from very early, early times. Do not disregard what is known as the primitive mind. Do not disregard that the mind, controlled by fear, creates forms accordingly. And those are the forms that you emit from your aura that go into the atmosphere and, like a great bombardment, descend upon any channel that is open and receptive to these other frequencies and wavelengths.

We've always taught that life is only the effect of our own attitude of mind. And so if your days are beautiful and heavenly, they are the effects of the angelic forms that have been created by your pure motive and selfless attitude of mind. Peace, and peace alone, is the power of God, of health, of wealth, of happiness. And when that effort of peace is made, over and over again, each moment, my students, not now and then—each moment you face your personal responsibility to be the instruments through which unadulterated, pure, divine Energy may flow through your consciousness, creating angelic forms of goodness, beauty, and joy to the world. That is the great responsibility that you all have earned in your evolution. And so you have come to the earth realm with a heavy, seeming, cross to bear. But you have also come to earth with a crown that waits to lift you to heavenly heights.

When you face, moment by moment, your personal responsibility as a creator—for that, my students, is what, in truth, you are. Constantly creating the good, the peace, the joy, and the happiness or destroying the goodness, which is the true home of your soul.

Thank you. Please give your understanding of graciousness.

Graciousness is the joy of dignity. And when the mind is free and clear, the character of the soul rises and you have a heart that's filled with joy and a soul that emanates the dignity, the true character of life eternal, freed from all self-concern.

Thank you. Please expand upon the deception of the mind when it says, "Those things never bother me." And please discuss the law one sets into motion when one flatly denies that one has a hang-up about money or another thing in particular.

To deny that we have this—or have not that—establishes the mental law and our denials become our destiny. It is through an error of ignorance that our minds choose not to face what we have judged is existing in another and is repulsive and intolerable to our minds. And because we have made the judgment and because we have found it repulsive and intolerable, reveals unto us that we have yet to open, in that respect, the first soul faculty of duty, gratitude, and tolerance. And so the law goes to work and it brings up from the depths of our own being the very level of consciousness that we have chosen, from our seat of judgment, to declare that it does not exist within us.

We must ask ourselves the question, when we say that we have no interest and no problems concerning what man calls money, we must ask ourselves what that means to ourselves. Does it mean that we do not entertain the thought or the interest of material supply? Or does it mean that we do not entertain the thought or the interest of material supply in the ways that we find others entertaining the interest and thought of supply? For it is not possible, my good students, to express in a material world without material interest to some degree. For if energy, which flows through the vehicle of thought, is not directed to some degree to a material world, a material body, you, your eternal soul, will not long exist in a material body.

We must take a new view in reference to material supply, for it seems that so many souls, expressing through these limited minds, have viewed spiritual sustenance as something to be enjoyed and entertained by the minds of men and that material sustenance is something that is to be viewed with a repulsive and intolerant attitude of mind. This is a separation and a creation of two powers at work in the universe. Now, the two powers, which are, in truth, the duality of creation, reveal to man, when man is in creation, the good and the bad, the positive and the negative.

But it is within the right of man to rise in consciousness to the divinity of neutrality. And we spoke earlier this evening on being in a world and not a part of a world, on being with a thing and not a part of the thing.

To entertain the thoughts that you have no interest in material supply reveals that there is a problem in your viewing of your material world. It is only in bringing a balance between the material world of substance and the spiritual world of substance—when that divine amalgamation takes place, a perfect balance is achieved and the soul is then able to rise above and beyond, into the freedom of the Divinity while yet encased in the forms of creation. And so, my students, do not deny, for, in so doing, you are establishing your destinies. Do not be intolerant, for in the intolerance, you guarantee the law that is necessary to educate your mind. Bring a balance between your spiritual and material worlds by viewing them as the manifestation and the effect of divine Energy, intelligently expressed, known as God.

Man, in his errors of possession, has forgotten the Source of his life. And, having forgotten the Source, he views a material world as the direct effect of his own personal efforts and energy. Man, without the divine Source, disintegrates into the nothingness, for the forms of man, in truth, have come up from the nothingness to return to the nothingness.

The Divine Spirit is self-aware as an effect of expression. And expression is an effect of the Divine's energy. When we permit our minds to forget the Source of our life, we are no longer life: we are but the shadows thereof. And each time we permit our minds to forget the true Source of our life, in those moments, which, sadly to say, are so frequent, we become the shadow and lose the true self.

Thank you. Would you please comment on the tendency of the students in class to tune out the lectures and the understandings given?

Whereas the minds of men are well likened unto a radio or television set, it is within their right of choice to turn whatever dial they choose to turn.

The great sadness of the turning of a dial to any station that is broadcasting—and even stations that are not broadcasting—is when the dials of the television set decide when to turn. And so it is with some who make the statement they don't remember what a lecture was about, they tuned out what they had made the effort to attend and to hear. The sadness, my students, is this: you, by conscious choice, rarely tune out what you have made the effort in the first place to come to hear. It is the dial on the television set, by its own volition, likened unto your subconscious, that has turned to a different station. And the sadness of that is the station that it tunes into maybe likened to one that no longer is broadcasting: it's all static.

And so supposedly you come to listen. Supposedly you think you've tuned out. And yet, you can't even remember what thoughts you had in the hour that passed. And so it reveals that there is indeed much effort, for those students, much effort yet to be made.

For no soul, no soul in any universe, ever consciously chooses to be so victimized by a temporal, created vehicle through which it is temporarily expressing. And to those who are so victimized by their mental body, my heart goes out, for I know from centuries of experience that your needs are so very, very great, that your little souls, in keeping with the laws established, have wandered so very far from their home, from its true source, that a mountain of needs has risen in your minds, that your soul cries out day and night, that it cries for its own freedom, that, surely, in keeping with the divine grace of God, someday your cries, though already heard by a compassionate Divinity, are registered and recorded. And each cry reveals a little more effort is being applied to the second soul faculty of faith, poise, and humility.

And that someday in the centuries perhaps yet to be, but someday, your soul will rise beyond the mountain of created needs. And you will find that you're not alone, that your fears and feelings of being alone were a deception and a delusion created by your minds, that in your long journey of evolution, you slipped and stumbled on the way. And when you stumbled, the mind rose. And when it rose, it declared its importance. And in declaring its importance, it put you, the true you, into prison. But the key to the cell block in which you find yourself is a golden key representing the wisdom of eternity. And you gain that key, my good students, through your efforts of gaining understanding. And that understanding, you gain through whatever effort you make in opening your soul faculties.

Remember that the law known as acceptance is the divine law. It is the will of God. And in keeping with your own acceptance will you, through understanding, gain the key of wisdom and unlock the cell block in which your beautiful soul waits to be free.

Good night.

JULY 1, 1976

CONSCIOUSNESS CLASS 126

Greetings, students. This evening we shall spend some time in discussing change, the Law of Repetition, the path of evolution, on which the eternal soul is constantly moving.

We note in our daily experiences the beautiful demonstration of the Law of Change, called repetition. And if we take the time to objectively view these experiences, we will find that, in essence and in truth, they are identically the same experiences that we have encountered years long past. And so it is that as the soul, evolving, reviews again, again, and again certain experiences until the day comes that the effort is made to face the experience for what it truly is and not what it appears to be. Experiences are, in truth, the golden opportunities for the evolving soul. For when the experiences, governed and controlled by the Law of Repetition, continue to bombard the consciousness, so to speak, in time, man surrenders to the divine Law of Acceptance and, in so doing, truly faces his personal responsibility as the sole creator of all his life's eternal experiences.

When man evolves in consciousness to the acceptance of the immutable Law of Personal Responsibility, then man begins to change. He evolves to a higher level of consciousness, where this repetition of past experiences no longer is affecting his eternal being. For man, not having accepted this divine Law of Personal Responsibility, continues to express through levels of consciousness known as delusion and deception. And man continues to freely give his divine power and peace to so-called experiences and does not truly accept that they are the effect of his own simple transgressions of natural, divine law. In time, in this evolutionary path, slowly, but surely, that acceptance comes to each and every soul.

We have stated many times that total acceptance *is* divine will. And divine will is supreme. And divine will is the will that man, in time, shall bow to. For only in bowing, through the second soul faculty of faith, poise, and humility, does man become the demonstration of personal responsibility. Only through the expression of those soul faculties does man awaken and accept his divine birthright. So think, my good students, in all of the words that have been freely given, think and apply the Law of Personal Responsibility. Take rein—take hold of the reins of the mind, that, in so doing, you may truly become the captains of your ship, that you may truly become the masters of your destiny.

Each time that you permit your mind to entertain the thought that something outside of you, something outside of your right to control in your own consciousness, that something outside, beyond your control, is causing you peace or is causing you grief or is causing you sadness, is causing you happiness or anything else, each time you permit your mind to entertain that type of thinking, you are sinking, your eternal soul, deeper into the bondage of so-called creation.

To go home, the home from whence you have wandered, is in your power and your right this moment. The going home is not something that you have to wait for, for untold centuries yet to be unless you have established laws that will cause that to be so. Going home—the key to your true home is the acceptance of the immutable Law of Personal Responsibility. When you accept that key, you open the door to the paradise, to the heaven that is waiting for you in your own consciousness. There is no need to go through the many realms of difficulty and struggle which are the effect of giving power to creation. For each thought that you entertain in creation releases energy and feeds that realm of consciousness. That does not have to be so.

However, it is true that untold millions of souls living in those realms continue to remain in them century after century after century, because they are entertaining what is known as regret. To entertain thoughts of regret is to entertain self-related thoughts. To entertain thoughts of discouragement is to entertain thoughts that are self-related. It is the self-related thoughts that not only ground one's universe, but it is the self-related thoughts that keep the soul bound in creation.

We have taught many times that the only path to spiritual illumination is the path of selfless service. And any effort which is the release of divine energy through your being that is directed to selfless activities is freeing you from bondage. Remember that the magnetic field is only balanced by the electrical field. And so it reveals to those who are grounded into the self that sufficient energy is not being directed into selfless expression.

My good students, my purpose and my work, so to speak, is to share that which is workable and demonstrable to free those who listen from realms that are truly, some of them, beyond description. Awaken within your consciousness the untold centuries that you can save yourselves by making the effort to redirect the divine, intelligent, neutral energy that you may truly flow in an unobstructed stream of life, known as heavenly consciousness.

Each time the mind rejects, it guarantees acceptance. So it behooves all souls to let go and let be. To do so under the guidance of reason will not place you into a so-called passive state of consciousness, for reason, the power that transfigures, will guide you in a perfect balance between your soul faculties and your sense functions. And in that balance will you truly be the being that you were designed to be.

Your world is awakening, slowly, but surely, to the demonstrable truth that man is an inseparable unit of a divine whole, that man, in truth, cannot survive separate from the whole, that all that is on your earth has been placed there for the good, the enjoyment, and the evolution of the evolving souls. You have already experienced the so-called lower kingdoms. You have experienced them in keeping with the divine laws of evolution. And your soul, moving on in so-called time, will experience many forms, personally, yet to be. To those who have built, so to speak, a strong attachment to creation, their suffering shall be not only intense, but very great. For as the soul moves in its evolution, the movement and evolution is only possible by letting go of that that used to be.

And it is the pain of letting go that is man's true suffering. It is true suffering because man has entertained the thought that he is owner and possessor of forms. And because man has entertained the thought, has believed it, and become it, man's lessons continue on and on and on.

Therefore, my good students, surely you can see the value and the wisdom of the divine will. Whatever you choose to hold to, you are bound by. And that, my good children, is when your suffering truly begins.

You may ask your questions at this time.

Thank you. Please discuss the chakras. What are they, their purpose, and where are they located? How do we become aware of them?

The question concerning what you call the chakras, or actually, in truth, energy centers within the body, is not something that we have discussed in public classes. And the reason that we have yet to discuss them in public classes is because we have found that anything that directs the attention of the mind to the personal body in such a way as to permit the mind to think that, by certain manipulations of the mind, it can gain spiritual illumination, is indeed far from the truth or benefit to the eternal soul. Therefore our efforts in bringing to you this philosophy of truth and freedom has always been, and continues to be, to reveal in many ways the effects of what the thinking process does to your lives.

Things of a spiritual nature are discerned by a spiritual effort within the human being. And so, my good students, when you have made the effort and, in making that effort, have risen to a level of consciousness known as selfless service, then time will come to discuss that that you are questioning.

Thank you. It is my understanding that in view of the teaching, "God is the source of my supply," the supply is limitless. Can there then, in truth, be any waste as in waste of food, money, or materials?

That is dependent upon the evolution of the individual and the questioner. Those who have evolved to a level of consciousness known as the God consciousness and have become unobstructed vehicles for the divine flow, to those souls, in truth, there is no lack and there is no limit. However, we find in your earth realm that there are very few souls who have reached and who sustain and maintain that level of consciousness of limitless supply. Therefore, to the many souls, the multitudes who have not reached that level of consciousness, there is lack and there is limit, because their reliance is not on the divine Source of limitless energy. Their reliance is still upon the limited mind.

Thank you. It was given in an earlier class that motive is our accepted faith to our duty. Would you please elaborate further on both motive and duty and how a law is set into motion?

Yes. Motive reveals the true essence, the true cause. And whenever man makes the effort to find his true motive, he will understand all of his experiences. A motive, the essence, the very initiation of the law itself, is where man stands in that instant and chooses the path of freedom or the path of bondage. It is in that moment in consciousness that man makes that choice. And there he faces the Law of Payment and Attainment or he faces the law known as divine flow.

How can man become aware of that moment in consciousness? For it is only a moment in which you have the choice of choosing the left, the path of darkness, or the right, the path of light. Man may become aware of that moment in consciousness by freeing his mind from all self-related thought. As man frees his mind from all self-related thought, man, in that moment, has the vantage point of objectivity and there he sees the energy as it first flows through the form. At that moment, he may choose to direct that divine intelligent energy through the soul faculties or the sense functions.

We have stated, and state again, that man's difficulties are the effect of an imbalance in the consciousness: an imbalance between the energy flowing to sustain the soul faculties equal to the flowing and sustaining of the sense functions. Motive reveals whether that energy is going through the Law of Creation or is being directed through the parallel law, called the Law of Life. Therefore, my good students, I am sure that you now see the great benefit of directing the mind to selfless endeavors that you may, in time, bring about a balance in your lives that you may flow freely in the stream of consciousness.

Thank you. What is the "white Light" that we have been advised to follow at the time of transition?

The white Light referred to many times in our teachings—and also in other philosophies—is the pure intelligent energy from the Source itself. When leaving the form, this white Light appears. In truth, this white Light is ever before us. It is that man rarely views it until he encounters the experience of transition. Now, the reason that man rarely views this eternal white Light, which is the pure, unadulterated, intelligent, divine energy, the reason that he rarely views it until his time of transition is because self-related thoughts are like a dark wall between man and the divine Source or this eternal, white Light.

When you follow this white Light, which is the divine Intelligence expressing itself, you are safe and secure in all that you do at the time of following it. For you are, in following this white Light, in a state of consciousness known as total acceptance. And the divine will, unobstructed by the duality of creation, guides you ever onward, ever upward, through the peace that passeth all understanding.

So many people in their endeavors and efforts to meditate and to concentrate seem to have so many and so much distraction of forms and things. That is because they have not gotten through the wall of creation and entered that great peace and that beautiful white Light of Intelligence. It means that their attention is directed to self. Although they try to meditate and to concentrate upon peace, they have not pierced the wall, the veil of creation. But someday they will. And they will go beyond form, for the white Light is beyond form, for it is pure. It is the true being.

Your affirmation clearly states that you are spirit, formless and free. My good students, only that which is formless is free. For freedom does not have boundaries or limits. Only form has boundaries and limits.

And so in your efforts to concentrate upon peace, it is not a matter of mental strain, for concentration is not a mental activity. It is not. The greatest concentration that you could ever experience comes as an effect of total acceptance—that means a whole and complete surrender.

Many words have been written and published concerning meditation and its benefits. Few words have been written concerning meditation and its detriments. Let us understand the process of meditation and concentration perhaps a little clearer than we have. When you go into your daily sitting for the purpose of concentration and peace and you are not becoming that which you are concentrating upon, in this case, peace, then realize the truth you are not letting go. Your mind is trying to control the process. Because true concentration is beyond the power and the control of the human mind, it is the human mind that must surrender and give up in order that that something, that something above and beyond the authority of the mind may manifest itself. And when you let go, you will experience true concentration, which is the key to all power. And you will experience the greatness, the beauty, and the true joy of meditation: the at-oneness with all, the essence of all. Because you are, in truth, one with the all, it is possible for you to have the experience of that allness, of that oneness. But that experience cannot come to you until you, through your surrender of the authority and superiority of your mind, let go and let God in.

God, this divine intelligent energy, cannot enter your being in its fullness until you, the identity, get out of the way. Man is an identifying, intelligent being and whatever man identifies with, he becomes a part thereof in creation. It is because man has given the mental process, known as "identifying," power over him, man has scattered his true power—the true power being concentration.

And so when man strives to do anything, in his striving there is untold millions of distracting forms in the ethereal waves. They are there in keeping with the Law of Association. Those are the things, my good students, we all have to evolve through.

You know how you feel when you are truly relaxed. You know how good you truly feel. But you also know that you are not able, you think, to have that experience of goodness and allness at your own choosing. But you can. You can if you will truly concentrate and truly meditate.

Now, we have stated that concentration is the key to all power. Not that concentration, in and of itself, is all power, but the *key* to all power. For it is through concentration, true concentration, that you open the door. And then you move from that state of consciousness and that open door into what we call meditation. Now, meditation is the all power, because meditation is where your soul enters the united whole. That is the process in which you, your true being, is awakened and aware of its own inseparableness with the Allness. And it is in that realm that you can do your part and the greatest good for the united whole, of which you are an inseparable part.

Now, many minds and intellects have tried to understand by what process are some people capable of affecting, without thought or act, the movement of an animal or another person. I tell you that it is through and in what is called meditation. But man, from his unawareness, he thinks that meditation is dependent upon a person being by themselves. It is not dependent upon that. It is dependent on how you are able to concentrate, to let go, and to surrender your mind that you may enter a state of meditation and be with the world and not a part of it.

There is a grave responsibility as you pass through the doors of concentration into the realms of meditation. For those who are not initiated cannot enter and those who are not initiated are the ones who still entertain self-thoughts and self-interest. And so the beauty of God's divine laws are once again demonstrably just. For in the realms of true meditation, there is no pollution, for there is no self-thought.

Good night.

JULY 8, 1976

CONSCIOUSNESS CLASS 127

Greetings, students. This evening we shall speak, for a time, on the great white Light.

At our last meeting, we discussed this white Light that appears to all souls as they pass through the so-called doorway of death. We also discussed that this white Light appears to us as a direct effect of what is known as surrender. This white Light that appears to those who surrender is, in truth, the essence of all life. It is, in truth, the Divine Intelligence: whole, complete, formless and free. This white Light, which, in truth, we really are, sustains all form in all dimensions in all universes.

We also spoke of the benefits of meditation. One of the greatest benefits of meditation is the experiencing of this eternal Light. For in the experiencing of this eternal white Light, there is a readjustment that takes place in what we call our priority values. However, this readjustment process of our priority values, unfortunately, is not a lasting or enduring effect unless we make a great, great effort. And so to those who make the effort in their daily meditations to experience what is known in some philosophies as nirvana, known in other philosophies as the cosmic consciousness, is something that should be experienced by all sincere students as a direct effect of their own honesty and sincerity in the spiritual path that they are endeavoring to walk upon.

This Divine Intelligence that is ever with us, that is blocked from our awareness of it by the creating processes of our own mind, by the unwillingness of our minds to surrender the thoughts that it entertains—this mind of created substance has bound us for untold centuries to mental dimensions.

Many times students have asked, Was it, and is it, necessary for all souls to experience what your world refers to as the realms of hell? My good students, realms known as the realms of so-called hell are mental realms. They are not spiritual realms. And for one to experience those realms of darkness is only possible while the soul is expressing through a mental body that is attached to forms.

Now, the attachment to form is the effect of the attachment to the thought that is entertained within the human mind. Therefore it behooves all sincere students to make this daily effort, this daily effort to free themselves from their own mental realms, for each effort that is made in the here and the now is saving centuries of experiences in the so-called hereafter.

The seeming difficulty in releasing a thought is the effect of the mind's declaration that it is the creator of the thought. To those who truly believe in an Infinite Intelligence expressing without pause at all times through all forms, to those students who've accepted that demonstrable truth, they, in truth, have the greatest potential of freeing themselves from the mental realms and the addiction to so-called form. For they have not only recognized, but they have accepted that there is, in truth, nothing new under the sun, that an idea passing through their consciousness is not theirs personally—originating within their own being—that they have simply become, as a receiving channel, receptive to those frequencies.

And so, my good students, when the need for attention, when the need for self-importance no longer exists within your consciousness, then the doors of opportunity will open for you. And you will accept the demonstrable truth that you are, we are, that all are, the servants of one Divine Intelligence, that we all are receptive to different levels of consciousness, that this Consciousness, this Infinite Intelligence is expressing through us, through all form. Then, my good students, you will no longer be the vehicle, but you will become the driver of the vehicle. You will then be ready to move on in evolution, in the here and in the now, to a greater and fuller life. You will no longer be a part of the mental realms of obstruction and of form, that simply, in your evolution, delay the process which is inevitable.

All that is necessary for your journey is already within your universe. The teachings given to you so freely are given with the motive of service: to serve not man, nor the minds thereof, but to serve the eternal Light that never stops shining no matter where we are.

If you use what has been given—and continues to be given to you—if you use it with reason and total consideration, it will serve you in the way that it has been designed to do so. And that is the greatest benefit you will ever find. However, if you use what has been given to you, if you use it only with the mind and you do not apply it in the heart, then you have not used it with reason, nor with total consideration. Therefore, you have abused what you have received. And that that you have abused shall, in truth, abuse you. For man is responsible for what man does with what man receives.

So, my good students, that that comes from the Light shall, in truth, return to the Light. And that which is Light and eternal, kept by a mental realm only and never, through the law of effort and application, moved into the vehicle and expression of your eternal being, known as the soul—if you do not, through application, permit these teachings to enter your heart, where application makes the living demonstration, then you are using and abusing that which has been designed to free you.

Thank you. You may ask your questions at this time.

Thank you. Could you please elaborate on the detriments of meditation?

Yes, indeed, my students. The detriments of meditation. Whenever man, in his efforts to meditate, refuses to bow the superiority of his mental conceptions, then the detriments are beyond the imaginations of the human mind. So very many people, in their mental interest to gain something better, go into what is known as the process of meditation. And in their efforts of becoming receptive, before making the efforts to find their true motive for meditating in the first place, the student becomes receptive to the level of consciousness known as priority value.

Priority value—being a mental conception given birth and controlled by what the minds of men believe they need, being governed and controlled by self-interest and self-motivation, limited to a particular level of consciousness, not even considering the other eighty levels of consciousness, man slowly, but surely, becomes controlled by that which he thinks and believes that he needs.

To permit the mind, which is the seat of judgment, to dictate to the eternal being known as the soul, to permit the mind to dictate need is to permit the mind to declare denial. For it is through the mental gymnastics of our mind that we deny the eternal white Light or Divine Intelligence. And so man, deluded by his own mind that has judged and dictated need, is now motivated by a level of consciousness known as need and, therefore, is controlled by that particular desire and is not only becoming receptive to his own level of consciousness in the meditation process, but is now becoming the receiver of all the realms of consciousness that are in rapport with that level not only on your physical earth realm, but in the astral-mental realms where untold millions of souls who are striving to evolve.

So often in this process of misguided meditation man believes that he hears a voice or voices. One of the earliest experiences are the voices of one's own suppressed desires on that particular level of consciousness. As time progresses and greater effort is made in continuity for the experience, there are the discarnate, so to speak, voices—that is, the voices of those from the astral realms—that man begins to hear.

Now, because man, in this misguided process of meditation, is in self-motivation and self-interest, lacking in the total consideration of all his levels of consciousness, man has established a rapport with those entities within his own mind and without in the universe who he believes are wise, who he believes are looking out for best interests. This is one—if not the greatest—detriment to the untold millions of souls who are now in the processes of so-called meditation.

When we look at our motive and we ask ourselves the question, "Am I ready, am I willing, and do I have the patience to accept a greater authority in my life than my own suppressed desires?"—before entering into a process of meditation, it behooves the student to ask himself that question and to be receptive and honest to his own answer. Until man is willing, until he has entered a level of selfless service, until he is freed from the fruits of his own actions, until such time as man places the work of the Divine first in all his thought, first in all his acts, and first in all his endeavors, until that day arrives in the consciousness of the student, it is not—I repeat—it is not beneficial to go into meditation.

Now, how does man free himself from this self-interest, self-motivation, and self-reliance?

For many years we have taught in many different ways one simple truth: it does not behoove man to enter the receptivity of meditation—because he will not enter true meditation—until he is in divine will. And man cannot enter divine will until man enters the level of consciousness known as total acceptance.

Now, our day-to-day activities are constantly revealing to us whether or not we are in total acceptance or whether or not we are in limited acceptance. If we find that we have to be forced to do what we know we should be doing, then, my good students, we are not in divine will or total acceptance.

The reason that we have taught in many different ways this one simple truth is in order that one of those ways would be able to enter one of your levels of consciousness and slowly, but surely, this beautiful light—the true you—would rise into your consciousness. And you could, in truth, at that moment, be in your true being, whole, complete, and perfect, beyond the dualities of creation.

We have watched here these past few months with great interest your reactions to the greatest truth ever revealed to your world. And that great truth has been placed into one word. And therefore we speak forth once again this word of great truth known as "surrender."

If you will spend the time each day and you will objectively look at that word in your consciousness, the moment you speak the word, you will see what level of consciousness inside of you that rises to the fore in immediate self-defense. That level that rises immediately in your consciousness in self-defense is the level that is controlling you. When you face it for what it is, you will move in consciousness through it.

One of the most interesting ways of learning a bit more about oneself—and that's where truth is truly found—is to entertain, as we do each day, thoughts of desire. At the moment of entertaining the thought of a particular desire, speak forth the word to the desire, "Surrender." Become aware of your emotional reactions. Become aware of your irritations. And you will indeed become aware of your priority values, of your obstructions in life, and what you must grow through.

Therefore, my students, in the detriments concerning meditation—for pure and true meditation is not a detriment. It is what man does with it. Without surrender, you are trapped in so-called meditation, not only trapped by the deceiving thoughts of need that are in the consciousness, but you become the victim of those many entities who are on that level of consciousness.

Wise men have always known to be patient: to see what grows from the seed before digging it up. So take another view concerning your efforts in meditation. See what is growing from the seed you have planted. But give it a chance to grow. Water it faithfully. And care for it. And the caring for it is the degree of surrender you are able to attain during the process. And the water of it is the organization necessary to do it on a regular basis in a continuity, not permitting it to be dictated by the fluctuating desires of the human mind.

Any voice that enters your consciousness that is not instrumental in its dictates to help you to stay in the Light that is serving and doing good in the universe is not an entity of light, but it is an entity of darkness that will feed your selfish desires.

When you decide that you have given all, then remember, you have yet to give. For he who decides that he has given all to God, to the divine eternal Light, has given nothing, but has loaned something. You can always tell, my good students, when you have given, for when you have given, there is no thought of it after you have given it. If you have loaned it, it becomes like a chain around your neck ever pulling you to you in disturbance and grief.

So remember, my friends, meditation, properly done, is a total surrender and a beautiful experience of your true heritage. And when you enter that realm of Light, you become that Light. And there you know and don't have to be told, for there you are one with everyone.

Look at your givingness to see for yourselves what is binding you. Any mind that entertains the thought of what it thinks it has given has never given to God. For those minds have but loaned with dictates, with self-interest, with self-motivation, and therefore must live in those realms until the day dawns that they enter a level of peace within themselves.

The opportunity for all is given freely. The opportunity for life *is* life. And with it comes the Law of Personal Responsibility: to do, to be the instruments through which the evolutionary process takes place harmoniously, peacefully, and joyously, to blend with all of life, for we are, in truth, an inseparable part thereof. The symphony of the spheres is the perfect balancing of the many dimensions of expression, not overly expressed, not under expressed.

To care for the physical body at the sacrifice of the spiritual and mental bodies is not only foolhardy, but bears a great price to the transgressor.

The difficulty of the human mind in accepting is the reliance we have permitted the mind to place upon the mind. It is because of our denials that we rely upon the human mind as the source of all our supply. It is our denial of the divine

Authority that cares for all of its children. And this denial is an over expression of the thought of I. Therefore, over identification with the self destroys the self and, in that sense, in time, serves the evolutionary good.

But there is a more harmonious path to the joyous expression of life—and that is a balanced identification with our many levels of expression. But balanced identification, which is, in truth, the reason that transfigures us, takes total consideration, known as divine love. It takes total acceptance, known as divine will.

Therefore, my students, whereas the mind is an instrument characteristic and necessary to identify, take control of that process of identification and identify in balance. And let the light of eternal expression, known as reason, transfigure you and free you and bring you the eternal joy that is not only your birthright, but your duty to life.

Good night.

JULY 15, 1976

CONSCIOUSNESS CLASS 128

Greeting, students. This evening, in concluding this semester, we will continue on with discussion and expansion of the process of meditation.

It should, by now, be evident to you that meditation, in truth, is a total surrender of the mental process that stands between you and your eternal being. We have spoken much on divine will, which is total acceptance. And to be in the flow of divine will, man must make the effort to surrender any and all thought that enters his mind. For only when that takes place is man truly in meditation and in divine will.

Much effort has been made and much emphasis has been placed upon the process of moment-by-moment surrender of mental thoughts and activities. Without that first being accomplished by the student, that received in so-called meditation is not only ofttimes detrimental, but it places the seeking student under the control of mental and astral forms. Meditation, which is, in truth, surrender, is something that all people shall have to evolve to someday.

In order to go to the essence of life itself, you must first remove all form that stands between you and the eternal Essence, which is intelligent Life itself. Whatever you are permitting to entertain your minds becomes, for you, the control of your life, not only on earth, but in time yet to be, when you leave the earthly realm.

We have also spoken on the viewing of your priorities and we have given to you a simple technique, so to speak, of viewing your desires and surrendering them and being the observer of the emotions and the feelings that rise in their defense. For those are the very things and forms that have you as their victim in this, the eternal moment.

Each time that you permit your mind to view outside and declare that that which is taking place outside of you is robbing you of your peace and your divine right of happiness and freedom, each time you permit your mind to dictate that falsehood, you grant unto that form greater power over you, your true being.

The needs that exist within the human mind are not only many, but extremely varied. And because they are so many and because they are so varied, when we view them, we project them—their lack of fulfillment—to circumstances beyond our control. And so without a surrender of that falsehood, man moves in a universe ever the puppet and the victim of the thoughts that insist upon playing their tune within his own mind.

In life, we call to us, like a great magnet, all of the experiences and all the lessons that are necessary for our souls' evolution. When those lessons come to us and we do not joyously accept them and surrender them, then we call forth greater lessons and greater struggle until we accept, which, in truth, is ours. The world offers these opportunities and these lessons not only to the human race, but to all forms of life.

In this philosophy much has been given concerning the forces of the mind. And it behooves us to understand the true cause of what is known as the emotional forces. Whenever man experiences the effects of the infallible laws that he has, through his ignorance, attempted to transgress and those effects knock at the door of his consciousness, if his eternal being, his soul, is in a process of surrender, of meditation, of total acceptance, then the light of reason shines clearly over the effects and he sees clearly the just, the beauty, and the living demonstration of God's infallible law.

However, when man, his eternal being, is not expressing through a level of total acceptance and is not in the process of meditation, then man goes into what we call the emotional forces, because, in those levels of self, man cannot view the impartiality of the divine law, for man is viewing life through the limitation of his own experiences and is striving to reject the experiences of this infallible law. And in his effort to reject the experiences, he goes into what is known as the emotional forces.

Acceptance is not something that we are going to attain through a mental process, for acceptance, the divine will, flows unobstructed when the thought of I is dethroned to the temporary, created substance from which it has been created.

For any student to attempt a process of meditation without a constant effort of surrender is one of the most detrimental things that any person could possibly do. In the many years of revealing this philosophy to your world, we have repeatedly stressed the importance of letting go of these forms created by your minds. And I am sure, as this teaching continues to expand, you will gain a greater insight into what is taking place in the mental substance in which your souls are striving to evolve through.

We must not look at the human mind as something distasteful, for without it, you would not have a vehicle of expression in a physical or mental world. It is not the vehicle that is faulty: it is the driver who is driving the vehicle.

And so, my good students, as you, your true being continues ever onward to express itself, you, in that evolution, go seemingly backwards in so-called time. But remember that there is no time in truth. And you are going to the Light, but before entering that eternal Light, the effect of total surrender, you must pass through, and are passing through, all the forms created from your feelings and attitudes that have risen in their priorities greater than the Light itself. And so you will find yourselves, as many of you already have, passing through the experiences of childhood, through the fears and the trauma, projecting ever outward the complaining and the blaming, for that is what you did as little children. And those obstructions, you must pass through, for all that has been created by your mind must bow to a greater intelligent and infinite authority than the thought of I.

If you make the effort to understand what you are, in truth, passing through, then it will not be as difficult or such a great struggle for you. Each and every one of these obstructions that have been created by your mind were created from fear. And the forms created by your mind were placed in front of your soul by your mind to defend what your mind thought was the I. And so the human mind, the most tenacious of all minds, of all forms, ever strives to defend and to protect that which it thinks it is. And because there are eighty-one levels of consciousness and because each level thinks what it is, is different from all the other levels of consciousness, man finds himself defending one moment what he is ready, willing, and able to surrender the next moment. For man's true being is fluctuating through these many levels of consciousness.

And finally in this evolutionary process, man enters a realm in consciousness where he wants to get away. That is a good sign for man, if he has a bit of understanding. For what we want to get away from is the levels of consciousness and the entities that we have created to defend those levels of consciousness. And that, in truth, will serve its purpose to drive us ever upward and ever onward to greater good, to greater peace than we have yet known.

In our efforts to evolve, let us have a bit more consideration for those around and about us. Let us not only recognize, but realize that our complaining and blaming things outside of us is a sad, a pathetic, and a pitiful level of consciousness that our eternal being is temporarily trapped in. Let us, instead of looking outward for causes, let us instead accept the truth of the philosophy of life that we profess. Let us accept the personal responsibility of our thoughts and of our acts. Let us be the living demonstration by our acts in life. For to speak forth one thing into the universe and to demonstrate its opposite is not only a guarantee of absolute failure, but it is also a guarantee of an ever-increasing lesson to come to us until the lesson is so great and so big that we view the obstruction, a mountain so high, we sink our souls into a realm of discouragement and become hopeless to life, to love, and to light.

Let us become what we profess to be. If we are teaching tolerance to others, then let us first demonstrate it unto ourselves. Let us not use the beauty, the glory, and the goodness of this philosophy against itself. And by that I mean, let not our minds speak this great freedom and truth and leave our hearts hollow as sounding brass. For only when this teaching enters your heart, do you move in application. And in that application, you demonstrate the Law of Gratitude, the very first soul faculty through which all souls must pass. And without duty and without tolerance, there is no gratitude. And that reveals unto us that our heart is not yet there.

It is a known truth that in all teachings, in all times, the teachings are first received by the minds of men and the heart comes along in its humble way. But unless we bow what the mind thinks it has, then the heart cannot receive it and the soul cannot move with it to the realms supernal. So in all your thoughts of meditation, in all your thoughts of spirituality, consider what your heart is doing. When you see there's work to do, your heart tells you. Don't let your mind, in its addictions and attachments to its mental patterns, deny your heart, which is the expression of your eternal soul. Do not permit the thought of I to deny your soul the opportunity of the lessons that it is crying, like a voice in the wilderness, to receive.

The only thing that causes the soul to cry like a voice in the wilderness is the human mind that refuses to permit the eternal being to do the work that the eternal being knows it must do: to face the adversities and the attachments the mind has created.

In all of life we move and breathe by the grace of Divine Intelligence. And without it, we would not be. But we must demonstrate it by applying the first soul faculty. You have entered this class by laws established before you entered the earth realm. You have earned what is offered in this school. And if your minds are entertaining that you have earned better, pause and let your heart speak, for the doors are open not only to enter, but to leave. But in your thinking and in your decisions, give your eternal being, expressed through your heart, the opportunity to speak.

For no matter where you go, my dear students, you will always find, whenever you're in self, you will always find something wrong outside. No matter where you wander in all of God's universes, you will always find someone and something to blame for your frailties in life.

Here, in this school, we offer unto you the opportunity of facing yourselves. The self is not often happy with that golden opportunity. But without facing yourselves, you will never find truth or freedom.

And so, when the self rises in its supremacy over your beautiful eternal soul, remember you have a good opportunity to look at it: to know that it is a temporary created thing, that it was designed by Infinite Intelligence to serve your soul and not for your soul to serve it.

So many times the mind, in its great authority and its cunningness and cleverness, tries to find a better way for its mental expression. We are not here, in this school, to find a better way for mental expression. We are here to find the way out of it, to find the way to the essence of Life herself. For only in going home can you be what you are designed to be. Each time you blame and complain outside to things and people, you permit your mind to be the authority and the throne of judgment. And in so doing, you establish a law that shall judge ye as ye have never been judged before.

We have often spoken on the Law of Divine Flow, known as gratitude. But man cannot be grateful for what he does not accept. And it is that which you refuse to accept in life that takes you to the depths of so-called hell.

We all have earned our so-called positions in life. We have earned them, and if we use them wisely and don't abuse them, then they will be the instruments through which our soul expresses itself. But whenever we permit our mind, the thought of I, to decide in which ways our eternal soul shall serve God, the Light, and we do not consider what our eternal soul has earned and opportunity has come unto us in keeping with those laws, when we refuse to view the opportunity as a direct effect of the laws established in our evolution and we permit the thought of I to decide how we will serve the eternal God, then we are not serving the eternal God, and the bells of freedom will not toll for us. We are serving the mental substance which conceives a god, but does not perceive the formless, divine intelligent Essence.

And when we speak forth the word that we have done enough work for God, that we are not going to do any more work for God and when we dictate those things, we become the victims of those mental conceived gods. For we are attached to conception and, therefore, cannot flow in perception.

My good students, in concluding this semester, many are called, but few are chosen. We will continue on with another semester, as we have done so in the past, for our interests are not in numbers, for, if they were, we would sell our soul to that mental conception and, in so doing, continue to live in the shadows of life.

We have often striven to encourage your souls, but not ever at the sacrifice of permitting the mind to think it has it all. I have witnessed and viewed with interest these past years and I have seen many minds decide they now had arrived and had it all. For them at that time that is what they had earned. And so it is in life we move from one thing to another. Because we are viewing from a level of things, we believe we are the things.

Change is not only necessary, but indispensable in evolution. And as the mind views a changing process taking place within us, it projects out to the world a need for change in the things in which it is involved. That reveals a soul in the form expressing through realms of personality. But in time this change that is, in truth, taking place will someday be accepted by your minds. And when it is, you will get on your knees and thank the Divine Light that finally you have accepted that change is the Law of Evolution, that it is inevitable, that it is, to some degree, taking place at all the times. And the change, when you finally see the Light, you will know that it's all inside. And because it is *all* inside, the only salvation is to surrender it to the Divine.

If you like someone, it's your thought. And if you hate them, it's your thought. If you blame them, it's your thought. You can do something with your thought, but you cannot, and you will not, do something with the thoughts of others. It is the greatest of all deception to entertain the possibility that you can change the thought of another human being. You may be the instrument through which a thought is introduced, but no man's power is so great that he can change the thought of another. So, my good students, is it not foolhardy to blame others and complain? Is it not the epitome of deception to permit your minds to entertain the possibility that you have such authority to change another soul?

God, and God alone, in his divine and infinite mercy, through laws inevitable and infallible, opens the way to all of his children. So whatever it is that you are experiencing in life, accept it. It's your child. They're your children. They're knocking at your door. You are the mother or the father and they will cry in your consciousness until you open up the door and let them in. For they are your children, no matter what you think. Accept them—your children, the effect of laws that you have established in your ignorance. Open the door of acceptance and let them in before they grow to manhood and they become stronger than you. That is known as personal responsibility.

And remember, my good students, when you truly surrender, you will no longer have need for recognition. When you truly surrender, you will no longer concern yourself with glory and success. When you truly surrender, you will no longer drive yourself and concern yourself with everyone's life and everyone's business. For you will be too active in working in your life and you will do what your heart, not your head, knows you must. For to postpone that which is inevitable is only to create a greater struggle, a greater suffering.

Many people say they believe in God. But to believe, is to accept. And to accept, is to demonstrate. So when we say we believe in God, let us take a look and let us see if we truly have total acceptance. For God leaves nothing out of his acceptance, not the ant that crawls the ground, nor the lion that roams the jungle, nor the snake that crawls is left out of God's love and God's universe. If we say we believe in God, then let us view our acceptance, then let us view our surrender, let us view the soul faculties, which are the instruments through which we are expressing our godhood, our goodness.

Kindness, a soul faculty, is so often forgotten when we are expressing through the thought of I. Kindness comes after understanding, not before. So let us, in the getting of our understanding, think more often of why people do what people do. Let us think more often of the errors of ignorance of childhood and before, that are causing them to strike out and blame others for their frailties in life. Let us look with compassion and with reason, for they, someday, shall rise through those realms of delusion. Someday they, too, shall surrender and, in so doing, live a life of true meditation.

Let us ponder well. The universe is the law's meditation and man is an idea of it, as mind is ever one in substance. Let us view the idea. As mind is ever one in substance with the whole, so man and the law and the universe are one and the same. You are an idea, a meditation of the Divine Law. And through meditation, which is, in truth, surrender, divine will, and total acceptance, you will, in that process, claim your divine right and become it. You are not the form. The form is an effect of the idea. You are an idea of the Divine Law. And when you return to that idea, you, then, are aware, for you are the essence of all life. And when you, in your return home, are then the true essence of all life, you become all life. But you cannot gain what you refuse to give.

And so, as the many centuries that lie before you pass as hours upon your clocks, your soul, slowly, but surely, is moving through your destiny, to your home, which is eternal.

Good night.

JULY 22, 1976

CONSCIOUSNESS CLASS 129

This philosophy teaches that the soul is evolving through the universes; that this earth realm is but one of the many planets on which the eternal soul has expressed and will express; that we have entered this earth realm in keeping with laws that we, and we alone, have established; that we have come to this earth realm to learn the lessons that are necessary to free us from the dictates and the bondage of what is known as human judgment.

We all know, also, that our minds are in a constant process of what is called choice. The moment we make a decision, we establish the Law of Judgment. And being the creators of that law—that's known as man's law—we must follow the law that we alone have established until, through the experiences offered in the law, we are freed from it.

This philosophy teaches that acceptance is the divine will. Life itself demonstrates to all of us that the Divinity, the Infinite Intelligence, known as God, does not reject anything; that this Divine Intelligence accepts all things and respects the divine right—God's right—of its expression.

We also know that whenever our minds reject in consciousness anything, we establish the Law of Judgment. The experiences that are offered to us here on this earth realm are the experiences that have become necessary for us in keeping with the laws that we have established in evolution by our own choices. We cannot relive that which is already passed, but we can, in this the eternal moment of consciousness, move ever forward by directing what all philosophies have taught, known as faith. There is no consciousness that does not experience what is known as faith. We have faith in many things and in many things we demonstrate our faith. That faith is an expression of what we, as individuals in evolution, have accepted. So in keeping with our own limited acceptances are we slowly, but surely, freed from ourselves by ourselves.

We have often taught that man is his own best friend and man is his own worst enemy. In any given moment, we may direct, through our own mind, the happiness and peace and abundance of life that is, in truth, our divine right. That choice is ever left in the hands of man. God, the divine Infinite Intelligence, does not choose, for to choose would make our God, the Infinite Intelligence, partial and a god created and known as personality.

Man does not have, in truth, a personal God. The God that is offered to all worlds is a God of principle in keeping with demonstrable, natural law. Man finds that truth within himself when he accepts, without reservation, the demonstrable Law of Personal Responsibility: the ability to respond to each and every thought, act, and activity that he chooses to do.

The delusion, created by the human mind, is the delusion that there is anything outside of our inner being that is changing in any way our lives. Many philosophies are offered to the world, but no philosophy can transform your lives unless you are ready: by accepting a greater authority in your life than has already been demonstrated. The acceptance of this greater authority is dependent upon your constant efforts to accept something besides yesterday's experiences. To accept the possibility of something better is to establish the law which will guarantee, through your own efforts, that something better in your experiences. To dictate to an Infinite Intelligence that holds all the planets in space is not only foolhardy, but extremely detrimental to the peace, the health, the wealth, and the happiness of any individual.

Fear has been demonstrated, by all species, to be the control of the mind over the eternal soul. The only thing that stands between us and the fullness of life is fear. Fear is used by the mind to preserve the limited accepted experiences of yesteryear. For it is the nature of the mind to preserve everything and anything that enters it. And so we find our lives, today, the effect of yesterday's acceptances and rejections. And fear, used as the instrument to protect those experiences, which no longer have value in our lives today—rise, those fears, constantly from the depths of our subconscious into our conscious mind. Man is only freed from fear—which, in truth, is negative faith—by the conscious direction of his own mind to accept and not be moved by the experiences that he is going through at the moment.

We have taken, already, centuries to reach this point in evolution. It will take as long as we are willing to accept something greater to move forward and fully enjoy what this life truly has to offer. It offers unto us what we are willing to accept. And so the teaching is, "To those who have, yea, even more shall I give. And to those who have not, even that shall I take away." Our wealth is in our consciousness. Our health is in our consciousness. Our joy is in our consciousness. The difficulty in finding this health, this wealth, this abundant good is because of yesterday's experiences.

Man's journey is in keeping with man's acceptances. Everything necessary, in truth, is taking place to free us, that we may enjoy this abundant good. Let us not be deceived by these experiences. Let us fill our hearts with gratitude for the opportunity that we are experiencing to free ourselves. Remember, my good students, that he who dictates to the Divine the necessary path to attain what he seeks to attain has, in that moment, limited himself and established a law that [he] must pass through all the experiences that stand in the way, like obstructions, all the experiences not only of earth life, but of his many lives before. And this is why man tests himself by himself in what is known as patience.

[At this point, Mr. Goodwin goes into a trance.]

Greetings, students. Once again it is indeed a pleasure to visit with you in this way.

And beginning this new earth year of yours, we shall speak for a few moments on the method of freeing oneself from the experiences of yesterday. For he who chooses with the full acceptance of change frees himself from the control of yesterday's negative experiences.

When we first came, years ago, to speak with you, we stated at that time, "Be ever ready and willing to change *[Discourse 3]*," for the Law of Creation is a constant, changing process. If you will make the effort to choose with full acceptance of the possibility of change, the suffering and struggle shall soon become a thing of the distant past. In order to awaken our eternal being, we must view life, our life, as it truly is. And in the viewing, encourage ourselves. Encourage ourselves in the true awareness that we have the right, the divine right, to goodness, which is godness.

No one in any world consciously chooses to suffer and to be denied the goodness, which is their right. Through this awakening process that is offered to you, through a constant exposure to the eternal light of reason, the emotions, which are the rigid judgments of yesteryear, those emotions, they calm themselves and bow to a path of light and truth.

And so, in beginning this semester, I want you to know, as students, that I view your eternal life and not the limited, temporary moments. For earth years, to me, are but fleeting moments. I view a part of myself, for I know, beyond a shadow of any doubt, that you are inseparably a part of myself.

I no longer have this need of identity, for it is no longer serving. And so, my good students, as you rise in consciousness to God, so, too, I rise. Inseparably a part of the whole, we shall all rise together. Be not so discouraged in what the mind has to offer, for it, too, shall pass, as it is doing so in this eternal moment. Lift up your heart and your eyes will see there is but one Light, one eternal Life, one divine Love.

Let not the veil of illusion separate you any longer from the Light that is your goodness. Let it return to the earth and all that the earth has offered. Let it return to creation. For creation is for those children who are pure of heart: to use what is offered and not abuse what is offered. Be in the worlds of all creation and be no longer a part thereof, for, my good souls, you are indeed greater than all the worlds have to offer, for you are eternal. You have always been. You shall always be. Be that freedom, which is the true you. Be no longer bound to that which, in truth, is not a part of you. For your eternal soul has evolved and is the covering of infinite Spirit. Go beyond the form of thought. Go home now and experience the eternal joy of your own goodness.

You are free to ask the questions that you have prepared.

Thank you. Why does doing exercises gently and slowly with particular attention to breathing, as recommended by some Eastern philosophies, help bring about feelings of harmony and balance?

Because, my good students, concentration is the key to all power. And so your mind is directed to graceful movement. And as your mind is directed to graceful, rhythmic movement, there is a stillness that comes over the mind. And the thoughts of contradiction go to sleep. And your consciousness rises above and beyond the duality offered by the human mind.

Thank you. As we descend through the subconscious mind during the unfoldment process, do we then experience to any extent old illnesses, etc., in order to grow through these levels?

In keeping with the divine law that nothing is ever lost, that all experience is indelibly recorded within the consciousness, we do indeed experience all of the accepted experiences of yesteryear, including so-called discord or disease. However, in this process of descent, under the proper guidance of those who have traveled the path, this discord, this disease, and yesterday's experiences can be but fleeting moments of awareness.

Thank you. Please explain "manifestation" in the concentration, meditation, manifestation triangle.

The triangle is concentration, meditation, manifestation. As man directs the divine energy through the mental vehicle, known as thought, this divine energy, directed through the mental vehicle to the source from which it cometh—the source being the peace that passeth all understanding—rises man's consciousness to spiritual heights and man, through total acceptance, surrenders to the divine Authority. And in that surrender, manifestations or experiences do not rise from the depths of the subconscious mind, but they descend from the heavenly realms of pure spirit.

Thank you. Please explain the saying, "When of naught desire is, / In vain doth sorrow speak [Discourse 2]."

"When of naught desire is, / In vain doth sorrow speak." We understand and we teach that total acceptance is divine will, that total consideration is divine love, that desire is the divine expression. And so when desire, the divine expression, enters the human mind, man possesses it for his own. And so we brought to you some time ago, when of nothing desire is, when it is of the nothingness, which is the allness of infinite Neutrality, Divine Intelligence, when it is that, and not the possession of the human mind, in vain shall sorrow speak.

When man takes possession of desire, man establishes, in that moment, the Law of Choice, the Law of Judgment. And the Law of Judgment, being a mental law, not a divine law—for God judges nothing and accepts everything—being a mental law, the Law of Choice, the Law of Judgment, man establishes the duality of creation by a created vehicle known as the human mind. And as he establishes that law through possession and judgment, he experiences what is known as need. When desire is taken by the mind, the law is established and man experiences need. The only need that exists is in the illusion created by the dual laws of the human mind. For every possession, there is a want; for every good, there is a bad; for every white, there is a black only in the dual mind of man.

Thank you. Please further explain the meaning of the teaching, it is through the faculty of tolerance that opportunity doth flow.

It is through the faculty of tolerance that opportunity doth flow. Without tolerance, the mind constantly expresses rejection. And it rejects an untold number of opportunities. When the soul faculty of tolerance is unfolded, man will view the untold multitude of opportunities that are entering his consciousness each and every day of his life. But without the faculty of tolerance unfolded, man does not accept and, in not accepting, does not experience the golden river of life's opportunity.

Thank you. What is the word for clear smelling, as clairaudience, for clear hearing?

In reference to the question, it will behoove the questioner, and all students, to place attention upon the clairsensing, the clear sensing of these supernal so-called dimensions. Let us not, in our lives, be seeking the effects. Let us have the wisdom in seeking the cause of effects. Let us, my good students, no longer be blinded by the effects of creation. Let us, through our hearts, search deeply within, where we may experience the Intelligence, that cause, that upholds all things. For he who seeks the effects shall constantly be in want and shall never be fulfilled.

The philosophies of your earth have ever taught to seek first the kingdom of heaven and all things shall be added unto you. In all your thoughts, in all your seeking, in all your searching, seek first the cause, known as God. Man's problems in life are effects of his forgetting the Intelligence that is life itself. Desire rises within the human mind, and man possesses, judges, and is in need. If you will only place God in your consciousness the moment desire, the divine (God) expression, enters your mind—put God there. Judgment shall fall by the wayside and ye shall be eternally experiencing the fullness of life.

Good night.

JANUARY 6, 1977

CONSCIOUSNESS CLASS 130

Greeting, students. And this evening we shall discuss the divine trinity of love, will, and expression, for man is the living demonstration of this divine trinity.

And once again we wish to speak on love, which is, in truth, total consideration, will, which is total acceptance, and expression, which is divine desire. Man, being the living demonstration of desire, will, and love—total consideration, total acceptance, and desire—awakens within his consciousness that he, in truth, is an effect of an infinite, eternal Intelligence, ever seeking to return to the fullness and goodness which he knows is his true home. In this journey, seemingly backwards in consciousness, man faces many obstructions, which are but the effects remaining of his own judgments.

But man does not have to reexperience anything that he has truly, through the divine trinity, already passed through. By this I mean to say that man can, by the trinity of truth, by full consideration and acceptance and desire, move forward in this, the moment of his own awakening. This process is known in this philosophy as divine grace.

The human mind is never without the expression of God, known to man as desire. Because desire, in truth, is the right of the Divinity to express, no mind, created from the gray substance of earth and its earthly aura, is greater than this Divine Intelligence.

Some time ago we brought to you a saying, which clearly states, "When of naught"—or nothing—"desire is, / In vain doth sorrow speak *[Discourse 2]*." When of no thing man desires, then man is freed from sorrow, for the divine expression, known as desire, is total consideration and total acceptance. And so when man, expressing the Divinity, has desire for no thing, then man, in the expression of the Divine, known as desire, is freed from judgment, which is, in truth, a dual law of the mental universes.

We have spent many centuries in efforts to help souls to rise in consciousness above and beyond the mental universes. For the nature of mind substance is a dual nature and it is where the authority and the throne of judgment truly exist. For many centuries, I spent my time as a magistrate or judge. For those centuries of experience, I am indeed most grateful, for I know today that they were all necessary for me in my evolution.

To lift the consciousness above the duality of mental universes is a process that takes the continuity of effort and the lack of concern. Without these mental universes, the eternal souls would not have the opportunity of serving the eternal Light and being the instruments through which the mental substance can, and is, refined. Do not look with disdain upon any level of consciousness or universe, for they are indeed, in the divine plan, all necessary.

In the freeing of the true self from these various dimensions, the struggle and suffering is the effect of the hold upon your true being. And the hold by those various levels is equal to the energy that you have permitted to flow through you in those directions. We have often spoken upon the value of encouragement. And we have often spoken upon the great value of constant prayer.

My good students, you are not the things that you believe you are. Accept in this moment that great truth. Demonstrate it for yourselves through the avenue that is opened to you: the avenue of hindsight. For, through that avenue, you may view your beliefs of yesteryear. And in the viewing you will see slowly, but surely, the inevitable law, known as change or evolution. This constant process, known as change or evolution, is beyond the power of any mind to stop. He who views for a truth what he cannot stop, stops making the effort to do so. That process is known as acceptance. In the moment that we accept, we become, in that moment, the clear channel of divine will. And in becoming the clear channel of divine or God will, we indeed are freed.

The seeming difficulty with students in our classes appears to be the refusal of facing personal responsibility. But man cannot face the responsibility of his person until he accepts the experiences, without question, that his person encounters. There is no other path to the freedom of our eternal being than the path of what man calls God.

And we must view what is around and about us and ask the simple question, "What is sustaining the variety of creation?" Whatever is sustaining this great variety must be intelligent. Whatever this Intelligence is, it must, by the living demonstration of variety and seeming contradictions in creation, this Intelligence must be a total acceptance of everything. The moment you stop the battle between the desire that you have limited and the obstructions that you are viewing, you will rise from the dual consciousness.

Many questions have been asked over these years on healing. When we view the discord or disease as we view the harmony or health, when we view it beyond the effect, we become above the effect in consciousness. When we no longer concern ourselves with our so-called merit system in life, we rise in consciousness beyond the dual experience. Rise, my good students. Rise up and view the illusion of experiences for what they truly are.

When we find ourselves plagued with poor health, when we find ourselves plagued with what you call a lack of supply of substance, do not permit your mind to view that illusion. Rise above and beyond and you will be in harmony: Arisen to the source from whence *all* doth come. But that takes the path of total consideration, total acceptance, and divine expression. Remind yourselves, my good students, that you, in truth, are the source, for the God consciousness within you *is* the source. If your problems are material or mental, then go within yourselves, beyond, to the cause, not to the dictates of the limited mind, for those dictate contradictions, in keeping with the substance from which they are created. It is the oneness of the consciousness that is the power of God, for, in truth, it *is* God.

My journey of many centuries and much experience has brought me here to earth to share with you these simple teachings that have come as the effect of a long, long, long journey. Let not your journey be so long in the realms of illusion. For it is not necessary for you. For in your evolution, you have earned an awakening, but it is up to you to do something with it that is constructive and worthwhile.

The mind serves the purpose for which it was designed: designed to preserve all information that is fed into it. And it is through the efforts of the mind to preserve that it rejects in order to defend what it thinks it has. It was not designed to reject. The rejection, the effect of an error in consciousness, began when the thought of I separated the mind from the Divine. This separation took place eons ago and in many philosophies it is known as the fall of God's angels. It is the thought of I that has closed the door to the fullness of life. It is the thought of I that keeps man in need. For it is the thought of I that causes the level of consciousness known as possession. It is the thought of I that rises from our depths, the defense judges, known as fear, who rise up to protect what the thought of I thinks that it possesses.

My good friends, it is within our grasp in this, the moment of truth, to remove the illusion and delusion of the thought of I. And in removing that delusion, you will become, in the moment of its removal, once again in consciousness, a part, through awareness, of the allness of the Infinite Intelligence.

Now, my good students, for Intelligence to be infinite means beyond a shadow of any doubt that it is not limited in any way, shape, or form. That means that all desire, the divine expression, flowing through that level of consciousness is fulfilled. That means there is no shortage in the material, mental, or spiritual dimensions for you who make the effort to enter that consciousness.

Many people, viewing the many experiences and effects of their lives, make judgment of how things could have been. They make judgment that their prior judgments were in error and so continue to entertain and to experience yesterday's laws of mental creation. The time has indeed come for us, in the many efforts that have been made, to surrender the thought of I and gain the true fullness of life. I assure you, my good friends, there is no other way to gain the wholeness, the pureness, the goodness, and the beauty of life.

And as I said earlier, it is not necessary for you, as students, having come so far in evolution, knowing the way and holding the Light—there is no reason to go through the centuries of error any longer. Whatever you desire, if you judge not how it shall be fulfilled, is God expression. And being God expression, it is good. And being good, it shall fill and fulfill your lives. But it cannot do so as long as you have the thought of I. For from the thought of I, the throne of judgment is built.

You may ask your questions at this time.

Thank you. What advantages are there in coming to class, as opposed to listening to the class tapes?

The benefits for any student in being present is in keeping with what is called priority value. The demonstrable law clearly states that we get out of anything what we put into anything. If we put the effort to push a button to hear a class, then that's how much we've put in to receive it. If we put the effort to walk a mile or drive a hundred, then that is what we will receive. There is benefit in hearing the class by recorded tape, but, yea, there is greater benefit by making the effort to be present.

It's like a person in business and they have a strong desire to make a sale. The effort that they make on calling the person and talking to them may or may not be sufficient to fulfill them. The effort that they make on driving to their home, spending whatever time is necessary and energy and effort will serve, yea, even more in their own fulfillment.

Thank you. Would you please explain why it is that familiarity breeds contempt?

Familiarity breeds contempt. Whatever man becomes familiar with, he tempts. And what does he tempt? He tempts temptation. When man tempts temptation, man becomes the throne of judgment. And becoming the throne of judgment, he breeds contempt in keeping with the dual law of that realm.

Thank you. According to my understanding, we are responsible for others as well as ourselves. How can this explain tragedies and illnesses befalling many in our families? How can we help prevent these occurrences as one individual?

By accepting the truth that we are not one individual. For the statement, "We are one individual," is contradictory. It is more correct to say, "I am one individual." But that is the delusion that keeps us in the realms of duality. To remove the thought of I—and, in the removal of the thought of I, we are then awakened to the truth of being the whole. And being awakened and a part of that great truth of the wholeness of all life, we are then not only qualified, but in a position to help another part of ourselves.

Man does not establish rapport with anyone or anything without some degree of surrender. I am sure that my students, married and single, will certainly be in accord with that. A rapport with any person is a surrender to some degree and extent of the thought of I. The greater the rapport, the greater the surrender. But let us remember, in our surrender, let us remember the one divine Intelligence that is formless and free, whole and complete.

We cannot, until we are qualified, be the instruments through which another may be lifted to God's heights. And so we brought to you a saying, some time ago, which states, "I helped a soul to heaven's heights that it may see a brighter light, and know that I am not unkind but only lost in troubled mind." Of which "I" does the statement speak? Not the "I" of the mental realms, for that "I" is dependent upon the seat of judgment and that is the I that deceives us. It is the eye of eternity of which we now speak: the eye that never closes; the eye that sees all and knows all, for it is total consideration and acceptance and expression.

I now speak to those who have so many money so-called problems, for in your world you have failed to study a spiritual significance of what you call money. You have not studied your own coinage, nor have you studied its currency, its paper. For had you done so, you would view without question, the eye of eternity that is so imprinted. And you would view the spiritual signs that are clearly upon it, that you may ever remember, "In God I Trust." It was so designed by awakened souls that those who handle what you call money may ever be reminded of the true banker of life.

We stated before that man is the greatest borrower in the universe. He borrows because he entertains the thought of I and cannot become a part of the wholeness and goodness. The thought of I views in ways that others have or have not. It does not view the allness, which is the truth.

If you go to a bank for a loan and you entertain the thought of I, then you have thoughts of fear. For you question and you doubt. But if you go to a bank and you know—and you know through your own acceptance—that you are a part thereof, that you truly are, for you have accepted that you are, and therefore you become, then concern no longer exists for you, and neither does fear, nor worry, nor all the things that the mind has to offer.

In your desires in life, it behooves you to pray for divine guidance. For that prayer and that affirmation is instrumental in helping your mind, one: to recognize something greater than the I, the thought thereof; to accept the possibility of another Intelligence that is sustaining you and that which you desire. And it is through those efforts of flooding the consciousness that you are freed.

My good students, the subconscious minds of all men are in a constant broadcasting process. In time, through your efforts of meditation and to still your mind, you will begin to hear the repetitive broadcasting of your own subconscious. This is taking place day and night: it never ceases. It is a radio station that is as powerful as all the minds of the universe and it broadcasts constantly. Becoming aware of that helps man to make greater effort in flooding his consciousness with positive broadcasting in all his thoughts, acts, and activities. In order to bring about a balance in that dual realm—for when the positive and negative are in perfect balance, you rise in what is called the divine neutrality: where all things *are*, nothing is in want.

Thank you. We have been taught that the sense function of procrastination is balanced by the soul faculty of unity. Would you please explain the effect that lack of unity has on the soul?

The lack of unity—a house divided cannot long stand. And so the lack of unity is a demonstration of a house divided.

Man, in the level of consciousness known as procrastination, is simply demonstrating what is known as priority values. We are constantly bombarded by the desires of yesterday. For, as I spoke earlier, we are the instruments through which the Divine is expressing and that divine expression is known as desire. So man, in truth, is never freed from desire, for man, in truth, is never freed from God, for man, in truth, *is* God. The Divinity is expressing through these forms.

Never being freed from desire or divine expression or God, then it behooves man to take control of the limited patterns of his desires. For without doing so, through a total acceptance in consciousness—which is divine will—man becomes what is known as a procrastinator. Dividing the temple of his soul, known as the human mind and body, and, in that division, does not long stand and falls into the darkness of delusion, through the errors of ignorance.

Thank you. What is recommended for a healing channel to entertain in mind while the spirit doctors are working with the person?

To be free from mind. To be free from mind. And how does man get freed from mind? By purity of heart and through our evening's discussion.

Thought is the obstruction. Thought is the obstruction to the fullness of life. For man's thoughts are the expressions of his limited acceptances, which are the effects of man's judgments. And so man must learn, in time, to control his mind. Slowly but surely, the struggle of life will help us all to do that.

Through this constant affirming of peace, we gradually, but surely, rise beyond the mental *thought* of peace. We become the peace. Then man, as an instrument, is clear and free, for the Divine to flow through them and the healing is accomplished.

We stated earlier that in order to establish a rapport with anything or anyone, man must express some degree of surrender. The purpose of a spiritual healer is a total and complete surrender to the Divine Intelligence. The recipient has the same potential of total acceptance and surrender to the Divine Intelligence.

Now, stop and think, my good students. We are affected by what we are exposed to. Call it good, bad, or indifferent in your minds. When a person goes to a spiritual healer for healing, by the very act of going, they are, to some degree, receptive to what is being offered. The spiritual healer bears a great responsibility to the Divine. Therefore they must consider well—and in sincerity—what they are about to do in their surrender to

God. For in that surrender, there is no judgment. In that surrender, there are no dictates. There is the peace, which is the healing power.

Good night.

JANUARY 13, 1977

CONSCIOUSNESS CLASS 131

Good evening, students. This evening our class will be a little different from the norm or normal. And in keeping with the basic foundation of our own philosophy—Be ever ready and willing to change—we will have a different type of class this evening.

This evening we are going to discuss here what most of us are spending most of our mental consciousness in, and that is the physical, material world. And in keeping with that class discussion this evening, I have an announcement that you, as members, students, and friends of this Association, have been anxiously waiting to hear. After nearly eight years of effort, the Serenity Association broke ground on its own home today.

I know that some of you have been very worried and concerned whether or not this was going to be possible. Now, it is one thing to say that it is simple to have faith, because we all have faith. But the question has to arise within our consciousness, "In what direction are we placing our faith or our energy?"

So often in life we are deluded and deceived by what is known as the stepping stones to attainment. We are deceived by the stepping stones to attainment because we judge the stepping stone as an obstruction to what we desire to attain. These stepping stones of attainment are ever in keeping with where we have been directing what we know as God's energy or intelligent energy. And in directing this intelligent energy to the minds' judgment, we constantly are viewing in our lives the obstructions to our physical desires.

This Association began eight years ago August 20, 1968, with a group of four people, myself included. It began with the savings that I had at that time of $100. Today, we are grateful, with God's help, that the assets of—the physical assets—of this Association are over $120,000.

Now, many people, in viewing the history of Serenity, have made many judgments, because they repeatedly view the stepping stones and do not see its true goal. There has always been in the world an illusion by people that spiritually minded people should walk around the Earth in sack cloth. Some have granted them the right of sandals, depending on the climate in which the spiritual leaders are living and working.

You cannot reach the soul unless you can work your way through the mental obstructions, which are judgments that exist within our mind. Therefore, in working with people, you must first have the motive that will grant you the consideration, which will, in turn, bring you understanding of what is standing in the way of the divine right of the eternal soul to experience and to enjoy the goodness of life. The goodness of life, as we all know, has been, and continues to be, dictated by the limited experiences of our own mind. To those few who have been with us since the beginning—and indeed they are few—they know something about the steps of evolution.

In this philosophy, many classes have been given and much has been spoken about the spiritual and the mental realms. You cannot reach the soul of anyone unless you can first establish a rapport with a level of consciousness that their soul is usually expressing on. To look at the material, physical world as something that is distasteful and an obstruction in the path of your spiritual evolution is total deception. I have always taught that because I have always believed it. And I still believe it.

When, in my own evolution, by laws that I did not think I had consciously set into motion, all my material possessions were taken from me, I did not, from that experience, reform myself and say, "The material, physical possessions of creation are of no value."

The first thing a person does when, after years of effort, they do not have fulfillment of their desires is to reform. We know what happens to the ex-smokers and the ex-drinkers. The same thing happens to people who are not yet sufficiently awakened to the light of reason. The same thing happens when their desires for physical possessions, for things, are not fulfilled. What they do not realize is, in their blindness, they have not viewed—because they have not accepted—what is behind and beyond the physical world.

This philosophy gives many affirmations, which can be beneficial to its students if the students are willing to use them not when the mind thinks that it needs them, but to use them as a daily and constant effort. He who views beyond the physical—which is an effect of a mental and spiritual realm—he who views beyond it, sees the cause of it. And he who sees and accepts the cause of anything, places himself in a position to direct it for the goodness of his own life.

So many times, in this church and in these classes, this Association has asked not man, but God to demonstrate his divine flow through an individual. If the individual says no, then the person who was asking has not yet gotten past the mental obstructions in his own consciousness. I have never had the experience in life to ask for God's guidance in anything—be it spiritual, mental, or material—that I have not received, because I would not permit my mind to dictate how long it would take. When we ask for God's guidance—whether it's a house or a new coat or an automobile—we are asking to make the effort to come into rapport with the principle of divine and immutable law.

Therefore, when man asks for guidance for a house, then he must view the principle of that law, which is its essence and be ever ready and willing to accept what he and he alone has earned. For to do anything else is to build the wall that stands between man and the divine good, which is his eternal right. So let us take, in this special class this evening, an honest view of our own efforts.

When we find a difficulty within us to give, we are demonstrating difficulty within us to receive. And if, on the other end of that united pole, we find difficulty in receiving, then we know that we have, in truth, difficulty in giving.

The things in our life are the direct effects of laws that we alone establish. If man, in his error of ignorance, views life and relies upon his *mind* to bring him what his *mind* desires, then that's all that he can grant to another. Therefore he places his eternal being under the control of dual, opposing law. The only thing that stands in our way is the will expressed by the accumulated experiences of this our Earth life. To tell a student that, "God, in truth, is the only source of goodness and supply in my life," is not to reach the soul unless the mind that is covering the soul has demonstrated unto itself that truth.

All of the experiences that you are having in your lives are revealing to you, as your personal truth—as truth is individually perceived—that you and you alone, *you and you alone*, are making your world. To accept that truth is to inspire the soul.

I remember once, when I had lost everything, an Earth teacher said to me, one day, "Richard, you are getting exactly what you have merited." I used to be known to have a good deal of temper. I still have it. I pray for a little control of it, for when she spoke those words to me over the telephone, I wanted to ring her neck, because she was certainly not a poor woman, either spiritually, mentally, or materially. Therefore, my mind dictated in that moment, number one: she had no compassion;

number two: she couldn't understand the experience I was going through, because she was not in it. Then I had a moment, hopefully, of light and reason. And I knew something of her history and I knew when she had not the material things of Earth. But my temper still expressed itself. And from it came great good.

I made up my mind, beyond a shadow of any doubt, that if what I was experiencing was, in truth, what I had merited—and I obviously had accepted that I had merited it or I wouldn't be so mad about it—then I would merit something better! That it was in my power to do so with God's help.

To experience this life and deny the goodness of life is certainly foolhardy. I ought to know, because I have done it. I did not do it by a conscious choice, to my understanding at the time. I did it in the errors of my own beliefs. Through the errors of ignorance, I had dictated that the things my mind called goodness could come in such and such and such a way. So I know how the mind works in that respect.

Since I lost my Woodacre home many years ago, myself and this Association has had to pay monthly rent. It has had to be the victim of the fluctuating minds of men. And that day, with God's help, is coming to an end. But let us stop and view our lives. And let us not delude ourselves, because we think and believe we have not, that someone else should have not.

Instead, let us ask the question, "What are they doing to be so receptive to the things that I desire for myself?" Let us ask that question in honesty. I can assure you that our lives are in keeping with our own beliefs: they are no greater and they are no lesser. And so when you seek for all the good things that Earth has to offer—as the Bible says, "Seek ye first the kingdom of heaven," for it is in the spiritual consciousness that what we call God flows unobstructed.

Let us look to the essence: the principle of the law. Let us no longer dictate by the dual mind, through which our soul is expressing. For in so doing, you will rise to material heights and descend to material destitution, for that is what the human mind, a dual vehicle, offers to the eternal soul. Learn the benefits, for your good, of the Law of Giving. For the benefits of the Law of Giving are many. And when you ask for the things which—the mind is always asking for something. Because, you see, the mind asks because the mind is in control. And the mind knows that it alone cannot fulfill your desires. The mind does know that. And that is why, when the mind says, "I am in want. I am in need," the mind asks. But your soul never asks, for your soul already has everything.

Through your effort, you may bow the dictates of your mind and experience the fullness of what the realms of material, mental, and spiritual substance have to offer. But no one can do that for you. To be poverty-stricken and destitute in a physical world is no indication or revelation of spiritual illumination or awakening. If that were true, the poor masses of the world would be in the fullness of God.

We must honestly ask ourselves the question, "What kind of a God do we, as students of the Living Light philosophy, truly believe in?" If the God that we are believing in, deprives us and denies us of the goodness of life, then our God is a false god, created by limited experiences of the human mind.

We do not *need* anything. When we rise in consciousness, we flow with the law of everything. But to look in and about a world and see the good that we seek in a another is to deny that same God to flow through ourselves. It is a matter of reeducating or reprogramming the human mind.

And so remember, my friends, knock and the door shall open. Ask and ye shall receive. But what door do you knock on and what do you ask for? That is the question that we must ask ourselves. If you ask, in all honesty, to be the unobstructed vehicle of the Divine Intelligence and if you knock, in that asking, upon the door of reason, then you shall be transfigured and you shall never again be in want or need. That takes an absolute and total acceptance of an authority that is greater than the thought of the human mind.

Each experience in our life—and every experience in our life—is absolutely necessary for us. The repetition of the experience is a revelation that we have yet to accept a greater intelligence than our limited mind. However, through the repetition of the experiences that are not tasteful to us, in time, we bow. In time, we free ourselves. The wall of illusion is very thick: it is dependent upon what man calls his self-will.

A few months ago, I was informed, after a twenty-five-year-old desire, that this Association would have a new car. I said, "That's fine." We always have a new car: we lease one every two years. But that was not what the Spirit was talking about—a lease. They said, "You're going to have a Corvette, the church's property," as all things are in this church. And I said to the Spirit, "I no longer want a Corvette. That desire is worn out from twenty-five years. I don't need one and I don't want one." Because, you see, I know enough about the human mind to know the payment of those levels of jealousy, envy, and greed. But I listened and I did what I was told to do, just like opening the doors of this church. I didn't want it, for I knew what it had to offer to my mind: personality, dissension, and self-interest. That, I had already viewed in another church.

I did it because I was told to, because it is the living demonstration. Considering my salary is $50 a month, it is the living demonstration that there is something greater than the human mind. Because the total donation's of our Sunday offerings do not even make the monthly payment on the church car! So there has to be something greater.

Many months ago, when we were looking for a lot, we asked for support, for our own church to get it. And we got some support in some areas. And then the day came that your organization was to purchase a lot. We had actually found the physical land. And from the years of experience working with a voluntary system—for this organization has no tithing—a fair share assessment was placed upon its membership. And it was a wonderful experience to view. Some responded. The majority of the membership of this Association did not. But those members who didn't, their right to membership has not been denied them, that they may learn by a living demonstration that this church does not depend upon a material world for its existence. For all of us, our true being knows the truth.

And so that little lot—we made a deposit. My mind viewed the few thousand dollars that were in the savings account—and there were very few: less than four. And it said, "You've got to raise at least so many thousands." And it didn't come in. And in the process of all of this, God and his administering angels brought us another lot—a bigger lot, higher on the hill. And so we made the change. And we got closer and closer to having to pay the amount in full at escrow closing and it still wasn't there. That's when you truly must demonstrate your givingness. That's when I really gave it to God. And I said beyond a shadow of any doubt, "If this is in your plan, God, then I know, and I accept, that you will bring it. And no mind on Earth—or any dimension—can stop it." And so we closed escrow on over an acre and a quarter of land and we purchased the lot for $16,000 plus closing cost. Anyone that has been up on that hill knows that the lot is worth over some sixty-some thousand dollars without any improvements.

I stood on that hill one day to dedicate that land with a few students. Following the dedication, one of my students said, "How do you know there's any water here?" And I said, "O Lord, oh man of little faith, oh man of little faith." For I could not believe that God's angels would take us to any lot where we would not be able to build his home. But that statement introduced into my consciousness what is called fear, for we all have a mind and we have to work through it.

And so I worked through that little fear. And we called the well company to come and drill us a well. On the day the drillers came, a stake had been placed at the exact spot that the Spirit had dedicated the land to God's work. And the drilling company had been instructed that you place your drill exactly on the stake or we don't pay you. That's the way I am in this material world: you do the job you're paid for or you don't get paid. So he placed the drill and he chewed up part of the stake, but he went in the exact spot.

While they are in the drilling process, some neighbors came up and said, "I guess you know that this hill is bone dry. There's no water here." And I said, "That's already taken care of. Thank you." And then they said, "I guess you know you can't get a sewer line up here and they don't allow septic tanks on the hill." I said, "Oh, we already got that permit." And we hadn't even *begun* with those permits. But I knew that to shut off those negative entities of the brain was in the best interest of your church.

So the well drillers drilled. And they drilled 100 feet, 150, 200 feet, 250 feet, and there's no water. And even the drilling company was negative. The owner of the company told me he couldn't understand: all of the material, called sandstone, was the right material, but there was no fracture. That is a crack in the sandstone through which water flows from who knows where. God and his angels know.

So I told him to keep drilling, he would get some water at 270 feet. And at 270 feet, we got some water. But it wasn't sufficient. In case you don't know, a well must produce so many gallons of water a day or you don't get a permit in this county. And so I said to him, "Keep drilling. After all we're the ones that are paying you. Just keep drilling." They had to drill through over 300 feet of solid rock! They broke three $500 drilling bits. But I told him to keep drilling.

One Sunday after church, I went up there. They were now at 350 feet! And the driller had stopped drilling. I said, "I want to go to 360 feet. Then, you can stop." And he said, "You won't get any more water. When you're this far down in this kind of stone, you just won't get any more water." You see, man has advanced greatly in his technology, but he can't see underground. And that bothers his mind.

And so I asked him to go down another 10 feet. He was very hesitant. I said, "We're paying for it, just go down another 10 feet." Well, the drilling pipes are 15 feet long. So if you go down 10 feet, you might as well go the other 5, because you have to pay for it anyway. At 360 feet, they hit water again. And they went to 365 feet. The well produces 1,800 gallons of water a day—more than sufficient for four houses, much more than sufficient for Serenity home. The water has been tested by the state of California: absolutely pure.

I went up one day and the pump man was putting his pipe down—365 feet. Because you've got to put a pipe down in the ground to the bottom to pump the water up. And he's putting down this plastic pipe. And I said to our contractor, "They're using plastic pipe." And he said, "That's what they use." And I talked to the pump man and he said, "We've used this for fifteen years. It's proven to be the very best." The Council that runs your church from the spirit realms said they did not care for that plastic pipe. And I said to them, "Well, shall I have him pull it all out?" Because, you see, there's quite a difference in cost between a plastic pipe and steel pipe. And they said, "No, they'll pull it out."

So they get the whole thing together and the water is pumping beautifully and all of a sudden it spurts and stops. Starts again and stops. And finally dies. No more water. That's what it appeared to be. So the well man was very upset, but he was willing to take all the pipe out. He had to, he's paid for the job: to find out what was wrong. That had to be the next day. And he told the contractor—he called him that night and he said, "I am willing and prepared to put in steel pipe, if necessary."

Well, he must have known it was very necessary because the next morning at eight o'clock he came with a truck filled with steel pipe. Now, if you can't visualize how much 365 feet is, just visualize a foot ball field. It's 65 feet longer—underground. So he takes out the plastic pipe and it had burst at the joints at two places. He said moisture must have got into it somehow—a little air bubble maybe. And I said, "Well, aren't you grateful that, whatever it was, it happened yesterday, rather than have you called back to re-do a job six months from now or three months, when the house is built?" And he said, "Looking at it that way, I certainly am." He took out all the piping—an all-day job, of course. And he's putting down, now, all his steel pipe.

And I left the hill and I came back a couple hours later. He was just getting the last two pipes connected and I said, "How are you doing?" And he said, "You know, I'm doing great since your encouragement." What it meant was, I simply said, "Aren't you grateful that you could come back the next day, that it happened now rather than six or three months from now?"

So the steel pipe gets in. The pump is pumping beautifully. The water is flowing at 1,800 gallons a day. And the pump won't shut off! And it was a bit upsetting. So—because there's so much water flowing underground there—there happens to be a lake under there larger than Lake Michigan—two-thirds larger, in case you want to know anything about what it looks like under earth in some places. He puts a governor on the pipe. That's to control that only so many gallons a minute will be pumped. But he knows what's wrong. He says, "It has to be the electrodes." Well, the way this thing works—and I'm not an electronic engineer—is that the electrodes trigger this pumping somehow and the water was too pure.

The report back from the state of California reveals that there's less than two point two mineral content in the water—below what is needed for the electrodes to work. But that's no problem, because they just put a little different kind of mechanism on there and get that straightened out.

Now, what's important is this, friends—this is what your class is about—because we all live in this earth realm and we have physical bodies and we are interested in physical things, as well as spiritual things, and we must not deny them. It's called an acceptance and an absolute belief that there is an Intelligence that's greater than all of the judgments of man that's working. And because this Association, you are a part of—for that's what it really is. It's important that you get some information of what goes on behind the scenes.

We live in a rented house and what your church has is equipment, not furniture. And for those you of who have been to where we presently live, I'm sure you will agree—I don't know the square footage of the house we're renting, but I do know the one that God is building, through your efforts, is 6,400 square feet. It's a fairly good sized place to do God's work. That means that it's got to have some kind of furniture in it—don't worry, I'm not asking you for a donation. We already have the furniture sufficient unto the present need, if you can call it need. Unless you want to eat on the floor and ruin the carpets—which anyplace I live in, I wouldn't allow anyway.

And so it was a few weeks ago, perhaps four weeks ago, it seems to me, that I was sent down to a furniture store where they sell bare furniture to buy furniture for a house when the loan hadn't even been approved! I thought it a bit awkward, but I'm used to working that way. So it didn't bother me too much, until they sent me back several times and I saw the money going out.

And then I had to stop and think. Thousands of dollars had been spent on a table and chairs, a few end tables, china closets, and buffets, that have to be refinished—because it's all bare oak—and I thought, "Now isn't this just great. I live in a house that you can hardly fit another toothpick into. What I am I supposed to do?" My mother said, "Now, Richard, you've got a house to build for God. It's going to take a lot of effort and a lot of energy and a lot of money. We have a magazine to publish and we're suspending it for four to six months, along with all printing, including church programs, in order to get God's home built." Because there are not that many workers in this church.

And so here I am with this furniture sitting in the living room, a few pieces. And all the staining and sanding and everything else to be done, and my brain thought, "Well, the loan hasn't been a approved yet. The building permit to build the house hasn't been approved yet. And all those other things haven't been approved yet."

Now, that takes a little faith. It dawned on me after we had already bought the furniture. It dawned on me, well, that would take a little faith. You see, because I'm used to accepting what the Spirit tells me to do, it didn't dawn into mind, until after I got back home, that it was quite possible that the loan would not be approved. That it was very possible that even the building permit wouldn't be approved. And then I had to take view of what would happen. And it was very interesting. What would my students think, let alone do, if they saw all this bare furniture and the loan wasn't approved? Where would we put it? What would we do with it? We had already paid for a large portion of it—$3,000 worth of it. What would we do? And the Spirit said to me, "You would have the greatest awakening of your evolution." And I said, "I'd be grateful for specifics." [*The class laughs.*] And they showed me three students. And I said, "Well, are they workers?" And the Spirit said, "They wouldn't be standing in front of you spiritually if they weren't." I said, "Well, God keeps the church together. If he's got three workers, then that's wonderful." And I just went on about my business.

The man in charge of the sanitation department came up to look at the feasibility of putting in a septic tank. And the next day, he went into the forces. I went up to meet him when he wasn't in the forces. I let the contractor talk to him when he was in the forces. Because I have had so many experiences with these forces and our contractor needed the help to strengthen his own faith in God. The contractor told me, "He's really in the forces." Everything was wrong: the slope was too much, this was wrong, that was wrong. Everything was wrong! The next morning, according to the contractor and God's angels, the man in charge of the sanitation permit became an angel over night. And the permit was issued.

As students, where is our faith? When the bank informed me that the loan for $90,000 could not be granted—because if you think you can build anything for $10,000, you won't even get a garage nowadays. I said to the student who had called me from the city, "We can build it for what God will grant." And we accepted what God did grant: $60,000.

Now, friends, you see, our class tonight is the stepping stones through life. Let us think about the stepping stones of our own life, our personal life. God's home is being built in keeping, in keeping with the acceptance of the students and the workers in God's house. To the degree of our own acceptance that God, and God alone, is the true and only source of our supply shall that goodness flow into our lives.

We have many steps yet to go through. We only broke ground today. All the permits are issued, but not all the work is done. Not all the brains have bowed and accepted an Intelligence that can do the job.

In some ways, I felt sad knowing that the $30,000 shortage could be made up easily by honest, sincere, volunteer help. But that's not the way that it can be. Because my students are not yet united in motive and in purpose for God's work: there are too many judgments of how a shingle should go on a wall. There are too many judgments of how much something costs. There are too many judgments of why Richard needs such a big house.

Yesterday morning the directors of your Association went to the title company to sign the final documents so the loan could be recorded so the bulldozers could break that ground today.

Before I got to the title company, I told one of the directors of this organization, I said, "You know, I only asked God if I could have a room with a bath," because I have no privacy and I haven't had for many years. And I said, "You know, that desire to have just a little privacy of a bath of my own, even that," my brain says, "All this hell isn't worth it!" And that was one half-hour before I was to sign the final documents!

Now, what is the hell? The hell is the faith we demonstrate in the human mind with all its limitations. The physical structure of your church would have been built years ago if we, as friends, members, and students of the church, would unite in purpose. And if each time we had seen a difference in thought, we put God in front of that difference, you would already have the physical structure of God's temple.

The obstruction is the dictates and the judgments of our own minds. That's why it took so long to get to this point today of breaking ground. For we judge and we dictate how our own church should spend a penny. The listing in your magazine [*The Serenity Sentinel*], which is being temporarily suspended for four to six months that the work may be done, of how much money is in the building fund has been used, not abused: it has paid for equipment, fine equipment to do the jobs of ten or twenty people, for we only have two or three working in that area. So we had to have electronic equipment that could produce with fewer workers. That's where those funds have gone that the light may go on the printed page to the world, that the light that frees the soul may go in the recorded voice on tapes and cassettes to the world. It hasn't been sitting in bank, gathering dust. It has been working for the purpose it was truly given in the first place.

If you have a lot of money sitting in the bank, you have a lot of fear. And your brain has not yet bowed to accept there is an Intelligence that will not let you go hungry or cold. To have security is to have God in your consciousness. I don't have a lot of money in the bank. I don't have *any* money in the bank. I don't have any there, because I don't need any there. I am not starving and I am not cold. But to those who need a lot of money in a bank, then that is what they need and I can see their right to do so.

Because we're not all on the same rung of the ladder of evolution—but let us truly think, my friends, where does it all go when you leave this physical body? The only thing that goes with us is the thought of it. If we have not enjoyed it in the physical world, we certainly will not enjoy it in the world that we go to when we leave here. For it is physical substance and can only remain in a physical world. Learn to use what the physical world offers you, for it offers you everything the physical world can offer. But don't deny the mental and spiritual worlds. For your time in the physical world is very short.

You're here, and I am here, a very short time. The years pass very quickly. We don't like to view them, because as we get closer to what our brains will permit us to say is, "Well, I could go any year now." Yes, that depends on our minds and what it will say. Why, you could go ten minutes from now. There's no law that says you must be old to leave the physical world. Open your eyes and view the multitude of souls that pass on—the little babies and children and young adults. There's no law that says you're going to stay here this number of years. That's dependent upon the laws you have established in evolution. And you can't even view those laws until you can accept there's something besides the tapes of experiences of the Earth years.

You see, my friends, there's great benefit in acceptance, the divine, God will, for when you accept the possibility of anything, you come under the law that will grant it. Now, you accept poverty, you'll always have poverty. You accept affluence, you'll always have affluence. It's dependent upon your acceptance, not upon the dictates of how you will get it. There's the difference, my good students. And that's what the Bible teaches: "To those who have, yea, even more shall I give. And to those who have not, yea, even that shall I take away." To those who have and remember the law, yea, even more is added unto them. To those who have not and remember the law, even that is taken from them. It is the dictates of the mind that does that to us.

You know, a lot of my students think that I'm a poor businessman. But that's fine with me. I never had any intent of being any businessman, unless you call a salesman a businessman. Some people have said all churches are a business. And I've said, "I hope so. If not, they'll not long exist in a physical world." And so, what benefit would they be in a physical world? No, I do admit that I am a salesman, because if I wasn't, there wouldn't be anybody here tonight. But I'd rather sell you on God, which is goodness, affluence, and abundance than on poverty and destitution. I am working to sell myself on the abundant good of life! And the more effort I make on selling you the divine right of abundant good in your life, the more I support that level inside of myself. I think a few trinkets are the necessary demonstration for the human mind. If it's possible for me, with a $50-a-month salary, it's certainly possible for you! Why, I blinked my eyes the other day when I heard that a worker made $72 a day! I said, "Why, that's more than I'm getting in a month!" But yet, it seems, I have more, because I have accepted no limit in my life.

I am trying to sell you—it is true, whether it's a Thursday night or a Sunday morning—to sell you on your right to have the goodness of life. And not to tell the goodness of life how it's going to work. Because I spent some years in telling that goodness of life how to work. That's how come I know the difference! And I'm learning slowly, but surely, that it's better to have, to give, and to receive than to have not and live in hell.

To those students and members who have been to our present residence to have dinner, they certainly, surely from their own physical sight, will admit it is a table of abundant flow. For me, to invite people for dinner and demonstrate lack and limitation is to be a hypocrite, for I do not teach lack and limitation. I have never taught lack and limitation since I have been teaching. Therefore, I can only teach what I personally make an effort to demonstrate.

If you, the ladies amongst us, want mink coats, accept your right to have them. Don't dictate to God how you will get it. Just accept it. If you want Corvettes—or maybe some of you prefer Porsches—accept your right! Entertain in consciousness that kind of God. Get rid of the miser! He's making you such a slave and victim to his realm of delusion. Don't tell God what you must do to have God's goodness. For in the telling, you have risen in consciousness greater than God and what you receive comes from the mental realms.

I have often said, and I say again, the gift without the giver is absolutely worthless. I wouldn't want it, for it brings me no good. The greatest gift you can ever give is the gift of yourself. And the gift of yourself is in your acceptance of something greater.

Thank you.

JANUARY 20, 1977

CONSCIOUSNESS CLASS 132

Greetings, friends along the path. In tonight's discussion, we are speaking of identity and the Law of Destiny.

As you will recall, we have spoken before on becoming the very things with which we do identify. And so it is that man, ever facing the eternal moment of choice, identifies with the things that permit his consciousness to view. In a world of form, known as creation, there is such a variety of things and forms with which the mind may identify.

As the infinite law of intelligent energy flows through all minds, man must constantly make a choice in the direction of his own thought. For in that direction is, in truth, his inevitable destiny through creation.

It is foolhardy for anyone to identify beyond the point of freedom. To identify and maintain and sustain freedom is the path of a wise and sensible man. But how does man identify and follow along the path of destiny and yet not be bound and controlled by the multitude of things and experiences with which his mind is constantly identifying? It is known as the peace that enters the consciousness in the very moment of identification.

Without this process, man believes that he is the things that he identifies with. And believing that he is those things, he becomes limited and bound by those very things, which are, in truth, a creation in his own mental universe.

It is not without a constant, moment-by-moment effort that man may become objective and free. The purpose of life itself and the evolution of the eternal soul is to awaken the very things that we identify with; to awaken them in our own consciousness, for they do not, in truth, exist beyond the consciousness.

In keeping with that simple path that lies before us, known as destiny, we must ever be on guard and alert and awake to the many things that our minds create. To attempt to stop the mind from its process of creating is also foolhardy. Peace is something that is above and beyond the human mind. It is when our desire, which is the Divine's expression, it is when that desire flows through us unobstructed, unidentifying with form that man's soul rises to higher levels of consciousness and views the forms that pass before it—views it from an objectivity, a realm of reason, a realm of light and understanding.

We all are exercising what is known as control, for we are controlling, in truth, the very experiences that are taking place in our mental consciousness. We are controlling them because we have accepted them. And that that we accept in truth comes under our own effort or control.

The great need that rises within the human mind is the need for the fulfillment or goodness of life. The obstruction to this abundance and goodness is the things that we identify with. This identification process is the judgments of the human mind. Therefore, as we judge, we control. We control the very thought of judgment by the judgment. And in so doing, we become controlled by that which we have initially established as a law of control.

Many times we have spoken of the human mind. And now we will speak more of the eternal journey and the destiny of the true life, known as soul. The mind is often asked about young souls, old souls, souls that have journeyed for centuries and souls that have not. My good students, it is a very simple and easy thing to awaken to whether or not your soul has journeyed for centuries: if you have journeyed for centuries, then your acceptance of life and all that it has to offer is very broad and encompassing, for in the experiences of centuries do we awaken, slowly but surely, to the eternal right of the divine expression. We learn, in those centuries, the foolishness of the human mind: to dictate and to judge. We learn, in those many centuries, that our destiny is the direct effect of mental thought processes. We also learn that to accept is to free from the seat of judgment. To accept is to permit an infinite, eternal Power to flow unobstructed through the mental form and, in so flowing, to bring unto us the goodness, the fullness, the abundance that, in truth, is our heritage.

Learn to accept each experience for what it is, in truth, offering to you, for it is offering to you a broader and a brighter horizon. Without the darkness on the path, there would not be the value for the light that, slowly but surely, begins to shine.

From the great eternal Oversoul we all have journeyed and many are the centuries that have already passed. Through experience without number, we have viewed what creation truly is: a mental attitude of mind. Remember, my good students, that creation is a mental attitude of mind. What it brings into your life is dependent upon your choice of attitude. It is within your power and right to sustain an attitude of goodness, of success, of all that life has to offer. Through your attitude of mind shall you reign supreme over all creation. It is your attitude. It is nothing, in truth, nothing else. Health, wealth, and happiness are the direct effect of your own efforts to maintain and sustain an attitude that is in keeping with those immutable laws of peace and harmony.

But, my good students, in this great evolving process, the steps are ofttimes painful. The dictates of the human mind are ofttimes very great. But no matter where you wander, no matter what you do, you shall, in time, forever and ever return to the Light that shines within you. There is no magic key to the success of life unless you can call an attitude of mind magic. The attitude is the Law of Vibration. The attitude is the essence of what you seek. For in your attitude of acceptance of your right, in that attitude of acceptance of your divine right shall you experience your divine right.

It cannot happen to you, no matter what you do, unless you change your own attitude. In the changing of your attitude is the transformation that will take place and flood your consciousness with what is rightfully yours. You have that right to the fullness of life. The thing that deprives you from that is the throne of judgment that exists within the human mind. To separate yourself in consciousness from that throne of judgment takes a little effort. I know. I spent centuries as a judge, but I first had to judge myself, before I could judge another.

So let us view what the throne of judgment truly has to offer. Through an error of ignorance in human consciousness, we think we are judging experiences taking place without. But each and every judgment that we entertain in thought is judging a level of consciousness that exists within us. The judgment, in turn, must bow, in time, to divine right, for it is the right of the Divinity to sustain the eighty-one levels of consciousness of the human being. And because that right belongs exclusively to the Divinity, our judgments concerning those levels shall bow through pain and suffering, known as experiences.

My good students, so often I hear your souls cry out to be free: to be freed from the multitude of experiences that are no longer pleasant in your consciousness. And, I assure you, that freedom is waiting patiently for your own acceptance: your acceptance of your right to an attitude that is beneficial to you, to an attitude of mind that will not fail you. For whatever you choose for your attitude, God, in all his power, shall sustain it. For so often we wish an experience to pass from our consciousness and yet we find that it remains: its tenacity is beyond the mind to believe. But its tenacity is sustained by the Infinite.

Over the universes you have traveled. And over many yet to be shall you continue to travel. There is no escape from that which you choose to entertain in your mind, for you alone are making the choice. The patterns of yesterday are long worn out. What is better—waiting for you—is your own acceptance, freed from dictate and judgment, your own acceptance of something better. When the mind says, "There must be something better," it goes into the mental processes and from the depths of the subconscious and magnetic field rise the patterns of yesteryear. That does not bring you something better. It never did. It never will. For your eternal being moves onward, not backward. In spite of our own individualized wills, our life moves on and on and on. It always has and it always will. We must learn to let go by accepting the possibility of something better.

So often the mind likes to say, "At my age, it's difficult to change." That's how the mind works to preserve the illusions of yesteryear. Waiting in front of you, so clear and simple that it blinds the view of your own mind, is all you could possibly desire. The veil is so thin. It's only a matter of acceptance. Accept the right of all of life and change your attitude towards it. And in those changes shall you lift your consciousness to a great peace and abundance of life in this the moment of your expression on a earth realm.

Some time ago I shared a bit of my history with you in a few words, for the very recall to my consciousness is still painful. And that has been many, many, many centuries ago. But my duties in the present are not only pleasant and enjoyable, but very worthwhile to me. For my duties are the expression and fullness of my own life and they bring me the fulfillment known as good or God.

So often we entertain in our lives desires for many things. And the years pass and we do not see their fulfillment. Be patient, my children, for no desire can be entertained in consciousness that does not establish a law in consciousness. And you will experience the fulfillment of each and every desire you entertain. Although the years will pass and, yea, even the centuries shall pass, but the law shall not forget and the law shall not fail.

In my many centuries of experience, though I had long forgotten certain desires, they were indeed fulfilled—not in my way, but in the way in which the law was established. Choose wisely, through your attitudes of mind, for all that you have asked for shall enter your consciousness and, with it, the payment. And the payment precedes each attainment.

And so how does man, a vehicle through which divine energy expresses, known as desire, free himself from so many laws that he alone establishes through his own errors of ignorance? Through an attitude known as acceptance. Remember, my good students, that all things shall pass. And all things shall forever pass and you, the witness of eternal life, have already viewed that.

Whatever disturbs you, remember, it too shall pass. Whatever brings you pleasure, remember, it too shall pass. Man does not know the day or hour when it shall pass. Ofttimes he has indications of when it may pass. Hold not to things, for they too shall pass. Dictate and judge not in life, for it all shall pass. Man's only security is in that that shall not pass. Man's security is on the shifting sands of time if he believes that he is secure in creation, for it all shall pass. Therefore, a man does not hold to things in his consciousness.

Man quickly learns, in his evolution, to possess is to bind. Man learns that it is the path of suffering and discouragement. For in his possession is his own denial and rejection. For what man possesses, he binds. And what man binds, he denies its right of freedom. And in the denial of that right of freedom, he rejects its expression. And that rejection comes back to him and he is the one who loses.

Do not hold to thoughts. Free them, for that is the path of wisdom. Do not hold to people. Free them, for that is the path of love. Do not hold to experience. Free it, for that is the path of common sense. Hold not, and ye shall be bound not. Hold not, and ye shall not be rejected.

Let all things that enter your mind flow through your mind to the Divine, to God. Then, you shall never be in want and you shall never be in need. Accept as freely as you give and you shall be the instruments through which the intelligence of God itself floods you with goodness and happiness and joy forever and ever.

Open your heart by opening your mind. Let nothing stand in the way of the infinite, eternal flow. Let it pass, as you let the very air you breathe pass through you. Because, through error, you have denied, you are being denied by the Law of Denial. From the error of ignorance you have held. And from the error of ignorance you are rejected. Blame nothing outside, for it exists not there.

View the animals and the plant kingdom. Their acceptance is a living example and demonstration for the human being. They walk upon the green Earth that has been placed there for all. Their acceptance is your example. Their sustenance, their minds are concerned not with, for they accept and therefore receive.

My good children, free yourselves from denial, free yourselves from rejection, free yourselves from possession, and you will be a free instrument and a light unto the worlds.

The many souls that have gone before you have returned to you to whisper in your consciousness a better way. You hear them not unless their whispering is in keeping with your judgments. You see them not unless your view and theirs are in keeping with your possessions. But that has not yet freed you. It never will.

So often the demonstration of judgment is so very clear. We can always tell what a man desires, for he judges the right of another to have or have it not. We can always see the hidden desire, for the demonstration is so clear and so easy to view. But remember, my friends, he who seeks that which is the right of another denies, which is his right to have. Judge not the rights of others to have or to have not, for that very judgment shall deprive you of greater good in your life. Judge not that a man has a right to moccasins or not, for in the judgment you establish a law for yourself to be without.

And so the prophets have well stated, "To those who have, yea, even more shall I give. And to those who have not, yea, even that shall I take." For those who have not insist, through judgment, on directing their energy—God energy—through their thought of judgment of God's infinite, eternal, and divine right to care for all his children. God does not fail man, plant, or animal. Man fails because he has judged what is right and what is wrong. Man fails because he has become, in consciousness, greater than that which sustains his consciousness. It is man's self-important judgment that deprives him of a life of beauty.

My good students, look to God. Don't look to man. For if you look to God, God will look to you. And God not only has everything, God *is* everything. So look to that which truly is what you desire in life. It will never fail you if you free yourself from the dictates of the human mind. Good night.

You may ask your questions.

Thank you. Would you please explain the teaching that guilt is nothing more than rejected desire?

Man, rejecting the Divinity, its divine right of expression, known as desire, awakens, in that moment, what is known as the conscience. The conscience—a spiritual sensibility with a dual capacity, knowing right from wrong, having not to be told— knows that in its own judgment it has risen beyond the Divine, experiences what is known as guilt. As this divine, intelligent energy, flowing through the consciousness, to express itself as divine desire, restricted by the judgments of the human mind, man is consumed by the cancer called guilt.

Thank you. Would you speak more on the seventy-two gods and goddesses who control the form within the seventy-two hours after physical death?

In reference to the natural law of nature and in reference to the teaching of the gods and goddesses of nature, which you understand, of course, is intelligence expressing through form, their explicit duty is to be the instruments of the care of the elements of nature.

Once the eternal soul leaves the temple, the earth temple of God, known as the physical body, there is a process, a process of withdrawal or return to nature, that takes place. That process does, and must, take place in keeping with the law which is known as the Law of Seventy-Two Hours. To go into further detail would require a special class on the gods and goddesses of nature and the multitudes of nature spirits and their explicit duties in creation. Because it is not in the best interests of the students present to give this type of detailed information, we shall not discuss it further during public classes. Thank you.

Thank you. How would you define success? How can it best be attained?

Success is the effect of an attitude of mind. How can it best be experienced? Man is already successful. He is successful in what he has chosen to be successful. If he thinks he is not successful, then he is viewing the effects and has [not] made a change in his own consciousness.

Now, many people say that success means to them such and such. They have dictated what success is. Therefore, because of the judgment and dictate of what success is, they do not view the success that they are already experiencing. What they mean to say when they say they are not successful, what they truly mean to say is they are not experiencing the fulfillment of their judgment.

All men are successful. They are successful and life reveals to them which level they are successful in. The level maybe viewed as a level of negativity, but it is a successful level. Or it may be viewed as a positive level, but it, too, is a successful level. We are all successful. And the experiences of life reveal the levels in which we have spent most of our time and energy. If we wish to be successful in other ways than what we are now experiencing, we need but to change our attitude of mind.

Thank you. When we go to spirit, will we be able to be with those who went before us? Does it depend on levels they and we have risen to?

It depends entirely upon levels that they and you have risen to. Though they may descend to lower levels than they are presently on, no soul may ascend to a level higher than it, through its own efforts, has earned. You will not be alone, for you have already accepted your right to company. And because you have accepted that and you have established those laws, company, ye shall have, but no man in no universe can tell you what that company shall be.

Thank you. Would you please speak further about friendship?

Friendship—respecting the right of difference. Friendship indeed is a rare experience for anyone whose thought of self is greater than his thought of God. For he who cannot accept God cannot accept anything beyond self. Think of that, my good students: he who cannot accept God cannot accept anything beyond self. To have a friend, you must respect the rights of difference. To respect the rights of difference, you must accept something different. And to accept something different is to go beyond the self. And to go beyond the self is to go to God.

Now, many people think that they accept friends and they don't believe in God, nor do they accept God. Whenever you accept anything that is beyond the dictate and judgment of the self, in that moment you have accepted God. And in that acceptance are you on the evolutionary path of your own freedom. But look wisely at the fine line of distinction. Look wisely at the line of principle. Are you truly accepting something beyond the self or are you merely accepting an *extension* of the self?

Man, knowing the self, becomes freed from the self. For you cannot free what you do not know. And so man's greatest job is an inside job: knowing the self; accepting all that it has to offer: the so-called good and bad and indifferent. And in that accepting of all that self has to offer shall man, through the soul faculty of reason, transfigure himself and view beyond his limited horizon, that he alone has created.

Make the effort to consider the possibility of success in a greater life for you. Make that effort without the judgment of how, why, or when it shall be.

To view the obstructions is to judge their worth for you. To view the Intelligence above and beyond the mountain of your creation is to fly to the fullness of Life herself. Let us use reason in all our endeavors. And reason clearly dictates: To God—or good—all things are possible. Flood your consciousness with that truth. Get closer to goodness, get closer to the Source that sustains everything, get closer to it inside, that you may experience what you are, in truth, searching for.

Good night.

JANUARY 27, 1977

CONSCIOUSNESS CLASS 133

Greetings, students. For discussion at this time, we shall speak on the function of reliance, the expression of self-will, and the faculty of acceptance, the expression of divine will.

It has been stated, by many, that, "As a man thinketh in his heart, so he becometh." As a man thinketh in his heart is known as believing, and as a man believeth, so he shall becometh. For man relies upon his beliefs and in the reliance is his suffering and his true bondage.

As we pass through these many experiences of our lives, we, slowly but surely, change our beliefs. We, slowly but surely, broaden our reliance until such time as the reliance and dependence is so broadened that it encompasses all and leaves out no thing. At that point in evolution, we pass through the gates of eternal acceptance. And in that passing, do we free ourselves, for that passing is a separation of truth from creation or form.

In the experiences that we are encountering in life, there is a process taking place that is, surely and firmly, freeing us from our own attitudes of yesterday, from our beliefs and reliances upon what is known as creation. And so man, in all his endeavors and in all his thoughts, acts, beliefs, and deeds, placing in his mind the acceptance of all, is freed from things. To be freed from things does not mean not to use them for the purpose they have been designed. But it does mean an acceptance that they are, in truth and indeed, on loan for a time. To dictate the length of time that anything you experience or think you possess, to dictate the length of time it shall remain with you is to establish the Law of Reliance and, therefore, a guarantee of the experience that is known as loss.

Look wisely, O man, at what you call loss, for it is only the passing in consciousness of the things that have, like magnets, been attracted into your universe to serve, in truth, a good purpose. Some time ago we stated, "Hold not to form for form doth pass [Discourse 3]." And now, perhaps you can accept the true value of that statement. Enjoy those things that move in and out of your universe, of your sphere of action, for in the enjoying of their movement of coming and going, do you flow and evolve to the great freedom in this the moment of your experiences. If you will but joyously permit yourselves to let go when things, by the laws established, are going, to feel the same joy in the going that you feel in the coming. That is where your peace and happiness truly lies.

The reliance is not only a cross of suffering, but it is that which holds you back from the movement of divine awakening. So often students, over the years, have asked if only they could see beyond this physical world of your Earth—to see beyond is to accept. Man may say, "I accept that there is something beyond." To experience it, one must demonstrate that acceptance in all their mundane, earthly, physical experiences. And in the accepting of an Intelligence beyond the earthly experiences of your mundane work activities—to accept it in the small things helps you to awaken until you view clearly beyond the veil that presently stands between you and the life that is true.

Reality is ever dependent upon your degree of acceptance. Your earthly experience is dependent upon your reliance upon that level of consciousness. Without that reliance, which binds you to Earth, you could not experience what Earth has to offer. It is in the broadening of your reliance that the other dimensions that you are truly expressing in open clearly to your view.

As the years have progressed in these classes, we have, in bits and pieces, given to you the various parts of the human anatomy and their relationship to the soul faculties and the sense functions. The attitudes of mind reveal the directing of this intelligent energy through your form.

To be a free and clear channel, one must accept a universality in consciousness. Accept, ever and forever, the possibility of something greater. It is in that accepting of the possibility of something greater that you begin to direct the universal intelligent Power to move through you and bring about your own acceptances.

Life is filled with a multitude of varying experiences. Those you may rearrange by your choice, to a certain degree, but you cannot stop what is known as experience. You can rise above experience in this your moment and you can view its coming and you can view its going. And when your efforts are made in that direction, you will no longer be concerned. For you will no longer question the why's and wherefore's of immutable law. You will rise above the effects and you will know what is and what is yet to be.

It is the demonstrable, divine plan that all men shall know the cause of all things, for that is man's eternal right. Look above the passing of so-called time and you will not have the need to wonder, to worry, nor to fret. All things in creation are governed by the cyclic pattern. Remove yourself from the effects of experience and view the pattern, and you will know when to go and when to come in all things.

Many are the centuries my eyes have viewed. And all of the experiences, for me, were necessary. For as I, in my efforts to do my duty, view the many experiences that you, as students, are going through, I know you shall pass through them. I also know that, for you, they are necessary, though painful and difficult. They are surely wrenching you free from that that has bound you. Therefore, in that understanding I have striven to encourage all in the sound of my voice. For I know, from many years ago, how beneficial a voice can be. For I know how it is to hear none for untold years. So listen, my students, when any voice speaks, for God, in his mercy, is speaking to you. Listen attentively regardless of what your minds dictate, for your minds do not know the good that is taking place. Do not, through your own awakening, remain on the seats of judgment, for that error in my evolution cost me untold centuries of suffering.

Whenever you have a choice and a decision to make, accept the possibility of its opposite, and accept that possibility of its opposite graciously and as joyously as you would accept what you choose. For in so doing, will you save yourselves many centuries of unpleasant experiences.

Sometimes my channel becomes discouraged on the untold thousands of words that are spoken on this philosophy. But he is not discouraged for long, for he has many friends in our realm to encourage him and once again place his sight straight ahead. The discouragement in our lives comes from the dictates of judgment, as all minds are easily trapped in the attachments to the fruits of action. Our channel is not infallible and therefore sometimes slips back to those mental realms that cannot view the great, eternal evolution.

I have never considered myself a wasteful person, nor do I consider myself this day a wasteful person. And though many, many students come and go, and though there appears to the human mind that is limited with its view, though it appears the growth seems not to be, I know that it is taking place in ways the minds of men cannot see.

You cannot introduce the simple light of truth to any consciousness that it does not become recorded indelibly in memory par excellence. And it is in that memory par excellence, indelibly recorded, that you will take with you when you leave your earthly abode. And as your experiences continue without number, there, in the depths of your being, is recorded the simple truth. The day will dawn that you will grasp it as a light upon your path, for it will be the only light you have to grasp. Therefore, do not be discouraged. You are doing what is necessary for you to do and, in truth, you are doing it very well. Though your experiences are ofttimes contrary to the experiences of another, they are the things that are pulling you to the bondage that is necessary that you will lift yourselves up ever higher than before.

And so in keeping with that truth that the climb is never higher than the fall, remember, that that falls has served its purpose. And it has fallen for a time only to rise again, again, and again. We all know that truth, for we all are making effort in our way to rise, to change. But those patterns of yesteryear cry out again and again and again. The day will come—their voices, like a distant echo, will be faintly heard. And then you will hear their cry no more. And time, time shall pass. And you, rising ever higher in the light, shall once again meet those patterns of yesteryear. But you will view them differently than before. You view them for what they really are, not what you used to think they are. And that difference in your viewing, as your soul rises higher in the light, that difference is the absence, the total absence of reliance upon them. And it is the absence of reliance where your freedom truly lies.

This process is taking place within you now. Not in some distant future, but now is this process taking place. You cannot stop that process for it is a part of Divine Intelligence. And as you will recall—that freedom is the direct effect of self-control. Man can only control what man relies upon, for that is man's belief. Therefore, it is the control of oneself that frees oneself. It is the control of what the dictates of your mind are relying upon.

When you experience your desires and they are not fulfilled, the lack of fulfillment, the obstruction to it, is your judgment. Only your judgment stands between you and prosperity and goodness and all the beauty that Life herself has to offer. There is no other obstruction in your path, there never was, there never will be. Take control of your mind, broaden your reliance, and you will indeed step down from the throne of judgment and know what life truly is.

You may ask your questions at this time.

Thank you. Do people with similar physical characteristics have similar attitudes of mind?

Absolutely and positively, they do.

Thank you. Would you please discuss communication within the animal kingdom? Do plants also communicate with each other?

Indeed, they do. There is no place, no form, where Divine Intelligence is not expressing. And Intelligence is Intelligence. God is limited in the sense only of the form through which it is expressing. The Intelligence flowing through the human species is identically the same Intelligence that is flowing through the animal, plant, and mineral kingdoms. There is no difference in the Infinite Intelligence.

The seeming difference to man is the form. Because man views in personality from the seat of personality, man looks at the plant and cannot communicate with it intelligently. The obstruction to man's communication with other forms of life—plant, mineral, animal, human, spiritual, astral, etc.—is man's judgment. Man dictates. That Intelligence *is*. And in his judgment builds the limits of what he will accept as intelligent. That judgment is man's obstruction to the flow of intelligent expression and communication with all forms of life. Slowly but surely, on your earth realm, is the acceptance, in man, that other forms of life not only exist, but possibly they are intelligent. Because that acceptance is ever growing on your earth realm, you will live on Earth to experience more and more of what you call facts and reality of communication.

Many times we have spoken on the language of the soul, known as love: to love all life and know the Light. To love all life is to judge not, for you cannot judge all and love all. Therefore, to love all life, you will know the Light, for you will communicate intelligently with all life, for you will have accepted, wholly and completely, all life. Man's universe, or life, is very small, for his judgments are very great. Therefore, his fences of obstruction are many and very, very high. But they will not always be that way. For experiences in life, gradually but surely, chip away at the throne of judgment that has been erected by the human mind on the shifting sands of time.

Thank you. In what way are we the creators of our own experiences, when that includes fatal accidents and illnesses happening to our loved ones?

We are responsible unto ourselves. And those within our sphere of action become, through the law established, known as like attracts like and becomes the Law of Attachment, responsible. Fatal accidents and illnesses are the effects known as experience. Their causes lie deep in consciousness.

So often man has an experience and he says, "*I* never treated anyone that way. Why, O God, should I have the experience of someone treating *me* that way?" Have we considered, truly considered, an acceptance of that level of consciousness? Or have we rejected the right of that level of consciousness and, in our rejection, become superior, by intolerance, to that level's expression? We have. We have judged the right of that level to express. We have judged what man shall do and not do. And in those decisions have we established the laws that are necessary to help us to awaken and accept the right of Infinite Intelligence to express through everything.

My good students, in these years much has been spoken, and shall continue to be spoken, on God's will, called by the minds of men total acceptance. I am well aware that those words are not pleasing, nor readily accepted by certain levels of consciousness. The reason that they are not pleasant nor readily accepted by certain levels of consciousness is because those levels fear losing their authority over your true being. Those levels of consciousness have convinced you that they are you. And because *you* have permitted them to convince you that they are you, you believe it. And in your belief, you rely and are dependent upon them. That is what is in the process of being changed. That is the cross of suffering that man has to bear until the day dawns that man accepts the right of all eighty-one levels of consciousness, which is the totality, the allness of God.

My good students, as those levels dictate to you, remember there are moments when they don't. And if you were truly those levels of consciousness, then where would you be when they are not dictating to you? You would not exist. But you do exist. Therefore, in that delusion, remember the simple truth: there are moments when you're free. There are moments when you're happy. And those levels are not dictating. Separate those experiences from you by casting the light of reason upon them.

When you are angry, remember the moments when you were at peace. For in that conscious awareness, you will, slowly but surely, accept that that is but a tape in the mind that's in the play mode. You pushed the button. You alone can stop it, for you alone can start it. Do not look out and blame someone else. They did not push the button that made you angry. You accepted an experience of years ago and are playing that experience in your present moment. You are not those things. Make that effort in accepting that truth and you will no longer be controlled by thought patterns that are not serving you well.

Thank you. Please give your understanding of judgment. Does it relate to projection and paranoia?

There are many names, indeed, that man has given to the throne of judgment. Paranoia. Schizophrenia. You can call it many things, but you will not change what it is. It is the throne of authority that, in the darkness of reliance, man has called his god and, in so doing, has become the servant, the slave of it.

And think, my children, whenever you judge, forgive yourself, for you shall be judged and you'll not like it.

We've stated before, and we state again, the God we understand is not a God of judgment. But man is judged by man's god. Man is judged because he judges. Therefore, man must face his judge. And his judge is as cruel or as kind as he has permitted it to be to others. It is no more, nor less, considerate than you have been in your efforts to understand the frailties of all creation.

We stated in one of our other classes that the greatest gift you can give to the God that frees all his children is the gift of self. For the gift of self, my students, is the giving of the throne of judgment to the God that brings you all good.

Good night.

FEBRUARY 3, 1977

CONSCIOUSNESS CLASS 134

Greeting, students. This evening, for our discussion, we shall speak on possession, a mental illness known as fascination.

As man, through the vehicle of thought, chooses the thoughts that stimulate his senses, he establishes a law unto himself and directs intelligent energy, known as the life force within the human being, to an image or images that, by his choosing, he has created. These images or thought forms, fed the life prana by continued entertainment of thought, strengthen these forms in the aura of the individual. As time and the frequency of thought continue to direct this energy, these images, which contain all the intelligence of the human mind, which is their father, become stronger and stronger.

Through this process or illness known as fascination, these forms, in time, begin to dictate to their creators. As they do so, these forms become the instruments through which depraved and unillumined astral entities enter, gaining control over the original creator and, in so doing, strengthening themselves in the levels of consciousness of what is known as license. Slowly but surely, man, in his suffering, which is, in truth, his awakening, begins to realize the folly and error of such mental so-called games.

Because he has yet to open his sight, he continues with the license of the desire, forgetting, by denial, the infinite right of God to express through the soul faculty of reason.

We bring this discussion to you at this time in your evolution because it stands as a solid wall between you and the Light that will illumine you.

To make effort, no matter how small, in your present Earth life is to save you untold centuries of life in the astral realms. The human mind, undisciplined by its own license, is adverse to the very process necessary to free the true, eternal being. It is adverse for it has gained control, through error of ignorance.

We can clearly see what level of consciousness we are expressing on by taking view of the thoughts and feelings that are entertaining our mind at any given time. As the student evolves along the path, the struggle becomes greater, for they have much to free themselves from.

The imbalance caused by the mental illness of fascination deprives the necessary energy to sustain the soul faculties and bring about a transformation in our lives. The process of daily effort: the way of placing goodness in every thought is putting God ever at the helm and, in so doing, free, slowly but surely, oneself from the untold created armies and astral entities that, by their own license, refuse to awaken. In placing, in all your thoughts and feelings, in all your acts and activities, the Light, known as Goodness or God, is a simple discipline that all may do. But in making that effort, you will soon see how your mind is controlled by things you have not hitherto considered.

And so it is as the students make the effort to speak forth the spiritual affirmations, to affirm their consideration and respect of a greater authority, known as Goodness, in their lives, something happens within the human mind to distract you, to irritate you, to cause you to forget. But remember, my good students, there is no way but the way you have chosen. But your choosing is ever subject to change.

Let us, on this path of evolution, keep our eye, which is, in truth, the awakened consideration, single. Beyond the form, you view the formless, free Spirit where all goodness is the principle of Life herself.

I cannot overemphasize the value and importance of affirming the divinity of your eternal soul over the dictates and demands of changing creation. Through your constant affirmation of truth, you will begin to view form as an ever changing effect of an infinite Light that is sustaining it. Move with the Light that does not faileth. If, in your efforts, you have failed to gain the discipline that you have sought, do not be discouraged, for truth that is crushed to earth shall ever rise again. And no matter how many times creation crushes you down, you, divine and eternal, shall rise again, again, and again.

Let that that is be. Do not try to change the changeless. Do not blind yourselves to the untold eons of time that you have already witnessed. So many things have passed your view in just your short Earth-span of time. But they have passed your view so many times before. And they will continue to pass your view until you place the Goodness, which is the Light, in all of it.

As you find yourselves in your struggle to be freed from this disease known as fascination, look for the Light and not for the panorama that entertains your senses. As that illness takes control of your mind, pray in that moment for the Light of eternal truth and you will witness the transformation of your being and you shall know the way, for the Light that is within you shall reveal it.

Do not permit those forms to justify your need for illness, for they are temporal, created by thought, deceived by thought, and their very life is dependent upon your bondage. And so it is understandable that as you, in your efforts to rise to freedom, must pay the price of the hissing hounds. For their very existence is dependent upon your slavery and they, in keeping with their self-preservation, shall do all within their power—and their power is your mind—they shall do all within their power to survive.

As you continue on in evolution, as you rise in consciousness above that which that stands between you and the transformation caused by the faculty of reason, you will know that you, your home is a heaven that no mind could design, that no mind could build. There, as you stand at the threshold of eternal Light, you wonder at the centuries that it has taken.

So often the students desire to view the angelic beings that serve the humble Light known as God. But we cannot view them as long as we remain in levels of consciousness that bring a wall between the united Oneness, known as God. For the mind is limited by its own choosing and cannot view the limitless. What the mind cannot view, it cannot experience. And so beyond the mind is where heaven lies, beyond thought, beyond form.

And to go beyond, man must learn to still the mind. To still the mind—so often the students ask, "How can I still my mind? It's filled with so many thoughts and things." The mind is filled with the children of judgment and there are millions of those children. How does man rise in consciousness to keep the eye single, to view and experience the paradise within? He who accepts everything, denies no thing. And when you accept *everything*, you are flooded in God consciousness. It is the demonstration that is ever amongst you. You all know that God accepts everything and denies no thing. In your rising to your paradise within, at the gate of understanding, the direction reads, "Acceptance, the will of God."

In your efforts in meditation, as you are plagued with so many forms and thoughts, they plague you from denial. They do not plague you from acceptance. It is in your acceptance, my children, that you shall be freed. For in that demonstration is God consciousness flowing through your vehicles unobstructed.

The illness of fascination is the limitation or denial caused by the judge on his throne that sits with his multitudes and armies. When you accept in totality, there is no longer the fear of self-preservation of the forms of your created mind.

Many philosophers have stated, "As you believeth in your heart, you becometh." The heart, the very vehicle through which the soul expresses, is the totality of acceptance, the essence of God Law, known as Principle. We have stated some time ago, it is our denials that are our destinies. Our acceptance is our freedom. You have no need for concern when you accept. You have no need for worry, you have no need for money, you have no need for the stimulation of your senses, for you have accepted. And God, the cause of all good, flows freely and life becomes an abundant joy.

View the heavens in all its glory. View the trees in all their beauty. View your life from a different perspective. He who accepts does not dictate. He who accepts does not fall, for he has nothing to fall, being freed from the dictates of the mind.

You know, my good students, as you view your lives, that in creation your adversities have become your attachments. And because they have become so, it is difficult to remember when you were adverse. That that we hold, we lose. And so we have taught, "Hold not to form for form doth pass [Discourse 2]."

Beware of judgment, for it soon becomes your king.

In these many centuries of experience, untold millions have I viewed accepting God's right of expression, for I spent so many years with the effects of denial.

Remember, when you have the sense functions of jealousy rise within you, when you experience the sense functions of envy and greed and fear, remember, you are in, and on, the throne of judgment of denial of God. For you have, through the error of dictate, judged and, therefore, experience need. For in the judgment you have denied, and in the denial are you destined. And in your efforts to be free from those functions of jealousy and envy and greed, in your efforts, remember, the will of God: acceptance, not dependence. Man depends on his denials and therefore establishes his own destiny.

When you entertain thoughts of self, you experience the limited stimulations of your senses, ever equal and in accord with the dictates and judgments of your mind. You have closed, in that moment, the door of acceptance that can free you. And because you have denied yourself, you will not grant to another—only the denial. If you feel lonely and uncared for, remember, in your throne of judgment, you have left out God or Goodness.

Bow and step down from that imperial throne that sits on the shifting sands of time and enjoy the life, the laughter, the goodness that is the true you. For time in your dimension passes very quickly. And your Earth life is a school. Your years within that school are numbered by laws long ago established by yourselves. And so you have many lessons to learn, many so-called tests to pass, that you may graduate. For you've waited so very long.

Balance these soul faculties with the vehicle known as the senses, through which you are expressing. Balance them not by the thought of your mind, for the thought of the mind deceives us, for it is dependent upon its own denials. Balance will bring the goodness that your heart long cries for.

Lift up, my good students, lift up, by the thought of lifting up, your being. Love is the language of the soul, for there are no boundaries to true love. For the love of God is true love. There are no boundaries for there are no denials. And therefore it is pure and it is love. Let it flow through your consciousness, for it bears with it not only the Light, but the very Life of which you are an inseparable being. Love conquers all and Light lifts all.

Some time ago we gave to you that simple truth, "Love all life and know the Light [Discourse 51]." Many times students have said, "It's so difficult for me to love all life." The only difficult—the only difficulty is your mind and its judgments. God loves all life for God *is* all life. Therefore, God, having no denials, God has no destiny. God *is*. Truth *is*. Love *is*. It is not dependent upon the thought of man, for it is above and beyond the thought of man.

Be, my good students, the living demonstration of higher levels of consciousness, where Goodness is in all things.

Many times, I know, your minds entertain thoughts—you've heard it all before. And, in some ways, that is true. We give in different ways that some level of receptivity will experience its benefits. But if your thoughts are frequent that you've heard it all before, then it only demonstrates the change is yet to come. For when the change in consciousness within you comes, you will know that repetition is the law through which change is made possible. There is no other way.

You may ask your questions.

Thank you. When one gives a check for which there are insufficient funds in the bank to cover, what spiritual law is being transgressed?

In reference to your question, we must first consider a simple statement, given to you many years ago. And the statement says that hell is paved with good intentions and broken promises. There are several laws involved with your question. There is the Law of Intent. There is the Law of Deception. There is the Law of Personal Responsibility. One must first consider, in the question, whether or not it is a pattern of mind. Is it a frequent demonstration? Is it a periodic demonstration? There are many factors that must be considered. But remember, my good students, it's only a level of consciousness. Pray for guidance, for understanding, for the strength to stand upon principle. And pray for God's compassion and forgiveness, for it is an error of ignorance.

Good night.

FEBRUARY 10, 1977

CONSCIOUSNESS CLASS 135

Greeting, students. Whereas experience is the effect of directed energy, we shall discuss at this time the Law of Obstruction, known as procrastination.

As the human mind is the instrument through which divine, intelligent energy doth flow and whereas the human mind, a dual vehicle, is constantly bombarded with choice, man establishes the Law of Obstruction as a self-preservation device. Because the effort has not been made by the mind to control itself from the effects of bombarding, contrary desires, man procrastinates on the things he knows that he should do. And because of this procrastination, he directs energy to other conflicting desires and builds these walls of obstruction.

In order to be free, in order to accomplish what one desires to accomplish, it is absolutely necessary to gain some degree of control over the human mind. Because man does not yet understand, nor accept, the way that this energy passes through his mind and creates these many forms in order to bring unto him that which he desires, that error of ignorance keeps man in a state of disappointment, confusion, and regret.

We all know, in truth, that as this infinite, intelligent energy passes through the human consciousness, it creates the very form of the thought and feeling that you entertain at the moment. Because it is an infinite, intelligent energy that is encased in the form of your thought, it is capable of accomplishing that which you, in truth, desire.

In working with this created vehicle, these forms leave your so-called sphere of action and they go out into the universe to do the work that they have been sent to do. However, because you have other forms constantly being created, the ones of your desires ofttimes suffer from lack of sustenance. And so, working through the mental spheres of action, man soon learns to release this energy through higher planes of consciousness in order that he may free himself from the contradictions of the human mind.

The efforts—no matter how small—that are made to discipline your minds will bring you just reward in due time. But you alone must make those efforts. You alone must become aware of these multitudes of forms that are, in truth, the armies of your efforts.

It is our purpose, and has always been our purpose, to encourage the soul. For to gain in one area is to lose in another. He who accepts graciously that truth—that is constantly being demonstrated to all of us—flows freely along the streams of eternal life. He who strives to swim against the tides of evolution only suffers the pain of his own folly.

Without constant repetition introduced into the consciousness, there is no effort, no effort being made to evolve.

So many times the students have entertained the thoughts of discouragement, for that, in truth, is the last effort made by the patterns of yesterday to keep control of your lives. Of what benefit is the viewing of our realms when the effort to enjoy them is not made?

To pause to think has often been the counsel of the Light itself. To pause to think, to become aware of what, in truth, is really happening. My good students, in these many years of experience, in time, they offer to one an acceptance of everything. They offer, in time, freedom from creation. They offer, in time, a peaceful sail through a jungle of duality. That, in truth, is what all souls are seeking. For that, in truth, is the home of the soul. Let us awaken within our being that simple, yet great, truth: that life was designed by the great Architect to be enjoyed.

Each and every experience is the living demonstration of the level of consciousness that is receiving the most of divine energy. Let that level of consciousness be a level that lifts you to the heights of joy and happiness. It is within your power to gain control of your mind. It is within your power to break the back of procrastination, to free yourself from the Law of Obstruction, and to be the living demonstration, a light in the world for all to follow.

And remember, my good students, we all follow someone. Whether or not we think about it, makes no change in that truth. For we, in truth, are followers, and our following takes us into many experiences in life. But we know before we follow, we know deep inside whether or not it's a detour, a dead end, or a way. Let your life be a way, for that is what it has been designed to be: a way upward, a way onward that all may follow the principle of joy, the principle of eternal freedom, in this the moment that is truly yours.

Many schools have offered varied ways of discipline. All true spiritual schools offer discipline as an integral part of illumination, for without discipline of the human mind, there is no light, there is no illumination. When you face this discipline, view carefully what is your greatest obstruction. And that is revealed by your procrastination in your efforts, for that will reveal to you the struggle of untold centuries. Whatever it is that you dislike the most, whatever it is that is your greatest adversity, sit back and ponder the truth. It has become your greatest dislike, your greatest adversity, not in these few short years that you recall on Earth, but it is the effect of directed energy for centuries that have already passed. If you make that effort in the here and now to view that obstruction wisely, you will be freed, through your efforts, of the centuries that wait to unfold before you. So remember, my students, what great opportunity you have in this moment!

You know and see the way, and there's always a voice from heaven to guide you, but you must learn to listen attentively. You must learn to pause and be at peace. You must learn to gain control of those things that have controlled you for so many centuries. But that that you wait to gain is waiting for you. And what you have to lose has already served its purpose in your evolution. Judge not that which waits on your horizon, for in the judging is your struggle. Let it come and flow into your consciousness graciously, for you, in truth, are moving through it.

You are not the things of life. You are the essence of the intelligence of the Divine. Let it flow in ways that will do you justice in your days and years ahead.

Remember that it is our conscience that judges us. And we have the conscience of the educated mind and we have the conscience of the eternal soul. You will face that throne as you already are facing it, but you will face it in ways that you will gain more understanding of its true purpose. For each thing that is judged waits as your child to judge you. And every law that has been transgressed waits patiently for you. Be encouraged that you are making some effort to awaken within you the demonstrable truth that there is no escape from any thought, act, or deed. Be encouraged in your prayer for peace in all your thoughts.

Often we have stated that God, the Divine, is the peace. So put peace in each thought and feeling. There will be a light that goes with each form, and the form, having the light within, it must bow to it. And in so doing, God or Goodness will be the wings of all your thoughts. And as they return onto you, those wings of thought, there will be that eternal light that comes with them. Therefore, the good, going from you, shall ever and forever return onto you.

We have given you a prayer of divine healing. And let us, step by step, walk through the evolution of the eternal soul as it passes through that affirmation of truth. "I accept"—the identity, the I, the form accepts. It accepts "that the Divine Healing Power,"—above and beyond the dictates of the human mind—"is removing all obstructions,"—all procrastinations—"from my mind and body and is restoring me,"—the restoration of the Divinity within you—"And is restoring me to perfect health, wealth, and happiness." Think, my students, what is truly taking place when you speak forth from your heart that affirmation. "My heart is filled with gratitude"—the heart is filled with the supply of goodness. "For the Divine Healing Power"—Think, my students, and think more deeply.

When you flood your consciousness with the true meaning that is contained in that healing prayer, all obstructions will melt before your view, because they have melted in consciousness within you. There is no greater—or simpler—declaration of truth than to declare the infinite, divine right of goodness in your lives. [*See the appendix for the text of the "Divine Healing" prayer.*]

Why entertain that which does not bring you the wealth of goodness that is truly yours? Remove from your minds the need to suffer. Root it out as you would root out a negative or cancerous growth. Accept your right. But remember, your right is not the right of denial; your right is the right of God's will. Your right is not the right of limitation; your right is the right of God's abundant flow. Your right is not the right of judgment; your right is the right of acceptance of all God's children. Do yourselves that favor. Do it and be the living demonstration of what God can do.

To dictate your misery and suffering is to deny the right of your eternal life. You are greater than all creation, and you know it deep within your consciousness. Sit humbly on the foundation stone of truth and look at creation come and go.

Whatever words are spoken to you here are recorded indelibly within your consciousness. They will serve you well in your times of need, for they are words of truth that you can use and lift yourselves up.

Remember the value of thought and also remember, it must never exceed the value of prayer. Let us begin to pray by placing good in all thought, for then all thought becomes the servant of prayer to God. And then all thought will bow to divine right and then it will not plague you as it has done for so very, very long.

Let us begin to demonstrate God's love: it's known as total consideration. He who considers everything is bound by no thing, for he stands in God's love, under the light of reason, that which transfigures the human being.

Remember that you already have long endured that which plagues you, but you do not have to endure it anymore.

There are no secrets in God's universe, and everything is in God's universe. And when you try to hide your thoughts and feelings, you feed them thrice the energy by your fear, and they become, yea, even more blatant than before. All minds fear, for fear is the authority of the mind or brain over the eternal life. But its authority is very temporal and in a constant process of change.

Throughout the universes, you have journeyed already and will continue to do so. The more you identify with your Earth planet, the more difficulty you will have in your journey onward. Learn the wisdom of not overidentifying with form, for the pain in your evolution is the direct effect of your overidentification. You are, in truth, the universality of consciousness. Pray for the broadening of your horizons that your passing from moment to moment shall not be so difficult and painful.

For we all experience death. Each and every moment we die to something, only to be born to something else. Accept the death as you accept the birth, for it is the law that you cannot change. Through an acceptance of that death-and-birth cycle, which is constant in creation, you will, gradually but surely, be released from the hold and the chains that overidentification have upon you.

Often we have spoken of the forces that the souls are struggling through—the forces of our own emotions. Because of the lack of discipline of our minds, we experience those forces, the effects of overidentification. The mind must identify. Then, let it identify with universality. Let it identify with constant change, for that is the law that your minds cannot change. Accept the coming as you accept the going—the loss, the gain, the loss, the gain again. Let it be, for only a fool tries to stop the unstoppable. Only a fool stands rigid in the Law of Constant Change. So if you must stand in the human mind, then be not rigid: be flexible. And from that flexibility in consciousness, you will begin to identify with the Allness that is, in truth, God's kingdom.

You may ask your questions at this time.

Thank you. Would you please explain why self-will is judgment? And does judgment lead to fascination?

Yes. The question is, Why is self-will judgment? "And does judgment lead to fascination?"

In order to express what is known as self-will, the will of the self, we must first understand that self is identity; that the identity known as self establishes the Law of Separatism and, in establishing the Law of Separatism, by the identification with what is called self, the mind must judge in order to preserve what it has identified with and establish the Law of Separatism. In so doing, from that throne of judgment, it, slowly but surely, begins to tempt in order to build a kingdom for its throne. Usually in creation, there is a kingdom and someone takes the throne. But in the throne known as self-identification, there is not yet a kingdom—only the throne called self. In order to fully realize its throne, it must now establish a kingdom. And in order to establish its kingdom, it must have slaves or victims. In order to gain these victims, it uses the law that has been designed for that purpose, and that is known as the Law of Temptation.

Now, we all know that he who tempts another is as guilty as the one who is tempted. And the Lord Prayer's, given to you so long ago, states, "Lord, lead me not into temptation, but deliver me from evil for thy name's sake." As the throne gathers unto itself its victims, through the law known as temptation, the victims in the kingdom, working for the throne, begin to want and to need more energy, more food for their labor. And so the demands of the kingdom upon the throne ever increase. As the son looks to the father for support and sustenance, so these sons, these children created by the throne of self, look to the self for their sustenance and support. In time, their demands become so great that the throne begins to awaken to the light of reason, the throne of self begins to realize that its kingdom is no longer the servant, but the throne has become the servant and the slave.

Now this is not something that is a passing fancy of the human mind. It is the *reality* of the human mind. And all you have to do is to think about your daily activities. All you have to do is to ask yourself why did you have a let-down feeling after you were compelled to do different things. Because, my friends, the truth is that it is not you who wants to do these different things: it is your kingdom of self, the children that you have created. And they are becoming more demanding. They gain their strength and sustenance of energy the way that they were born. They became your sons and daughters through the Law of Temptation. And they have served you in those times. And now the law—so just and beautiful—the dual law of the mind, they now have become your kings and you, once sitting mightily on the throne of self, are their slave, their victim. And so you are tempted in a multitude of ways. You are constantly tempted, for they demand—the slaves who have now become masters—they demand their sustenance in order to survive. They are very real, my children. They are, oh, so real. And so they cause you to tempt and to fascinate that you cannot pass through one single day without their control. That, my friends, is why the soul waits to serve in the depths of bondage.

But be encouraged, for they once were your slaves. And because now they are your masters, give up your throne, for it is a prison of your creation. Give up your throne that created them and, in giving up your throne that created them, you will be freed from them. There is no other way to free yourselves from the dictates of those who once were servants and now are masters over your life.

Think of what life has already revealed unto you. You make the slightest effort to change, in keeping with the divine of Law of Evolution, and your kingdom screams to the very depths and your pain gets ever greater. And each time you try to do what you know you should be doing, they, in keeping with what you have done, build the wall of obstruction, known as procrastination. But you shall pass through it by giving to God your greatest gift: the gift of self. By giving that, you give the kingdom that has made you slave.

Good night.

FEBRUARY 17, 1977

CONSCIOUSNESS CLASS 136

Good evening, students. At this time, we are discussing destiny and how it works for you.

Because we frequently refuse to accept the experiences in life that we encounter, we establish the Law of Denial and, therefore, follow the infallible law known as destiny. Through a conscious effort of relating experiences in life to the true cause, which is an attitude of mind within, we are then enabled to establish new and more beneficial laws, known as our destiny.

The seeming difficulty with the human mind is its tenacity to hold to the decisions it has already made. When all of life is unfolding before your very view, it is indeed foolhardy to remain in attitudes of mind that repeatedly prove, from their own demonstrations of experiences, to be not beneficial to oneself.

How does man make the necessary effort to accept the personal responsibility of all experiences in his life? By first accepting that he, and he alone, is the cause and the effect. To accept that simple truth is to make the first step in walking upon the path of Light and freedom. It is necessary to repeat, in untold thousands of ways, the simple truth. For, slowly but surely, we begin to accept level by level. So often our minds question. So often we fear, because our attention, our energy is directed to yesterday's experiences and we are not looking to the horizon that is awakening before us.

We have spoken before that before every victory come the hounds of hell. Being the hounds of hell—the tenacity of our own denials in life. Each denial that we entertain in thought is a judgment before the right, the eternal right of God. And for each denial we must pay the just dues. And those just, impartial dues are the very things that cause us so much grief in life. When a moment to pause would grant us the opportunity to rise to other levels of consciousness, where the light of reason would guide our footsteps. It is a matter of programming our mind to make that pause to think. To become the actor in life—and not the reactor—takes a degree of discipline, because we are the way we are from disciplining of the past.

The truth is, we all are disciplined. We have disciplined ourselves to certain attitudes of mind. We have disciplined ourselves to certain denials and judgments. So it is not a matter, my friends, of introducing into the consciousness a new principle. The principle of discipline, we already are well familiar with. For we have already well disciplined ourselves to our own attitudes. It is the discipline of reason of which we are speaking.

It is the cause that we are searching for in all things. To work upon the effects is a waste of time and energy. And so we find these obstructions before us, which we know, in truth, are the effects of procrastination. And remember, my good students, that he who fascinates, procrastinates. And so we see the chain of events as we move in consciousness and in life's experiences from temptation to fascination by the way of procrastination. Let us view these simple, demonstrable truths. Let us view them and let us use them. We use them by going inside, ever searching and ever seeking for the cause of the experiences that we are having.

The centuries here seem to us, sometimes, very short. But there are times when they seem very, very long. That depends upon the pleasure or distaste of experience. For that which is distasteful to the mind is long enduring and that which is pleasurable to the mind is quickly fleeting.

My students, in many ways we have strived to encourage you and continue to do so. The changes are taking place. Perhaps not as quickly as those who have so much impatience would like to see. But the time in eternity that is passing, through the small efforts that you are making, is more than rewarding. For many attitudes already are in the process of change, known as transformation.

You must accept, with the fullness of gratitude, those little crumbs of change, for it is in that acceptance that the change will increase. It is in that acceptance that your attitudes will broaden and view a greater life. For those whose minds insist on discouragement are simply directing the energy to the self-defense mechanisms, created by the old patterns, in order that they may return to that which has served its purpose and is passing on its way.

As all of life is the direct effect of Infinite Intelligence, expressing through what is known as a vehicle called thought, let us broaden our horizons in consideration, divine love of the thought of the animal, the bird, and the tree. For all expresses God, the Divine. And to accept that truth is to place you, the true you, in communion with all of life. It is all of life that will lift your soul. To think otherwise is to deny the right of the Infinite Intelligence and, therefore, bring upon yourself the destiny and the payment of that judgment.

It is through a constant reminder, a constant call from the eternal soul to the limited human mind—the call to understand. To understand is to broaden your horizons. To understand is to lift you to heavenly heights of peace and harmony. But man cannot understand without, because without is the effect of the within.

To forgive the attitudes of mind that you entertain is to free those denials in consciousness and, in so doing, to gain a greater understanding of yourself. That greater understanding will open your eyes that the Intelligence, known as God, will have a clearer and freer channel through which to express.

How does man, bound by the illusion of form, view the Infinite? By the one thing that *is* the Infinite: it is known as Peace. To think the word and become it is your eternal birthright. In the midst of all change, be your true being. In the midst of all experiences, be the peace that is you.

In your prayers to the Divine, may they ever be for formlessness, for, in so doing, you rise beyond creation and its dual, opposing laws. May your prayers be more than words. May they be the call to the Divine that the light of reason may shed upon your eternal being today. Be not concerned with the tomorrows, for they shall ever be the effects of your todays. Work with this moment, take care of this moment now. Let not your thoughts drift backward or forward, for it is the drifting of thought, backward and forward, that binds you and pulls you in opposite directions—a house divided. This is the moment. The moment of the now *is* your success and your fullness of life.

When you find your mind drifting back and forward, remember that it always drifts backward in so-called time first. For it is the magnetic pull of yesteryear that has the greatest hold upon you. And when it pulls you backward, as it does each moment of each day, its projections forward are in keeping with the same dual law. It is a matter of the now. That is your most valuable asset: the moment of eternity. To drift backward and forward is to review an illusion known as experience. The only thing it may serve is to help awaken you, but it only awakens a wise man. It awakens a wise man because a wise man uses it for the sole purpose of being an instrument to help others. The greatest asset is your eternal moment. That is the treasure of the universes and in the eternal moment you will awaken to all eighty-one dimensions. You will no longer dream: you will become. Heed well, my students, the power of that eternal moment, called now. For in the heeding, you shall become what you truly are.

You may ask your questions at this time.

Thank you. Please distinguish between revelation and judgment and, or gossip.

The question to distinguish between revelation, judgment, and gossip is very simple: if you have revelation, you have reason. And with the other two, you do not.

Thank you. How do we honestly begin to open the first two soul faculties?

By honesty.

Thank you. Is it motive that determines whether or not one is in fascination?

Well, if one is in fascination, one is in procrastination. And so it is very simple to view whether or not a person is in fascination. You cannot be in fascination without demonstrating the Law of Procrastination. Thank you.

Thank you. Are there spiritual significances that incline one to have reference over the hours of time? The expression is frequently used, "I am a day person" or "I am a night person." Does this tell us anything about our spiritual nature?

It does not in any way, shape, or form reveal your spiritual being. It does reveal your judgments.

Thank you. When a child is fearful of the dark, is this an indication of the soul's innate aversion to spiritual darkness?

Not necessarily so. However, it is a revelation of a denial in reference to darkness from past experiences.

Thank you. In this age of narcotics, where marijuana is fashionable, could you please us tell us if the drug is spiritually detrimental? Please be explicit in telling us what it attracts into our lives from the other side of the veil. Could you describe the invisible attractions, if you could, please?

What is important is whether or not the drug is detrimental in any way to one's own evolution. Anything that causes a person, by their own use, a lack of the full use of the faculty of reason is detrimental. And in reference to the latter part of the question, the law is very clear and simple: that likes attracts likes and becomes the Law of Attachment.

Thank you. Is alcohol, including wine, a spiritual detriment when used in moderation? And how does it compare to a drug like marijuana used in moderation? What invisible forces, if any, does alcohol, in moderation, invite?

It is in keeping with the answer to your first question. Anything that has a detrimental effect upon the faculty of reason is not beneficial to the evolving soul.

Thank you. If a person whose home is burglarized but is not a thief himself and he never set the Law of Temptation into motion because he locked his doors and windows, can you please tell me what spiritual laws he has transgressed to merit such an experience?

Any person who has the experience of someone stealing from them has stolen. Otherwise, the law could not fulfill itself that likes attracts like and becomes the Law of Attachment.

The question is, that man, in this particular question, has not stolen, that is, in his judgment, from anyone and has taken great precaution not to place temptation before another soul. That is in keeping with the statement you have read. Any person, any person who takes a desire is known as stealing. Desire is the divine expression. When man entertains desire, he is entertaining God. When the desire, in keeping with the laws that he has established, is not fulfilled in keeping with the judgment of his mind that it should be and he continues to entertain the desire, he has stolen from the Divine. For he has stolen by dictating to the Divine that it should be fulfilled. He has not given it back to God, because from God it has come. It does not belong to man.

Now, man is the vehicle through which the Divine expresses itself and that divine expression is called, by man, desire. When man judges how and when it shall be fulfilled—this energy that is flowing through him—and holds on to the desire, he is stealing from God. Consequently, when man asks the question, "I have never stolen. Why am I stolen from?" it is simply a lack of awareness of the divine, demonstrable law. Let us think a bit more deeply, my students, in reference to stealing.

Can we, by our thought, change the hair upon our head? We know, in truth, we cannot. We delude ourselves by thinking we can. But, in truth, each hair is accounted for by the Divine, in keeping with law established.

We entertain many thoughts and we do not place God or goodness with them. And so we steal daily. And because of our unawareness of this demonstrable truth, we do not pray for forgiveness. We hold to thoughts and we do not free them. We do not strive to become the examples of what we know in our hearts. So we must consider a bit more than we have already considered.

We stated many times that the greatest gift is the gift of self, for it is self that stands in the way. And it is self that makes a judgment that the divine expression is our sole possession. And in so doing, we steal many things and, therefore, are stolen from in many, many, many different ways.

Let us never forget that we are loaned much by the Divine. But because all things are sustained by God, God may call at any moment. So it is only pure common sense that we accept all things. For in the accepting of all things, we are bound by no thing, for we are no longer stealing from God.

Good night.

FEBRUARY 24, 1977

CONSCIOUSNESS CLASS 137

Good evening, class. This evening, our class will be a little different than the usual.

Our philosophy teaches that truth is taught through indirection, demonstration, and example. And whereas you are all students of the Serenity Association and whereas many of you are members of the Association, we all know the Law of Personal Responsibility.

And so this evening, you are being informed that the American Legion has raised our rent—an increase of $150 per month. Now, as your pastor I receive $50 a month for my own survival and that's not going to spread that far. We also have $51,000 to raise to complete God's home. That is a personal financial responsibility of every student and every member, who has already received so much and continues to do so.

We have refrained—ever since the founding of this Association—we have refrained from compulsory tithing. We have only at one time placed a direct assessment—a fair share assessment—upon our membership in order to purchase the lot that we have. Many of our members have not yet responded.

Therefore, this evening, we're going to have to face the responsibility that justly and rightly belongs to each and every one of us.

I have absolute faith that God will see us through these seeming obstructions. This morning, at eight o'clock, the Civic Center came up—their inspectors—to stop the construction of God's home. By 9:00 a.m., I had our attorney at Civic Center and that obstruction was melted away.

Now, this evening, we must face how much value we have in keeping these church doors open and in facing the financial indebtedness—that we *must* raise. And so I'm going to go to each and every student, to each and every member that is present and personally ask here, in front of God and man, what their feeling and intention is in remaining as students and members of this Association. Now, if we are limiting ourselves by our brain dictates of experiences of yesterday, then we have yet to gain the truth that has been shared with all of you over these years.

This home will be completed in approximately thirty days. We will move into it. But we are going to have to unite in consciousness, in motive, in principle, and become a united whole. If we are interested in what this church offers, then we must do our part, not only spiritually, but mentally and materially. I assure you, no matter how few, or how many, are left in this Association, God will find a way of keeping these doors open. But you are given the opportunity to demonstrate what you have been learning and what you have been teaching.

And I'm going to begin with the group on my left. We all know that our membership is approximately thirty-six members. And if any of you have taken the interest, then you know exactly how much money comes into the Association and you know exactly where it goes. Any clothes upon my back or anything else that you think I have did not come out of the funds of your church. I'll begin with the group on my left. Will you rise, please?

[*The sound level of the recording made it very difficult to accurately and completely transcribe the students' responses.*]

How would you like me to speak?

You know that our rent has been increased—I officially received the notice this evening—from $200 a month to $350 a month. And you also know that we have an immediate indebtedness of $51,000 to pay off. Would you like to speak on how or in what way you feel that you will, or you can, help your Association, for its doors to stay open?

I sincerely pledge that I will do my part spiritually, as I saw demonstrated today how it works. And in the physical world, I pledge what I can give—my income tax return is coming and from the sale of some property. And if you'd like an estimated amount at this time . . .

Mr. Vice President, would you take note? No, it's not necessary. It's on tape. Yes, that would be most helpful to all of the rest of our students. Remember, friends, this church doesn't belong to any one person. It is, and we are, a united part of it. Yes, please.

At this time and with God's help, I feel that I can get together at least $1,000.

Thank you very much.

Thank you.

The next student, please.

Yes, Mr. Goodwin, I would like to help . . .

Thank you so much.

I don't have—don't know how much . . .

Thank you. The next student, please.

Yes, sir. I'm most grateful for what I am continuing to receive from this organization. And I can state at this point that I will be very happy to pledge $2,000 in the next few weeks, but I will not put a ceiling on it, because I would like to give more.

Thank you very much.

Yes, I'll do what I can. I can come up with a couple of hundred of dollars right away. And is there a deadline on this?

In reference to the $51,000, we have approximately thirty days. Thirty days.

Well, by then, I could get some more. But in the next couple of months for sure.

Thank you very much. I would like to say one thing. We have, a month ago, placed the Serenity Camp lands on the market for sale. We have had several offers. The latest offer to us was $33,000—$7,200 down and a mortgage. Now, I know that we can receive $36,000 from the sale of the camp lands, but we would have to take a mortgage. And there are very few people that have been bidding on the land that have $36,000 cash. But we will do the very best that we can. And I know between that sale, which will go any day—there are so many people bidding on it—and with the help of this membership and the students and friends of this church that we will be able to carry through.

Now I'd like to go to the next group, please. I'll just go group by group. The next student, please.

Well, I'm very grateful for the philosophy and the laws that have been demonstrated on the job and throughout the time that I've been here. My wife and I have already pledged $3,000 and we can borrow another $5,000 in our capacity from borrowing from the bank.

Thank you very much. Next, please.

I second the motion. We'll set into motion to have the $8,000.

Thank you very much. Next.

Well, I'm very grateful for what I've learned since I've been here. And I can state that I'm working that. And I feel that I will work to do as much as I can and give all that I can to support these efforts. They have really benefited myself and people around me. And I think I can pledge $1,000.

Thank you very much. Next.

At the moment, I'm at a crossroad. I'm unemployed. And financially, things have been difficult for me. The one thing I can pledge is self. I have always been successful as . . .

Thank you very much.

As far as ready cash is concerned, I can immediately give $150. That's all that I feel that, that I can at the moment. However, I will make my property available, if a loan, a sizeable loan is needed.

Thank you very much. Next group, please.

I have much gratitude to the Association, Mr. Goodwin, having known you, perhaps, longer than most people here. I know the philosophy has worked for me and I try to pass it on to people that I've been associated with. I've already pledged $2,000, within the next two months, after the property that I've sold goes through, and I will add another $1,000.

Thank you very much. Next, please.

Yes. I am quite encouraged. As a matter of fact, tomorrow I have an appointment for a loan. I'm three months behind in my rent and I was going to borrow that and try to get a few more—a hundred for Serenity along with it. I just won't tell them where it's going. And so I'm hoping I get $200 or $300, if I can get that much.

Thank you very much.

I'm very grateful for the philosophy.

Thank you.

I'm very grateful to the philosophy, too . . . [Although the student continued speaking, it was not possible to transcribe her comments.]

Thank you very much.

Mr. Goodwin, I am grateful to you and this church. I just pray that . . . $412.50 . . . another $37. And I believe that I'll have another check . . .

Thank you very much. Would you start off your group, please?

I'm very grateful for all that's happened in my life since walking in these doors . . .

Thank you very much.

I am grateful for the philosophy. I think I'm going . . . anything past . . .

Thank you very much. Next, please.

I'm very happy for everything that I have received here. And I pledge $100 for . . .

Thank you.

I'm very grateful for what I've learned here. And I'm very happy to be here, a part of this class. And right now, I'm not working, but I would like to pledge $200.

Thank you very much. The next group, please.

Within the month, I'll be able to pledge $100 for the church, even though the mind . . .

I understand.

I think it'll work.

Thank you.

I was thinking much about what this church has given me, what you've given me. And I'll pledge $1,000.

Thank you very much.

My gratitude is boundless. It really is. My responsibilities at this time are very great because my desires have been very great. And I will pay . . . for the blessing of the gain. I have no ready cash, but my father is, you all know, is not . . . And my father has always supported this church and he and my brother almost help build the church . . . I believe they will be quite sympathetic. And I will call and see what they can give . . . Don't know what to say. I will ask for a thousand—maybe more. I'll ask for what I can get.

Thank you very much.

Sir, at this time, I can pledge $500.

Thank you. That includes the other student. Thank you.

Since my introduction to Serenity, I have received great benefit. And I only came here about last spring. At this time, unfortunately, my cash flow is practically nonexistent. But if I ever get any, you'll hear about it.

Thank you.

I'll pledge $3,000 based—pending on sales and . . .

Thank you very much.

Thank you. I, in attending Serenity, have but one purpose: and that is, the aiding of myself in fulfilling the true purpose of my life. In keeping with that, I will pledge to you all support that I can. I can pledge to you at this time $500.

Thank you very much.

Yes, Richard. First, I want to thank you and everyone for the response that I've seen here. It's prompted me, I guess, to, to respond more than what my mind would let me. I'm not—I would rather not make a financial commitment. I know I can easily come up with some cash . . .

Thank you very much.

Well, I'm very grateful for Serenity. And it has meant a lot to me to be here. Again, I think the philosophy is just beautiful. And sometimes I say to myself about money problems, "You now have the opportunity to see what you love more, God or money." And there's always that funny feeling in my stomach, when I write out that check . . . and I always . . . what a surprise. I'm not very good at finances . . . but I will pray for some inspiration to . . .

Thank you.

Mr. Goodwin, I give you what I can . . .

Thank you.

[*It is not possible to transcribe the student's remarks.*]

Thank you very much.

Now, I know with the students' motives that have been demonstrated this evening and with our prayers on the divine guidance of the sale of our camp lands that we will meet this financial commitment. Now, the additional $150 a month that the Legion—it is effective the first of April. I got the letter tonight when I came to class. We will pay that because that is the thing to do. We use the hall on Thursday evenings, we use it on Sundays, and we now have brunches every Sunday morning.

These things are a wonderful demonstration of how the law impartially works. For many years, we have taught that just before the victories in life come all the hissing hounds of hell. So it serves a very good purpose, because it helps to remind us what truly has value for us. And we all know how much we have received in this simple, down-to-earth, and practical philosophy.

And because we have received it, we bear the responsibility to share it with those who are seeking it. That does not mean to transgress the demonstrable law that says that unsolicited help is to no avail. But when people solicit help—and help is solicited in many ways—it is our responsibility to share that which has helped us.

Now, I'm going to ask all of you, as students, for your daily prayers in guidance concerning the building of God's home. I know that many of you are not aware of the protests that have been going on daily at Civic Center in reference to building that house, in order that we may continue to serve God. There have been, since the day we first stepped on the land, daily protests at Civic Center, with the public works department, with the building department, with the planning commission. Now, these protests, we know—and knew from the first day—where they were stemming from. As you drive up the dirt road up that hill, there is one house that sits there. And it belongs to a Swedish boy who is living in Holland. There are several people that are tenants in that house. And they have lived up there on that hill all by themselves. And they didn't want anybody up there. And so from the first day, they made that very clear. We never said anything. We went on about our business.

At the insistence of the Council of your church, we had that land surveyed—one and one-quarter acres. And the survey revealed that the road easement, which is legally forty feet wide, that that house at that corner was forty feet into our road easement. The survey proved that. Now, we said nothing to Civic Center or to anyone else over the illegality of that house that belongs to those Swedish people.

The protests reached such a point at Civic Center that this morning, at eight o'clock, one of the planning commissioners came up to put a stop construction on God's home, making the judgment that the house was being used for church services. It has never been, nor is it, nor will it be the intent of your Association to conduct religious services in that house. We tried to inform the planning department of that truth. They would not accept that. The judgment has been made and those tenants in that house have enforced it at Civic Center five days a week for the past two months that we've been up there working.

Now, today I had the treasurer call the parents who purchased the home for their son, who is now in Holland. They were very upset and were not aware that their tenants had been making these complaints. Because the truth of the matter is, the owner came up on the hill and spoke to our contractor because he received a notice from the public works department that their property was encroaching on the public road easement forty feet. And, of course, that is their problem.

And so with your prayers, I am sure that we will, we definitely will finish building. We will move in. And we will continue to operate our church.

Our attorney, this morning, was informed by one of the commissioners that if we ever applied for a use permit in order to do our printing of our church programs, he would close us down. What we must accept is truth: he is one person at Civic Center, one of the many workers in the planning commission. Now, the truth of the matter is that there are thousands of use permits for running a business in a private home in a residential area. There are thousands of permits. We happen to have a permit. It costs us $10—a use permit to run our little printing press in our present residence in Corte Madera. It is a well established principle in Marin County for anyone owning a home—architects have use permits. Designers have use permits. Untold numbers of people operate a private business in this county in a private residence. So I am not worried, nor concerned, about that.

We placed—we put in a 1,600-gallon holding tank for our water. We put in such a large amount because the fire hydrant is a couple of miles down North San Pedro Road. For any type of fire protection, it will take two fire engines with connected hoses that long a distance to protect the home. And so at the request of the Fire Marshall of Santa Venetia, we placed our water tank—our 1,600-gallon water tank and pump—in the place closest to the road. So that not only our home would have fire protection, but that Swede's cottage across the street would have fire protection. Today, we found out we must have a variance in order to have that holding tank that close to the road. And it's several feet from it, by the way.

Now, tomorrow morning the contractor is going to see the Fire Marshall. The contractor went today to speak to the planning commission—is that correct? And the book—and going by the book, as they do, requires that we have a variance. Now, if possible, they're going to try to get us on the agenda for Monday, March 28.

Now, unless you're familiar with the different laws of this county, when you apply for a variance, anybody—any property owner or anyone that is interested in your property—appears to either protest or to help you get the variance. And so I am asking the students of this Association to be present. We will let you know for sure—we should know tomorrow morning if we will be able to get the variance for the present placement for our water tank. And it would behoove you to make that effort, whether it be March 28 or the following month.

The water is connected. What we went down for—we were not aware that you had to have a variance to put in a water tank.

What we went down for was a permit to build a shed around the water tank, because it looks like some kind of a spaceship from Mars, the way it's made. But it's very modern. But that's what it looks like. And so we were going to build a little shed around it, so it would be more in keeping with the house itself.

And so, remember, March 28. And we will know Sunday for sure if we're able to get on the agenda. The only ones that I know of that would try to protest that variance are those tenants at the Swede's cottage. But I also question that there'll be many more protests at Civic Center considering the parents of the owner—a man and his wife—who bought that cottage for their son, who is in Holland, are very unhappy because so many problems have risen from their tenants making so many complaints about the building of your church home.

And so those are the things that we must look at. I know that, financially, with God's help and with your prayers, we will meet our commitment.

Now, I know that many of you have not been up to the hill to see that home and its building. And I would like to have all of you up there all of the time, but we have tried to be considerate of all the neighbors—and we only have, really, one. There's only one on that street. And unfortunately, their home is illegally on top of the street. But it's been there for about forty years. I am convinced that the planning commission would not force them to tear their home down. If they would go and apply for a variance—because it has existed there for so long. And they had no neighbors to protest the variance.

Now, the reason that we have been very strict about the building of that house is because we have tried to keep the flow of traffic down. Because, you see, when you drive up a one-mile dirt road, it makes quite a dust—a lot of dust. And so with all of the work and all of the hammering and the sawing and all of that going on, we have, every Saturday, for those who have shown some interest and who have asked, we have taken up groups of people to work.

And the ladies and the men of this church have done a great deal of work up there. You cannot move from foundation to roof in three weeks without a lot of help. If you don't believe me, when you go up and see the house, you'll understand.

What the problem with the minds of some people is, we have built a home that will accommodate the storage of our church. Because we have no place here in a rented hall [*the American Legion log cabin*] to store anything. And we have a great deal of things. We have a little printing press. We have an IBM composer. We have a duplicator to duplicate all of these classes. And we needed a workshop where the men could make things and the ladies could make things, you see. And so it *is* a large house and it looks like a large house. It's 6,800 square feet. But because it's such a large and beautiful house—and it's the largest house in Santa Venetia—it's caused, what we all know, is a little bit of jealousy.

The minds cannot understand how one man could live in such a big house. Well, if any of you have been to Corte Madera, you can't say that one man is living in a big house because I have many students that come to work. So it is a very rare occasion that the house is ever empty of people.

Now, I am very grateful to God that the students that are present in the class, that show some interest in this philosophy and church and its continuity, are willing to do all that they can to keep it going. Because I certainly will continue to do all that I can to keep it going, because I know that it has great value. I also know that we all have a human mind. And I know that we have eighty-one levels of consciousness and we have to have great understanding and tolerance to understand when someone is trapped in one of those levels of yesterday's experiences.

You see, you must have compassion for people. You must understand that those kids—those tenants in that house—they're filled with fear. They're afraid. And they're afraid because they have to do something in order to stay in that house. And fear causes us to do things that are not sensible and not practical and not reasonable. It is the fear, you see. We try to preserve certain levels of consciousness that are destined to be changing, for we have evolved through them. So we must let these levels of consciousness—that disturb us so greatly—we must let them pass so that we can move on in consciousness to something more peaceful and harmonious.

I have always taught that a seeming bad experience ofttimes, ofttimes produces excellent results. And so the disasters of this day have already produced excellent results. For excellent results are a uniting in consciousness for a spiritual purpose. We have nothing to fear at Civic Center, for the planning commission is not our God. But we do have to do our part. It must mean enough to us. It must mean enough to us to go to that meeting, requesting a variance for a water storage tank that we placed where the Fire Marshall asked us to place it. So their fire truck could come up and just connect. We're even going to the expense of putting on a special faucet so their hoses can connect. Not only to protect our property, but to protect the property across the street. Even the Fire Marshall said, "How fortunate those people over there are that you're putting in this 1,600-gallon water storage tank." We did that at the request of the Council of your church, right in the midst of their daily protesting the building of that house. But we did it anyway. And so, you see, if you do what is right because it is right to do right, then only good can come from it if you have the patience and you have the faith that is necessary.

It would have been very easy for me, this morning, when I was called at 8:00 o'clock and informed of the situation with that inspector—I immediately decided that *I* would go to that Civic Center. How dare they threaten to close the building of God's home, when every legal permit, *every* permit had been granted and approved by the county. And so I started to get ready. And my mother came to me and said, "Richard, you're not going to Civic Center." But I had already decided to go, because, you see, it triggered in me the self-preservation tapes. And she said, "This is the reason that we have an attorney. That is an attorney's job. That is why you pay them." And so I had to wait from 8:00 o'clock until 9:00, because I tried, immediately after, to reach the attorney and there was no answer. But I reached him at two minutes to 9:00. I explained the situation to him and he said, "I will leave in five minutes." I asked him to go up, first, to the hill to see the house and the property that the county was insisting that we were going to hold church meetings in. And he came up. And he saw it. And he went to Civic Center and he talked to an individual. And that individual admitted that he was trying to scare the hell out of us. He said that he would do everything to stop us from moving in to that house. But, you see, right is right and just is just. And I assure you, we are doing everything honest, aboveboard, and legal. And we will move in.

I understand—I have not met that individual—but I understand that he has a judgment and he's made his decision. I realize that. I realize that the man has prejudice and he has many problems. But they are not ours if we do what is right.

And so in reference to the $150-a-month increase on your church rent, there are many ways to raise funds—many, many, many ways. And every door has been opened so that our doors, to serve God, may remain open. Because all who enter these doors benefit, then it is our responsibility to encourage those who are not in the class this evening to do what they can so that each and every one of us may be a part, a part of something greater. Because that's really what it's all about.

If we unite in our efforts, then we are with God. And nothing can stand against God—and God means good and right. And that's the way that it will be.

We have—as I said earlier—we have brunches every Sunday morning. That's one very fine way of raising funds. The average of those brunches is approximately $100 a week. Now, we did that in order that we may help defray the cost of the monthly mortgage on that home and that we could continue on with our work. So we should not be discouraged because the Legion has raised our rent.

And you know—may I have the letter, please?—and you know what is so interesting—the Legion has been kind to us. We've been with them six years in May. But I want this letter read to you to see how the mind has to justify in order to do things. They didn't have to tell us that we leave the hall dirty on Thursday nights. We never have. But that's what they told us. They didn't have to tell us that we use more water than we should, because, you see, when this man who signed this letter, when he called me months ago and the American Legion needed this hall on two occasions, I said, "Well, we'll have to make out advance publicity and everything." And he said, "Well, Mr. Goodwin, I certainly would appreciate it, because this is a very important meeting for us." And I said, "When, then, we will just do that." And he told me at that time how grateful the Legion was that we always left this hall as clean as we did. Now, I think it's important that the letter be read to you, as members and friends.

It's addressed to Serenity Spiritualist Church:
Ladies and Gentlemen,

I have been instructed by the Commander, Officers, Members, and Executive Committee of the membership of this post that effective April 1, 1977, your fees for the use of the log cabin will be increased to $350. There are several reasons for this decision: your increased use of the cabin on Thursdays, which originally *was for choir practice for a few hours, which has now been increased to full time use, including use of all facilities. We have had complaints, from the custodian, that the cabin was left in an unclean condition after the Thursday meetings, as well as the third Saturday of each month. Also, the increased cost of utilities and maintenance fees, plus the fact that, in spite of water rationing in Marin County, your group is using too much water.*

We are also increasing the rates for all of our regular renters, as well as for various reasons. So we are not discriminating against your group or any other renter.

We regret that we must take this action, but, under the circumstances, we have no other choice. We suggest that you reply promptly to this letter, addressing your reply to the Commander, San Anselmo Post 179.

Sincerely . . .

Now, you see, friends, in keeping with your philosophy, when you receive something like this, you can read it and you can say, "Well, Lord, yes, I can see the need here that the mind has for justification."

You see, it would have been much more in principle—and I'm sure you would all agree—if they simply sent us a letter and said, "We regret to inform you, but effective on April 1, your rent will be $350. Due to increased costs of etc., etc."

So the wise thing to do—it is very simple: we will send them a kind letter informing them that we have been advised of the increase in the rent and we shall pay accordingly. To do anything else is to move out of principle.

I happen to know, for an absolute fact, what rented halls rent for. And it is in our best interests to pay the rent and to continue on with our church. Does anyone have any question in reference to that? *[After a short pause, the Teacher continues.]* Because we could talk to them and go through all kinds of justifications and maybe get it knocked down $20, but it is better that we stay in principle and accept it in keeping with the laws that we alone have established and be grateful that we have a place in order to do the work that we have to do.

Now, I would like to ask for a show of hands, if it's in keeping for March 28, this variance meeting—and I would like to say this first: For those of you who make the effort to go that night, it will be an education of how your county operates. You may not have to say one word. Because, you see, when you go to a meeting where there are these variances and they're on the agenda, you're not the only one that's on the agenda. So you have to sit and have some experiences with other people's request for variances. Now, when our turn comes up, you may not have to say a word. There may be no protest and no objection to that little water pump and that tank that's sitting on the hill. But if there is, then we will at least be there united to speak for what we believe is right.

Now, those of you who are willing to go and who will be there, will you kindly raise your hands? I thank you all very, very much. I don't think we're going to have to battle. But remember, man must make the effort to stand up for principle. And our philosophy is a lot further ahead today than it was even five years ago. There's a lot less prejudice. It still has not been totally eliminated from the world, but there is a lot less prejudice to our religion than there ever was before.

And, as I said, I would like all of you to see that beautiful home. It isn't the most expensive, but it certainly is quality. The building inspector—I said to him today—he came up and gave us the approval for the close-in, which means the sheetrock can be put on the walls. I said, "How is the house?" And he said, "It's a fine house. It's not going to go anywhere. It's so solid." And it is solid. And you have a wonderful asset that will serve a very good purpose. And it's made of quality and you'll not find a more beautiful view than you have on that hill.

Now, any of you that would like to go to see it, I am more than happy to make arrangements to take you up to see it. But

I know you understand that we are trying to be considerate of the neighbors and not run thirty or forty cars up that dirt road. So any of you that would like to go, be so kind to let me know and I will make sure, personally, that arrangements are made so you can go up and see what's happening. Now, Saturdays, we do have arrangements where we meet and go up in a car pool from Lyon's restaurant, up there by the Emporium. And the ladies go up and—in fact, the ladies already have started to do all of the insulation, you know. There are many jobs that the women have been doing, and, of course, the men, too. And that's how come it's going along so very nicely.

And I want to thank you all once again that there is enough to keep it going, because there's enough people who really care. I know your class has been different tonight, but I'm sure the benefit you have received in going inside of yourself to see what it means to you is worth more than all the words that could have been spoken.

Thank you very much.

MARCH 3, 1977

CONSCIOUSNESS CLASS 138

Good evening, class. Before getting into our class this evening, I think it is very important to all of you who are present—especially last class—to be briefed on the present situation in reference to God's home that's being built on the hill in Santa Venetia. As you know, there were serious problems last Thursday, and I am very happy to report, through sticking to and standing firmly on principle, that peace is, once again, reigning supreme.

And I want to thank all of the students who have already come through with their pledges. And I know that this evening, before we leave, that we will be able to save the 2 percent, which is necessary to pay tomorrow. And 2 percent seems very little perhaps to some of us, but it adds to a great deal when the amounts are in the thousands. And I want to assure you, with your continued help and support, these classes and this church will continue to operate, and the work of God, of presenting this light and this philosophy to the world, shall carry on. I know that all of you want that to be.

And I assure you, as long as I am on Earth—and I intend to be here for some time. I know there has been some concern in reference to the financial aid and support of your church, what might happen should I leave this earth realm. I don't think that I have honestly been such a bad person that before I got a chance to move into a house with a private bathroom that God would send me on. I'm in excellent health. Some people think I'm a little heavy, but if you live up on a hill, you'd better be a little heavy or the wind will blow you off the balcony. In fact, it almost did to a couple of carpenters and the shinglers. In fact, they had to go home.

So please don't be concerned about my health or concerned about my wealth or any of the good things of life, because they just continue to flow. And they will flow for all of my students if you will just be so honest as to accept your right to experience the goodness of life. For if you make that simple effort, what you will experience is the power of God moving through your consciousness and all the goodness that you could possibly desire will take place.

Today, we had some visitors, as we usually do, up on the hill—a young couple. I was out there on the lot. And the man got out of the car and he said, "Do you think there's any chance of seeing this house?" And I said, "I don't see why not, if you stay out of the way of the workers." Because there are many people there working. And he said, "You know, we have driven from Rohnert Park because we've heard about the marvel of Marin." I said, "Well, what do you mean?" He already knew that that house was in the sixth week of building. He knew that a minister, he said, was living there. He wanted to know who owned it. And I told him the Serenity Church. And he wanted to know who the minister was. And I said, "Well, that's me." And he said—it was kind of interesting—he said, "Well, you must have saved a lot of souls to earn such a beautiful place." And I said, "Well, I don't know about that."

But, you see, that's the way most people think, you know. If you have any goodness in life, it's something that you've inherited. The consciousness can't seem to accept the possibility that it's something you might have worked for. So let us not forget that the workers win. And let us not forget that what one has, that we desire—let us not deny that to that soul, because, in denying the right of that soul, we are, in truth, denying the right of our own soul. So if we ask for the crumb in life, be rest assured if we have the faith and we're willing to work, the chances are that we'll get the whole loaf. And no one can tell me that in asking for a bathroom, a private bath, and bedroom of their own, perhaps without all the church stuff stored in it, is not a crumb to ask for. For none of my students that I know of have to wait in line to go to the bathroom at home. And so, you see, the crumb did turn into a loaf because God moved through, and continues to move through, a sufficient number of my students.

Now, God will move the same way for you if you don't tell him how to move. And thank you all very much. I thank God each day and I thank you as individuals for being clear channels to permit God's goodness to flow, not only for me, but for you, your church, and the work that it has to do. Thank you.

[*At this point, Mr. Goodwin goes into a trance.*]

Greeting, students. This evening we are discussing the beginning of form. And in that discussion, we must consider that, in truth, we are the essence of life itself. We are a sphere of energy in comparison, to your understanding, the approximate size of a pinhead.

And in this evolutionary process, in this expression and expansion of consciousness, through this microscopic form, you, through the laws of expanding identity, have, through the evolution of many spheres and planets, evolved to your present form. It is in the divine law that this evolution, through expansion, shall, in time, return to the whole from which it has wandered on its journey of continuing identification.

And so, my good students, it behooves us to accept everything, to deny no thing, for, in that expanding or broadening of your horizons, do you become the receptacle of the divine power of peace. For the essence of life is, in truth, the peace that sustains all of life. For he who accepts is freed from his judgments; he is freed from the dual law that governs and controls all forms.

Move graciously along the stream of consciousness. For if you will only do so, you will experience that peace that passeth all understanding.

You are today the effects of judgments passed. You are the effects of all your denials. And whatever the mind denies, it is guaranteed, by self-destiny, to accept.

In the multitude of experiences in evolution, do not permit your mind to dictate its value or its worth. All of these many experiences, you alone have made necessary that you may broaden your horizons, expand your consciousness. The pain and struggle of life is nothing more than the illusion known as judgment.

My good students, may the centuries pass quickly for you. For in passing quickly, your journey homeward is indeed more pleasant. Life is intended as good for all.

Remember that the mind, in its very nature of attachment, brings unto your consciousness awareness the eternal cycle in creation of pain and pleasure. Free yourselves, my good students, from that dual wheel of joy and sadness, of hate and love. The path of freedom is the path of divine will. Whatever comes into your life is called forth by you. Knowing that simple truth and demonstrating it is the transformation process that you are destined to pass through. Grant unto yourselves the right that is you. Rely not upon the dictates of your mind, for that reliance holds you back temporarily from the goodness that is waiting for you to experience. Become more consciously aware of those dictates. Separate truth, that which you are, from creation, the illusion, which you are not. For in so separating that true you from the untold limited identities, you will unite yourselves with the Allness that, in truth, you are.

When these dictates and disturbances of your mind scream out for their fulfillment of energy, take hold of your mind and declare the truth: the affirmation that was given to you so long ago, "Thank you, God. I am at peace." For the true you *is* that peace. The illusion that is temporarily blinding you has come to you by the Law of Judgment and it shall leave you by the Law of Forgiveness. Forgive that which disturbs you, forgive the illusion. Do not deny it. For in so forgiving shall you be freed from it. For to forgive it is not to deny it and its right of expression. Learn to forgive those levels of consciousness that no longer serve a beneficial purpose for you.

And the question rises within your minds, "How do I know they no longer serve a beneficial purpose? How do I know without judgment?" You know through forgiveness. For in the process of forgiving, you are giving forth to God, the power that sustains that level of consciousness. And in so doing you are the one who rises ever closer to the eternal Light, where harmony doth reign supreme.

Use that which is for you to use. Use it wisely and you will never be in want. Learn, my good students, not to hoard, for to hoard is to support the level of consciousness known as fear—the supremacy of the mind over your true being. Learn to use what you have, for not to do so is to waste, and to waste is to want. Learn not to depend upon people, places, and bank accounts. Learn to rely upon the essence of peace that is your true being. For that peace, once rising within your consciousness, brings harmony and health to your being. And remember, health *is* wealth, for that which is healthy is prosperous and multiplies its own goodness. So he who is healthy is wealthy, for he prospers physically, mentally, and spiritually.

Learn to prosper by your acceptance of your right. Learn to prosper in all your endeavors in life by putting peace, the power of God, in all your thoughts, acts, and activities. And in putting the power of God, known as peace, in your thought, you will, by a very natural process, forgive all the temptings of judgment that rise within your minds.

Look at all of Nature and view the living demonstration of how she prospers. Her multiplication of the species is without number. That is the law: to multiply and increase. For through that increasing process is the consciousness expanded and, in that expansion, more of God is able to flow.

Until we learn to open our minds, we can never experience the fullness of our hearts. Let new thoughts and new ideas enter your consciousness. And as you become ever-increasingly aware of the battle of the human mind in its effort to preserve what it has already dictated and accepted, pray in that moment for peace. For your simple asking for peace is recorded and registered by the Power that can accomplish it. Whatever thought you entertain is sustained by the power of the universes. Entertain the thoughts that prosper the goodness in your life. For we all prosper in that that we are truly willing to accept.

Think for a moment when something distasteful happens to you. Does it not grow and prosper within your mind? Does the thought not continue to repeat itself? Do not the judgments of your mind continue to speak? Is the law not simple and clear? You prosper in whatever your endeavor is.

Become more consciously aware of the direction of your energy. Look more closely within, during the course of your day.

Look more closely within, when you speak to another. Become aware of your feelings, become aware of your thoughts. And in that awakening you will know what controls you. Make that effort, my students. Awaken within and you will understand everything that is without.

You may ask your questions at this time.

Thank you. Is it possible to express acceptance and yet, at the same time, make a choice without going into detail?

In reference to the question of acceptance, man is in a constant process of acceptance, for he even accepts the right of his denials. One, faced with decision—and we are faced with decisions each moment of conscious awareness—may, through accepting the right path, instead of the left path, be freed by the power of forgiveness, granting the left path its right and experiencing the right path.

Thank you. You said that you did not fulfill what was given you to do when you were on our planet in physical form. Can you please tell us what it was you were given to do and in what manner your task was assigned to you and how each of us can best determine the highest way that we can serve God?

In those centuries past, when I entered your earth realm, my soul, in its evolution, had awakened sufficiently to know right, to do right. And as it entered the earth realm and through the experiences of early, early age that it had encountered, I chose, though knowing within it was wrong, I chose the easier—I thought at that time—the easier path. I knew that he who judges shall be judged. I knew that from my experiences before entering your earth realm. But my mind rose supreme and I became a judge in order, my mind dictated, that I would not be judged. And because, knowing what I had to do and choosing the supremacy of my mind, I had to return. And I still return. And it has been many, many, many centuries.

My seeming payment is just and good, for through the many experiences that I have, and continue to encounter, I have gained much. My responsibilities are greater than ever before, but those responsibilities are no longer a burden to me, though they were for centuries. No longer do I judge and no longer am I judged. Life, my students, is our judge, for we make life our judge. Because we judge life, life, in turn, respectfully responds. And so each experience, the effect of judgment, returns unto us. Each morning that we awaken, we are judged by life, for life, we are judging. Each person that we meet judges us, for we are judging them.

And so, my students, forgiveness, in truth, is the path of freedom. We have spoken to you before that freedom is the direct effect of self-control, and without forgiveness, there is no control of self. Let us look at life as an observer, a witness of all that passes before our view. And in being the witness, let us look beyond the illusions of form where we may view the eternal Light. Whether or not it is a blade of grass, a human form, or a bird, look beyond the form by looking beyond the self within. And as you do that, you will experience a great harmonious upliftment in consciousness. And as that experience increases, you will communicate with a part of yourself expressing through the bird or the blade of grass that your mind never knew existed. The eyes are opened. And we know when we go beyond creation, when we go beyond the limits of the human mind.

I speak to you here in this way, but I speak to many in the same moment in many dimensions. For I am not limited by the form and, being not limited by the form, I am free to express through many forms. I am as free to express through as many forms as I identify with. But I know the identity is the necessary illusion in order to reach those in the illusion. So let us not look askance at the identities of life, for we are the life and not the identity.

The separation in consciousness is the truth that you are truly seeking. You will find that truth, for it is, slowly but surely, rising within you. And in that opening of your minds, the angels of eternal Light are able to inspire you, to inspire you in keeping with the law of your total acceptance. For whatever we accept, we are. And because we are, in truth, the Allness, the Oneness, then our destiny is broadened and love, the power of the Light itself, emanates throughout our being. And those who come within the sphere of our consciousness become one with it, for there is only one Light, one Life, and one Love.

Good night.

MARCH 10, 1977

CONSCIOUSNESS CLASS 139

Good evening, students.

Before we start class this evening, it's always nice to have some good news, I'm sure. And I want to thank all of you for being willing to go to the Civic Center to the variance meeting for the pump house. And I also want to tell you that Civic Center has moved the date from the twenty-eighth of this month, in the evening, to this Friday, which is tomorrow, at 9:00 a.m. The Friends feel that it will not be necessary for the membership and the student body to go, unless they so choose to do so. Because most of you are working at that time anyway. But it will be most beneficial if you will just take a few moments at nine o'clock—we are the first ones on the agenda—and just give a moment of prayer and peace for what is in the divine right action for your church. I am sure that there will be no problem.

I spoke to the Fire Marshall today and he hand delivered his recommendations to the Planning Commission for the tank of water, the holding tank, to be where it is, close to the road. Because Serenity is the only one that has any water on the hill at all. And in case of a fire, that's where the fire department would have to go, because the nearest fire hydrant is 3,000 feet down North San Pedro Road. And it would take three fire trucks to connect their hoses in order to protect any homes on that hill. So those of you who wish to go, it will be at Civic Center at 9:00 a.m. I believe it's room 361. Is that correct? Yes. And we are the first on the agenda.

Now, tonight we'll conclude this semester. There have been occasions in the past that our semesters have been ten weeks. And this year, that is one of those occasions. So we will have our class this evening. And if you are wondering why it's one of those occasions, then all you have to do is listen to the tapes of this semester and ask yourself the question, Do you feel you got your money's worth? And if you don't, please see me at anytime that you feel that you didn't.

Now, our next semester, beginning in May, will include all the tape cassettes. Corrected fees have been made by the Association in order to include your cassettes, because there are so many students who have not been receiving them. And I know that the human mind cannot consciously, cannot consciously recall the many different laws that are revealed in these philosophy classes. And so those of you who are interested in attending our next semester, it will behoove you to make your reservations as early as possible.

Now, this Saturday, as you all know, is our Finlandia Dinner. And that is one of the many ways in which all of us can support the philosophy that we believe in.

I want to thank the many who have come forward with their pledges. And I also want to thank those who are in the process of doing so. Because I know that it will come at the right time and in the right place and through the right people. And when we accept life that way, then life becomes much more beautiful.

Now, in reference to the deadline established by the Council of your church—of moving to this new home—I'm happy to report that it is beyond a shadow of any doubt, the way that things are going and through our efforts—all of you—we will meet that deadline. And as I said before, at our last class, to those of you, as members, friends, and students, who have not seen the house that God is building, you are welcome to see it by making proper arrangements with any of the directors of your church. And we'll be happy to take you up there on a Sunday or make some arrangements for any other day, so that you can see what you are supporting physically, as well as spiritually and mentally.

Thank you.

[*At this point, Mr. Goodwin goes into a trance.*]

Greetings, students. In our discussion this evening on the divine principle of giving, we shall speak on the gift and the giver.

You have all heard from varying philosophies that the gift without the giver is of no value and worthless. What does that great, but simple, truth really mean? We have spoken in this philosophy about the greatest gift we can possibly give—is the gift of self.

As your soul, in its evolution, is often inspired to do, to act, these inspirations, rising from your eternal being, passing through the limited experiences of your present life, are contaminated by the judgments, restrictions, and reservations of past experiences. It is this contamination of the human mind that separates the gift from the giver. This separation or contamination, in turn, establishes the dual law of the human mind. And so it is that man, often with good thought, yet, in the error of ignorance in the unawareness of the contamination of his mental substance, makes a loan, instead of a gift.

Whenever we give—whether it is the spoken word or things we think that we possess—if we give them with reservation, then we have contaminated them and they constitute what is known as a loan. And because the gift is now separated from the giver—separated because the giver has not given the gift of self—then they, in their experiences, receive unto themselves all that is necessary that they may free themselves from the illusion and the delusion of placing the human, limited mind as the higher or greater authority in their own lives.

For example, say that you have the inspiration to give of your time, of your energy, and your efforts to something that you truly believe is worthwhile and good, first, for yourselves and then for the world. For unless you first accept that it is good for you, you cannot be qualified or in a position to accept that it is good for another. And so you give of your time, of your energy, of your efforts to something that you believe in. And in that giving, if you have thoughts of what you will receive or what is yet to be, then you can be rest assured that your gift is contaminated and now constitutes the principle of what is known to man as a loan. For you have placed upon the pure motivation of your eternal soul, you have placed a reservation, a limitation. And so in keeping with those laws that you alone have established in your givingness, shall you experience all of the obstructions and difficulties necessary in receiving.

It has been often said that it is better to give than to receive. Now, what do you think, my good students, that the philosophers of old meant by that simple truth? 'Tis better to give than to receive, for to give, man is in a position to know, in truth, whether or not his gift is contaminated by the reservations, limitations, and mental dictates of his own mind. Ah, but to receive is something that takes a greater degree of effort, for to receive anything is to place yourself at the mercy of the laws that you, in error and ignorance, are accepting. Unless, through your own prayer, you honestly accept the gift from God the Divine, then only the purity in your receiving can enter your sphere and zone of action. So let us consider this Law of Givingness. Let us consider it in all of its aspects. And in this Law of Receiving, let us never forget that there is one Intelligence—and one inseparable Intelligence—that is flowing through everything.

This philosophy, for many years on Earth, has taught that total consideration is divine love; that total acceptance is divine will. My good friends, we all, each moment, demonstrate divine love and divine will. It is in the broadening of our horizons that we speak, for when we have a thought or a desire, we totally accept it and we totally consider it. So in our own desires from our mind, we demonstrate each moment divine love and divine will. But we have limited ourselves and therefore must broaden our horizon in granting that divine right to all of life.

As our souls have entered these many realms of consciousness, they have brought with them all of the experiences of the centuries past. Some time ago we stated to harbor a thought is to feed a form. And so it is that these many forms, these attitudes of mind that we have directed energy to, have been created by us. Now, our souls entered into certain forms that would offer to us the necessary lessons in life to free us from all of these children that we have created over these many, many, many centuries. These created forms are not something that have been created by your thought, just from the moment that your soul entered the earth realm. Oh no, my good students, these various patterns and attitudes of mind are something that you have carried with you for many, many, many centuries. They are, slowly but surely, in the process of change, as each and every soul is evolving into the wholeness and the fullness of their eternal life and joy and peace.

We must ask ourselves the question—and learn to pause to think, to broaden our horizons of consciousness, for we are these many eighty-one levels expressing. But we are expressing in an error of ignorance in the sense that we, by our total consideration and by our total acceptance of limited thought patterns, we have reduced our horizons to a microcosm, so small and so minute. Man, in truth, knows that he is as small, or as large, as his God, and that his God is ever dependent upon the broadening of his horizons of God will and God love.

And so, my students, as we conclude this semester, we encourage you to continue on with your daily efforts, for it is through your daily efforts that these changes, that are inevitable for you, will take place more harmoniously, more graciously. Your horizons have already been broadened in just this short semester of class. They have been broadened in many ways. Although many things that have been spoken have been rejected by your limited minds, those thoughts, those ideas have been introduced into your consciousness. They are indelibly placed there and will live with you. They will serve you in your times of need. And though today we reject many things, we find, as the years and the centuries pass, that those rejections of yesteryear have become the acceptances and the very foundation stones upon which we climb, yea, even higher into the heavenly heights of consciousness in the eternal moment of now.

Look more objectively at thought. View it for what it truly is: a form created by your mind. Look at life. You all view it differently, at different times, because we are viewing from so many different levels of consciousness. Remember, as you communicate with all of life, that all of life is inseparably a part of you. That if you find things distasteful, it is simply because you do not yet understand the cause behind them. And the very level that is distasteful to you is revealing to you your own need to educate the limited mind, known as the human ego. For that which you find unpleasant in life is waiting within your consciousness. And some day in this eternity you will experience it in order that you may be freed from it. For that that man does not understand, he guarantees, by the Law of Not Understanding, to call it forth into his life that he may be freed from the obstructions that wait upon his path in consciousness.

Remember, my students, some time ago in our discussion of adversities—the immutable law that makes them attachments and the necessary efforts to be made by each and every student, each and every day, in every way to be freed from the mental law that lifts you one moment and drops you the next. If you are experiencing extreme difficulties in any level of consciousness, view them objectively by entertaining the thought of what is behind the experience. Go beyond the feeling and the thought, go beyond that cloud of delusion created by mental substance. For in your efforts to go beyond it, will you find the true goodness of all life.

Though thousands upon thousands of words have been spoken to you in this school, there are an unlimited number yet to be spoken.

When we first came to Earth to share with you our understanding, one of the first things that we stated was our request, to all Earth, to broaden your horizons. For it is in the broadening of your horizons that the fullness of life will rise into your consciousness. It is in the broadening of your horizons that your health and your wealth will abundantly flow. For, in the limited views in life's experiences, we deny the possibility of something better to be. It is in the dictates of these patterns and attitudes of mind of yesteryear, it is the dictates of the mind that keep us in our bondage. Life is truly beautiful when we stop dictating how it should be. Pause in your activities, that you may become aware of how often your mind dictates to God.

We understand that God is goodness and all that man could possibly desire. Think, my students. Think how many times our mind rises to dictate to Goodness. It is those dictates to Goodness that keep goodness from us. It is the authority of the mind that is our true obstruction in life.

Earth offers much in its education of Earth people, but it has yet to offer how the mind should be wisely used. It is the abuses, through errors of ignorance, of our mind that cause our difficulties. It is because these patterns and attitudes are running wild. We have lost control of them. But we can once again gain control. It is the very purpose of this academy to help those students who are sincerely seeking to find the way to once again gain control of their vehicle of mind and, in the control of that vehicle, will they be truly freed. No longer the victim through errors of ignorance, but rise supreme to do their duty that they alone have earned in these many centuries of experience.

My good students, learn the lesson that is before you. We stated in one of our other classes that he who fascinates, procrastinates. So become aware of how many times in the course of a day that you procrastinate, for it is the revelation of how you fascinate with the thoughts of your mind. Success is dependent upon the willingness to move harmoniously forward with the divine Law of Evolution. Whenever man fascinates with his mind, he is simply playing with a computer. He's not moving forward in consciousness, but standing still in a stagnant pool.

My good students, untold centuries has passed in fascinating with your minds. Surely, the time has come, for you have earned the way and the Light has dawned within you. When you have something to do, do it. It is fear, the control over your soul, the authority of the mind, that breeds fascination. Long ago it was stated, "Dreamer, dream a life of beauty before your dream starts dreaming you [*The Living Light* or *The Living Light Dialogue,* volume 1]." I assure you, my friends, that he who fascinates is no longer the dreamer, for the dream is dreaming him.

So remember to be the observer and not the observed. Be the captain of your ship and not the ship itself.

Think more deeply, more often. Awaken even more that which is truly you. You are not those thoughts. You are the cause behind those thoughts. You are that which sustains the thought. That is you. You are not the illusion; you are that which sustains the illusion. You are not the feeling; you are the very cause of the feeling. And because you have had, and continue to have, many thoughts—those which are pleasing and those which are not—and you have had, and continue to have, many feelings—what you judge to be good and what you judge to be bad—then you, the true you, can move on either path, accepting those things that exist, for they have a right of existence. Accepting them passing through your consciousness, without *you* being deluded that they are you. You are not the hair upon your head, nor the hands that you use. You are the essence. Remember, through identity is your destiny established. And man identifies with his denials and his denials become his destiny.

Why does man identify with his denials and not his acceptances? Man identifies with his denials for in identification with man's denials is the superiority of the human mind over the eternal soul established. That, my good students, is the lesson of eternal life. Think on it well during your semester break.

Good night.

MARCH 17, 1977

APPENDIX

The Divine Healing Prayer

I accept that the Divine Healing Power
Is removing all obstructions
From my mind and body
And is restoring me
To perfect health, wealth, and happiness.
My heart is filled with gratitude
For the Divine Law of Acceptance
That is healing both present and absent ones
Who are in need of help.
Peace, the power that healeth,
Is guiding my thoughts, acts, and deeds
As God and I go hand in hand
Living a life of joyful abundance.

The Total Consideration Affirmation

I am the manifestation of Divine Intelligence. Formless and free. Whole and complete. Peace, Poise, and Power are my birthright.

The Law of Harmony is my thought and guarantees Unity in all my acts and activities, expressing perfect Rhythm and limitless flow throughout my entire being.

Without beginning or ending, eternity is my true awareness and sees the tides of creation, as a captain sees his ship.

As the Light of Truth is sustained by the faculty of Reason, I pause to think and claim my Divine right.

    Right Thought. Right Action. Total Consideration.

        Amen. Amen. Amen.

Divine Abundance

Thank
(Gratitude)

You
(Principle)

God
(Divine Intelligence)

I'm
(Individualizing)

Moving
(Rhythm)

In
(Unity)

Your
(Realization)

Divine
(Total)

Flow
(Consideration)

God We Love

O God, we love the roses,
The weeds and thistles too;
O God, we love the butterflies,
The snakes that crawl are you.
O God, we love the ones who hate,
The ones who live in fear;
We love them more each day we live
For all to Thee are dear.
O God, we love the ones who see
But even more the blind;
For in our love we hope and pray
Their sight may be Divine.
O God, we love all paths to Thee,
For in them we can see
A light that shines to all mankind
In varying degree.
O God, we love the sunshine,
The darkness and the night;
O God, we love the weak and strong,
For in them is Thy might.
O God, we love all things in life,
For in them we find Thee,
A shining light that's dim or bright
For all mankind to see.

www.ingramcontent.com/pod-product-compliance
Lightning Source LLC
Chambersburg PA
CBHW020635300426
44112CB00007B/124